Our Beleaguered Species:
Beyond Tribalism

Our Beleaguered Species:
Beyond Tribalism

Elizabeth Crouch Zelman

To my friend, Tom,
as we wish for
more years of fun
and fellowship.
Affectionately,
Liz

Library of Congress Control Number: 2014918689
Zelman, Elizabeth Crouch
Our beleaguered species: beyond tribalism
Includes annotated bibliography, notes, references, index
Human origins, social evolution, tribalism and war, cooperation,
morality and religion

ISBN-13: 978-1502769336 (CreateSpace-Assigned)
ISBN-10: 1502769336

Printed in the United States of America
First edition, 2015

Interior design by C. Leon McGahee
Cover design by Sophie Binder
Author photograph by Claire Anderson
Cover photograph by Elizabeth Crouch Zelman

Dedicated to my grandson James

and to other children of his generation

and beyond

Contents

Acknowledgments

As part of a personal lifelong quest for understanding the natural world and our place in nature, I began this project as a series of essays based partly on classes that I presented as a volunteer in Washington University's Lifelong Learning Institute. The project evolved into its present form as I taught, listened, and wrote. My first debt is to participants, to administrator Katie Compton and to Henrietta Friedman who was the brainchild behind this Institute, founded in 1995.

Questions and comments from class participants about the subject matter, centering on understanding human institutions and ethics through how we evolved as a species, helped me to refine and expand my own thinking. Specific individuals helped me to clarify content. Among them were biologist Don Cohn and physician and genetics educator Ben Borowsky.

Susan Balk and Tom Crouch read and gave feedback on early drafts of the Preface and Chapter 1. Writing maven and friend Marilyn Lipman provided valuable editorial and stylistic comments on intermediate versions of the Preface and Chapters 1 and 2. LLI colleague Tom Mitchell, with grounding in mathematical sciences and wide interests and knowledge, carefully read later versions of all chapters, offering valuable editorial comments on both style and content prior to final editing, and later advising on formatting.

My freelance editor, Kathy Clayton, retained her patience and sense of humor with my sending revisions of revisions, a few times in close sequence. Her suggestions for changes in organization within chapters added to the overall coherence of the book. Her questions regarding content helped me to recognize and identify particular areas that needed clarification, which led me to changing details that clouded my explanations.

LLI colleague and friend, Professor Emeritus of Psychiatry at St. Louis University School of Medicine, C. Leon McGahee, was my greatest and steadiest source of support during this project. He kindly read and provided a wealth of commentary on early versions of all chapters, and willingly discussed, agreed, and disagreed with various issues of content as they came up during these years of pruning and rewriting, adding much to my own thinking and to the book. His depth and breadth of knowledge of the biological and social sciences, particularly neuroscience, and his keen interest in the human condition and human ethics informed our many discussions. He reread the book in its entirety prior to my sending it to my editor, and, in the last phase, applied his skills and his time to its final formatting for publication.

For additional technical assistance, I thank website designer Heather McGahee, Internet wizard Marian Zelman, anthropology graduate student Margaret Buehler, proofreader and indexer Robert Saigh, and cover designer Sophie Binder. I take full responsibility for all errors that occur within the book.

For ongoing encouragement and support during my preoccupation with this project for the past five to six years, I owe special thanks to several other friends. James Hoggard for some years encouraged and invited (prodded) me to share my perspective in presentations and in writing. Claire Anderson, Ellen Green, Roberta Stolz, Ruth Schwartz, Eleanor Sullivan, Julie Schmelz, and Margaret Kuhn have been staunch friends and supporters throughout this project. I received encouragement also from St. Louis Ethical Society's leader Kate Lovelady, evolutionary psychologist David Barash, and archeologist Sarah Nelson.

About the Author

My path toward the study of anthropology and human evolution began with my childhood in Farmington, Missouri, a town with a population of about 5000 in the 1940s and 1950s. Bicycle treks and family jaunts into nature's haunts piqued my curiosity, along with encouragement of interest in nature's creatures by my physician-ornithologist father, and the ready listening ear and thoughtful responses of my mother. Even then, I was struck by similarities between ourselves and other animals.

I entered Grinnell College in 1960 as a biology major, but studying history and philosophy pointed also to a world of interconnections. The mysteries of nature and human nature fueled a growing skepticism toward ready-made solutions. Discovery of the holistic study of the human animal, the perspective of anthropology, suited my outlook and temperament.

After completing B.A. and M.A. degrees at the University of Missouri, I moved to the University of Michigan, earning a Ph.D. in anthropology in 1974, based on cross-cultural research on pregnancy and childbirth ritual in relation to women's roles and status. My growing concern with women's issues, injustices connected to ethnic identity, and the lengthy Vietnam War reflected those times and my other role as mother of two young children.

Now in a later stage of life, moved by today's worldwide misunderstandings and conflicts, applying the anthropological perspective in book form became a personal imperative.

Elizabeth Crouch Zelman
January 8, 2015
zelman@beyondtribalism.com
www.beyondtribalism.com

Preface

An Anthropological Odyssey

The origin of modern humanity was a stroke of luck—good
for our species for a while, bad for most of the rest of life forever.

    —Edward O. Wilson, 2012[1]

In this book, I explore how we human animals evolved as part of
the natural world, how we changed during the first several million
years of our tenure on earth to become who we are today, and where
we might be headed. No one knows what our future will be, but it
does seem clear that we are on the brink of large changes. Although
my book's title—*Our Beleaguered Species*—suggests a rather pessimistic
view of *Homo sapiens*, this is countered by its subtitle. *Beyond Tribalism*
hints at a path toward solving the problems our species faces; this
path emerges as we come to understand how we got here and what
capacities we possess for constructing a new path.

    Historically, a hallmark of anthropology has been its holistic per-
spective, that is, viewing our species as a biological creature and a
creator of symbolic culture simultaneously. While our common biology imposes limits, it also enables symbol-based language and verbal
reasoning and, with it, sociocultural variety. Anthropologists try to
understand how these pieces fit together into a whole. As the only
creatures that study ourselves, we can hardly be objective observers
of our subject material. The ways of acting that we call culture feel as
natural to us as the impulses and behaviors that originate directly
from our biological selves.

Because of this evolutionary legacy, most members of *Homo sapiens* are curious about themselves, about how other people feel and think, and about the quirky behaviors we all have. Few of us are engaged in unraveling the mysteries of exoplanets or decoding DNA, but most of us do think about why we and those around us act the way we do. Anthropology's main contribution may be in understanding our species' diverse ways of life. This book is an attempt to interpret and apply this to some of the problems we face *because* we are human.

Language-based culture, added to our primate legacy of upright walking and highly mobile hands and fingers, enabled us to craft tools ranging from ancient stone hand-axes to iPads, and transformed us into "artificial apes."[2] With these tools, we have successfully taken over most of the planet, occupying even extreme environments. At the same time, evolution gave us bodies without fangs or claws, helpless babies and long childhoods, and a great need for cooperation with other humans.

As highly social creatures, we bond strongly with, identify with, and favor members of the social groups in which we find ourselves. This bonding, however, has been coupled with less positive feelings toward outsiders. Our impulses toward caring about and helping others, and toward a sense of fairness that feels almost instinctive, do not always stretch toward those we classify as outsiders.

This part of our evolutionary heritage is a tendency toward *tribalism*. I use this term *not* to denote small-scale society organized as a tribe. Instead, I define tribalism as a perspective that values people of one's own society or group more highly than outsiders (members of outgroups), judging and treating them differently. This stance toward others worked to keep small, scattered groups together in the past, but its consequences are wreaking havoc today, threatening our future. With more than seven billion of us jammed onto one small planet, if we are to survive as a species, we must escape the bounds of this small-group orientation and move beyond the tribalism that circumscribed our past.

Whether it is unthinking loyalty to a group of kin, nationalism carried to extremes, notions that skin color affects our common humanity, or religious allegiance run amok, the tribal mentality imposes extraordinary costs and dangers on our twenty-first century world. We see its effects every day in our communities and in the news.

But there is hope. The cognitive capacity that enabled our species to probe the universe and plumb the secrets of our brains can help us to extend cooperation and empathy outward from the people we know best to the larger world. Our emotional capacity to imagine how life might feel in circumstances different from our own, and to empathize with others, gives us the potential to extend caring to all people and even beyond, as Charles Darwin envisioned over a century and a half ago.

As we evolved in a rapidly changing natural world, *Homo sapiens* emerged as an adaptable, generalized animal whose big brain-culture-language complex enabled migration into a wide range of environments. This legacy endowed our species with a high degree of adaptability. Just as genetic variety provides the raw material for biological evolution, cultural and behavioral variety provides the ingredients for cultural change. Our evolutionary heritage gave us the means to act tribally, but it also endowed us with the means to act globally.

We must now tap into this adaptability, making use of our diverse perspectives and institutions that provide a vast pool of creativity beyond that of any single culture. We can put these to the service of overcoming small-group tribalism. With knowledge of who we are and where we have been as a species, we can tinker with our own cultural evolution and work at replacing our easily triggered sectarian tendencies with life-affirming and planet-affirming principles. Our future as a species on a planet of shrinking resources depends on our overcoming the ancient tribalistic perceptions and emotions that divide us.

To move beyond tribalism, I suggest (in Chapter 9) a range of specific prescriptions that involve perception, cognition, social, economic, and political institutions, and overall outlook that can serve as a basis for a common ethics, centering on issues that confront all of humanity.

In the final chapter of this work, I explore how we might approach our status as self-aware creatures who are part of nature. A sense of meaning can come from an ongoing quest to understand ourselves and the world we live in.

Finally, I offer a personal disclaimer: As anthropologist and writer, I am reporting mainly the primary research of others. I have gleaned information from all areas of evolutionary science, and new findings appear almost every day. Because of the lag time between research, its publication, my writing, and appearance of this book, some details presented here are sure to be outdated. I see my contribution not mainly as a research summary, but as a particular interpretation of how developments in evolutionary anthropology can enhance our understanding of the human condition and suggest a path forward.

This project has been, in one sense, a personal odyssey that expresses my understanding of life as a journey in asking questions and searching for understanding. From another point of view, my project may represent something else entirely. In the words of philosopher Daniel Dennett: "A scholar is just a library's way of making another library."[3]

PART I

INTRODUCTION: LIVING THE QUESTIONS

In the distant future I see open fields for far more important researches. Psychology will be based on a new foundation, that of the necessary acquirement of each mental power and capacity by gradation. Light will be thrown on the origin of man and his history.

—Charles Darwin, 1859[1]

1

Science, Evolution, Biology and Culture

Science is not just another enterprise like medicine or engineering or theology. It is the wellspring of all the knowledge we have of the real world that can be tested and fitted to preexisting knowledge. It is the arsenal of technologies and inferential mathematics needed to distinguish the true from the false. It formulates the principles and formulas that tie all this knowledge together. Science belongs to everybody. Its constituent parts can be challenged by anybody in the world who has sufficient information to do so. It is not just "another way of knowing" as often claimed.

—E.O. Wilson, 2012[1]

Are we a beleaguered species? In this chapter I lay the groundwork for understanding this notion from the perspective of evolutionary anthropology. In its first section, I review the power of the scientific approach in searching for knowledge about our species. The second section describes how Darwin's theory of natural selection jump-started the growth of knowledge about living things that we use regularly in our everyday lives. Since his time, technological breakthroughs in acquiring, observing, and analyzing information have filled in details of the evolutionary process. In the third section, I describe how sequencing of genomes of living and ancient organisms and the burgeoning field of evolutionary developmental biology (or Evo Devo) rest on the strong foundation of Darwin's concept of natural selection, and the evidence that all living things are interconnected.

Two dynamics characterize both biological evolution and human cultural evolution and history. One is an interplay between competition and cooperation, and the other is a tension between adaptive specialization and adaptability. Each can be seen as a continuum that requires a degree of balance for an organism or a social group to maintain itself and to be responsive to changing conditions.

In exploring this application of science to ourselves, we must recognize the value of maintaining an attitude of skepticism laced with humility regarding our importance as a species. *Homo sapiens* is one among many forms of life on our planet; accepting this is critical as we search for answers to questions regarding who we are and where we may be heading. It is likewise critical in our struggles to solve problems, act ethically, and prepare for a viable future.

Science

Anthropology, as both a biological and a social science, attempts to make sense of the human condition from an empirical perspective with the scientific attitude of skepticism, and in the context of our biological and cultural heritage. As an anthropologist, I like to think of our ancient *Homo sapiens* ancestors, subsisting for hundreds of thousands of years on wild plants and animals, as the very first natural scientists. They certainly amassed a large body of empirically based knowledge about our earth and its inhabitants during everyday activities. The value of this ancient body of knowledge, conveyed for generations through oral traditions, is being recognized by today's medical and nutritional scientists, and it is being tapped with a sense of urgency as the knowledge disappears along with the people whose traditions carry it.

In the European tradition, Aristotle is often mentioned for his contributions to the biological sciences. He observed, dissected, described, and classified living organisms into a hierarchal system that he based on their commonalities and differences. Using the same idea, Carl Linnaeus in the eighteenth century formulated a scheme of classification whose terms and overall outline we still use, with modifications, today. In studying living things, Aristotle introduced a "bottom-up" or inductive approach that differed from the "top-down" approach of his mentor Plato, who deduced particulars from "ideal forms." Yet Aristotle retained Plato's basic concerns with form, substance, and the idea of a purposeful world. Aristotle also emphasized the importance of function and change in understanding natural phenomena, and he clarified and classified types of causation.[2]

Although Aristotle's contributions were well-known in the Western world, a Muslim/Arabic philosopher, mathematician, and astronomer, Ibn al-Haytham (Abu Ali al-Hasen), not as well known in the West, outlined a method for studying nature that European scientists adopted as the scientific method several centuries later.[3] British physicist Jim Al-Khalili provides a history of this "Golden Age of Science" that was centered in the Near East beginning in the eighth century CE. This period lasted for six centuries and led to numerous developments, including Ibn al-Haytham's classic work on optics. This golden age began with the translation of ancient Greek thinking into Arabic and continued with original research in many fields by scholars from diverse traditions bridging Asia, Africa, and Europe. In the fifteenth century, however, Islam began a period of religious fervor and increased intolerance of other traditions coupled with cumbersome bureaucratic "involution," and with this cultural shift the scholarly tradition began to fade.[4] As scientific research floundered in the Arabic world, Italian scholars were beginning to translate older Arabic works of science into Latin. This began the scientific tradition that became a significant part of the European Renaissance.

Traditionally, the words *philosophy* and *science* were used interchangeably. The stated goal of both was to search for knowledge to understand the world. The term *natural philosophy* later came to be used for subjects that we now call *science*, and the phrase *natural history* is still used sometimes to refer to descriptive studies of our earth and its life, as in our many museums of natural history. The word *science*, used to refer to a specific type of discipline, was uncommon in western Europe until the nineteenth century. In 1833, William Whewell first suggested the word *scientist* as an analogue to the word *artist* to refer to one who does art.[5]

In discussing science, people commonly confuse the terms for fact, hypothesis, theory, and law. But scientists have very definite meanings for these terms. A *fact* is an observable phenomenon (an object, movement, behavior, process). It may be detected directly by one of our senses or by extensions of our senses such as telescopes, spectrometers, electronic sensors, and other scanning devices. For science, a phenomenon must be verified by multiple observers to be considered factual. As the ability to observe the world improves, our perception of facts changes. Until telescopes were strong enough to see Uranus and Neptune, for example, the accepted fact was that only six planets existed. A *hypothesis* is an educated guess about how a given phenomenon works. It attains the status of *theory* or *law* when the guess is tested and empirical (sense-based) evidence overwhelmingly supports the proposition in various conditions and in a large number of studies. The terms *theory* and *law* are sometimes used interchangeably, but a law has a connotation of greater strength than a theory and is often backed by mathematics.

Scientists sometimes define a law differently, as a phenomenon that consistently exists or happens. This definition, however, is easily confounded with the definition of fact as stated above. It also introduces the sticky issue of differentiating description from explanation. Isaac Newton's law of universal gravitation, for example, states that "any particle in the universe attracts any other with a force ... that is proportional to the product of their masses ... and inversely proportional the square of the distance between them."[6] This might be called a description, but it is also a proposition about a variable relationship that seems to constitute a level of explanation.

The hallmark of science is that all propositions are subject to change. Newton's law of gravity explains the movement of most objects. Albert Einstein's law or theory of general relativity moved Newton's understanding to a new level, and is now being reexamined in the light of quantum theory, string theory, and the notion of multiple universes. There are many questions, and science pushes on, searching for answers. Each new theory builds on previous work, clarifies conditions under which the earlier theory made sense, and extends the reach of the conclusions that are incorporated into the new understanding.[7]

In science, then, assertions about the nature of the universe, about life on earth, and about ourselves as biological creatures are tentative, subject to change as we learn more. Even what we consider to be a fact at one time changes with new evidence. Science is an ongoing process of attempting to understand the world we live in and who we creatures are by asking new questions as we uncover new phenomena. There always is something beyond what we know; mystery remains and we keep searching to make sense of it. A scientist can never afford to be confident that a theory is immune to challenges or refinement. The importance of this skeptical attitude combined with humility regarding one's conclusions was recognized by Ibn al-Haytham around 1000 CE[8] and is emphasized throughout this book.

As the only animals who study ourselves, we must recognize that this dual role of subject and observer implies a particular bias toward this subject matter. In our past, we have consistently overestimated our importance in the natural world and have deemed ourselves as superior to other life forms. We must remind ourselves that the human species is only one of many on this planet, which is itself an infinitesimal bit of the universe. A large dose of skepticism toward any conclusion we draw about ourselves is in order. Viewing ourselves through a broad evolutionary perspective can nudge us toward a healthy mix of humility and skepticism.

Evolution and Darwin's Natural Selection

The idea that living things have evolved over time was not new with Charles Darwin's 1859 publication of *On the Origin of Species*. His grandfather Erasmus Darwin and others had earlier proposed the general idea that living things change over time.[9] What Charles Darwin did is offer a carefully and thoroughly documented theory about how evolution happens, proposing a specific mechanism that he called *natural selection*.

Biological evolution simply refers to the changes that occur in organisms from earlier to later generations, so that descendants come to be different from their ancestors and eventually may become separate new species, in a process called *speciation*. Species are clearly not static. The world of nature looks different now than it did millions of years ago. Scientists today can see evolution in process, most easily in tiny organisms that reproduce rapidly, such as fruit flies or bacteria. But the same observation can also be made through careful studies of longer-lived organisms in nature, such as the classic study of finches responding to local climate change on the island of Daphne Major in the Galapagos archipelago.[10]

The process of evolution, then, is an observable fact; living things change over time, and this has been observed repeatedly in nature and in the laboratory. A fundamental piece of this idea is that all living things are products of earlier living things. Darwin's theory of natural selection, originally published in 1859, explained in great detail how this works in small stepwise changes over many generations.[11] In his words: "I have called this principle, by which each slight variation, if useful, is preserved, by the term Natural Selection."[12] This theory continues to explain how organisms change over many generations, providing the foundation for modern biological sciences, although we now have much more specific, detailed information than Darwin did in the nineteenth century. Discoveries since then clearly demonstrate the remarkable unity of all life and the fact that we humans share much of our DNA not only with other animals but also with fruits and vegetables and single-celled organisms.

How did Darwin come up with his theory of natural selection more than a century and a half ago without any knowledge of the existence of genes? He was influenced by many factors. He was a keen naturalist as a young man, and impressed by the immense diversity of plants and animals, even before his famous voyage around the world on the *HMS Beagle*. After that adventure, he was determined to make sense of what he had carefully observed, noted, and drawn.

Darwin also knew that plant and animal breeders selected organisms with different traits to modify subsequent generations, and he had studied the process carefully. Indeed, he bred pigeons upon his return from his journey, and carefully tabulated the results. In addition, he had read and been impressed by the essay "On Population" in which Thomas Malthus contrasted the faster geometric growth of population to the slower arithmetic growth of food supply, concluding that sooner or later population would come to exceed available food. The resulting famine or war would then decrease population and begin the cycle again.[13]

Finally, for years Darwin had observed evidence, apparent in different layers of exposed rock, that the earth itself had changed, and he had been impressed by geologist Charles Lyell's explanation of earth's features as having resulted from complicated, ongoing geological processes. The continuous pattern of building up and breaking down of earth's features over time is called *uniformitarianism*. That uniform forces have the same effects wherever and whenever they occur struck Darwin as an important feature, which he later applied to his understanding of how evolution happened. With this, too, Darwin came to understand that the earth was much older than indicated by the widely accepted biblical description of his time.[14]

His resultant theory shook the foundations of scientific thought. He explained that those organisms in a population that inherit traits helping them to survive and reproduce will contribute more individuals like themselves to the next generation in that population. In time, succeeding populations become different enough from the original one that, under some conditions, they become a new species.

This is the basic idea, but other factors are often involved. Geographical separation, for example, may keep two populations from blending again into one. Speciation is complicated and the details continue to be studied today. A key issue is where to draw the dividing line between an emerging species and the original species from which it evolved. But the fact that speciation occurs, that new species emerge through an evolutionary process, is clear.

Darwin's theory explains many biological phenomena, but its reach is being continually expanded as new evidence accumulates. Yet the success of his theory of natural selection in explaining so much in biology is a testament to the role of skepticism and humility in science and to Darwin's almost obsessive thoroughness and caution. He was not satisfied with results of his reasoning until he had researched every possibility available to him in his century. His writings display the passionate sense of curiosity that moved him forward.

A clear demonstration of evolution in action is regularly seen today in the field and in the laboratory with rapidly reproducing bacteria. We see natural selection at work as new, antibiotic-resistant species emerge, leaving scientists watching with horror and hoping that they can out-maneuver these species and prevent bacterial ascendance. Another easily observed example of evolution's results lies in the fact that some of us can digest milk as adults, while others cannot. The cultural trait of herding of large mammals was developed in parts of Africa, the Near East, and Europe. Modern human populations with ancestors from these areas include a large percentage of individuals with a mutation in the lactase gene that enables them to drink and digest milk as adults. Populations with ancestors from other areas, on the other hand, usually lack that mutation and have trouble digesting milk of other animals.[15] This exemplifies recent human evolution and illustrates how human culture, animal domestication in this case, can influence the distribution of a variable genetic trait.

Darwin did not know the actual mechanism that produces changes in living organisms from generation to generation, but today scientists understand the process. One key was the discovery of DNA, the long molecular strands that include the genes that encode our biological inheritance. Mutations, errors in copying or replicating this DNA, generate the variation that provides the raw material for the work of natural selection. Mutations occur randomly. Most make little difference for survival, and others cause death or serious impairment. But occasionally a mutation changes a gene or set of genes in a way that enhances the survival of a developing organism. When enhanced survival results in improved reproductive chances, this change is transmitted to the next generation. Over many generations, the frequency of that gene in the population changes and evolution has occurred. The synthesis of population genetics with Darwin's theory dates back to the 1940s and is considered a breakthrough in understanding evolution.[16]

New Developments in Evolutionary Biology

With the giant first step of Darwin's theory, followed by development of population genetics and discovering of DNA's double helix structure, we now are witnessing another important milestone in understanding how life's incredible diversity evolved. In his 2005 book entitled, after Darwin's words, *Endless Forms Most Beautiful*, geneticist Sean B. Carroll describes the basic outline of a field of study, *evolutionary developmental biology* (often called Evo Devo). A basic idea of Evo Devo is that much evolutionary change occurs when genes, held in common by many life forms, are activated and deactivated at different times and locations during embryonic development.[17]

In that book, Carroll presents a lucid description of how the design of organisms often changes through a kind of evolutionary tinkering with existing biological forms rather than invention of new forms from scratch. Major design features present throughout much of the animal kingdom include modularity (segments), repetition, symmetry, and polarity. This organic design is itself a product of evolution, just as design in nonliving substances such as crystals is a product of physical laws. These design features and more detailed biological traits of a given organism appear at particular points during that organism's development.

Each embryo is a work in progress, constantly changing. If a particular gene is switched on or off at a particular time and in a particular location within the embryo, this event determines the resulting feature. As Carroll puts it, animal forms evolve through changes in embryo geography. He uses this phrase to describe the embryo as a kind of dynamic, four-dimensional map or globe whose axes denote events in time (one dimension) and space (three dimensions). These events are directed by toolkit genes, and within these, the homeobox (HOX) genes are particularly important for the sequence and patterning of development in bilaterally-organized creatures, including ourselves and others with a vertebral column.

In addition, there have been major advances in genome sequencing and molecular genetics. Genome sequencing has enabled scientists to read the genetic code in various organisms, including ourselves. This advance showed us, much to our surprise, that we share 98 percent of our genes with chimpanzees and a very high percentage with other creatures as well. But because the genes are switched on and off in varying patterns and at different times during an embryo's development, we are quite different from frogs and different as well from our close relatives, the chimpanzees and bonobos. Using these concepts and the tools of modern genetics, Carroll and others are coming to understand surges of evolutionary development, such as those seen in the Cambrian Explosion and also in smaller surges as evolution proceeds.

A major contribution of evolutionary developmental biology is the notion that as organisms evolve, it is often development itself that is evolving, rather than individual traits. Aiding this study has been the discovery of *epigenetic factors*. These are materials in a cell's nucleus that are not genes but that influence how genes are expressed in particular organisms. Focusing mainly on arthropods (for example, insects, spiders, lobsters, shrimp) and on vertebrates (humans, frogs, birds), which are all bilaterally organized creatures, Carroll shows that the ancient, conservative toolkit genes that regulate body-building can be switched on or off by other genes and by epigenetic switches. This complex, dance-like coordination of embryonic space-time coordinates, genes, and epigenetic factors enables even a small genetic mutation to occasionally produce a large difference between species.

Beyond these developments are further observations, reports, and behavioral experiments that are adding new information about behaviors of our living nonhuman primate relatives and other human beings from around the world. Observations of modern human hunter-gatherer populations have stimulated questions and hypotheses about the lifestyle and behaviors of our ancestors. Current methods of locating, extracting, dating, analyzing, and comparing ancient fossils and artifacts use DNA, advanced imaging techniques, and bombardment of material with light or heat to release radiation accumulated in buried items. These techniques are combined with relative dating, in which the date range for a given fossil or artifact is estimated from the geological strata or tree rings from its surroundings. Paleoanthropologist Chris Stringer has a good summary of new methods of dating fossils and artifacts in his book, *Lone Survivors*.[18] In Table 1.1, I outline new information sources and insights gained as a result of each.

Given the profusion of recent research, we now know that evolutionary changes depend on a complex interaction of organisms with their particular environments. The old *nature versus nurture* controversy, which posed a choice for any given trait of having been produced

Table 1.1. New Information Sources and Related Insights	
NEW INFORMATION SOURCE	**INSIGHT ABOUT EVOLUTION**
Genome sequencing	Preponderance of noncoding DNA
Genome comparisons	Relationships of diverse species
Molecular biology	How DNA, RNA, proteins interact
Fossil and artifact discoveries, and new dating and imaging techniques	A tangled web, not a straight-line pattern, describes human evolution
Evolutionary developmental biology (Evo Devo)	Evolution of "design," role of toolkit genes and genetic switches
Science of epigenetics	Influence of environmental switches on gene expression
Behavioral observations and experiments using living great apes, humans, and other social animals	Inferences about evolution of behavior

by genetic inheritance or by the environment, has become outdated. Interactions are far too complex to be understood in terms of this dichotomy. As anthropologist and physician Melvin Konner states, "Genetic determinism died long ago, and now environmental determinism is dead too. Long live complex, measurable, and mainly deterministic interactionism."[19] Similarly, neurophilosopher Patricia S.

Churchland refers to this interaction as "a dense thicket of complex-ity."[20]

This new information and perspective enable a more holistic un-derstanding of humankind than was possible ever before. Edward O. Wilson coined the word *consilience*, which refers to bringing fields of study together to understand the world in all its aspects, and it is now crucial to understanding human evolution and culture. Philosophers are talking about neurobiology; neuroscientists are attempting to un-derstand and make sense of philosophical notions, and so on.

Since *Homo sapiens* is the dominant species on the planet today, we need more than ever to make sense of who we are, where we are going, and how we are influencing other life on our planet. My goal is to contribute in a small way to thinking about how we might move beyond our current state of world misunderstandings into acknowl-edging that current behaviors of our species have considerable influ-ence on what will happen next on planet Earth.

Moving into the last section of this chapter, I look at two im-portant dynamics or themes at work within evolution, each requiring a balance between two poles. Understanding each dynamic is im-portant for coming to terms with where our species has been, who we are today, and where we may be headed. Here I apply each dy-namic to cultural evolution and human history as well as to biological evolution.

Dynamic Themes in Evolution

Cooperation and Competition

The phrase "survival of the fittest," coined by Herbert Spencer in 1864 and often used in conjunction with Darwin's theory of natural selection, is quite familiar to most of us and refers to the notion of competition between individuals. The individual with the fittest ge-netic makeup will have features that will enable it to win in the search for food, defense against predators, and mating. Unfortunately this concept, and particularly this phrase, fueled a movement called *social Darwinism*, which confused fitness with the value-judgment "best" and then attempted to apply the notion to sociology and politics. Employed in the nineteenth and early twentieth centuries, it became justification for genocidal policies, including Nazi atrocities in Germany and forced sterilizations in the United States and elsewhere.

This misinterpretation and misuse of evolutionary theory caused a backlash among many mid-twentieth-century social scientists, who came to reject any evolutionary approach toward understanding human culture. This prejudice was not broken until late in that century when more social scientists came to understand the complex interactions between competition and cooperation in the evolution of social animals.

Matt Ridley calls the balance between conflict and cooperation "one of the great recurring themes of human history," as exemplified by Lewis Carroll's Red Queen in *Through the Looking Glass* informing Alice that despite running as fast as she can, she can only keep her place without making progress because everyone is playing the one-upmanship game. Ridley's book focuses on sex as the main stage for conflict, but competition happens in all arenas, down to the genetic level in one's own body.[21] Research on embryonic development is updating this notion, demonstrating that a kind of tug-of-war exists even between mother's and the father's genes, with each competing to deactivate switches that would favor the other parent's influence on embryonic development; this process is called *imprinting*.[22]

Darwin, in *The Descent of Man*, explains how our own "complex instincts" rest on the social emotions that we share with many other animals. For this, he draws from Adam Smith's conception of sympathy as the basis for human cooperation.

A Scottish philosopher of ethics and logic as well as the founder of the economic views that made him famous, Adam Smith expressed his understanding of sympathy in a book, *The Theory of Moral*

Sentiments, first published in 1759 prior to the better-known *The Wealth of Nations*. In the sixth edition of the earlier book, he describes "sympathy" as the part of human nature that is concerned with others, stronger in some individuals than in others. He explains his view of how it works: "By the imagination we place ourselves in his [another person's] situation, we conceive ourselves enduring all the same torments, we enter as it were into his body, and become in some measure the same person with him, and thence form some idea of his sensations, …" He continues by describing its application to positive feelings as well, i.e., feeling another's joys.[23] His definition is similar to what we today call empathy although he lacked today's knowledge of its neurological underpinnings.

Darwin viewed this sympathetic sentiment as a product of group selection in which "those communities, which included the greatest number of the most sympathetic members, would flourish best and rear the greatest number of offspring."[24] Different forms of selection will be explored in more detail in later chapters.

Adam Smith also emphasized issues of fairness and justice, and he recognized the importance of maintaining and encouraging good health and the general welfare of citizens. These concerns are apparent in both of his major books. He went to great length in *The Wealth of Nations* to describe every form of taxation and its effects on fairness and justice for different social groups, for production generally, and specifically for laborers and owners of land and businesses.[25]

In *The Theory of Moral Sentiments*, Smith emphasized the importance of altruism and cooperation: "And hence it is, that to feel much for others and little for ourselves, that to restrain our selfishness, and to indulge our benevolent affections, constitutes the perfection of human nature; and can alone produce among mankind that harmony of sentiments and passions in which consists their whole grace and propriety."[26] Today many people associate his thinking only with human competitiveness and the "invisible hand" of the market, but an actual reading of his extremely nuanced work demonstrates that this grossly simplifies and distorts his writing.

Others have spoken of the tension between cooperation and competition informing historical ideas about political philosophy. Recent students of economics, politics, and law are recognizing that economic policy in the past few decades, in the United States in particular, has emphasized the centrality of competition based on self-interest while ignoring other human motivations. Today this overemphasis is being recognized and corrected, as researchers from different fields increasingly demonstrate the significant influence of prosocial emotions and other motivations on reciprocal relationships, including everyday economic decision making. Researchers also address the cooperation versus competition dynamic in studying behavior of other animals. Primatologist Frans de Waal adds a third dimension—a sustainable environment—to cooperation and conflict.[27]

Examining the dynamics of cooperation and competition demonstrates that impulses toward both are present in human biology and in sociocultural interactions. The dynamic they create continues to inform human affairs today and influence how we define and shape ourselves.

Adaptive Specialization and Adaptability

Although most people understand the differences between cooperation and competition, the distinction between adaptive specialization and adaptability is not as straightforward. All organisms adapt to their environments; through natural selection they acquire features that increase their survival and reproductive success in the particular environment that they inhabit. Some adaptations are fine-tuned to a particular set of features of that environment; an example of this is a beak that can extract a seed of specific size and hardness. However, a finely tuned adaptation such as this, an example of *adaptive specialization*, can eventually make it more difficult for an animal to cope when environmental conditions change.

Other traits can allow for greater flexibility of behavior; one example is the ability to digest varied foods. Such a trait gives an organism adaptability. Over the course of evolution, and particularly during times of large environmental shifts, having a generalized set of traits can enable a species or a society to survive and even thrive in the midst of a changing world. This is the meaning of *adaptability*.

Two different terms are currently being used in the evolutionary literature to describe how organisms adapt and evolve. Many traits that evolved in the past in response to particular circumstances and perform specific tasks for an organism, in later generations come to be used in different ways. Some of those become modified through further selection to become different adaptations. Various writers have attempted to clarify terms and ideas for distinguishing older adaptations from newer versions either by using the older term *preadaptation* or the newer term *exaptation*.[28] Following Ian Tattersall's observation that almost all evolutionary variations arise from something used before in some other way, and thus most adaptations are in fact exaptations,[29] I shall simply use the term *adaptation* in this book to indicate evolutionary change in response to particular stimuli.

With this, I return to the dynamic between adaptive specialization and adaptability. Matt Ridley's explanation of the Red Queen phenomenon refers to the general notion that progress is relative. He states that "time always erodes advantage. Every invention sooner or later leads to a counter-invention. Every success contains the seeds of its own overthrow. Every hegemony comes to an end. Evolutionary history is no different."[30] The generalization that progress is relative applies to both dynamics identified here, and it applies to biological and cultural events.

The phenomenon is evident in the rise and fall of dominant species and human sociocultural units over long periods of time. Indeed, the rich concept of natural selection itself is currently being applied to various nonbiological systems that influence each other through time. Increasing understanding of coevolution is based on the dynamic interaction between competition and cooperation. Short-term success does not guarantee long-term success. Cooperation within a group can make it stronger in relation to other groups, perhaps bringing them into competition with each other. Competing organisms or groups can discover that joining forces and cooperating can benefit both.

But the world changes. Environments are dynamic, ice ages come and go, periods of drought and rain come and go, and neighboring species or sociocultural groups change. Changes in one species or one culture influence surrounding species and cultures. It is in this context that the *second* dynamic, between adaptive specialization and adaptability can be understood through the Red Queen analogy. In the long run, as natural or cultural environments change, nonspecialized organisms and societies have greater staying power; flexibility is strength.

Anthropologist Elman R. Service, in an essay published in 1960, proposed a "law of evolutionary potential" to refer to what he saw as a tendency of *unspecialized* or *less-developed* societies to move forward and develop new forms as other more *specialized* or *developed* ones became stagnant or too "married" to their specific adaptive niches.[31] He cited several historians who had introduced the notion earlier: Thorsten Veblen spoke of the "penalty of taking the lead" and Leon Trotsky of the "privilege of historical backwardness."[32] More recently, archaeologist and historian Ian Morris completed a detailed analysis comparing political and economic development in the West and the East, supported by a wealth of data. He offers a similar thesis that he calls the "paradox of development."[33] Finally, naturalist Geerat Vermeij notes that dominant species in one time period often give way to previously subordinate ones in the next, and he suggests that similar transitions happen with dominant and subordinate human societies.[34]

We might view both dynamics as an evolutionary dance involving sets of partners: adaptive specialization and adaptability, and cooperation and competition. This suggests a question of whether evolutionary success is definable and measurable. Christopher Lloyd in an entertaining book designed for children and adults[35] devised a measure that ranks organisms according to five criteria: (1) evolutionary impact, (2) impact on human history, (3) environmental impact, (4) global reach, and (5) species longevity. Using these, he ranked the most successful 100 organisms. The earthworm, also recognized by Darwin as a significant actor in evolution, is at the top of Lloyd's list, with algae in second place, while *Homo sapiens* is ranked sixth. Of course, this list was compiled by a member of our species; perhaps a dolphin or a crow would rank the species differently.

Summary and Conclusions

We shall see in the following chapters that our human heritage as mammals, as primates, as apes, and finally as hominins (bipedal apes) tells a story of the evolutionary potential of adaptability and behavioral flexibility. As mammals, our warm-bloodedness, parental care, and ability to learn gave us adaptability. As primates, a generalized body plan with flexible digits, opposable thumbs, semi-upright stance, well-developed vision, and a relatively large brain were also critical. These features can be used in diverse environments and circumstances, unlike hoofs or bills, for example. Primate dentition is also generalized; our four kinds of teeth perform different functions. Our specific human adaptation of two-legged walking, use of freed hands to fashion complex technology and to mediate changing environments, and a large brain that completes its development during a long childhood, bequeathed to *Homo sapiens* still greater adaptability.

I shall return often to the themes introduced here, which provide clues for understanding who we are as human animals and how we might work together to construct a viable future. I close this chapter with two quotations that highlight the centrality of evolution for understanding life on our planet and our species in particular:

Nothing about biology makes sense except in the light of evolution.
　　　—Theodosius Dobzhansky, 1973[36]

Nothing about culture makes sense except in the light of evolution.
　　　—Peter J. Richerson and Robert Boyd, 2005[37]

PART II

THE HUMAN ANIMAL EVOLVING

I assert ... that the long-sought missing link between animals and the really humane being is ourselves!

—Konrad Lorenz, 1963[1]

Part II is about how we became who we are; its three chapters provide an outline of human evolution. Chapter 2 focuses on our overall place in the natural world as animals: vertebrates, mammals, primates, and apes. It looks especially at our common ape ancestors and the split of the human branch from the branch to which our modern cousins, the common chimpanzees and the bonobos, belong. The first and longest phase of the human evolutionary narrative after that split, beginning between five to perhaps nine million years ago, was our ancestors' journey toward becoming two-legged, bipedal apes. The second phase was the transition into creatures with traits that brought our ancestors closer to ourselves, close enough to be classified into our own genus *Homo* and to be called early humans. Walking on two legs put us on the path to becoming human. One consequence of becoming bipedal was the development of consistent toolmaking and use, the beginnings of human technology, and a second consequence was the modification of childbirth and infant care.

Together, these adaptations set the parameters for our further transition to full humanity, for becoming *Homo sapiens* (the subject of Chapter 3). The major development of the third phase of becoming fully human happened in our skulls and in our behaviors: Our brains increased in size and in complexity of interconnections, much of it happening through changes in the timing of brain development and in novel uses of ancient neurochemicals. The human *culture-language complex*, and with it human behavior, coevolved with the brain, each simultaneously a consequence and a cause of change in the other.

I call Chapter 4 "The Moral Mammal" because our mammalian evolutionary heritage bequeathed to us the basic social sentiments that underlie human morality, although the seeds of this development are even more ancient than mammals. One defining feature of human morality is a concern with sharing, giving, and cooperating with others, or an altruistic impulse. A second defining feature is a concern with fairness. Both features are seen in mammals (and some other animals), and both are concerns in all known human societies, expressed in different ways and extended to others in varying degrees. All human societies have means of enforcing these features, sometimes informal and sometimes more formal. We will look at some of the ancient brain features and neurotransmitters that support the emotions that move us to behave morally, at least some of the time. Advances in the neurosciences, economics, and even mathematical game theory have added to the understanding of morality. Human morality, while having ancient roots and universal themes, is widely variable within our species, and it also has a dark side, to be explored in later chapters. I define human ethics as language-based ideas about how people ought to behave, an add-on to mammalian morality.

2

The Bipedal Ape: Our First Steps

There is power in the idea that the struggle for life can lead to so much variety and creativity; and there is unity in the phenomenon of adaptation, which through emergence and selection is the foundation of evolution and of the scientific way of knowing.

—Geerat Vermeij, 2010[1]

We saw in the previous chapter how Charles Darwin, lifelong naturalist, serious thinker, and skeptical scientist, gave us a powerful theory for understanding how living things evolved. In studying our own evolution, we use Darwin's theory, recent developments in evolutionary biology and genetics, discoveries of the last few decades in paleoanthropology and archeology, and new analyses of older discoveries. In addition, we continue to analyze knowledge about modern hunter-gatherer lifestyles.

Changes resulting from natural selection in any population, of dandelions or earthworms or humans or mushrooms, depend on how well the organism's physical and behavioral traits enable it to survive and reproduce in its environment. We human animals evolved in the same way that other living things made their appearances. The overwhelming evidence for our evolution comes from study of anatomy and physiology, genetics, embryology, the fossil record, the archeological record, psychology, anthropology, medicine, and even geology.

The Human Animal in Context:

Our Biological Heritage

Linnaeus classified all life on Earth into kingdoms and a series of nested groups within each, with organisms grouped by observable physical features. Today's picture is more complicated. Newer classification schemes are based on dynamic evolutionary relationships determined by genetic analysis. The resulting bush-like branching diagram (*cladogram*) yields groups that often resemble the older ones, but are modified regularly as research uncovers connections.[2] Because of this and the juxtaposition of older and newer schemes, terminology is used inconsistently by different researchers and writers. In reality, any classification system is only as good as ongoing knowledge, and it is subject to human biases of various sorts.

Today, all life on earth is divided into three domains, called Archaea, Bacteria, and Eukaryota. Eukaryotes include all organisms with nucleated cells, as opposed to the Bacteria and Archaea domains, whose cells have no nuclei. Some members of our large eukaryote domain are single-celled organisms; others, like animals and plants, are multicellular, meaning that they have multiple specialized cells that are sometimes compared to a society of cooperating specialists. Humans belong to a rather tiny branch within the eukaryotes called the animal kingdom. Within this, we are vertebrates (animals with backbones), and within this division, we are mammals.

In Table 2.1, I have simplified and summarized our place in nature. In this table, I include only the sequence of major evolutionary events that are significant for human evolution. Only members of eukaryotes are included, followed by those groups to which we humans belong. Each table row is a subset of the group above it. The dates are approximate, and for ease of comprehending time relationships; I use "ya" to denote "years ago." For reference, scientists place

CATEGORY	WHO ARE INCLUDED?	APPROXIMATE DATE
Table 2.1. Humankind: Our Place in Nature[*]		
Eukaryotes	Cells (single or multicellular) with nuclei	2 billion ya
Animals	Moving multicellular creatures	600 mya
Vertebrates	Animals with backbones	500 mya
Mammals	Animals with live births, mammary glands	200 mya
Primates	Lemurs, tarsiers, monkeys, apes	75 mya
Catarrhines	Old World monkeys, apes, humans	30 mya
Hominoids	All apes, lesser and great	28 mya
Hominids	Great apes, including humans	15 mya
Hominines	Chimps, bonobos, humans	7 mya–6 mya
Hominins	Bipedal, prehuman and human apes	3 mya
Homo	All human apes, ancient and modern	2.5 mya
Homo sapiens	All modern human apes	500 kya–200 kya

[*] Abbreviations: ya=years ago; mya=million years ago; kya=thousand years ago

the formation of Earth at approximately 4.5 billion years ago, and the earliest single-celled organisms emerged around 3.5 billion years ago.

Evolution Before the Primates

I am indebted to several researchers and authors for the background data provided in the next sections, especially Ian Tattersall, Chris Stringer, and others as noted.[3]

Early life forms, like many modern organisms, reproduced asexually. Cells reproduced by simple duplication of chromosomes, then division (*mitosis*), resulting in offspring genetically identical to the parent. At some point during the evolution of life, sexual reproduction evolved in some species. This adds a second form of cell division, *meiosis*, that occurs only in formation of the specialized sex cells (egg and sperm). Beginning with chromosome duplication, each chromosome then exchanges bits of genetic material with its unlike counterpart (from opposite sex), before *cell* duplication. Then comes the meiotic division, in which the new cells each divide, this time *without* further chromosome duplication. Then each daughter cell again divides by mitosis, producing four sex cells (eggs or sperm), each containing half the number of chromosomes of an ordinary body cell. When egg and sperm later combine, the fertilized egg contains a full chromosome number (46), half from each biological parent.

Although asexual reproduction uses less of an organism's energy, allows all of an organism's DNA to be transmitted, and provides no chance for sexually transmitted diseases, it provides little genetic variety (although some organisms have evolved ways of getting around this). Since diversity is the raw material for evolution by natural selection, it has been argued that sexual reproduction is widespread because it introduces diversity. This diversity facilitates adaptation to new environments, helps eliminate unfavorable mutations (hybrid vigor), and may aid an organism in its struggle with harmful parasites.

Biologists have begun to define the specific conditions that make sexual reproduction especially advantageous; these involve mutation rate, environmental selective pressures, and degree of variation in a population. There are some organisms that actually shift between asexual and sexual reproduction as specific conditions change![4]

Within the animal kingdom, we *Homo sapiens* are bilaterally symmetrical creatures, as are butterflies, spiders, crustaceans, worms, crocodiles, and many others. Many of our body-building and regulatory genes and on-off "switches" were present in ancient bilaterally organized creatures that are easier to study than larger animals. We humans are further classified as vertebrates because of our segmented backbones, along with fish, frogs, and others.

Within the vertebrates we belong to the category (class) of mammals, and the definitive mammalian features are especially critical to understanding human evolution and development. These include the following:

- Mammary or milk glands (evolved from sweat glands)
- Live births to immature young (rather than external eggs)
- Length of gestation related to brain growth
- Constant body temperature (warm-blooded and active)
- Body hair
- Changes in vocalization (anatomy and position of larynx) and hearing (middle and inner ear/cochlea)
- Importance of learning and play, particularly in the young
- A neocortex superimposed on an older, reptilian-like brain

Of particular note, the mother-child bond of attachment, connected to the infant's need to be nursed, is most likely the basis for human sociability, cooperation, communication, and morality. These behaviors are grounded in changes in the brain that occur during development, and in the coevolved capacities for vocalization and hearing that define mammals. As an aside, two of the middle ear bones of mammals, incus and malleus, evolved from the bony jaw angle of our reptilian ancestors; a third, the stapes, once was a bone connecting the upper jaw to the braincase in ancestral fish.[5] Mammals are quite recently evolved, and we humans are extraordinarily recent and "jerry-built." I borrow this term from neuroscientist David Linden, who used it to describe the human brain, indicating that, in evolution, the new builds on top of what is already there, rather than predesigning structures as an engineer might do.

Within the mammals, we humans belong to the primate order ("primate" denotes prime, or first, so it's clear what we think of ourselves). Most of the defining features of primates are related to the arboreal (tree-living) lifestyle that characterized the earliest members of the order and typifies most subgroups of living primates. The importance of primate traits for understanding changes in our own evolutionary line becomes clear when we consider human childhood, posture and gait, toolmaking, language, and culture. Defining features of primates include the following:

- Omnivorous diet, generalized teeth, and a relatively flat, expressive face

- Grasping hands and feet with opposable first digits (thumbs and big toes)

- Tendency to semi-upright posture related to living in trees

- Unique tooth patterns for different primate groups, important for classification (teeth frequently fossilize)

- Increased visual acuity, with color and binocular vision (two eyes used together, giving depth perception), and forward-facing eyes

- Fingernails and toenails instead of claws

- Intelligence, relatively large brains, and awareness of others to varying degrees

- Prolonged gestation and development, with learning as an important factor

Primate Evolution and Classification

The earliest primates were generalized creatures that evolved around 55 million years ago. They were traditionally classified as *prosimians;* this word describes them well because they preceded the monkeys and apes although there are also modern representatives. The newer cladistic categories and terms are different,[6] but are not crucial to understanding the major themes of this book. The largest evolutionary branch of living primates, traditionally called *anthropoids*, includes all monkeys and apes, including *Homo sapiens.*

Evolution of monkeys was characterized by increased emphasis on and improvement of vision in contrast to smell. The New World monkeys are distinguished anatomically by different dental patterns, direction of nostrils, and *prehensile*, grasping tails in most species. Old World monkeys, from which our ape ancestors evolved, have tails without the ability to grasp, and apes have no tails at all.[7]

Within the apes, the highly arboreal forms that move around by brachiation, or swinging through branches using the arms, include only the *lesser apes,* the gibbons and siamangs. The larger orangutans, gorillas, chimpanzees, bonobos, and humans are now placed together and officially classified as *great apes* or *hominids* although many writers still apply the word hominid to a smaller grouping of bipedal prehuman and human animals. Cladistic analysis based on genetic similarities rather than physical features group the two species of genus *Pan* (common chimpanzee and bonobo) and upright apes (ancestral and modern humans) together as *hominines.* We three species are separate from the gorilla and orangutans, which are less closely related to us than members of genus *Pan.* Increased genetic understanding of monkeys, apes, and humans has made the current terminology quite confusing. Various researchers and science journalists prefer different terms.

Because bipedalism (walking on two legs) separates our branch from that of our chimpanzees and bonobo cousins, I shall use the term *hominin* to refer to all fossil and modern bipedal great apes (the human branch), in contrast to the branch featuring genus *Pan*. That genus includes *Pan troglodytes*, the common chimpanzee (with three subspecies), and *Pan paniscus*, the bonobo, formerly called the pygmy chimpanzee.

In contrast to some writers who stick to the traditional word *hominid*, I prefer *hominin* because it is more accurate and specific, highlighting bipedalism as the defining feature of our branch. The other important term I use frequently in this book is *Homo*; it is the genus name for our entire human branch after the earliest prehuman, bipedal apes (the australopithecines and transitionals). The term *hominine* is included in Table 2.1 only for reference; it is the official cladistic term that includes chimpanzees, bonobos, and humans, distinguishing this subgroup from the other great apes.

An important but sometimes misunderstood fact about human evolution is that we did not evolve from any species living today. Instead, we share with the chimpanzees and bonobos a last common ancestor (LCA) that lived seven to ten million years ago and perhaps earlier. Each of the modern species evolved separately since the split, at least after the early years around the split. Yet as human animals, our genomes are remarkably similar to those of our living ape cousins. And we share considerable genetic material with all life on earth.[8]

With this, I turn to important findings within the fossil record of human evolution, beginning with the earliest fossils representing our hominin branch after its split from our last common ancestor.

For convenience, I group hominin fossils into three rough phases. The bipedal locomotion unique to our hominin branch began with small-brained prehuman specimens exhibiting a wide variety of features. All representatives of this *first phase* were walking on two legs some of the time and had anatomical features related to this form of locomotion. Overlapping in time with these first hominins, there appeared fossils of more efficient bipedal walkers with larger brains. These were the original members of our own genus *Homo*, which I describe as part of the *second phase*. I lump discussion of other, still more advanced pre-sapiens fossils, including Neanderthals, into a *third phase* of human evolution that includes the appearance of *Homo sapiens*. There are fossils that do not easily fit into one of these phases, in keeping with how evolution proceeds. But each phase illustrates an important transition in human evolution.

The Hominin Fossil Record

When considering the fossil record, many science writers have discussed the minuscule likelihood of organic remains surviving decay to become fossils in the first place. When the even less likely chance of a fossil being found by a paleontologist is added, the odds of locating a particular specimen become nearly impossible. Science writer Tim Radford, in a brief, entertaining article calls this likelihood "improbability squared."[9] The fossil record is only a tiny sample of the life that existed in the past. Each time a new fossil is found, scientists must rethink their hypotheses about animal and human evolution. Nevertheless, even that tiny sample adds up to many fossils, enough to give us a reasonable outline of what happened in the last approximately ten to seven million years since the human branch diverged from that leading to modern chimpanzees and bonobos.

At some point, some members of the hominin branch of apes began walking upright on the ground more frequently than apes had done previously. This was not a smooth process. Many anatomic changes were necessary and many false starts occurred. But by three million years ago, bipedalism (two-legged walking) had been established. Most of the early populations of hominins (sometimes called prehumans) that went through this transition have been assigned to the genus *Australopithecus*, while the very earliest are often called *transitionals* and they provide insights into the earliest portion of the first phase of becoming human.

It was only following achievement of life on the ground and habitual two-legged walking that major changes began to occur in the brain structure of various prehuman populations; these changes mark the second phase, whose members are placed into the genus *Homo*. We modern humans belong to this same *Homo* genus but our species, *Homo sapiens*, is the only one to have survived through the third phase of evolution.

This evolutionary process seems clear and simple when summarized in this way. Exploring the details and the rate of new developments creates a more confused picture, but it tells us much about how evolution works. Each fossil is just a small sample of what was going on in the past, and evolution does not invent organisms from scratch. We humans are fond of categories because they help us think about, talk about, and manage the world around us. We invent and impose these categories onto a complex reality to make sense of the complexity. But to understand how it actually happened, we must recognize that every organism is built from pieces of other organisms and has been modified from what came before. Categories must change as knowledge is gained. There are ongoing differences about where different hominin fossils fit, which ones are direct ancestors of modern humans, and which are merely offshoots that became extinct before more modern forms emerged. In fact, all of us could be called transitionals in the sense that our species continues to evolve.

With this as a backdrop, I next survey some of the details that make the picture so muddled, but so exciting as well. An important piece of the story started during the ancient Miocene geological epoch, which stretched from about 25 million years ago to approximately 5 million years ago and ushered in significant worldwide climate change.

Environmental Changes and Challenges

The natural environment in which our ancestors lived played a large part in human evolution. During the first part of the Miocene Epoch, much of the African continent was covered with lush forests that were home to many ape species. But later in that epoch, about 16 million years ago, the climate began turning cooler and drier. As this happened, vast forested areas were replaced by smaller patches of woodland interspersed with grassy stretches. These conditions changed the availability of food and its variety by reducing supplies of accustomed nuts, fruits, and tree insects. The new conditions also increased danger from predators because there were no longer as many trees for shelter when these large predators approached.

The later Miocene, especially in eastern and southern Africa, featured more rapid climate changes and greater climatic variability. Then, later in the next (Pliocene) epoch between two and three million years ago, a shift in the tectonic plates deepened and widened the Rift Valley of East Africa; this rift and its branches are still geologically active today. But then, there were numerous upheavals and volcanic eruptions. Geologists James Wood and Alex Guth argue that these events further accelerated the pace of local climatic change, increasing the challenges of staying alive and therefore the selective pressure on our ancestors.[10]

As outlined earlier, the already existing traits that originated in our mammalian ancestors (live birth, care for young) and our primate ancestors (opposable thumbs, binocular vision, posture, large brain for body size) were critical to how our ancestors adapted to various challenges. The environmental shifts set new parameters for survival and reproductive success for the many Miocene apes. In his latest book, Edward O. Wilson argues that it was the accidental sequence of changes in these traits that led us through a kind of "evolutionary maze" that resulted in our improbable evolution into apes who came to dominate the planet.[11]

Ian Tattersall, too, emphasizes the combination of challenge and promise of the new and different food resources that these homeless but fairly brainy apes faced during the long period of unpredictable climatic changes and retreating forests.[12] These ongoing shifts would certainly have increased the value of adaptability.

PHASE	DESCRIPTION	EXAMPLES
Table 2.2. Phases of Hominin (Human) Evolution		
I Africa 7-2 mya	Beginning bipedalism Apelike body and brain proportions	Transitionals: (*Sahelanthropus, Ardipithecus*) Varied australopithecines (*afarensis, sediba, robustus*)
II Old World 2 mya-?	Full, efficient bipedal walkers and runners. Enlarging brains	*H. habilis* *H. ergaster/erectus*
III Entire World 200 kya	Large reorganized brains Culture-language complex	Archaic neanderthals, denisovans, others? *Homo sapiens*

Key geological events and their connection to our biological heritage are beautifully illustrated and summarized in several timeline charts within Chris Stringer and Peter Andrews's book, *The Complete World of Human Evolution*.[13] Determining the climate, terrain, and vegetation from several million years ago is complex, and scenarios and dates are constantly being revised. In this section and Table 2.2, I draw from those geological guidelines for large era and period estimates, and I continue to draw from Tattersall and Stringer as well as other paleoanthropologists (see Notes).[14]

Of the many upright and semi-upright apes that existed at some time during the past seven million years, some were ancestors of later upright australopithecines and a few ended up as probable ancestors of all of us modern humans. Many more, however, were evolutionary dead-ends, even though they may have survived for many thousands of years, and some for a few million years. This is why many speak of a family bush rather than a family tree, with branches going in many directions, but mainly ending with no offshoots remaining today. Nevertheless, some patterns have emerged.

In this discussion I present a rough picture of what we have learned by emphasizing patterns of traits that define especially significant evolutionary breakthroughs, using the word *phase* to group fossils, as explained above. But this simplifies a much more complex evolutionary story. In reality, the fossils assigned to each phase show a wide range of anatomical variation. Because of this, different researchers may place them in different genera and species. It is often hard to tell where a given fossil best fits. Analyses of a group of fossils from the country of Georgia (in the Caucasus region), for example, is indicating how easily individual variation can be wrongly interpreted as species variation. Secondly, some fossils assigned to different phases overlap in time. Finally, as new material is analyzed, interpretations change and a given fossil may be reassigned to a different place on our complex family bush.

All discoveries provide clues into how our hominin ancestors may have lived and died. Table 2.2 outlines each phase to introduce the discussion that follows. Emphasis is on major trends that influenced who we became; these patterns continue to influence who we are today. Each phase is marked by major anatomical changes that reflect a new way of dealing with the world, an adaptive transition. But specifics are being revised regularly.

Phase I:
Hominin Transitionals and Australopithecines

Evolution of bipedalism took millions of years to happen. The first clear evidence for its emergence in African apes dates to around 7.0 million years ago in the late Miocene with the transitional ape *Sahelanthropus* and continues with a few others, including the prehuman ape popularly called Ardi (*Ardipithecus ramidus* from 4.4 million years ago), which some now classify as an australopithecine.[15] Evidence for bipedalism in *Sahelanthropus* comes partly from the position of a structure called the foramen magnum, the opening at the base of the skull into which the vertebral column fits.

In humans, this opening faces the ground when we are standing, and our backbone is roughly perpendicular to the ground. In contrast, the vertebral column of a four-legged animal is approximately parallel to the ground and fits into the back of the animal's skull rather than at the base. In many monkeys and apes, semi-upright in the trees, this opening is halfway between these two positions. When the crushed fossil skull of *Sahelanthropus* was reconstructed and later scanned, it was determined to have a downward-facing foramen magnum, as we do today. This animal also had remarkably smaller teeth than most great apes (especially canines) and a flatter face. These features alerted discoverers to its importance as a transitional ape and possible human ancestor.

The first discovery of an australopithecine fossil was by Raymond Dart in 1924 of the "Taung baby," which he named *Australopithecus africanus* (Southern African ape). We now know the fossil was that of a three-year-old child. But in 1924, few of Dart's contemporaries believed it could possibly be related to us at all. The earliest definite member of the australopithecines is dated to 4.1 million years ago. The most famous representative of the australopithecines appeared a bit later. This was "Lucy," an example of *Australopithecus afarensis*, for which many specimens have been discovered since she was found. Lucy's anthropological fame rests on her relatively complete skeleton and the Laetoli footprints that look almost identical to modern human footprints. Naming Lucy after a Beatles song that was playing on a portable radio at the time of her discovery contributed to her fame as a fossil.

The famous Laetoli footprints, left by a member of that species, were uncovered in 1976 by Mary Leakey. Continuing for about eighty feet, and looking almost like modern human footprints, these indicate a narrow foot with low arch, and a big toe in line with the other toes. These are traits of humans but not of other modern apes, who have opposable first toes. Updated recent analysis of the *A. afarensis* foot has reconfirmed that description.[16]

A more recent discovery of a quite complete australopithecine fossil, *Australopithecus sediba*, is proving to be important, and it illustrates the large anatomical variety during this period. The *A. sediba* group demonstrates a lesser degree of *sexual dimorphism* (male-female differences in size and build) than that of chimpanzees and closer to the degree of size difference between in *Homo sapiens* females and males. If this holds up for other australopithecines, as some evidence is indicating, it suggests that female-male pair bonding and reduction of male fighting for females began earlier than previously thought.[17] In general, species in which male fighting is important show greater sexual dimorphism.

The discoverer of *A. sediba*, Lee R. Berger, proposes that this particular species is the australopithecine link to early *Homo* forms.[18] Others claim that the link is Lucy and her relatives, or perhaps even the Taung child.

The early australopithecine representatives were mostly small, *gracile* types that subsisted on an omnivorous diet. Some later australopithecines, in contrast, are classified as *robust* forms because of their large jaws and thick skulls with large ridges for attachment of powerful jaw muscles.[19] The latter were originally thought to be adapted to diets of mostly harsh, fibrous vegetables, but recent studies of tooth wear are suggesting a more omnivorous diet for them also.[20]

There is overlap in time between several of the robust australopithecines and the fossils that may be early representatives of genus *Homo*. The degree of variation may reflect different microenvironments on the African continent during this time of massive and rapid climate change. The combination of features in a given fossil is sometimes interpreted as a form of natural selection's "experimentation" that produced some odd-looking upright apes (from a modern human point of view). Eventually, however, greater efficiency stabilized the bipedal adaptation. But some of the fossil variation may represent individual differences.

Given the climatic change and environmental shifting of those times, the fact that some fossils were found in densely wooded areas, while others lived in mixed woodlands separated by grassland, suggests that these prehumans were on the edge of a changing world. They were attempting to make the most of their well-developed arboreal skills and their newer terrestrial skills, perhaps moving from one terrain to another. Some would have been better at moving in trees and others on the ground, and the same is probably true of their skills for exploiting different food sources.

Remaining upright while standing, and moving smoothly without wobbling sideways with each step (as we observe in modern chimpanzees and gorillas when assuming an upright stance), require considerable coordination. Adaptive modifications in leg and arm muscles, bones, and ligaments; in foot and knee structures; and in configuration of the pelvis would have been important. Upright posture and gait also entailed modifications in the skull and jaw, in relative length and flexibility of legs and arms, and the finger, hand, and thumb complex.

Given the diversity of fossils, physical features common to the australopithecines include the following:

- Small size compared to modern humans (Gracile and robust forms are distinguished by differences in skeleton and skull shape and thickness of bones.)
- Brain sizes in same range as modern chimpanzees, perhaps slightly larger
- Variable degrees of bipedalism, ranging from intermittent to fairly habitual, with part-time arboreal lifestyle, particularly for nesting and safety
- Variable (and controversial) degrees of sexual dimorphism

With different mixtures of primitive and advanced traits in specimens, there is considerable uncertainty about where exactly each fits into the family bush. Certainly the evolution of bipedalism was more complex than originally thought. A number of ancestral sequences have been proposed. As new fossils are unearthed and analyzed, the scheme changes. We know that at least one of these prehuman australopithecines gave rise to the second phase, the first of the *Homo* genus, the first "real" humans.

Science writer Katherine Harmon provides a summary of these early hominin "experiments" and proposes a tentative family bush that incorporates recent developments, discoveries, and interpretations of this early phase of human evolution.[21] She emphasizes the wide range of variation and the messiness of links among specific fossils. We await further advances in genetic analysis for a clearer picture of our common ancestry.

Features Related to Bipedal Locomotion

Most differences between Phase I hominins and the branch that gave rise to chimpanzees and bonobos are related to walking on two legs. They include modifications in body proportions (for example, arm and leg length), degree of sexual dimorphism, pelvic structure, straightness of leg bones, opposability and degree of alignment of the big toe, articulation of arms with shoulders, size and opposability of the thumb, curvature of the fingers, and position of the head in relation to the backbone.

Of these, the story of the human pelvis is unique and particularly significant. In modern women, the pelvis is broad compared to the chimpanzee pelvis, while that of the australopithecines falls somewhere in between. Also in moderns, the sacrum (the back portion of the pelvis that is formed by the fusion of five vertebrae) is tilted forward and the center of gravity lies directly over the vertebral column. This results in curvature (lordosis) that keeps the center of gravity of the upper body directly over the pelvis. The thigh bones are then better aligned with the hip sockets for walking bipedally. The human pelvis is often described as a kind of "basin" or "armchair" and our lower abdominal contents (intestines, fetuses, etc.) rest in it.

Walking on two legs is facilitated by swinging the legs under the pelvic sockets, and this movement involves muscle attachments as well as bones. During human walking, balance must shift from one leg to the other while the walker maintains an upright stance. Without these pelvic adaptations, upright posture with a human-like gait would be impossible, and we would wobble with each step. Structural pelvic changes, in turn, influence the dynamics of childbirth, which must happen through the smaller pelvic opening resulting from the adaptation of upright posture. The staggering amount of fossil material now available and the new techniques for analyzing it will continue to invite new hypotheses regarding the evolution of hominin bipedalism. What is clear, however, is that it took place in Africa, where all fossils representing this phase have been found. Darwin had suggested an African origin for humans long before any ancestral fossils had been discovered there. This is further testament to his insight into the workings of evolution.

The evolution of bipedalism set us on the road toward becoming human. We still do not know exactly why it took hold. After all, the changes it caused in the pelvis made childbirth more difficult. And until the switch to an erect posture was complete, locomotion on the ground was probably awkward and inefficient. Recent work that models energy use suggests that bipedalism in australopithecines with their short and somewhat curved leg bones would have been less energy-efficient than modern human walking and running on straighter and longer legs.[22]

We do know that most primates are arboreal and accustomed to being semi-upright when moving around in trees. Some researchers have related hominin bipedalism to a more distant common ancestor of all the great apes, including the semi-upright, branch-standing arboreal orangutan.[23] All modern great apes use bipedal or tripedal stance occasionally during threat or sexual displays, while carrying infants, fruit, and other objects, and while reaching for hanging tree fruits or nuts. But chimpanzee and gorilla knuckle-walking is quite inefficient, and probably was an adaptation that evolved in those apes only after the split from our human or hominin branch, perhaps separately in each species, but this too raises questions.

There are disadvantages to bipedalism. Yet, to have evolved, it must have worked a bit better on the ground than other modes of locomotion.[24] Numerous hypotheses of why this happened despite disadvantages include the observation that a small animal can see predators or food sources at a greater distance if it is standing on two rather than four limbs. Another is that eye contact between mother and child, and between female and male, may be easier for a bipedal animal than for a quadrupedal one, and this would have been important in development of empathy in youngsters, and in adult human communication as well. Also, overheating of the body and brain in a savannah environment may be less likely for a fast-moving bipedal creature than for one walking or running on four legs.

In any case, moving over the ground between patches of trees on two legs, simultaneously walking, foraging, and eating would have been an early form of multitasking. An animal on two legs can carry things and can also throw objects, a marvelous new way to defend oneself from predators, and later to hunt animals less dangerously.

Regardless of exactly how two-legged walking came about, we know it did evolve, and we have a rough picture of what life may have been like for these early prehuman bipedal apes.

Inferring from the available evidence, we can develop an image of a probable australopithecine lifestyle. These prehuman apes must have been fairly well-adapted as scavengers in this new world of forest clusters separated by grassland, subsisting on tree fruits, insects, and nuts when those were available, and probably eating tender shoots, roots, and grubs near the ground at other times. Sometimes they would happen upon a small animal that they killed for meat or a carcass left by carnivores fleeing from the site of a kill. At night, these australopithecines would probably have sought trees for a safe and restful sleep.

Under these challenging conditions, the healthiest, cleverest, and the most skillful at using a bone or wood digging stick or a modified stone with their hands would have had an edge on survival. So might those who were best at hurling stones accurately to hit a target. There are sites where such stones seem to have been stockpiled. Finally, with group living, the most socially adept individuals probably had an advantage. This would have been a dangerous lifestyle, but it was successful for over two million years, ten times longer than any of us modern humans have been around.

The most successful of the australopithecines incorporated most of the traits listed above and set the stage for the second phase of evolution and the emergence of the first members of our own genus, the first humans.

Phase II: Early *Homo*

Running, Cooking, and Expanding Brains

The earliest fossils that fall roughly into the early *Homo* grouping of ancestors have features that suggest regular and more efficient bipedalism. By the time this transition was complete, the human post-cranial skeleton (everything below the head) had become what it is today, except that the skeleton was more robust than that of modern humans. And human brains had expanded significantly.

Early members of our genus *Homo* appeared between two and three million years ago, with their tenure overlapping that of the later australopithecines. During this period, East Africa was experiencing unprecedented heat combined with drought, so that some of the remaining forested areas were becoming savanna or grassland. *Homo habilis*, or "handy man," is the best-known fossil representing the beginning of this second phase of our evolution. Several other fossils similar to this one are sometimes referred to as *habilines*; they display differences from the australopithecine fossils without quite matching all features of the later representatives of the second phase. The habilines demonstrated three notable changes: (1) definite evidence of stone tool manufacturing; (2) an enlarged brain; (3) more efficient bipedal walking.

I group later representatives of the second phase together for convenience and, like some others, use the combination term *Homo ergaster/erectus*. This combined term uses the current species name of two of the key species associated with activities important to understanding this phase: fire making, long-distance running, and increasing cooperation. As with the australopithecines, there were varied representatives of the *Homo* genus, and many were evolutionary dead-ends. Yet some differences among fossils represent individual diversity rather than different species. As a whole, these early members of our genus were extremely successful, surviving for more than several million years, and at least one tiny population (*Homo floresiensis*, whose designation and genus remains puzzling) survived to almost 15,000 years ago, much longer than previously thought possible for any human species except *Homo sapiens*.

The following features differentiate the second phase (early *Homo*) from the first phase. They are grouped into two clusters, the first directly related to locomotion; the second related to brain and behavior. All are interconnected and typical of most *Homo* forms prior to the emergence of *Homo sapiens*.

Getting Around

- Increase in body size and height; longer legs and relatively shorter arms

- Modified angle of knee and hip joints; related soft-tissue changes

- Decrease in degree of sexual dimorphism (probably)

- Further decrease in jaw and tooth size

- Persistence of sloping forehead with brow ridge

- Long-distance endurance running and walking

- Loss of body hair, increase in sweat glands, and possible changes in blood circulation in the skull

Brain and Behavior

- Increase in brain size up to 1,200 cubic centimeters

- Incipient Broca's speech area; beginning of reorganization of brain

- Beginning of standardized stone tool traditions; transition from rather crude Oldowan stone tools to sharper, oval Acheulian hand axes.

- Beginnings of fire making and cooking

- Relative prematurity of infants; longer childhoods

- More cooperation and sharing; growth of empathy (inferred behavior)

- Wave of migration out of Africa; geographical distribution changes from narrow to wide

Besides the features related directly to upright walking, much of which enabled gravity to take over the work of keeping the skull in place, other physical traits saw considerable modification in early *Homo*. Teeth and jaws became smaller, faces became flatter, and the musculature supporting the jaw and neck became less massive. This overall trend toward dentition and jaw reduction had begun sporadically with the gracile australopithecines but became more pronounced and consistent during the lengthy tenure of early *Homo* forms on Earth.

Hands became more adept at carrying and manipulating tools, food, and infants. The earliest stone tool tradition was eventually superseded by the more refined stone tool construction that we see in the sharper-edged hand axes of the Acheulian tradition. There is also evidence of fire use and then fire making.

The increasing use of tools and their substitution for teeth in tearing and cutting food as well as defense against predators or other hominins would have allowed evolutionary changes in dentition. Large teeth and the bony and muscular jaw support for their use became less critical for survival, reducing selective pressure for sustaining these energy-expensive features and freeing more energy for the hungry brain.

Michael Hopkin summarizes Hansell Stedman's research into a particular gene (*MYH16*) related to jaw musculature. A mutation in this gene, probably during the time of early *Homo*, apparently inactivated (switched off) the gene's production of a protein that stimulates growth in the temporalis muscle, which moves the lower jaw. This muscle, very large and strong in chimpanzees, is considerably smaller and weaker in our own lineage. A muscle this massive must attach to a hefty, thick bone. Stedman suggested that the *MYH16* mutation, in reducing muscle size and strength, also enabled reduction of the mandible (jawbone) and thinning of the braincase, allowing more room for an enlarging brain.[25] His hypothesis is that this small genetic change enabled other critical differences.

Dentition and jaw reduction are also related to diet. The first use of fire, and then making fire and cooking food during this period, influenced the evolution of dentition and the jaw complex. Cooked food is easier and faster to chew and digest than raw food, requiring less of an animal's energy for eating. This resulted in a decrease in the size and length of our digestive tract, preserving additional energy stores for the requirements of the enlarging brain. This is behind Richard Wrangham's hypothesis that cooking was critical to making us human.[26] We can see how cooking food; chewing less and more easily; reduction of jaw, tooth, and gut size; position of the head atop the spine; and brain enlargement all interacted in a kind of mutual evolutionary feedback loop.

We can observe the reduction in size of the gut by comparing the human ribcage with that of a gorilla or chimpanzee. While the sides of the human ribcage are almost parallel, those of other apes flare from top to bottom, accommodating a massive digestive tract. A well-preserved skeleton of *Homo ergaster* shows a ribcage with almost parallel sides that was closer to modern people than to the earlier habilines. And, although fire was apparently trapped and utilized by earlier representatives of *Homo*, we have definite evidence of fire making from around 500,000 years ago associated with "Peking man" (*Homo erectus*). Wrangham also ties food sharing and cooking to female-male pair bonding and to an aversion to conflict during mealtime despite periodic food scarcity. These shifts in eating patterns may be related to strong ethos of food-sharing between women and men still evident in egalitarian hunter-gatherer societies.

We do know that, below the neck, our early *Homo* ancestors were anatomically like modern humans, with arm and leg bones essentially the same as ours in shape and relative proportions, except that their bones were bigger and stronger than ours. Further changes would take place in our early *Homo sapiens* ancestors, but these later modifications were largely in the head, face, and brain.

Another important development marking the second phase, the capacity for long-distance running, probably evolved within the first two million years after the appearance of early *Homo*, and it was most certainly practiced by long-legged *Homo ergaster/erectus*. The well-preserved, modern-appearing, and quite complete fossil skeleton of "Turkana boy," is of a young man, originally estimated to have been twelve years old. However, new evidence suggests he was only eight years old at the time of his death. Looking at this fossil, with his long, straight leg bones and modern feet, one can certainly envision his long-distance running ability.

Biologist Dennis Bramble and anthropologist Daniel Lieberman proposed in 2004 that long-distance running was instrumental in transforming our prehuman australopithecine ancestors into members of genus *Homo*.[27] It enabled early *Homo* people to scavenge carcasses and eventually hunt during daytime hours on Africa's dry savannah. By about 2.5 million years ago, savannah covered much of the formerly forested area. Most carnivorous predators from that time, notably the large wild cats, were nocturnal hunters, sleeping in the day. This opened a daytime niche for human hunting. These authors name 26 specific anatomical features shaped by running, arguing that this activity made us human. Changes began with *Homo habilis*, were refined in *Homo ergaster/erectus*, and were eventually inherited by *Homo sapiens*.

These features remind us also that we modern *Homo sapiens* can run incredibly long distances and demonstrate a level of endurance not matched by other animals. The San people of the Kalahari desert in South Africa are well-known for pursuing and hunting large animals during long daytime hours, even into several days. The hunted animals become overheated and exhausted before the human hunters do, allowing the hunt to be successful. Quite a few modern city dwellers take part in long-distance marathons and triathlons, exhibiting this adaptation even though we no longer chase our meat.

Two other human traits evolved during this period and were probably related to endurance running. One was the loss of most body
hair. Simply walking upright is not enough to beat the heat if you
have a furry coat, as demonstrated in a recent experiment.[28] Hairless
bodies are more efficient at utilizing sweat glands to remain cool during heavy exertion. Other mammalian long-distance runners cool
their bodies mainly by panting. Human hunters have an advantage
during long-distance daytime hunts because we have up to two million sweat glands (many more than most mammals) and only sparse
body hair, enabling sweat to evaporate quickly, thereby cooling the
body. Many other animal predators hunt at night when it is cooler.

Without body hair, however, human infants are no longer able to
cling to their mothers as other infant apes do. Like many other adaptations, loss of body hair had advantages but also introduced new
problems.

Dating the loss of human body hair was enabled by research on
the two species of lice that infest human hair even today. Most
mammals have only one species of lice infesting their fur, but humans have two different species of hair louse, one found on the head
and the other in the pubic area.[29] The ancient single louse species diverged into two different species around three million years ago, as
determined by DNA analysis. Because these lice cling to hair, loss of
human body hair produced a "geographical divide" between head
and pubic areas that they were unable to navigate.[30]

The second feature related to loss of body hair was darkening of
skin color, a focus of research for anthropologist Nina Jablonski. She
notes that in our closest ape cousins, the skin located under the thick
coat of hair is pale at birth, while the areas of skin not covered by
heavy fur are very reactive to tanning. The exposed areas become
darker through ape childhood. This effect can be observed by comparing facial skin color in infant and adult chimpanzees. Jablonski
infers that this pattern existed in our last common ancestor, before
divergence of the hominin from the chimpanzee-bonobo branch of

our family tree. Without thick body hair, the skin is more vulnerable to damaging rays of the sun. A mutation resulting in a new variety of *melanin*, which darkens the skin, was favored by natural selection in early *Homo*. Darker skin provides greater protection from the tropical sun's powerful rays. She argues that the key selective factor was preservation of the body's folate reserves, which are easily damaged by these rays. Folate is critical to the developing neural tube (spinal column's enclosed nerves) and the immune system (See Chapter 8).

Jablonski and her biogeographer husband George Chaplin study different forms of melanin in modern human populations to determine when these genetic mutations took place. They show that the initial mutation occurred during this phase II; additional variants of melanin appeared later, after *Homo sapiens* migrated and settled around the world.[31] Putting the lines of evidence together, it appears that long-distance running, reduction of body hair, increase in sweat glands, and initial darkening of skin color took place between two and three million years ago. This coincides roughly with the date for the Turkana boy fossil (*Homo ergaster/erectus*).

A particularly surprising and enlightening collection of early *Homo* fossils from a variable population has enlightened paleoanthropology regarding ancestral human populations. This population represents a migration from east Africa into the area of today's country of Georgia that occurred around 1.8 million years ago. Many of the fossils found near the town of Dmanisi are thought to represent early members of genus *Homo*. Ongoing analysis shows that one individual had been disabled for some time before his death and would have required considerable help from others in daily life. This is the earliest clear evidence for this degree of social concern combined with an ability to provide regular care.[32] Dmanisi's rich yield of skulls of various shapes and sizes also provides evidence that some of the variability, originally interpreted to indicate different species, instead represents individual variation.[33]

Another surprising and much-publicized fossil was found in 2003 on Flores Island, Indonesia. These very small-bodied, small-brained early humans are still puzzling paleoanthropologists. This new species, *Homo floresiensis* (popularly called "Hobbit"), survived long after modern humans came on the scene, not becoming extinct until around 15,000 years ago. The fossils have prompted various hypotheses because of their odd mixture of features: The brain size is within range of australopithecines, even in relation to body size, but other features, particularly the beginnings of brain reorganization and skillfully made tools, resemble *Homo*.[34]

These discoveries illustrate the mobility and adaptability of these early humans that enabled them to occupy environments quite different from those of their predecessors. They were a remarkable success as judged by their wide geographical distribution and their total length of tenure on the planet. The expansion from Africa into other parts of the Old World probably began almost two million years ago, shortly after they appeared. Earliest migrations were to tropical, subtropical, and temperate areas, while some groups later reached colder parts of Europe and Asia.

Now, however, all pre-sapiens humans are extinct. We *Homo sapiens* are lone survivors. But we have occupied the planet for a much shorter time than our ancestors did, only about 200,000 years. What led to dominance of our own species? Some suggest that violent competition with rival human forms was important, but I will argue here that a more general quality, increased adaptability to different geographical settings and to a changing natural environment, would have enabled success in competing with other human and migration into new areas. We see the beginnings in these early humans.

Consequences of Bipedalism

I focus now on two significant consequences of walking on two legs. First was freeing of the upper limbs for diverse use: tool use and manufacture; carrying of infants, food, and objects; and aiding communication in the form of gestures and face-to-face interactions. Second was the influence of upright posture and gait on childbirth and child development.

Freeing of Arms and Hands from Locomotion

Given the primate characteristics of opposable thumbs, substantial brains, and acute three-dimensional vision, having two hands free from locomotion opened a world of opportunity. Most primates use this ability to manipulate materials and to carry objects, and some even make simple tools and stand upright temporarily to engage in sexual or threat displays and fighting. But we humans are the quintessential toolmakers. We changed the entire landscape through inventing, constructing, and using tools. At one time anthropologists argued that tools made us human, defining our species as "the toolmaker."[35] Timothy Taylor, more recently dubbing our species "the artificial ape," in a book of this title, gave the old argument a new spin.

Freeing the hands resulted in evolutionary changes in our anatomy first seen in transitional and australopithecine fossils of the first phase. From that point forward, the hand coevolved with upright walking. John Napier in 1956 pioneered study of how the human hand evolved.[36] He identified two basic human hand grips, *precision* and *power*, for which the human hand became adapted through changes in the thumb and fingers.

Richard W. Young reviews Napier's work, further analyzing each grip. He thinks they evolved largely in response to throwing rocks and using pieces of wood as clubs in hunting and defense prior to stone tool making. He points to small changes in finger and hand structure beginning inconsistently in transitional and australopithe-

cine hominins and a basically modern human hand beginning with
Homo ergaster/erectus. Changes occurred also in the wrist, forearm, and
shoulders. The motor cortex of the brain underwent modification
with increased area devoted to the hand and particularly the thumb.[37]
More recently, analysis of the *Australopithecus sediba* hand has shown it
to be quite well adapted to a precision grip.[38]

A tool, defined broadly, is any item that an animal makes and uses as a body extension to achieve a goal. With this definition, tools
refer to all products of technology, from baby slings and hand axes to
genome sequencing apparatus, iPads, and the Internet. Historically,
stone tools, which were easily preserved as other materials decayed,
were given the most credit for marking the emergence of humanity
and for shaping further human evolution. These stone tools were assumed to have been crafted by men. Anatomist and anthropologist
Raymond Dart, discoverer of the Taung child (*Australopithecus africanus*) in 1924 in South Africa, postulated that tools made from
bones, teeth, and horns probably came before stone tools.[39] Recent
researchers are again emphasizing that our ancestors probably used a
wide range of materials.

Anthropologists also have come to recognize the important role
of women in early toolmaking. Modern women in hunter-gatherer
societies traditionally used wood and bone digging sticks for tuber
and plant extraction, large eggshells and skin pouches crafted into
containers and water bottles, and gourds that were carefully hollowed
out for various purposes. Baby slings (revived in recent years and
used widely by individuals of both sexes) were used traditionally in
many societies around the world and may have been a very early human tool, probably manufactured and used first by women.[40] This
invention relates to a second major consequence of bipedal locomotion.

Modification of Childbirth and Childhood

As our ancestors increasingly relied on getting around on two legs, the pelvis was modified accordingly. One result was a decrease in the size of the pelvic opening through which birth takes place. Modern nonhuman apes usually give birth easily and alone, while we human females have more pain and difficulty, often requiring help from others.

Until very recently, the consensus was that this did not make a significant difference to childbirth while the hominin brain remained apelike in size. In this view, australopithecine females gave birth more easily than we moderns do, while more efficiently bipedal and larger brained *Homo ergaster/erectus* women were beginning to have difficulty because of the mismatch between increasing head size and decreasing size of the bony birth canal.

Current research suggests that this obstetrical hypothesis does not tell the complete story. It was based primarily on the Lucy fossil (*A. afarensis*). Ongoing analysis of Lee R. Berger's *Australopithecus sediba* fossil is indicating pelvic changes more typical of later hominins, specifically a broad birth canal.[41] Observations of births in monkeys and chimpanzees have also aided understanding of prehistoric obstetrics. The transition from ape-like to human-like childbirth began further back in prehistory than originally posited, in the australopithecine phase, rather than beginning with the second phase of larger-brained *Homo ergaster/erectus* types.

The bony passage through the *Homo sapiens* birth canal changes shape from top to bottom, requiring the fetal head to turn during birth, emerging almost face-down so that the *back* of its head usually presents to its mother. Because of this, a human mother cannot easily grasp and deliver her emerging infant as other ape mothers do, since their infants present *face* forward, making delivery easier for mothers to handle. Some researchers have pointed to the wider and more rigid shoulders of humans as another source of difficulty during childbirth. This anatomical difference has also become evident in recently discovered fossils. Nonhuman primates have more flexible shoulder girdles, not so good for throwing or clubbing, but better for swinging below tree branches *and* for exiting the birth canal.[42]

Also, compared to its mother's body size, a *Homo sapiens* infant is large and its behaviors are immature; modern chimpanzees and bonobos, in contrast, are small in size but possess some coping behaviors at birth, such as clinging to fur. Human infants lack grasping big toes that enhance secure clinging to mother in other primates. Thinning of the mother's body hair would have increased the grasp problem. In these ways, the first days of life are difficult for a hominin infant.

The birthing changes would have made some form of midwifery beneficial and often necessary even for some australopithecine females. It became more critical for early women of genus *Homo*.[43] The value of helpers, or *allomothers*, to assist not only with childbirth but also with caring for a relatively large, helpless infant unable to cling to its mother would have put a premium on any impulses toward helping and cooperation among women, as hypothesized by Sarah Hrdy and others (detailed in Chapter 3). It may also have encouraged female-male pair bonding. No doubt this story of birthing issues will continue to change.

Summary and Conclusions

Developments connected to evolving bipedalism remind us that human evolution is a story of multiple factors interacting in complex ways. This is why human ways of living can be so variable cross-culturally and so difficult to untangle. Eventually we acquired a greatly enlarged and restructured brain and all that it implies. But our bipedalism was critical for all that came later, making us human in the first place.

From early on, the dynamic of cooperation and competition played a large role in how we became who we are today. Reciprocity and caring for others originated through natural selection in the context of group living. The several hypotheses differ in details, but all agree that we became "human" during the several million years when our ancestors were subsisting on wild foods, before the advent of food production. Some emphasize the earlier australopithecine and early *Homo* periods discussed in this chapter, while others emphasize the changes apparent in the third phase of becoming *Homo sapiens*. In any case, how our ancestors negotiated each prehistoric challenge set the stage for those we face in the twenty-first century.

The third phase of human evolution concerns the modern human brain and the culture-language complex. This is the subject of Chapter 3. We shall see how the combination of long childhood dependency and material culture influenced and were further influenced by the evolution of fully modern brains and language. Chapter 4 will focus more specifically on the evolution of human-style morality. Evolution of these two attributes made us into modern *Homo sapiens*, the conflicted moral animals that most of us are today.

3

The Brainy Ape: Glory or Tragedy?

If the human brain was so simple that we could understand it,
we would be so simple that we couldn't.

    —Emerson Pugh, 1977[1]

The brain boggles the mind.

    —James Watson, 1992[2]

This chapter is about how we bipedal apes became fully human
and how this changed the face of the earth. Its title, "The Brainy
Ape" highlights the human brain as a product of interactions among
environmental pressures and existing physical and behavioral features
outlined earlier. And the human brain was the final enabler of the
complex, language-based culture that defines us as a species. Yet it
worked as much in the opposite direction, with burgeoning human
society, culture, and communication creating the large, complexly
interconnected brain. The environment, human biology, and human
culture changed each other, and produced our ancestors' future and
our present. As described through the Red Queen analogy, changes
in the organism are always playing catch-up. Then culture evolves to
make optimal use of the improved brain. In reality, this interplay is
too complex to specify directionality.

    In writing about human brain evolution I do not add to the spe-
cific knowledge that neuroscientists, biological anthropologists, and
other researchers have developed in this area. My goal is to review
these developments, offer a perspective on their significance, and
share the perspective that I have gained through incorporating this

into my reflections on the state of our species and prospects for its future.

The human brain has become a popular topic of discussion and research in recent years. Almost every discipline has something to say about who we are, focusing on our ape-derived brains. Not only has neuroscience become central to the social sciences, but science writers from various fields have invented catchy book titles such as Jared Diamond's *The Third Chimpanzee* (2006) and Richard Coniff's *The Ape in the Corner Office* (2005).

The prototype for this kind of name was Desmond Morris's *The Naked Ape* (published in 1967). Increasing fascination with brains has been fueled by technological innovations in research tools. Computers analyze huge volumes of data in short order, and scanners image brains at rest and in action, even producing images of probable brains within incomplete fossil skulls. Breakthroughs in evolutionary developmental biology and behavioral observations and experiments using animals ranging from fruit flies to flounders to humans have added to these efforts.

Neuroscience journalist David Robson reviews nervous system evolution beginning with the sensory movement responses of ancient single-celled organisms to their environments, through diffuse sensory patches in early animals, evolving into specialist cells called neurons, into crude neural networks of communication, and eventually into a brain centrally managing the whole thing. Other creatures evolved alternative forms that enabled learning.[3] I like to compare this sequence of an evolving central nervous system with the cultural evolutionary sequence of small scattered bands coming together to form loose regional or kin-based associations, and in some circumstances becoming or being incorporated into centrally organized states (see Chapters 5 and 6). Neither sequence applies universally, but both describe some trends over time.

The Evolving Brain

How and when did the human brain evolve? We saw in the last chapter that the evolution of bipedalism set the stage for subsequent changes in brain and behavior by freeing our ancestors' arms and hands and making childbirth more difficult for females. This first step began around seven million years ago when the diverse ape species on the African continent faced massive worldwide climatic shifts.

Prehuman australopithecines were the advance evolutionary guard, members of their small populations taking the first tentative bipedal steps (Phase I). Two to three million years ago saw development of greater local and seasonal climatic variability; this is associated with appearance of early humans, the first members of genus *Homo*. Improved mastery of bipedalism and its benefits eventually led to improved tools, greater ability to cooperate, mastery of fire, and long-distance running. The trend toward increasing brain size characterized evolution from the earliest habilines into the later *Homo ergaster/erectus* people who migrated into other parts of the Old World (Phase II).

Anthropologist Timothy Taylor describes the results of this development as "survival of the weakest" in which technology replaced bodily strength and bulk to make us who we are today.[4] Conditions put a premium on group living, bonding, communication, and cooperation. Behavioral and social flexibility, i.e., general adaptability, became part of the mix and is a key to understanding how our brains evolved further and how they work today. Certainly, the explosion of technology (toolmaking) was critical and dependent on the catalyst of freed hands that were a result of regular bipedalism.

Elaboration of the brain's motor cortex and other brain changes must be understood in the context of technology and society. While we became modern below the head during the second phase, the third phase is about the emergence of *Homo sapiens*. This is defined by changes in the size and internal organization of the brain and by emergence of the culture-language complex. Discoveries of complex, finely worked tools and decorated objects and spaces demonstrate related lifestyle changes. From this physical evidence, investigators infer the development of symbolic communication (human language), and other social, emotional, and behavioral changes that cannot be precisely dated.

There are several ways to compare the human brain to that of other animals. We can compare absolute brain sizes, relative brain sizes, and brain organization in different mammals, specifically in the primates. Neuroscientist Sebastian Seung points out that brain size was emphasized in the past because it could be measured and compared easily. Study of other features, such as complexity or neural circuitry, requires technology that has developed only recently. Size by itself tells us little about how the brain works or how it compares to the brains of other species.[5]

One debated issue in understanding evolution of the human brain is the degree of continuity between it and those of our ape cousins and our direct ancestors in the hominin branch. Some argue for greater continuity, while others emphasize unique processes and structures that define the human brain. My view aligns more with the continuity hypothesis, while acknowledging the significance of specific developments that changed our particular evolutionary trajectory.

Brain Size

In absolute size, human brains are not at the top of the list. Elephant and whale brains are considerably larger. But these animals also have larger bodies than we relatively puny humans do, and it takes a larger brain to run a larger body. In relative brain size (brain size in proportion to body size), human brains do come out on top, but not strikingly so; dolphins and whales are close behind us.[6] Yet as Edward O. Wilson suggests, we dominate the world, while dolphins don't, in part because our freed upper limbs, hands, and dexterous fingers enabled us to develop complex technology.[7]

When comparing Phase I and II fossils to ourselves, we see over-all increases in both brain and body size as we move from the austra-lopithecines, through the pre-sapiens *Homo* forms, and on to *Homo sapiens* and closely related archaic species that together constitute Phase III. Some of the extinct Neanderthals had larger brains than we moderns do. And some early humans with quite tiny brains (such as *Homo floresiensis*, the "Hobbit") were able to accomplish feats, such as hunting larger animals with bows and arrows, that have surprised researchers analyzing that discovery.

Table 3.1 Estimated Ranges of Hominin Brain Sizes	
HOMININ	**BRAIN SIZE (CUBIC CM)**
Australopithecines	400–550
Earliest *Homo* (habilines)	600–850
Homo ergaster/erectus	725–1200
Homo heidelbergensis/rhodesiensis	1166–1325
Homo neanderthalensis	1000–2000
Homo sapiens	1000–2000

Table 3.1 gives a rough comparison of the size range for brains characterizing different phases of our evolution, including a set of fossil skulls assigned to an intermediate species known as *Homo heide-bergensis*, with fossil representatives from Africa, Asia, and Europe. Brain size ranges in Table 3.1 are based roughly on estimates from Ian Tattersall's 2012 book.[8]

Robin I.M. Dunbar, in 1992, first published his hypothesis that typical group population size among different primates is a function of the average brain size of the species. He determined 150 individuals to be the approximate size of a viable group of *Homo sapiens* and more recently demonstrated that this number represents the size of social networks of urban people as well as those living in bands or villages.[9] Beyond that range, informal mechanisms for keeping track of, cooperating with, and managing individual interactions break down and require a more formal organizational hierarchy. For most primates, grooming is an important specific mechanism for managing relationships among individuals, and Dunbar thinks that talking, especially gossiping, replaced grooming in hairless *Homo sapiens*. This proposal stimulated further comparative study of nonhuman primate societies and behaviors in comparison to human groups, institutions, and behaviors across cultures.

Dunbar and Susanne Shultz more recently clarified the connection between brain size and group size in primates by statistically separating specific features of group living. They demonstrated that neocortex size correlates more strongly to social complexity (group size, social alliances, social play, social learning) than to environmental complexity. Their conclusion is that managing coalitions, dominance relationships, and social control within a population drives group size and brain size.[10] Having a large brain makes a difference in managing social behaviors, suggesting there are natural brain-based limits to one's capacity for recognizing faces, managing relationships, processing emotional information, and manipulating and coordinating this information.[11]

Another hypothesis regarding brain size is that of Daniel Sol, who sees the ability of a species to invade new territory as a critical factor in the evolution of large brains. He provides evidence showing that larger-brained birds and mammals have more success in taking over new territories and developing behavioral diversification.[12] One might wonder if population growth drives movement into new areas, which then drives brain enlargement and diversification, another chicken-and-egg puzzle. Perhaps evolutionary changes in brain size result from complicated interactions among many variables involving environment, population, and sociocultural factors. Size and complexity are often associated, which brings us to the next section.

Brain Reorganization

The other significant process characterizing human brain evolution has been reorganization of its structure, which involves the lobes, smaller regions within them, neurons, and the connections among them. How are human brains different in this respect? Work in this area is progressing so rapidly that what I present here will soon be updated.

As noted above, some researchers argue that differences between ourselves and other great apes represent a kind of "Big Bang." Historically, the European Upper Paleolithic cave art was interpreted to represent a quite different brain at work compared to those represented by earlier archeological findings. Others emphasize the continuity and buildup of small quantitative differences that eventually result in something unique. Melvin Konner, Sean B. Carroll, Sarah B. Hrdy, and others describe this point of view. With evidence from recent finds combined with better understanding of the effects of climate and geography on the preservation of artifacts, many researchers are moving toward the idea of continuity over time, while recognizing smaller surges in different areas at different times, all combining to create a complex picture. Ian Tattersall observes that "the reign on Earth of *Homo sapiens* started with more of a whimper than a bang."[13]

The variability of brain features inferred from fossil skulls also suggests a nonlinear pattern of evolution. Many natural experiments were happening during human evolution, and less successful variations were winnowed out. Moreover, we know today that what looks like a striking and abrupt change in an organism can result from the mutation of a single regulatory or toolkit gene that changes how old material is used. This is consistent with neuroscientist David Linden's description of the brain as "jerry-built." Evolution of new structures based on or attached to previously evolved structures came to result in what he calls our "accidental mind."[14] This form of complex interaction between a species and its environment, in which both are modified, is called *niche construction.*

Just as the major transition to bipedalism had significant consequences for what happened next, so did the evolution of our large and complex brains have consequences for further evolution. As new opportunities became available, unexpected challenges had to be faced. Today, as we navigate the twenty-first century, we are facing some of the long-term consequences of being a brainy but conflicted ape.

Carroll emphasizes that complex interactions among genetic and developmental sequences shaped human brain evolution. Our brain's *neocortex* (a relatively new outside portion of the brain) evolved in mammals, expanded in primates, and shifted during primate evolution from emphasizing smell to emphasizing vision. With this shift came changes in brain structures that coordinate vision and movement (e.g., manual dexterity). Brain asymmetry that is related to speech and language in modern human brains is apparent also in our great ape relatives, but it was modified in important ways in our hominin ancestors. Although brains are not preserved, they can now be analyzed through reconstruction of interior surfaces of fossil skulls.

Sebastian Seung, in *Connectome,* describes the significance of developing interconnections for understanding brain function and its evolution.[15] Today, brain activity can be visualized and measured, adding new technology to the older method of dissecting the larger neurons of simpler brains to understand brain evolution and development. The word *connectome* refers to a map, a wiring diagram, of neuronal connections. A brain's connectomes develop from progenitor neuron cells that first divide, then migrate to different areas and regions, then grow the branching dendrites and lengthy, wire-like axons that finally meet and make connections. A connection event depends sometimes on random encounters, but it also responds to the animal's experiences, such as observing or learning a behavior.

Connections are pruned as well as constructed as we live, respond to stimuli, and learn. Seung compares the early connectome of a child to a first draft of a book, from which the author deletes, changes, and adds portions as ideas are clarified through thinking, ongoing research, and the process of writing itself.[16] Paleoanthropologist Dean Falk coined the colorful term "braindance" to refer to the complex, sequenced, interconnected, choreographed events that occurred as human development evolved.[17]

Neuroscientist Michael Gazzaniga suggests that reorganization of connections, more than size, made the human brain unique.[18] Because connections use space and metabolic energy, evolutionary reorganization of the human brain involved decentralization into local networks, each containing numerous short connections, with a smaller number of interconnections between local networks rather than multiple individually interconnected neurons, which would make the human head too large to carry around.

We shall see in Chapter 10 that human consciousness is distributed throughout the brain, and reorganization into local networks is responsible for that distribution. Moreover, the cerebral cortex is organized into roughly horizontal layers and vertical columns. Its surface is highly convoluted rather than smooth, and this provides still more area for a larger number of neurons. Another twist to the story is that some neurons themselves are specialized in function and can be differentiated by their pattern of branching, size, and shape. Their evolutionary histories differ too, and are currently being explored.

Recent work points to total number of neurons as an important factor in human brain evolution. Science journalist Ann Gibbons summarizes the findings of Brazilian neuroscience researchers Suzana Herculano-Houzel and colleagues: The human brain has three times the number of neurons of any other ape. This number is related to brain size and energy use supplied by nutrition,[19] which brings us to another link in the human evolutionary chain.

In the last chapter, we saw that cooked food is digested with less energy than raw food, which frees some of the energy and space within the human body that is otherwise used for digestion and muscles in other apes (e.g., larger jawbones and muscles; larger digestive tracts). This leftover energy helped to nourish the growing brains of evolving early humans. At around the same time, genetic changes reduced size and strength of teeth and jawbones and the large muscle that attaches the jaw to the head. The bony crest at the top of the head to which the chewing muscles attached was reduced and is no longer part of the human skull. These changes, like the digestive changes, decreased the rest of the body's need for food energy.

Another genetic change increased the amount of energy going to the evolving brain by increasing the number of protein transporters of glucose (an energy source) in the brain, while decreasing the number of glucose transporters expressed in muscles.[20] Neurophilosopher Patricia S. Churchland aptly summarizes the advantage of this evolutionary strategy: "It is more efficient to build brains that can learn than to build genomes that build brains with reflexes for every contingency that might crop up during life."[21]

Further research in brain evolution has led to discoveries of mutations that influence brain volume (the several microcephalin genes), increase size and convolutions in the all-important cerebral cortex, influence speech and language development (the FOXP2 gene), and decrease the rate of maturation of neurons. In slowing the maturation of neurons, this last mutation enables neuronal development throughout childhood and into late adolescence. The connections made during lengthy human childhoods allow for more learning and more time for both building and pruning connections, thereby increasing brainpower.[22] Since researchers are now able to sequence genomes of ever earlier ancestors, researchers in paleobiology, paleoneurology, and paleogenetics work together to probe backward in time and connect evolution and development.

Mutations that differentiate members of the early *Homo* genus from *Homo sapiens* are particularly significant because several of the mutated genes regulate development itself. Their effects are expressed during embryonic and fetal development and through infancy, childhood, and adolescence. And each mutated regulatory gene can make a large difference in the resulting phenotype (actual body, brain, behavior) because it changes how the affected individual develops and functions in real life. Yet each gene represents only a tiny bit of an organism's genome.

In this way, a small change in a genome can sometimes make a large difference in outcome. We are indebted to researchers in evolutionary developmental biology for this understanding. Ongoing and further work will certainly bring more surprises, puzzles, answers, and new questions. This kind of process may have been significant for the increased rate of evolution during the third phase of human evolution, compared to the millions of years involved in evolution of bipedalism in our australopithecine and early *Homo* ancestors.

Evolution of brain size, brain to body ratio, body size, absolute and relative number of neurons, and relative size of local brain areas happened in concert. Each aspect can be viewed through individual development. In *Homo sapiens*, developmental changes are extended through adolescence and even into a person's early twenties as connections are pruned and made more efficient through learning and experience. In contrast, the same process in our chimpanzee cousins is completed near the beginning of adolescence.

Evolution, Development, and Neoteny

The phenomenon of *neoteny* is related to human brain development and evolution. It refers to retention of infantile and childhood physical features into adulthood. In 1955, anthropologist Ashley Montagu popularized the notion that this process was especially important in human evolution.[23] We can see that human adults resemble baby chimpanzees more than they resemble adult chimpanzees. Similarly, infant australopithecine skulls appear more modern than do adult australopithecine skulls. Through changes in development, these neotenous (infantile) traits were retained for longer periods of time as humans evolved. Neuroscientist V. S. Ramachandran and others suggest that the combination of "neoteny and plasticity" worked together in human brain evolution.[24] In this way, a connection to behavioral plasticity (being able to learn easily, as children do) certainly seems logical.

Melvin Konner further clarifies the idea of neoteny, pointing out that development itself evolves.[25] In human evolution, changes in the timing of development have been complex and important. Neoteny and relative immaturity at birth are both connected to the degree of learning required for a youngster to develop. In contrast to the long childhoods of *Homo sapiens*, australopithecines became mature more quickly. Transition to the lengthy childhood pattern of today had its beginning in early *Homo* species, perhaps related to the beginning of cooking, although continuing analysis of the Turkana fossil indicates that *Homo ergaster/erectus* matured considerably faster than *Homo sapiens*. *Homo sapiens* individuals remain immature through a uniquely lengthened middle childhood period into an adolescence that goes beyond 20 years. During this span, we continue to learn easily and quickly, and our brains are still maturing.

Konner uses evidence from brain imaging, comparison of endocasts made from fossil and modern skulls, comparison of genomes, and evolutionary developmental biology to support this point of view. The net result for individual development is a tripling of brain size between infancy and adulthood in *Homo sapiens*. He and others speak of a kind of "external gestation" in that we humans spend part of our fetal lives outside our mothers' bodies, developing behaviors during infancy that other mammals accomplish as fetuses.

He relates this to an inferred *bottleneck* in human evolution, that is, a contraction of ancestral human population size caused by the complex of circumstances related to bipedalism, birthing, increases in brain size, and child care (described in Chapter 2). This bottleneck has been confirmed by several lines of evidence, unlike other proposed bottlenecks for later *Homo sapiens* populations.[26] Carrying and caring for young infants while gathering wild foods would have been challenging, and this challenge probably influenced how all of us eventually became who we are today, with big brains, language, and all. Babies whose brains would continue to grow considerably after birth would have had a better chance of surviving and having a surviving mother.[27] Flexible intelligence would have helped and been part of the ongoing dynamic of adaptation.

Chris Stringer discusses birthing in light of new techniques for analyzing teeth and skulls, including electronic replication of these features, to understand the fossils of immature hominins representing each evolutionary phase. These analyses have provided further insights regarding childbirth and childhood in different human ancestors.[28] The need for help with birth and care of the young became progressively more important as brains evolved and as humans became more dependent on the culture-language complex.

We might say that the *development* of our brains made us who we are today. Brain development depends not only on protein-coding genes, but also on their being turned on or off at the right time by regulatory genes and by numerous factors outside the gene and even outside the body. These *epigenetic* (near the gene) factors influence individual development. Because of this, comparisons of modern human genomes with those of other apes provide only a partial picture of differences between human brains and those of our nearest ape relatives. An understanding of human brain development during our lengthy childhood and adolescence is crucial to understanding how the *Homo sapiens* brain evolved.

Specific brain changes and related features found in *Homo sapiens* include the following:

- Specialized neural networks
- Various neotenous features, such as a flat face and large eyes
- Reorganization of interconnections
- Change in proportions within the brain (of lobes and specialized regions), such as the enlarged prefrontal cortex
- Increased importance of visual cortex
- Communication through symbolic language, reflected by increased regional organization in the brain; e.g., Broca's and Wernicke's speech and language areas
- Prolongation of myelination of axons beyond adolescence, into 20s
- Layering and columning of cortex in response to vast connectiveness

The third phase of human evolution is as much defined by the associated expansion of symbolic language and cultural institutions as by changes in the physiology of the human brain. Material evidence of fossils, artifacts, and DNA analysis together indicate cultural and brain changes, although cultural changes such as the advent of full-blown symbolic language and culture followed the anatomical changes. As during the two earlier phases, some small populations— sometimes by accident— would have been more successful than others at surviving and contributing genes and cultural traits to new generations.

The Culture-Language Complex

Human society and the developing social networks within it, cultural advances in technology and ideas, and changes in the human brain happened together; they coevolved. Researchers are attempting to put together pieces of how this unique *Homo sapiens* adaptation came to be. Assembling the puzzle requires learning what ancient cultures looked like, what prompted their development, and how changes in the environment, the brain, and human groups resulted in diverse cultures around the globe.

A Few Hypotheses

There are as many hypotheses for why a *culture-language complex* evolved as for why bipedalism became established. I note a few of them here. Many researchers have their pet hypotheses, but the actual transition probably involved numerous factors in different combinations depending on local circumstances. Earlier hypotheses emphasized mostly male roles, while more recent ones acknowledge and emphasize roles of women, men, and children.

The best-known mid-twentieth century hypothesis was systematized in a 1966 symposium entitled *Man the Hunter*. Group hunting of large animals by men and male competition for females were viewed as driving forces behind cooperation and communication among early prehumans and humans.[29] This followed an earlier formulation and book from British archeologist Kenneth P. Oakley called *Man the Tool-Maker*, which focused primarily on stone tools with the assumption that they had been invented and manufactured by our male ancestors.[30] Both hypotheses saw males as the center of the culture-building process.

An alternative view, described in a collection of essays edited by Frances Dahlberg, *Woman the Gatherer* in 1981,[31] highlighted the importance of female food gathering for provisioning families. It demonstrated also how different local environmental challenges, from limited natural resources to population pressures, influenced roles of females and males. A more recent hypothesis and book, *Man the Hunted*, posited that our earliest hominin ancestors were prey more often than they were predators or hunters.[32] Other hypotheses

suggested that fire and cooking (Wrangham), long-distance running
(Bramble and Lieberman), or even weaving (a "fiber revolution")[33]
made us who we are today.

Primatologist and anthropologist Sarah B. Hrdy proposed a sharing and caring (cooperative breeding) hypothesis as basic to evolution
of human culture. In her view, the long period of infancy and childhood put a premium on sharing of child care (allomothering) in humans. This was a solution to the problem faced by hairless human
mothers who needed to gather food, carry, nurse, and nurture babies
and toddlers for such a long period of dependency. Hrdy calls us
"special needs" primates because of these extraordinary needs.

Most students of human evolution now recognize the importance
of allomothering and development of human empathy as keys to understanding how we became fully human. The early seeds of cooperation with others spread eventually to female-male relationships and to
different local groups. Hrdy contrasts her view, sometimes called
"the mind-reading mums hypothesis" with the Machiavellian intelligence hypothesis. The latter emphasizes male jockeying for dominance, which we see prominently among chimpanzees and to different degrees in human societies.[34]

The notable features of human childhood are related to our being
altricial rather than *precocial* animals. Precocial animals are precocious,
able to fend for themselves shortly after birth. We, in contrast, are
altricial: We are quite helpless at birth, and have very long childhoods
during which we learn to be human (socialization) and to be members of a particular culture (enculturation). The results include language with arbitrary sound units and syntax, reliance on alloparenting,
teaching, and increased behavioral plasticity.

The notion of plasticity, so important in human evolution generally and brain evolution in particular, relates back to the old and outdated conflict between nature and nurture. Konner speaks of our genetically based, biological readiness to easily learn particular behaviors
and skills from a normal social environment. Nature, in this view,

prepares our brains to easily acquire certain behaviors. For language, this prepared biological platform is what Pinker, following linguist Noam Chomsky, calls our language acquisition device (LAD).

Every account of how we became who we are assigns a critical role to the evolution of symbolic language; some might say that language made us human. The 4,000 known languages of the world share basic features. Language development happens in all normally developing children, even in many with extraordinary childhood disorders. Particular genetic abnormalities affect this developmental process in predictable ways, which are being discovered as research proceeds.[35] We return to symbolic language in later chapters.

Many primatologists, anthropologists, and others now realize how important the changes in childhood and thus parenting were to our evolution. Interactions between infants, children, mothers, and other caregivers during human immaturity would have been critical to survival. In anthropologist Dean Falk's view, the inability of ancestral *Homo* babies to cling to their mothers' hairless skin resulted in the increased use of vocalization to maintain contact when mother and child were physically separated. This vocalization, a high-pitched universal baby-talk often known as *motherese*, may have served many purposes. Both Falk and art scholar Ellen Dissanayake propose that it may have been an important early step in the evolution of language and perhaps even music and the arts.[36]

Like Falk and Dissanayake, Hrdy gives vocalization between mothers and children a role in evolution of the culture-language complex. She ties it also to care by others at a stage when food other than mother's milk is beginning to supplement an infant's diet.[37] Kristen Hawkes proposed a "grandmother hypothesis," suggesting that older women were critical in providing both food and child care; she argues that this important role is partly responsible for the increased lifespan of women past menopause.[38]

Overall linking of physical evolution, environmental conditions, and cultural development is well recognized, yet specific features of language evolution remain hidden because the fossil record does not tell us directly how our ancestors were communicating. We do know that modern human languages are accompanied by nonverbal cues that include gestures, facial expressions, and postures. True spoken language, with long strings of sounds organized into words, sentences, and narratives, probably took its present form around 150,000 years ago.

Putting the Pieces Together

Researchers of different stripes are recognizing that multiple factors contributed to how we evolved and who we are today. The following list summarizes the behavioral traits related to changes in brain size and reorganization outlined above. Behaviors are inferred from archeological, fossil, and genetic evidence as well as comparative data.

- Cooperative or collaborative breeding with midwifery, prolonged child care, and help from others
- Extended period for learning and cultural acquisition, related to increased behavioral flexibility
- Manufacturing and use of tools from stone and other materials; fire making and cooking
- Food sharing and reciprocity, division of labor along sexual lines, intragroup cooperation
- Increased cooperative efforts; ethical and moral sentiments
- Mind reading and empathy; primacy of facial expression; pointing (shared attention); and learning by teaching as well as imitation
- Enhanced mother-child communication with melodic and rhythmic features
- Complex symbolic language using combinations of arbitrary sounds that form words and sentences (morphology and syntax)
- Storytelling and song expressing ideas about the world; autobiographical memory

- Long-term female-male bonding, extended kinship ties with recognition of ties with father and his kin, and beginning of inter-group trading contacts

- Self-consciousness: the idea or sense that each of us has the experience of being a "whole self" and not simply a collection of physical body parts[39]

The sociocultural features that had their beginnings in earlier ancestors came to full flower in modern *Homo sapiens*. We do not know exactly when each of these features began. Evidence from genetic and genomic analysis and comparison, fossil and archeological discoveries, and observations and interviews with historical and modern hunters and gatherers have converged to allow researchers to conclude that by approximately 150,000 years ago, *Homo sapiens* had appeared. Evidence for the transition to behavioral modernity comes from fossil and artifact remains and improved methods of analysis. These are bringing us closer to determining the amount of time separating anatomical from behavioral modernity.

Phase III: Fossil Evidence

The devil is in the details, and there are so many bits and pieces coming in that developing a comprehensive picture is ongoing. Unlike a jigsaw puzzle that has been scrambled but whose pieces can be fitted together, assembly of the evolutionary puzzle depends on pieces not yet discovered. This provides an exciting but sometime frustrating experience.

The earliest well-preserved *Homo sapiens* fossil is the Herto skull from the Afar region of Ethiopia, dated to 160,000 years ago. Chris Stringer compares this skull to two more primitive skulls from Omo Kibish of Ethiopia. The latter skulls have now been dated to a time earlier than previously determined, around 200,000 years ago, and may be loosely connected with north African Aterian sites.[40] The extent to which early, large-brained *Homo sapiens* (sometimes called archaic *Homo sapiens*) had modern human behaviors is not yet resolved. These include mind-reading (sensing what another human is experiencing), language, and ritual. The enlarged, reorganized brain may have predated these cultural developments.

Here the issue of abrupt or gradual change enters again. There is evidence for cultural features that most researchers tie to human language in African sites after this time. These include the use of pigments to decorate tools or living areas, the presence of drawings or engravings, repeated motifs, and objects placed with bodies and skulls after death. Use of multi-stepped techniques to form a substance (silcrete) or a hafted tool indicate planning and foresight. Evidence of widespread trade networks is another reasonable indicator of planning and intergroup relationships for trade. These activities make use of the ability to invent symbols that represent meaning different from, or larger than, the material object or its use. Connecting symbolic behavior with specific fossil remains is ongoing.

Early contrasts between the lifestyles of early *Homo sapiens* and *Homo neanderthalensis* were exaggerated. The two species shared the *FOXP2* gene (related to speech and language), and sexual dimorphism was less prominent in Neanderthals than was previously thought. Diets were not that different from those of modern *Homo sapiens* in of the European Paleolithic era. Consensus seems to be developing that many Neanderthal behaviors were close to those of modern *Homo sapiens*.[41]

Neanderthal skull size was greater, and skull shape and structure were somewhat different from that of *Homo sapiens*, but Neanderthal was quite a successful species as measured by its time span of 200,000 years and its wide Eurasian range. Because of the preponderance of limestone in Europe, coexisting Neanderthal and modern human populations are represented by well-preserved fossils and cultural artifacts on that continent.[42]

The several *Homo heidelbergensis* varieties found in Africa (*Homo rhodesiensis*) and Europe appear to be intermediate in anatomy and behavior between early *Homo* forms and *Homo sapiens*. Ian Tattersall calls them "the first cosmopolitan humans," who seemed to have migrated out of Africa to later spin off the local variants in other parts of the Old World, perhaps contributing to Denisovan, the Spanish Atapuerca fossil hominins, and even Neanderthal members of our genus; see Table 3.1. Stone tool kits vary considerably between different sites, indicating successful hunting technology and fire use, but indicators of symbolism for Neanderthals include only burials and perhaps use of red ochre. Finds have been puzzling and may reveal other surprises. It seems that moderns and archaic species may also have used some of the same sites and perhaps even mingled.[43]

Details for evolution of modern *Homo sapiens* are rapidly being modified by ongoing sequencing of DNA samples from fossil remains and from living modern people around the world, as summarized in a very readable article by Michael F. Hammer in *Scientific American*.[44] The most commonly accepted Recent African Origin model (RAO) that views sub-Saharan Africa as the sole genetic source of human genes throughout the world is being superseded by more complex models. The latter models account for small contributions of archaic DNA during migrations. Neanderthal contributions came as *Homo sapiens* groups passed through the Middle East into Europe and Asia. Denisovan contributions were added as modern humans made their way from central Asia, through Southeast Asia, then into Melanesian islands of the Pacific. Similarly, some modern African *Homo sapiens* also show small amounts of archaic DNA.

With this recently acquired information, Chris Stringer has modified his RAO model to a new one that he calls predominantly RAO, accounting for limited hybridization with archaic humans. He calls it limited because the sampling and comparisons are based on information from large selective sweeps that use particular genetic markers. This is another work in progress. The diversity of archaic humans for so many thousands of years on the African continent largely provided the material on which modern humanity was assembled. We continue to evolve today in various ways that are related to modern shifts in culture and the environment. These include the agricultural revolution, the birth of industrialism, worldwide travel and communication, reproductive technology, use of antibiotics, war and trade, new diseases, forced and voluntary migrations of people, and advanced information technology.[45]

Phase III: Archeological Evidence

The earliest archeological evidence for the culture-language complex of *Homo sapiens* comes from several South African coastal sites discovered and analyzed in recent decades. Several have yielded large amounts of material that is undergoing analysis. I borrow the apt words of historian and archeologist Ian Morris who describes the development at the Pinnacle Point site:

> *Homo sapiens* moved in here about 160,000 years ago. This is interesting in itself: earlier ape-men generally ignored coastal sites, probably because they could not work out how to find much food there. Yet *Homo sapiens* not only headed for the beach—distinctly modern behavior—but when they got there they were smart enough to gather, open, and cook shellfish. They also chipped stones into the small, light points that archeologists call bladelets, perfect as tips for javelins or arrows, something that neither Peking Man nor Europe's Neanderthals ever did.[46]

This site provided clear evidence of sophisticated stone tool making using a heat-based hardening process called silcrete firing in the production of thin stone blades dated at 150,000 to 110,000 years ago. This elaborate technology would have required modern cognition, advanced planning, and probably deliberate teaching of skills.[47] Some researchers suggest that the seacoast adaptation may have given the survivors an edge after any crisis, regardless of its cause. Curtis W. Marean, a principal player in the discovery and analysis at Pinnacle Point, considers current discoveries to be only beginning to tap the potential of the area for yielding information about early *Homo sapiens*.[48]

A second South African site, Sibudu Cave, revealed the earliest evidence for bedding mats composed of plant material with insecticidal properties, and also processed and fire-treated adhesive material used to attach stone points and blades to wood handles, all dated to around 70,000 years ago, about 25,000 years before previous dating of similar human sleeping mats in Spain and Israel.[49] Discovery at Sibudu of another ancient tool set, a bow-and-arrow combination dated to 64,000 years ago, is also indicative of modern cognition, planning, and behavioral flexibility.[50]

A third South African coastal site, Blombos Cave, produced sophisticated, sharp bifacial points for composite tools like spears; engraved bone tools; and tick shell beads decorated with red ochre dated from 75,000 to 80,000 years ago. In addition, the cave shows organization of living space within it. The decorated beads were widely distributed on the African continent and also east of the Mediterranean, indicating trade networks and symbolism. Symbolism is usually associated with language and ritual traditions, and wide trade networks indicate concern with relationships between different human groups.[51] These traits suggest artistic sensibilities and modern human behavior.

There is ongoing disagreement about the significance of these findings for understanding what happened next. At some point, the total *Homo sapiens* population may have plummeted to as few as 2,000 people, creating another evolutionary bottleneck. Several South African coastal sites were apparently abandoned around 60,000 years ago, and evidence is scarce after that time in that location. Some have suggested that this is related to the massive eruption of a volcano in Indonesia, but the timing seems to be off (although time estimates are questionable), so it remains somewhat of a mystery. It could also be that the reduction of forest areas curtailed the use of trees for heat treatment of silcrete.

Apparently, the smaller human population expanded again following this decrease, as evidenced by recent discoveries of tools, bits of human teeth, skulls, and post-cranial skeletal remains along the coasts of eastern Africa and across to the Arabian peninsula into what is Oman,[52] as well as north through east Africa, along the eastern Mediterranean coast and into eastern regions of Asia and Australia. Considerable evidence is emerging for the importance of fish and seafood in the diets of early *Homo sapiens*; recent findings on the coast of Australia dated to 42,000 years ago support this contention.[53]

Regardless of specific site data, we know that by around 15,000 years ago, modern *Homo sapiens* had increased in number and populated much of Europe, Asia, Australia, and some other Pacific islands.[54] Tattersall and Stringer also report other modern human migrations, as the North African Aterians moved east and other populations traveled north along the Nile to merge, perhaps, with Near East populations of 80,000 to 60,000 years ago.

Melvin Konner, Jared Diamond, Timothy Taylor, and others have pointed out that African human population expansion would have again reached a critical size for the flowering of innovation, which can be seen also in Europe around 45,000 years ago with the striking Upper Paleolithic artifacts and art that are associated with modern *Homo sapiens* in that area. These European paintings and delicate, carefully crafted tools appeared much later there than the South African art and artifacts described above. These authors suggest that a minimal population density may be necessary for an abundance of creative art to appear.

Once the culture-language complex had emerged, human life was drastically modified, and evolution continued. Cultural evolution, in contrast to biological evolution, can happen more quickly because it is based on the controversial and more easily changeable *meme* rather than the gene. It is multidirectional rather than moving only from parent to child, and can be transmitted to unrelated peers. Hence, cultural evolution results in a much more open and flexible system than biological evolution alone.

Summary and Conclusions

The behavioral changes that made us human all began on a tree-rich continent that was losing trees to climate change. In an area with fewer trees for our ape ancestors to find their accustomed foods, and to find safety from predators, group living would have had survival value. On the ground, they found safety in numbers. Babies and children were safer when mothers cooperated with others to care for and help provide food for their offspring. With hands freed as a consequence of walking upright, tool making could become more sophisticated, and objects and children carried. With changes in the pelvis and with enlarging brains, a premium was put on infant's brains being less mature at birth and capable of growing throughout childhood, prolonging dependency and enabling learning. This gave an advantage to those groups who shared food and child care, and who communicated efficiently. So the culture-language complex transformed our ancestors into different creatures.

In the third phase of human evolution, then, our modern human brain coevolved with the culture-language complex. We cannot separate individual strands of causation. Brain enlargement began gradually, with a growth spurt during early *Homo* times, and another between 750,000 and 200,000 years ago with the emergence of modern *Homo sapiens*. As happened with most australopithecine and early *Homo* variants, many early *Homo sapiens* probably did not contribute much genetic material to later populations. All of us modern humans, of course, have descended from ancestors that did survive to reproduce and eventually claim dominion over the earth, for better or for worse. Only time will tell.

My sense is that there must be a certain fuzziness to any definition of human nature, as there is for defining life itself, or separating pre-language from language. In evaluating hominin evolution, clearly differentiating ape nature from human nature and even fully archaic from fully modern, are ongoing tasks. Since we continue to evolve, future human nature may change and require a new definition. We human animals continue to impose categories and boundaries onto the continuous real world. We are modern only from our present perspective.

The three phases of human evolution outlined in this and the previous chapter resulted in human behaviors and processes that eventually transformed the face of our planet and all life on it. Cultural evolution interacted with biological evolution, with language as catalyst and mediator of this interaction. The benefits of flexible symbolic communication in negotiating harsh environments and co-operating to meet new challenges would have further increased the benefits of adaptability, rather than adaptive specialization.

Chris Stringer and Ian Tattersall stress the large influence of extreme Pleistocene climate changes on human evolution from ancestral australopithecines through all members of our *Homo* genus from *habilis* to *sapiens*. Beginning around 2.6 million years ago, the recurrent ice ages separated by warmer spells featured relatively rapid changes and extreme events. Around the world, striking local variability of temperature, precipitation, and plants and animals was typical.[55] This would have put a premium on any features that increased overall adaptability and behavioral flexibility. In this sense, environmental issues drove human evolution in general and human brain and cultural evolution in particular. With this eventually came human domination of the planet.

Today, we are again threatened by major and rapid climate change but with a vastly larger population and with atmosphere, oceans, fresh water, and soil in a vastly less pristine state. It is in this sense that I came to call us a beleaguered species. We return to this in Part IV (Chapters 9 and 10).

In the next chapter, I cover basic and social emotions, behaviors, neurotransmitters, and brain functions that help us understand how we became "moral animals" of sorts, yet continue to be "immoral animals" at the same time. I explore some of the values and capacities that push us toward tribalistic sentiments and at the same time pull us beyond those sentiments to consider ourselves a single human tribe sharing the same planet. We shall look in later chapters at the extent to which we modern humans continue to be influenced by the many built-in brain biases that inform our behavior and our thinking.

4

The Moral Mammal:

From Mammalian Morality to Human Ethics

[A] deeper understanding of the nature of our sociality may shed light on certain of our practices and institutions, and cause us to think more wisely about them.

—Patricia S. Churchland, 2011[1]

Everyone is a moon, and has a dark side which he never shows to anybody.

—Mark Twain, 1837[2]

This chapter's title reflects the fact that human morality is built on a basic mammalian template. I use *moral sense* for the biologically based impulses (emotions and feelings) that motivate us to care for others and treat others fairly. Although its evolutionary roots are more ancient than mammals, the particular behaviors that came to flower in our mammalian ancestors primed us to develop the moral sense that we recognize today. Our concepts, too, are products of evolution, and they are related to the dynamic between competition and cooperation (described in Chapter 1). In retrospect, we can identify several evolutionary events that were particularly significant.

Evolving Morality

Morality is about how we treat others, and it is an issue because we are social animals who live in groups. Group living requires a measure of predictability and it requires norms of behavior that enable social order. Some eusocial creatures, most notably ants and bees, are programmed, through genetic inheritance (instinct), to behave predictably and *prosocially*, for the good of their group.

The human animal has a more general biological program, a platform on which learning builds. This adds another dimension, influencing how morality plays out in particular cultural traditions and in the lives of individuals. Learning happens unconsciously and consciously during development and into adulthood, and it is sensitive to the emotional and social context in which it takes place. Other social animals fall somewhere between the eusocial insects and *Homo sapiens* in their degree of add-on to the biological programming of behavior.

Most of us recognize that we are ambivalently moral; we want to do what we think is right, but we are often pulled in the opposite direction. This ambivalence illustrates behavioral flexibility, and it is another expression of the cooperation and competition dynamic.

Bonding and the Evolution of Social Groups

If we define *bonding* loosely as coming together, we see that it is a basic process of the universe as a whole. Given a big bang or a less dramatic scenario, our universe's beginning involved a massive expansion of concentrated substance that precipitated infinitesimally tiny bits of matter. These tiny bits eventually merged, or bonded, as a result of electromagnetic forces and later on gravity. Multiple mergings produced larger bits, sequentially becoming atoms, elements and compounds, stars and planets, galaxies and universe(s). At some point on our remarkable planet, after the appearance of water, the highly bondable carbon atom combined with other elements to form a huge number of carbon-based molecules. A few of these molecules became the building-block nucleotides for more complex molecules.

In one scenario, a molecule within this chemical stew made a copy of itself. The beginning of replication, or simple duplication, was the foundation on which all life is built. Some scientists earlier posited a possible early RNA-dominated world, but specifics of life's origin remain open to further clarification. Others are investigating less complex, smaller molecules than RNA and simpler, more commonplace physical and chemical processes as candidates for the beginning of replication, the beginning of life. These feature an energy source, boundary or membrane formation that occurs spontaneously (think of water bubbles), ordinary chemical or physical links and reactions, some kind of catalyst or driver, and one of the several extreme but common environmental triggers present on our young planet between 4.5 billion and 3.5 billion years ago.[3]

We do know that once replication began, the race was on. The most successful replicator did what it could do best: It replicated. As this continued, copying mistakes (mutations) occurred, resulting in variation among replicators. Those replicators most successful at capturing energy would have outcompeted variants unable to do this.

The earliest replicators enhanced their own survival by joining forces, bonding again in various ways. Multiple clustered cells would be better protected from the environment (cold, for example) than single cells, enhancing the value of grouping and even specializing. To move toward each other, these early cells had to have been predisposed or attracted to other single cells or accidental cell clusters. Anything giving one cell affinity for another (temperature, chemical, a sensory patch) would serve that function.[4] And these features would have become coded into the replicator. Multicellular organisms thus evolved; there was no self-consciousness or purpose in this development, only a "selfish" replicator's drive to perpetuate itself and the value of safety in numbers.

Another key step in the grouping together of living things was the evolution of sexual reproduction, which probably occurred over a billion years ago, but only in some organisms. This resulted in greater variety for natural selection to work with, and it entailed a kind of early reproductive division of labor between females and males. Again, we see the role of attraction of one organism to another—sexual attraction—as a new kind of "glue" between organisms. Immature offspring of some species required nutrition, care, and protection, which created additional bonds.

Here we confront the question of motivation for attraction: what motivates adults to care for immature offspring? Understanding the answer to this question helps us to understand how all mammals, including the human mammal, evolved. And this rather torturous story returns us to the main topic of how morality evolved.

Multilevel Selection and the Cooperation-Competition Dynamic

To understand the role of Darwinian selection in the evolution of morality, we must look at the notion of the "selfish gene." This phrase is sometimes used to imply that *Homo sapiens* and other creatures are naturally selfish. But the word *selfish* describes what the gene does, not what the creature containing it does: A gene replicates itself without concern for other genes. Evolutionary biologist W. D. Hamilton coined the phrase in 1963, pointing out that nothing lives on between generations except the gene; it is selfish because its only goal is to perpetuate itself. Richard Dawkins further popularized this notion in his 1976 book, The *Selfish Gene*.

Genes need organisms to reproduce themselves. In real life, organisms compete and cooperate to survive, and thereby reproduce. Their cooperation with each other enhances survival and reproduction of genes. In the same book, Dawkins clarifies Hamilton's notion of *kin selection*. The fact that we share genes with our relatives gave rise to this concept. A simple example of kin selection is this: If a person risks his life, even loses his life, to rescue his child or his sister or brother, the rescuer is still preserving his genes and enabling them to be reproduced because these individuals have some of their genes in common. Considerable work has gone into developing mathematical formulas for determining probabilities of benefit for relatives of differing relationships. Unfortunately, it has proven quite difficult to apply these formulas successfully to real populations.

There is currently disagreement regarding levels of selection. The phrase *multilevel selection* still refers to Darwinian natural selection, but it is based on the fact that social organisms live in groups, that members of local groups tend to share genes, just as known kin share genes. It assumes that there are genetically based differences between the populations of more successful and less successful competitor groups. The notion of group selection originated with Darwin himself, who proposed that groups whose members are able to work together and cooperate would have thrived and reproduced, enabling population growth and expansion.

Controversy centers on the relative importance of individual, kin, and group selection, and about whether selection can happen at the whole-group level. I think of kin selection as a subset within group selection, but refer often in this book to multilevel selection, following D. S. Wilson, Herbert Gintis, and others, while remaining open to continuing developments in this burgeoning area of study.

In any case, grouping and even bonding, understood very broadly, go back to the actions of our earliest ancestors, who accidentally and unknowingly discovered a means of enhancing their chances for survival and reproductive success by clustering together and forming groups.

Selection favored genes that caused our more recent ancestors to share, to take care of their offspring, to foster connections with kin and neighbors, and to "do unto others as we would have them do unto us." It is easy to envision how caring and sharing enabled our children, relatives, and neighbors to survive, thrive, and reproduce.

We regularly do act kindly toward not only our children, but also toward others, even without thinking.

We have emotions that nudge us to live in groups, care for others, reciprocate favors, and act unselfishly and altruistically at times. These responses are rooted in how our brains assess and initiate behaviors suited to various situations. It seems reasonable that those early human groups able to work toward common goals without rancor or obstructionism would have thrived and expanded more readily than those groups unable to cooperate efficiently to accomplish tasks. A given group member's total fitness (ability to thrive and reproduce) depends on the ability to care for offspring and to foster connections with other group members. This relies on individuals having the kinds of feelings that encourage such behaviors.

The exchange of favors (prosocial exchange) that characterizes connections with another group member is called *reciprocal altruism*, or simply *reciprocity*. You scratch my back and I'll scratch yours. It governs all kinds of exchanges in human societies and may be one of the mechanisms driving group selection.

Among humans, we feel pleasure in many of our interactions with others based on the social sentiments of empathy and affection. This happens as we care for our babies and children, share and cooperate with friends and neighbors, and meet and greet strangers. These emotional responses are as much a part of our evolutionary heritage as are emotions associated with gaining things for oneself at the expense of others. Selfish and freeloading behaviors, whether motivated by jealousy, hatred of others, or simply pleasure in being "on top," are often thought to represent caring too much for self and too little for others. Yet these behaviors happen regularly. E.O. Wilson observes that the uncomfortable combination of selfish and altruistic motives within each of us results from multilevel selection; individuals compete against each other through individual selection and whole groups compete with other whole groups as part of group selection.[5]

We might view this ambivalence about motives as part of the co-operation and competition dynamic, as a means of achieving balance between selfish and altruistic motives in ancient groups. Today we display many behaviors that indicate conflicting impulses. These behaviors include cooperation, trade, alliance-building, peacemaking, love, and jealousy, rivalry, and war. While some of these ancient impulses have been tamed or pacified, we continue to express some and struggle to manage others.

We humans carry cooperation a level further than other animals, and we do it with the help of cultural tools as well as built-in biological tools. Cultural tools give *Homo sapiens* the tremendous flexibility that defines our behavior. The ability to learn, remember, problem-solve, and talk, combined with our built-in moral sense enabled us to create systems of verbally based ethics. The words *morality* and *ethics* are often used interchangeably. In this book, I distinguish *ethics* by its basis in and expression through human language. In all cultures, storytelling, gossip, concern with reputation, and ideas about what makes a good person influence behavior, and in large-scale societies written codes enforce these ideas. The details of how people ought to behave vary with specific environments and how particular sociocultural groups are organized (treated in Chapters 5, 6, and 7).

Can we consider ourselves to be moral animals to a greater extent than other animals? Sarah B. Hrdy asks us to imagine a bunch of chimpanzees attempting to travel by plane. This, she predicts, would result in many missing fingers and toes, ripped ears, and dead animals. In contrast, she describes how we humans peacefully "line up to be checked and patted down by someone we've never seen before, then file on board an aluminum cylinder and cram our bodies into narrow seats, elbow to elbow, accommodating one another for as long as the flight takes."[6] Chimpanzees could never accomplish this even though they do work hard at maintaining social ties, even sometimes consoling other after fights. But the ability of *Homo sapiens* to interact with strangers so readily in many situations may be a unique feature of our humanity. Although we are not perfect moral animals, we are capable of behaving decently much of the time.

I next focus on two components of reciprocity and cooperation that are basic to human morality and ethics. These behavioral features are caring for others and treating others fairly, and the ethical notions that developed from them are *altruism* and *fairness*. Observations and experiments with *Homo sapiens* in many different societies show that these components are essential for social living. Widespread support for the importance of a caring impulse and a sense of fairness comes from many ethnographic observations and reports, analysis of cross-cultural data from large samples of human societies, and experiments using reciprocity games. They are supported by the narratives of every major worldwide religion. The emotions that motivate and support impulses toward altruism and fairness include trust, love, attachment, anxiety, fear of separation, and social pain and pleasure.

Most humans would agree that although caring for others and a sense of fairness are vital for social living, we are far from a perfect species. Our ability to think, talk, and rationalize our behaviors makes us a conflicted species (or some say a "bipolar ape"). The following two sections focus on these two components of human morality.

Caring for Others

Neuroscientist Antonio Damasio, in his book *Looking for Spinoza*, describes the origins of social impulses and caring behaviors in our emotions. He ponders "how the world would have evolved if humanity had dawned with a population deprived of the ability to respond toward others with sympathy, attachment, embarrassment, and other social emotions that are known to be present in simple form in some nonhuman species."[7] He borrows Baruch Spinoza's insights from 1677 that ideas of virtue and good were built on a broad need for self-preservation. This is grounded in social relationships, and human happiness depends on it. Damasio likes Spinoza's formulation because it is based on observation of human behavior rather than religious revelation, which was the overwhelming basis of philosophy in his time. Spinoza was ahead of his times for recognizing the central role of social emotions in moral behavior.

Damasio suggests that emotions evolved originally as tools for managing life. The earliest single-celled organisms would have responded, like their modern counterparts, to outside stimuli (e.g., light, heat) by moving or changing their orientation. Whether these responses of early life indicate the beginnings of pleasure and pain is still an unanswered question. Early organisms, from single cells to multicellular creatures, had no central nervous systems or brains, and responses were reflexive. Eventually, the evolution of neural networks and then brains enhanced survival and reproduction in animals and centralized many responses and behaviors through what were to become emotions.

For Damasio, emotions and feelings were necessary but not sufficient for human morality to evolve. For this to happen, increased memory and a self-consciousness (sense of self) had to be added to the proto-morality that he attributes to other animals.[8]

Caring in Mammals, Including the Human Mammal

Mammals as a group require more parental care than most other animals. The kernel of mammalian morality is the mother-child bond of attachment, its associated emotions and underlying neurochemistry that involves hormones and neurotransmitters, social living, and intelligence. For an infant and her mother, attachment causes pleasure, and separation cause pain, and these emotions are basic to our relationships through life. Psychoanalyst John Bowlby demonstrated the importance of early emotional attachment (bonding) to a dependable caregiver for an infant to thrive and develop into an emotionally mature adult. This attachment, and the feelings of warmth and well-being that it conveys to both partners, is the basis for caring for others.

These responses and feelings, which Damasio sees as derived from emotions, happen via neurochemicals, which are produced in several ways. Hormones are released by various glands in the body to enter the bloodstream and influence physiology and behavior. Neurotransmitters are produced by the brain's neurons and are released into synapses (gaps) between neurons. They also mediate muscular and glandular responses. Interacting with each other, these neurotransmitter systems convey awareness of pain and pleasure, and produce various emotions that influence attraction and antagonism among social animals.

Emotions themselves are products of evolution. They are influenced by interacting genetic and epigenetic materials, social relationships in the context of environment and society, and, for humans, cultural values. Our infants become moral beings through the process of bonding with a trusted caregiver or caregivers. Other mammals seem to have an incipient sense of "fairness" and "reciprocity" which some call morality or proto-morality.

Patricia S. Churchland builds on this evolutionary foundation of connecting morality to attachments with others. She emphasizes the emotions of trust and caring that develop in mammals as part of nurturing the young. Like Damasio, she sees learning, social intelligence, and predicting others' behavior as important components of how social mammals adapted to their environments. I draw from her analysis in the next few paragraphs.[9]

The chemical tools for managing the lives of mammals include ancient neuropeptides that originally evolved in association with egg-laying and mating in amphibians about 700 million years ago. Churchland explains how two of these neuropeptide hormones, *oxytocin* and *vasopressin*, continued to regulate reproduction but were co-opted and modified for additional roles in mammals, including stimulating live birth and promoting bonding emotions in mother and infant following birth and during nursing. These two interact with female hormones and the neuromodulators that mediate pain and pleasure, including the pleasure of bonding. Other neurochemicals that play important roles in this complex interplay are dopamine, serotonin, and corticotropin releasing factor (CRF).

Although the hormone oxytocin has been publicized widely as a trust hormone, it was first understood to be present during mother-infant interactions, sexual activity, and other positive interactions. Some evidence suggests a link between the amount of maternal oxytocin present during a child's infancy and that child's ease of forming secure relationships later in life. Others who care for babies and young children, including fathers, tend to increase their production of this hormone. As oxytocin production increases in men, testosterone production decreases. The effects of oxytocin production are responsive to context in other ways. Besides its association with bonding, it is active during times of stress, increasing aggression toward intruders and playing a role in feelings of jealousy.

Peculiarities of Human Caring

Churchland uses an apt phrase to describe the complexity of interactions involving chemistry, neural connections, environmental input, and human consciousness: She calls it a "thicket" of influence; this word connotes the overwhelming tangled and dense nature of these interactions. The emotional pain and distress that mammals feel in response to separation from loved ones utilize ancient chemicals also, specifically, those active in simpler (ancient) creatures in response to physical pain. This too illustrates evolution's tinkering with existing materials to come up with something new, this add-on of emotional pain to physical pain.

If the mother-infant bond was the beginning of mammalian morality, then how did it happen that men as well as women are able to share, care, cooperate, and experience social pain? As described earlier, with bipedalism, changes in childbirth and childhood, and later, enlargement and reorganization of the brain, came changes in sexuality and parenting that influenced both women and men. In Chapter 6, I outline differences between the sexes; extension of caring to mates and others is basic to understanding human society.

Advanced learning and problem-solving enhanced the ability to extend caring outward. Such values are part of every human culture, and they motivate protecting, feeding, and teaching youngsters, enabling them to survive, thrive and reproduce. An important piece of altruism and caring as we evolved was providing and sharing food; generosity in provisioning others was a critical component of extending altruism beyond the immediate family.

Evidence that links neurochemical release to emotional and behavioral responses enhances our understanding of how natural selection has modified human emotions. Somewhere in our evolution, back in animals who appeared before mammals, there was a mutation that produced the first oxytocin molecule; it proved to be successful in getting offspring to be cared for and to reach reproductive age themselves. This started us on an evolutionary path that included pleasurable mother-infant bonding and moved towards other forms of caring and protectiveness, involving multiple hormones and neurotransmitters that produced and mediated our basic and social emotions and associated behaviors.

In these ways, our mammalian heritage primed us for becoming altruistic and generous. The human capacity for empathy and its cognitive twin, called *theory of mind* (ToM), honed human sensibilities toward differentiating kind from mean behaviors in ourselves and others. Primatologist and anthropologist Sarah B. Hrdy proposed that attachment, sociality, and empathy made our ancestors emotionally human before we developed modern brains and language, and that this facilitated attachments to people other than mothers in our ancestors (described briefly in Chapter 2). The birth of empathy transformed our relations with each other, extending our ability to care for strangers and, with effort, even for past enemies.

All of these bonding and altruistic impulses come with a flip side. Science writer Shankar Vedantam provides a wealth of information demonstrating that our feelings of identification with and affiliation to groups give rise to unconscious biases (tunnel vision) that influence our behavior toward outgroups (those not part of the initial bonding experience).[10] This downside, tribalism in its many guises, is the subject of Chapter 9 and a major concept of this book. This dual aspect of our humanity is manifested in the emotional ambivalence resulting from multilevel selection as outlined above. This dual aspect of being human is one reason that Frans de Waal calls *Homo sapiens* a "bipolar ape,"[11] Steven Pinker refers to the demons and angels of our nature, and David Barash, de Waal, and others describe our species as "Janus-faced."[12]

There is a battle of sorts within all of us between doing the self-indulgent thing and doing the "right" thing, between satisfying immediate or individual impulses and considering the needs of others and future generations, between having our rewards now or later. Being smart helps a lot, being able to predict and think about the future, learn, and be flexible in our responses is part of how we became fully human and who we are today. It distinguishes us from other apes and from our earliest pre-human ancestors.

The understanding of ethics or morality as a product of evolution is sometimes called *evolutionary ethics*. It recognizes that we are moral animals not because of a goal-directed process, but through natural selection that must work or tinker with the material at hand in crafting solutions to problems of surviving and reproducing. Its results are compromises that are not perfect. Evolution produced what we consider "bad" in our human nature, but it also produced what most of us call "good" in ourselves. In our species, caring for others comes from being attuned to another's thoughts (mind reading, or ToM) and being able to sense and even experience emotional states in another person (empathy). It evolved from ancestral behaviors of which we see traces in our modern cousins, the common chimpanzees and bonobos. Our particular evolutionary story is all about how the various sentiments or social emotions that came to be mediated by the culture-language complex define our species.

Treating Others Fairly

Caring for others and fairness are connected, with *reciprocity* as a connecting link. Their origins, however, may be rooted in different mammalian features. Fairness is expressed early during a mammal's developmental play, and all mammals are playful when they are young. Most investigators recognize that we first practice motor, cognitive, and social behavior in play. Along with play is the notion, whether verbalized as humans do or expressed solely through behavior, of fair play. Having a sense of fairness, like caring for others, is associated with cooperation and is necessary in social animals that require learning to become fully functioning adults.

I next outline the role of play and its connection to the development of fairness. Then I summarize its connection to caring for others.

Fairness and Play

The issue of fairness, sometimes framed as *justice*, has been discussed by philosophers for many years. Today, it is a topic of interest to a large range of disciplines from ethology and anthropology to mathematics. Its origin is obscure, but we see it regularly in the spontaneous play of young mammals. When bear cubs or kittens play-fight, for example, they often do so without causing injury, by biting gently or sheathing their claws. Two sources for understanding the role of play in the evolution in morality are observations of spontaneous play, and experiments with monkey, ape, and human subjects of various ages.

Animal researcher Marc Bekoff and others describe how animal play participants first agree by using a recognizable signal for play. This initial step denotes fair play. A fairness component can also be detected when animals refuse to play with group members who are somehow identified as perennial cheaters. Among animals, too, players regularly use self-handicapping (self-limiting) behavior that makes play partners equal. Bekoff concludes that play in young social animals is necessary for normal social development. He specifically notes the importance of bonding and tolerance of competition within wolf packs, which he studied over many years.[13]

Animals lacking play experience do not fare as well as adults. Assumption of egalitarian play norms or rituals seems to foster cooperation that is later required for more important social activities. Although nonhuman social mammals do not have the same concept of fairness as we do, the evidence indicates that they have a built-in sense and motivation toward it. Amazingly, 15-month-old human infants are able to detect fairness in others, and select toys on that basis. Developmental psychologist Elizabeth Spelke and her colleagues and students demonstrate this in their experiments with infants and young children.[14]

Stanley I. Greenspan and Stuart G. Shanker extrapolate their observations and experiments with human children to speculate about the nature of play in different phases of hominin evolution. They suggest that, through play and its temporarily relaxing of dominance behaviors, imagination is more easily expressed. This can further the growth of creativity and eventually spur cultural innovation. In an atmosphere free of status concerns, innovations come from any player, even normally nondominant or quiet individuals in the group.[15]

Robert N. Bellah draws from the work of researchers of human and other animal behavior in noting that dominance hierarchies and play co-occur, even though play requires the assumption of equality between players while dominance relationships are about inequality. Play and dominance behaviors are seen in species whose young require learning to become normal adults, in contrast to those species largely programmed genetically to know how to behave with little or no learning.[16] It makes sense that play is more prominent in species whose offspring require learning, because play provides practice for adult motor and social skills. Bellah characterizes childhood itself as occupying a "relaxed field," a period that provides time and freedom for practice and for novel behaviors and ideas to emerge.

He further connects this to human neoteny (retention of youthful traits, discussed in Chapter 3). Human children experience extended readiness to learn easily, through and beyond adolescence, and even into later years. Along the same line, neoteny might also be related to a kind of self-domestication of the human animal and to the use of shared care and teaching in contrast to the more rigid pattern of mother-only care found in most other apes. Human flexibility and the symbol-based culture-language complex may have been enhanced by this longer period for creativity, learning, and extension of play into later years. In Chapter 9, I return to this in considering the use of creativity in solving current problems facing our species.

Other Activities that Level Relationships: Making Things Fair

Other "leveling" activities can create and reinforce bonds. A striking example of leveling, the creation of a relaxed field of behavior, and a temporary suspension of "normal" expected hostility comes from World War I when an unplanned Christmas truce "broke out." In December of 1914, German and British soldiers were facing each other in the trenches when they spontaneously began singing and sharing greetings of goodwill, before resuming the fight.[17] If this incident could happen in the heat of war, if members of our species can sometimes agree to suspend hostilities, then the potential for peace and for harmonious social relationships must be lurking within us.

So, we have come full circle, back to the bonding and cooperation that require caring for others and fairness for their expression.

And we see the critical importance of communication, specifically language, in human expression.

In this light, I wonder if the behavior of grooming, such a prominent activity in nonhuman primates, also is a kind of leveling activity that utilizes neurocircuitry similar to that used in play. Grooming, like play, appears to foster reconciliation among social primates, even when there are differences in dominance. It bonds peers and cements friendships between adult females and adult males as well as parents and offspring. Did this evolutionary heritage of bonding through grooming make it easier for our hominin ancestral females, and even males, to bond with each other in collaborative child care? According to an old Yoruba proverb, "It takes a village to raise a child."[18] Perhaps the rituals of hugging, kissing, and even handshaking represent another version of bonding.

Robin Dunbar and his collaborators have proposed that the role of grooming in bonding was replaced by language as its human version.[19] In Chapter 3, I discussed the hypothesis that language evolved as a means for mothers and infants to keep in touch without touch, which was then extended to other relationships. We know, too, that language, the basis of human culture, enables verbal creativity, storytelling traditions, mythmaking, poetry, drama, and the rest. These human activities help to hold societies together and promote harmony.

In the last chapter I noted a connection of brain changes to the birth of human empathy and human cooperation, tying that to the long childhood dependency period during which much learning takes place. One foundation for its development is *shared intentionality* that we see in young human children who are developing language. This depends on *shared attention*, expressed in pointing and in interpreting pointing by looking at the object of the point. Young children acquire this, but other apes do not (yet dogs do). These foundations require communication and trust. Language is another critical foundation for development of human collaboration and sharing. The exact evolutionary sequence of these foundations is not yet clear.[20]

Group living requires organization, and in social mammals, dominance hierarchies are a common means by which group order is maintained. Wolf packs provide a good example. The importance of dominance varies with the mammalian species, and it also varies among individuals belonging to the same species. The interplay between fairness and dominance in groups also expresses the ongoing dynamic of competition and cooperation. Animals compete with other members of their own species, including members of their own social group, as in sibling rivalry, for example. Yet social living requires social order, as opposed to anarchy.

Science writer Natalie Angier summarizes and popularizes the importance of fairness in our evolution by speaking of the ethic of egalitarianism common to hunter-gatherer societies. Intolerance of stingy hunters is reflected by customs in which an individual hunter verbally insults his own bounty.[21] Angier reports that extreme hierarchy is not favored or tolerated well anywhere in the world. People have strong feelings about having a fair chance to meet common goals. She concludes "that the basic template for human social groups is moderately but not unerringly egalitarian." This impulse toward being treated fairly is evident in the powerful drive within most human societies to punish cheaters and freeloaders.

My choice of caring for others and fairness as two basic components of morality fits with the research findings of Martin A. Nowak and colleagues regarding reciprocity.[22] They use mathematical games (trust, ultimatum, dictator, prisoner's dilemma) to model strategies that people utilize in reciprocal exchanges. His team's analysis, based on computer simulations tracked through a large number of exchanges, indicates that some work better than others to foster and maintain cooperation. Most strikingly, the winning strategies, those resulting in long-term cooperation, involve both altruism and fairness. I turn next to these connections.

Fairness, Reciprocity, and Caring

Nowak and colleagues demonstrate through detailed analysis that, for win-win outcomes that endure over time, game partners must "be hopeful, generous, and forgiving."[23] These traits enable cooperation, in contrast to other traits that engender win-lose strategies that do not persist over time.

Reciprocity is about caring for others and expecting to be cared for in return. A simple example is giving a gift or hosting a party and expecting something in return at some point. In this way, caring for others and fair play are connected. In any relationship or group of cooperators, a problem develops in the presence of cheaters or freeloaders, i.e., those who are willing to take without giving back. An individual's or a group's willingness to cooperate depends partly on the likelihood of regular cheaters being punished. Freeloaders who get by without reciprocating receive some kind of punishment in most cultures. This pattern most likely began in the ancient cultures of our hunter-gatherer ancestors.

In keeping with the dynamic between cooperation and conflict, the benefit of a particular strategy for reciprocal interactions changes through time, because each strategy runs its course eventually, ending with an outcome that then begets a different strategy with a different outcome, which determines the next step, and on it goes. Some strategies have longer spans than others, but the dynamic is cyclical. Observing entire spans of history demonstrates that species, societies, and empires rise and fall. Statistically, Nowak's research demonstrates that extreme competition eventually begets cooperation, and extreme cooperation begets competition.

It may be that democratic institutions can protect human societies from the extremes, but this is speculation on my part. I see this complicated process as the balancing of cooperation and competition over time and space. This cyclical alternation between cooperation and competition demonstrates that we are an evolving species, not a perfect or a permanent species. And we cannot overcome our internal contradictions completely. At best, we can learn to handle them to increase well-being among people. A democratic form of government with plenty of regulatory checks and balances would seem to have fewer obstacles in the way of approaching this goal than one ruled by an elite or any group without checks to its power.

These conclusions regarding the competition-cooperation dynamic and the evolution of morality parallel the conclusions reported by Herbert Gintis and colleagues from interdisciplinary work with humans and with nonhuman primates.[24] The work presented in their collection utilized field and laboratory research from biology, primatology, anthropology, sociology, economics, and social psychology. The volume's beginning and ending chapters summarize evidence that human sentiment and motivation originated through coevolution of biology and culture over several million years. They contend that neither biology nor culture alone could have yielded the complicated mix of human motives and means that define us as bipolar apes. In their view, multilevel selection and coevolution of biology and culture produced these quintessential human traits and contradictory impulses, in line with Edward O. Wilson's 2012 description of the evolutionary maze through which our ancestors traveled in becoming fully human.

Gintis and others conclude that *strong reciprocity* played a large role in the evolution of successful cooperating groups, and they hypothesize that it may have a genetic component. Strong reciprocity is the tendency toward cooperating with others, while providing some kind of punishment for those who consistently do not cooperate. Such penalties are observed universally across cultures. This combination also "wins" in social dilemma game experiments done with members of diverse cultures, although there is cultural variation.

They also suggest that group selection would have been more important than kin selection in the real-life evolution of human-style cooperation in ancient times, since early humans most likely lived in local bands of varied composition (See Chapter 5). "Other-regarding" (sharing and caring) preferences and "inequity aversion" (a fairness norm) during human biological and cultural evolution would have produced this outcome.

There is good evidence from studies of brain activity and from social surveys and experiments that doing good (helping others without material incentives) gives most people satisfaction and helps individuals feel positive about their contributions to and participation in community projects. In the long run, this supports the contention that "groups with prosocial norms outcompete groups that are deficient in this respect."[25] In other words, selfish motives alone did not produce our existing human nature. Current research findings (and the observations of Adam Smith from more than two centuries ago) agree with this contention. Cooperation, economic productivity, and social living require a level of trust among group members.

Alan Page Fiske's description and classification of several different kinds of human exchanges add to this discussion; he describes the complexity of economic relationships and their roots in several different motives.[26] This current understanding of and evidence for multiple motives and exchanges emphasizes the value of a holistic anthropological approach that views economic relationships as embedded in larger social relationships and connected to moral values as described by anthropologist Marshall D. Sahlins (see Chapter 5).

Summary and Conclusions

Through natural selection, our species built on the traits that had their beginnings in ancestral apes. Some behaviors of other animals are similar to what we call moral or ethical sensibilities in ourselves. While human evolution continues today, our basic humanity was established largely during the several million years before we became food producers, when all humans were egalitarian hunter-gatherers.

The importance of other-regarding preferences that we call morality is evident as we regularly interact harmoniously with friends and strangers.

Here I have emphasized two evolved human impulses, one moving us toward caring (altruism) and the other toward fairness. The seeds of both were present in our mammalian forebears, evident in the mother-child bond and in play. In *Homo sapiens*, both impulses have been extended beyond mother-child interactions and beyond play to inform other relationships and exchanges.

Both appear in the several forms of reciprocity that constitute human kinship and social, economic, and political organization; they are mediated through language and interpreted through various cultural ideologies. The creativity of behavior and thought related to learning and play enable human adaptability. One consequence of coming up with diverse ideas is difficulty achieving consensus and getting along. Another consequence is that it enables us to use reasoning and language to problem-solve, enabling rapid change.

We are moral animals because we are social animals. We bond with others to reach common survival and reproductive goals. Morality arises from and enables group living, which requires cooperation. And when we cooperate with others, we act altruistically and fairly toward them. Many specific cultural norms are related to these two behaviors, but their specific flavor is acquired through learning and the particular culture-language complex that gives each of us a framework. Specific cultural frameworks need not restrict the reach of ideas. In keeping with Darwin's vision and that of Peter Singer, we can enlarge our circles of caring and fairness.

Finally, *morality* is about how we treat others, i.e., how we behave. One way of describing human *ethics* is its reliance on ideas about how to behave, as formulated through language. In this sense, ethics is a human product, while other animals have morality in the broad sense of sometimes acting toward others in a way that furthers their well-being. This distinction between ethics and morality may seem rather odd, but with evidence of our deep kinship with other animals and the compassion some of them show, even in the wild, it is hard not to credit some of them with a degree of moral sentiment. I have difficulty calling *Homo sapiens* the lone moral animal.

The next part of this book deals with the development of sociocultural variety, focusing on how different human societies are organized and how variable group norms can be understood in the context of varied environments.

PART III

PEOPLE IN GROUPS

We are ruled by our reason, but only until our hormones take over.

—Ian Tattersall, 2012[1]

How does our biological heritage influence the structure of human groups? Our needs for survival and reproduction are those of other animals. Yet our offspring require substantial care and learning to meet these needs. Group size and how we bond and band together, communicate, and organize ourselves influence and are influenced by specific cultural modes as well as human biology.

A society's particular environmental context includes terrain, plants and animals, water supply, climate, how resources are distributed, how abundant or accessible they are, and the degree of competition from other species and from surrounding or encroaching human societies.

Features of specific cultures develop in this context and contribute to how individuals develop and identify themselves. This happens through *socialization*, by which we become human, and through *enculturation*, by which we become members of a particular group. Learned, cultural patterns of thinking and talking about the world combine with a society's context to define the group's adaptation to its environment.

In Chapter 5, I discuss how different forms of social organization are responsive to specific environmental conditions. Technologies, methods of tapping resources and harnessing energy, organization of local groups, and ideas about the world develop in response to conditions. These features are intertwined. Hunter-gatherers, for example, usually have lifestyles and ideas about the world that differ from food-producing societies. And we humans were hunter-gatherers for the lengthiest portion of our tenure on earth.

Chapter 6 focuses on kinship as a universal means of pulling and holding people together in social groups. The original kernel of kinship seen in other mammals, and specifically in other primates, evolved in our genus *Homo* to extend mother-offspring ties to others, including fathers, in-laws, and larger groups. Studies of kinship in other social primates help us understand human kinship, but we humans stretch the concept into a wider social realm when we create groups that include persons who are not related. Biological and culturally defined differences between women and men are part of understanding human kinship and relationships among groups.

Human religion is discussed in Chapter 7 as another ancient means of holding people together. Since morality, one facet of religion, was covered earlier, this chapter focuses on two other components of every religion. One is ritual, and the second is narrative or myth. Religious narrative includes beliefs and stories about how the world, living things, and we humans originated, and about our place in the world. The arts, including music, visual arts, and dance, are almost universally associated with religion and will be included in this chapter.

The focus of Chapter 8 is tribalism, a central concept of this book. The same forces of bonding that hold people together often work to pull people of different groups apart. In becoming attached to our own groups and ways of living and thinking, members of *Homo sapiens* often use their strong small-group identities to denigrate other human groups. This attitude toward others defines what I call *tribalism*. This dark side of bonding underemphasizes our common humanity and the needs and goals we share. As such, it often hampers cooperation on a larger scale and breeds destructive conflict. Groups with "modern" technology and centralized government are not immune to tribalism, which comes in various specific forms.

5

From Foraging Bands to the Digital Age: Environment, Technology, and Organization

Civil government, so far as it is instituted for the security of property, is in reality instituted for the defense of the rich against the poor, or of those who have some property against those who have none at all.

—Adam Smith, 1776[1]

A man ought to be a friend to his friend and repay gift with gift. People should meet smiles with smiles and lies with treachery.

—Thirteenth century *Edda*[2]

Previous chapters focused on the evolution of universal features of our humanity, how we became human. Cultural variety, in contrast, illustrates human adaptability and behavioral flexibility. Our evolved culture-language complex enabled us to invent novel ways of approaching life's challenges. It enabled our enterprising species to explore and inhabit almost all environments of our planet. Some niches were easier than others for early people to occupy and utilize. As *Homo sapiens* spread out from their African home, multiple variables worked together to produce cultural diversity.

Making Sense of Cultural Diversity

Criteria for Classifying Cultures

We *Homo sapiens*, natural classifiers, regularly sort ourselves into categories. Western European explorers, reacting to the large difference they perceived between themselves and people they encountered in distant lands, put themselves at the top of the heap of humanity. From their perspective, the ability to produce many goods, sail around the world, and impose their own way of life on other human groups indicated superiority. This ethnocentric view led to difficulties but also to alternative ways of understanding humankind.

Leslie A. White, in two books published in 1949 and 1959, revived and redefined an evolutionary approach to understanding human culture by employing a "layer-cake" model with technology at the bottom, society in the middle, and ideology at the top.[3] In his view, technology, most closely related to environmental features, was causative, and causation worked its way upward. Tools and techniques for dealing with the environment (technology) influenced the structure of social organization and relationships in a given culture (society); ideas about the world and about how to live (ideology) were built upon the lower layers. This model was based roughly on the Marxian-influenced understanding of social forces that had impressed White as a young man.

More specifically, White viewed extraction and harnessing of energy from the environment as the basis of cultural evolution and cultural complexity. His model for understanding human society and culture and his emphasis on energy harnessing were particularly insightful. Yet today we have a better understanding of multidirectional causation and the interplay between biological constraints and cultural influences. White's view that symbolic language defines our humanity was another important contribution. He used *symbolling* as a verb to denote the inventing of arbitrary symbols and assigning them meanings that others could understand and use.

Most classifications of human cultural variety used today are linked to (1) technology and energy harnessing, (2) type of subsistence, or (3) complexity of social organization. Each emphasizes a different feature, but all three represent evolutionary transitions over time. As cultures evolve, change in one element often influences the other two.

Biological evolution is understood in similar ways: As some organisms become larger or more complex, they capture more energy and develop specialized organs or limbs that perform new tasks. In both cases, environmental change and stress are often the impetus for modification. In human evolution, early cultural transitions included increased energy capture through technology for extracting food, making fire, and cooking. Biological and cultural processes continue to coevolve.

It is important to view evolution as an ongoing process. It does not produce finished products and does not reach a peak and stop. Some of its results have a long duration with minimal change, and sometimes they become complex for a while. But over the long run the outcome is always extinction. So evolution cannot be equated with progress. It always happens in the context of other events, it often happens through a series of accidents, and it has positive and negative consequences, depending on one's point of view.

Schemes for classifying societies and cultures is imperfect and messy. For example, most hunter-gatherer societies are simple in organization, but if wild resources are concentrated and rich, local populations may become large and the social organization of groups more complex. Human societies, even state societies and empires, join together or break into smaller groups depending on circumstances; civilizations, like biological species, rise and fall over time.

Nevertheless, classification is useful, and probably necessary when we attempt to make inferences about how human groups change. It is a valuable tool for analyzing observations from past and present and studying large trends and associations among traits that vary around the world. Multivariate cross-cultural studies make use of statistical and digital techniques that can analyze large bodies of data, identify trends, and enable long-term projections. These can point to directions for further research and suggest new hypotheses for testing.[4]

One commonly cited scheme for classifying human sociocultural complexity is that proposed by Elman R. Service, who in *Primitive Social Organization* defined band, tribe, chiefdom, and state according to the size of the largest sociocultural unit in each type.[5] In this scheme, the *band* is a basic local unit with no formal organization uniting similar bands. Regional bands do share cultural features, including a common or similar language, and they often trade with and marry into other bands. Relatively egalitarian *tribes* have more formal social groups that are usually kinship-based, and they encompass several local groups. Ranked *chiefdoms* are characterized by a centralized focus on a chief and prestige-based ranking but they lack centralized power to enforce or sanction authority. The latter occurs only in *state-based* societies. Tribes and chiefdoms tend to be unstable forms of society that fluctuate in size and level of organization as external conditions change.

Type of subsistence has been important in classifying the cultures of prehistoric people because, until recent decades, the remains of tools and containers, marks on fossil bones, and wear on teeth provided the only data available to paleoanthropologists and archeologists. Archeologists first coined the designations for cultural evolutionary stages based on stone tools. The *Paleolithic* (Old Stone Age) is often used to refer to hunting and gathering, and the *Neolithic* (New Stone Age) to plant cultivation and animal herding. Because of the huge impact on human lifestyle, the Neolithic later came to be known as a food production *revolution* that marked the beginning of plant and animal domestication. Remains of early ancient cities, writing, and "monumental architecture" indicated a stage called *Civilization*, which developed independently in similar settings on different continents.[6] This chapter explores and compares these developments.

We shall see that along with the well-recognized features of a given natural environment, such as climate, terrain, plants, and other animal species, other human groups are part of a given society's ecological context. One's neighbors make a difference.

Baseline: Society and Behavior in Genus Pan

As a preface to describing human hunter-gatherers, I compare the social behavior of our two closest nonhuman, modern ape relatives: the common chimpanzee (*Pan troglodytes*) and the bonobo (*Pan paniscus*).

The bonobo/chimpanzee split took place about one million years after the hominin and *Pan* split.[7] Sequencing of the bonobo genome was completed in 2012, and ongoing analysis suggests that our human genome is equally close to the bonobo and the common chimpanzee although each of the three genomes is distinct. The common chimpanzee genome, however, has apparently undergone a higher rate of genetic coding changes than the bonobo genome since their split, suggesting to some investigators that bonobos may be a better model than chimpanzees for making sense of human behavior and society.[8] Primatologist Sarah Hrdy also reminds us "that all primates are social opportunists. Even those with nowhere near human levels of cognitive processing capacities, foresight, tool kits, or language are nevertheless adept at social compensation."[9] With this in mind, I compare these two species and then move back to *Homo sapiens*.[10]

Common chimpanzees combine foraging with some hunting of small animals, occasionally involving cooperation. They make and use simple tools by modifying natural materials to perform tasks. Physically, males are notably larger than females (sexually dimorphic) and are dominant over the latter. They also can become quite aggressive and have more pronounced dominance hierarchies than females. Males and females are sexually promiscuous. Intergroup relationships can and do sometimes involve cooperative violence that some have called chimpanzee "warfare." Melvin Konner reports that chimpanzees have much smaller home ranges than those of human hunter-gatherers, eat less meat, display ovulation clearly (in contrast to human females), and show little pair bonding. Also, grooming most often takes place between same-sex individuals.

Bonobos, in contrast, subsist almost entirely by foraging, with little or no tool use. They demonstrate a smaller degree of sexual dimorphism. Female alliances are common and they result in some cooperative domination over males. Bonobo females, like human females, are sexually receptive most of the time during the year and during most of each month, in contrast to other apes. Grooming between females and males is also more common in bonobos than in chimpanzees, and interactions within and between groups are more peaceful among these apes, even in all-male groups. Reconciliation of conflicts happens frequently through sexual contact that takes various forms: heterosexual and homosexual, genital and oral-genital, and even intercourse in a face-to-face position. It has been said that bonobos prefer to "make love, not war."

Eric Michael Johnson further reports that bonobos demonstrate more frequent use of bipedal gait and are closer to humans in body proportions, canine size, diet, group size, and aggressiveness within groups, than are common chimpanzees. In addition, hormonal expression and brain regions associated with empathy are closer to the human pattern. He concludes: "The killer-ape is our own creation and by holding on to this myth we are chaining ourselves to a pessimistic vision of human nature."[11]

Konner points out that human sexual dimorphism, development, and maturation patterns also resemble those of bonobos more than chimpanzees, and he also points to the importance of neoteny in human development. In both chimpanzees and bonobos, infant contact and care is provided almost entirely by mothers. This contrasts with infant care in humans, which is shared with other members of the social group although the amount of shared care varies from one human society to another.

Steven Pinker, in his work on violence, suggests that bonobos may be ape outliers, based on their exaggerated degree of neoteny compared to other living nonhuman apes and to the prehuman australopithecines.[12] That particular line of reasoning seems to contradict the generally accepted understanding of us *Homo sapiens* as the ultimate in neotenous development. Reduction in sexual dimorphism, too, had taken place by the time of *Homo ergaster/erectus* (the second phase of human evolution). Yet research on bonobos is ongoing, and we do not have a complete picture of this species.

The strength of different emotions and behaviors varies from one species to another, and it also varies in response to environment, food supply, and other factors. There are differences in typical behaviors between related species (e.g. chimpanzees, bonobos, humans) and within the same species. There are also large individual differences between members of the same species, and among humans from the same sociocultural tradition. With this background, we move to our human past as hunter-gatherers. This ancient adaptation characterized the ancestors of all of us and has provoked considerable interest over many years because of its persistence and because of the common threads running through these widely scattered cultures.

On Generalizing from Present to Past

One line of study speculates about how ape social groups were modified to form societies of pre-human hominins after the split with genus *Pan*. Because our ancient common ape ancestor cannot be observed, we must glean clues from biology, cultural anthropology, history, and archeology. Our ancestors were first hunter-gatherers, and this way of life lasted far longer than any other mode of subsistence to date. Moreover, almost all animals share this food-collecting way of life. The ability to *produce* food is rare. In *Homo sapiens*, the development and spread of food production and the domestication of plants and animals transformed our relationship with the rest of nature. This transformation is a key to understanding how human cultures evolved and will be a recurring theme in this chapter.

The Neolithic, or food-producing revolution, gave rise fairly quickly to civilization in some parts of the world, mostly in fertile river valleys. At the same time, humans in less hospitable areas continued to pursue hunting and gathering, sometimes in combination with simple food production. These hunter-gatherers remained outside or on the margins of state-based societies well into the modern era. Because of this, we have much to learn from observations, reports, and experiments with people living these once-prevalent hunter-gatherer lifestyles. The ancestors of every one of us pursued this way of life long before food production began.

Some investigators object to using contemporary hunter-gatherers to speculate about ancient people. Yet we do not hesitate to use our knowledge of the organization of modern state-based societies to help decipher archeological evidence regarding early civilizations. Likewise, it seems to me that refusal or failure to use knowledge of modern hunter-gatherers is unwise even if what we know does not fully represent the past. Making an effort to explain sociocultural diversity can help us better understand our sometimes puzzling impulses and behaviors. It can also help us recognize the significance of the agricultural revolution as a catalyst for the chain of accelerating events and processes that continue today.

At the same time, we must be wary of generalizing too broadly from hunter-gatherers to ancestral human lifestyles. Modern hunter-gatherer cultures have histories of their own, and these histories often include long-term relationships with societies of farmers and herders as well as colonial and modern state-based societies. All modern hunter-gatherer societies were at some point subjugated by other cultures and are now part of larger state-based societies. Robert L. Kelly describes today's hunter-gatherers as representing a spectrum of diverse adaptations.[13] Lawrence H. Keeley reminds us that since early contact with hunter-gatherers, Westerners have been thinking ethno-centrically about this way of life, simplifying its complexity either in the direction of Thomas Hobbes's or Jean-Jacques Rousseau's perceptions of human nature as violent and nasty, or peaceful and kind, respectively. In both cases, researchers and other observers have erred toward ascribing more uniformity of personality and culture to these peoples than actually exists.[14]

Despite diversity in these living cultures, we can make some generalizations by recognizing different varieties of hunter-gatherers, as suggested by anthropologists who specialize in this way of life.[15] Criteria used for developing hypotheses have included (1) degree of egalitarianism, (2) nomadism, (3) ability to store food (called "delayed return"), and (4) local climate. For comparison with food-producing societies later in the chapter, I assume that food storage, permanent settlements, and hierarchy or ranking developed later than an "immediate return" (no food storage), nomadic way of life.

Another caveat is that those hunter-gatherer societies that remained as entities long enough to be studied are those who retreated or were pushed into the most marginal environments of the earth, so we may never know how well this small sample represents our common past.

Primatologist Bernard Chapais, anthropologist Christopher Boehm, and others suggest that we humans were at some point able to override the strong dominance and hierarchal tendencies that were probably important in our ancestors. Doing this, these early humans improved their ability to cooperate more effectively and in increasingly larger groups. How this happened and whether it can continue into the future are important questions. Canadian philosopher Benoît Dubreuil describes a stepwise process involving multiple feedbacks involving technology, body form, brain, cooperation in child care, food sharing, and ongoing development of behaviors that made us human. Together, these interactions resulted in the strong egalitarian ethos common to a number of hunter-gatherer societies.

Only later, with modern *Homo sapiens,* was a new kind of hierarchy enabled, again fostered by brain changes related to creativity, cognition, and complex tools of the types being found at early *Homo sapiens* sites, such as Blombos Cave. Dubreuil argues that changes in temporal and parietal lobes and their connections increased individuals' ability to understand other perspectives, enabling cultural variability that incorporated advanced cognition. Re-emergence of human hierarchy occurred still later, among already modern humans living in areas that supported greater population concentration and tighter networks among different local communities.[16]

With this background established, I describe a lifestyle common to some historical hunter-gatherers that is thought to be the closest to that of prehistoric *Homo sapiens.*

The Paleolithic, Hunter-Gatherer Adaptation

Richard B. Lee and Richard Daly, in their comprehensive "Introduction" to a large volume of essays that comprise *The Cambridge Encyclopedia of Hunters and Gatherers,* define foraging as "subsistence based on hunting of wild animals, gathering of wild plant foods, and fishing, with no domestication of plants, and no domesticated animals except the dog."[17] While recognizing that actual societies fall along a continuum representing prehistoric and historic differences in degree of dependence on foraging for a livelihood, they isolate several basic cultural universals that apply to those societies that fit this definition.

One universal is organization featuring small nomadic bands of variously related kin that disperse and come together regularly in relation to resources as these shift throughout the year. This pattern is called dispersal and concentration, and is typical when food sources are unpredictable. A second feature is egalitarianism, with informal leadership based on popular opinion (often linked to sharing resources) rather than on force-based authority. This results in a kind of personal freedom that is rare in today's world but that also increases vulnerability to takeover by other societies. Common use of land, either unrestricted or shared through reciprocal arrangements, is a third universal (connected to being nomadic); related to this, inheritance of goods is unimportant. Fourth, a widespread ideology perceives the natural world as a mostly generous and often animated presence that exists in mythical relationship with people.

Consistent with this ideology, value is placed on human sharing and generosity rather than on accumulation, and the "cardinal sin" is hoarding food or taking too much credit for one's individual contribution. Sarah B. Hrdy and Melvin Konner, having researched childhood in particular,[18] describe egalitarian hunter-gatherers as usually gentle in their ingroup personal relationships and care of children, going out of their way to be inoffensive to others and indulgent toward children. Fighting within the group does exist although it varies among groups and appears to be associated with a combination of features related to environmental context. Both use details of childhood from several carefully researched and observed warm-climate foragers from historical times to make inferences about our hunter-gatherer past. These include the San of southern Africa, the Ache of Paraguay, the Agta of the Philippines, the Aka and the Efe of central Africa, and the Hadza of Tanzania.

Other researchers offer additional insights. In his book, *Moral Origins*, Christopher Boehm focuses on a much larger sample of hunter-gatherers he calls Late Pleistocene Appropriate (LPA) foragers. These are societies that he selected from a total of 339 that are adequately described in the literature.[19] For his study, Boehm eliminated all societies that could not have represented early hunter-gatherers, for example, the horseback-riding hunters of the American West whose observed culture developed partly in response to the European fur trade, and the hierarchal Northwest Coast Indians who harvested large runs of salmon and even had slaves.

Similar to Lee and Daly's markers of traditional hunter-gatherers, Boehm's criteria for selection were nomadism and lack of food storage. His culling resulted in a sample of 50 societies that he inferred to be similar to populations of *Homo sapiens* who migrated out of Africa to populate the rest of the world. After his detailed coding of features of these societies, he and his team developed a picture of early hunter-gatherer culture that was similar but not identical to those described by Lee and Daly, Konner, and Hrdy.

In 1972 Marshall Sahlins described this way of life as the "original affluent society."[20] His definition of affluence contrasts with the usual understanding of affluence as the ability to purchase and make use of many material goods. He saw the hunter-gatherer lifestyle as an alternative route to affluence: having little but also wanting little. It was based on a relationship between people, work, and goods in which a degree of scarcity was accepted. Generosity trumped accumulation in these cultures.

He cited fieldwork statistics showing that some hunter-gatherer people enjoyed more leisure than people living in the modern world, spending less total time working than many Americans (with jobs) and considerably more time telling stories, socializing, and relaxing. Sahlins's characterization provoked considerable argument and it stimulated much long-term research whose results are now available.

Even with a strong ethos of sharing among hunter-gatherers, the perennial problem of freeloaders exists among these people as it perhaps does in all social animals. While chimpanzees and other apes deal with these individuals through dominance relationships, human hunter-gatherers, thanks to language and culture, utilize other means, at least as initial responses to individuals who fail to share or who violate group norms in other ways. Boehm discusses this issue in some detail, suggesting that freeloading is suppressed partly through the generosity ethic and partly through informal social sentiments and sanctions.[21] Among early people, one must not only be generous, but must also be humble and avoid dominant aggressiveness within the group.

Boehm reasoned that as our ancestors evolved to be fully human, with symbolic language and culture, internalization of this ethos became what we call *conscience*. Among egalitarian modern hunter-gatherers, one's reputation is important, and storytelling, gossip, and humor encourage group members to suppress impulses toward aggressiveness and self-promotion. Deference and respect toward others, generosity, and fairness are encouraged, while extreme deviance is punished by group expulsion, shaming, and even death when other options have been exhausted.

The birth of conscience and the strong ethos of food sharing and egalitarianism associated with it may have evolved around the time that early *Homo* ancestors practiced a pursuit-type of hunting. It may have entailed an increase of self-control in those individuals who could manage it, and severe punishment for those who couldn't or wouldn't suppress these tendencies in themselves. Boehm further suggests that cultural suppression of freeloading behavior would have prevented genetic selection from completely eliminating "freeloader genes" from human populations.[22] Altruism and cooperation outside the immediate family were enabled because our ancestors internalized the strong sense of caring for others and not disrupting cooperation.

In early, small-scale human societies whose members recognized each other, this ethos, and repeated stories that tugged at individuals' consciences as they sat around their fires, were enough to enforce bonding by engaging emotions of shame, pride, and embarrassment. But this type of social bonding is not sufficient in larger communities. The elaborate ethical codes and ideas of justice that we see in large-scale hierarchical societies most likely were constructed on this earlier framework, and they drew on similar social emotions.

I find it interesting that Adam Smith, over two centuries ago, drew similar conclusions about the generosity of hunting and gathering people from accounts of explorers and missionaries who were often showered with gifts. Europeans did not understand this kind of generosity, often describing it as irrational and foolish, declaring that these people were unaware of the value of their goods since they shared without expecting payment. This was quite a puzzling attitude from the visitors' point of view. It was exploited by many early explorers, officials, and colonists, who filled personal and museum collections with such goods.

Thinking back on this past and on observations of contemporary hunter-gatherers, we see that human decency did not begin with the advent of food production, with the world religions, or with the European Enlightenment. It most certainly began with our hunting and gathering ancestors, and it was evident in indigenous societies "discovered" by Westerners on every continent.

Ethos of Generosity and Egalitarianism: Women, Men, and Children

Whatever the motive, generosity was central to human relationships and central to the degree of cooperation necessary for the tiny groups of relatively defenseless *Homo sapiens* to survive. The capacity for trusting and caring for others and treating them fairly is built into our species, as is the capacity for selfishness, competitiveness, and even cruelty. We shall see in later chapters how human societies that develop extreme hierarchy violate the basic sense of fairness that is part of who we are.[23]

Richard B. Lee and Richard Daly find it notable "that, despite marked differences in historical circumstances, foragers seemed to have arrived at similar organizational and ideational solutions to the problems of living in groups." They are impressed by the persistence of the forager way of life through an especially long prehistory and even into modern times despite domination by stronger and larger societies. It is partly this persistence and strength that has motivated so many observers to be drawn to and explore this ancient (and what some have described, longingly perhaps, as a more natural) way of living and what it can tell us about being human.[24]

Recent genetic research suggests that hunter-gatherers, in contrast to settled agriculturalists, may have greater genetic diversity than the latter, indicating mating over larger territories, although this is not proof in itself that relationships were friendly.[25]

Two other cultural features are often associated with egalitarian hunter-gatherers but in reality vary from one group to another, according to Lee and Daly. One variable feature is the status of women. These authors conclude that women in foraging societies have higher status than in many other types of societies, including many modern industrialized groups. They cite Karen L. Endicott's measures of women's freedom to move, their contribution to group decision making, and their relatively low rate of subjection to domestic violence. High status for women is not universal in these societies. Endicott notes that historical contacts also influenced female status, sometimes toward reduced equality and status, and sometimes toward greater status; the latter often through introducing educational opportunities.[26] Other researchers find that increased pressure on resources is associated with decreased status of women.[27]

Women's status is also connected to features of infant and child care. Sarah B. Hrdy and Melvin Konner describe common characteristics of managing infancy and childhood within warm-climate egalitarian hunter-gatherer bands.[28] Infancy generally involves prolonged mother-child contact and cosleeping, with frequent nursing and late weaning, and children are generally spaced about three years apart. Mothers are primary caregivers during infancy even in groups that emphasize shared care. Nevertheless, in contrast to other social primates, human infants usually have some care from others besides their own mothers, often fathers, grandmothers, or others from their local band. Children most often enjoy a carefree childhood and tend to be indulged by parents and others, while also practicing adult activities during play. Direct teaching of skills takes place too, most commonly by mother to daughter and by father to son. Acceptance of adolescent sexuality is another common feature of these cultures.

A second variable feature of hunter-gatherer societies is the degree of harmony characterizing interpersonal and/or intergroup relationships. Reports of peace and harmony among hunter-gatherers were probably exaggerated in some studies, particularly as writers responded to carnage during the two Eurocentric World Wars. Many people in the middle of the twentieth century were eager to find evidence of human goodness, and this bias probably influenced how they interpreted observations. Also, the fighting that was observed among hunter-gatherers would have looked quite different from wars between nation-states. Contests between men over women, or quarrels based on jealousy and other interpersonal issues, might have looked like unorganized violence.

The majority of egalitarian hunter-gatherers who depended on unpredictable food sources were by necessity nomadic or semi-nomadic. Secondly, land was public or shared rather than being private property among these egalitarian people. Prestige was more dependent on sharing or distributing than on accumulating food or goods. Inheritance was unimportant, since nomadic bands couldn't carry or store many items.

Ongoing studies of these peoples have focused on demographics, property and territory, environmental context, specific patterns of merging and dissolution of migrating units, and movement of individuals within and among local hunter-gatherer bands. These features influence each other. We saw that traditional egalitarian hunter-gatherers ended up retreating more often than fighting in response to pressure from dwindling resources or from encroachment on territory by other populations. It is hard to wage war if you are a small nomadic group, and small groups need friends more than enemies.

Konner concludes that among hunter-gatherers, as among human populations generally, difficulty obtaining food and population pressure are important causes of violence regardless of social organization. Emphasis on fighting was probably variable, with little or no real warfare among those groups as long as competition for resources was low, although individual homicides may have been more common. For perspective, we must remember that modern state societies also differ from each other in their degree of violence.

In speaking of war in early societies, Lawrence H. Keeley and Azar Gat note that historically, as other cultures moved in and became dominant, practically every hunter-gatherer society experienced effects of contact, if only indirectly through spread of disease.

In recent years, some anthropologists have looked more closely at small-scale societies that today are embedded economically and politically in larger state-based societies to determine whether sharing and reciprocity norms are retained under these conditions. Michael Gurven describes reciprocal altruism among the current Ache of Paraguay and the Hiwi of Venezuela, who now are embedded forager-horticulturalists.[29] The meshing of domestic and larger economies has resulted in imbalance among individuals and constriction of the circle of sharing to kin and close neighbors. Moreover, high producers take advantage of the opportunity to trade surpluses for other goods. It seems that we humans are alike in becoming who we need to be to survive in the specific conditions that surround us. Norms of sharing are part of specific sociocultural adaptations.

We turn next to a recent sociocultural adaptation that had revolutionary consequences for all life on our planet.

The Neolithic Revolution and Its Consequences

The differences between hunting and gathering wild foods, i.e., the Paleolithic adaptation, and producing food, particularly in combination with food surpluses and storage of food and goods, are profound. They involve energy use, technology, social organization, and human values. They reach into everyday life, influencing family and community, conflict and cooperation, ideas about the world, and overall well-being. How people make a living affects how they behave and relate to each other. With these points in mind, I describe the beginnings of food production and its consequences. Events associated with the Neolithic initiated a process that we are still experiencing today, almost 11,000 years later.

Beginnings of Food Cultivation

Between 12,000 and 10,000 years ago, a new approach to the natural environment developed that was to have a huge effect on humanity from that time forward. The economic and organizational changes modified how people viewed themselves and their relationship to the rest of nature. This set of events is called the Neolithic Revolution. I summarize here the widely known features of this cultural phase, limiting citations to particular or newer information.

As noted earlier, the Neolithic was originally identified and named by archeologists upon discovery of new and different artifacts dated first to this time period. Stone grindstones and mortars and pestles for grinding grains defined this New Stone Age. Sickles, pottery, and signs of textile weaving and basketry also appeared, indicating the beginning of plant cultivation. Early Neolithic people were not only collecting or hunting wild food; they were producing food and storing seeds for the first time. They were beginning to settle into semi-permanent or more permanent villages, replacing a nomadic lifestyle in some areas.

Food production developed independently in several areas of the Old and New World at different times. The best-known, probably earliest, and most heavily studied sites of the Eurasian Neolithic are located east of the Mediterranean in the Levant area. This area, known also as the Fertile Crescent, centers in the valley created by the Tigris and Euphrates Rivers (in what is now Iraq) and the surrounding hills. Here, large stands of wild grasses provided food for the various wild but mild-mannered grazing herbivores of the region. The hill-and-valley topography, combined with alternating seasonal rainfall and dryness, made a good setting for diverse self-pollinating annual plants with storable seeds. The same environment worked well to support sheep and goats.

Changes had begun with wider use of the abundant wild grasses and the cereal grains einkorn and emmer, which could be ground to mix with water and made into a new product, bread. Climate change, particularly drying, enabled safe storage of extra seeds. The activities of storage and planting define basic horticulture, or hoe cultivation, in contrast to the more advanced plow agriculture that developed a bit later. Wood digging sticks used by gatherers around the world could easily have been modified to become hoes for use in horticulture. After all, women had been digging and preparing wild tubers, stems, and seeds for many generations as gatherers. Women likely were critical players in observing, recognizing, gathering, moving, and experimenting with plants, developing early cultivation techniques, inventing storage containers, and finding new uses for plants.[30]

Researchers have asked why the Neolithic happened at all. Some hypotheses focus on demographic changes, such as population increase spurred by the abundance of wild food. Increased population would have pushed further against new resource limits. Others emphasize the role of climate change. Around 20,000 years ago, global warming, with retreat of the last major Pleistocene glacier, was modifying climate in this area. Hunter-gatherers were able to use wild resources quite intensely in this hill-and-valley context, so that some groups were becoming less nomadic. People were probably beginning to sow seeds or place stalks in the ground to save carrying food from one area to another.

A geologically based cool spell called the Younger Dryas had developed about 12,000 years ago.[31] Combined with more efficient human hunting, this widespread cooling probably contributed to extinction of large herd animals, particularly in north temperate zones. These species had been important to earlier hunter-gatherer economies, and their extinction would have required changes in subsistence. Changes were facilitated by increasing knowledge and use of varied plant and animal resources. The generalized adaptation, more accurately, adaptability to shifting food resources, gave hunter-gatherer populations in the area considerable flexibility in subsistence activities, at least for a while, and may also have fostered early experiments with cultivation.

The Neolithic, then, did not begin as a revolution but as a natural outgrowth of intensive use of wild plants and animals. Domestication of plants and animals happens through *artificial selection*, which is driven by human-selected features that can be identified by genetically based physical changes in new species. The word *artificial* simply distinguishes it from natural selection, which happens without human intervention. Artificial selection may have first happened accidentally. In carrying plant stalks from their natural hillside environment toward the valley for putting in the ground closer to where people lived, stalks with tightly connected seeds would be reproduced with greater frequency in the new environment, modifying the proportion of seed types in the next generation in the river valley.

Similar processes would have modified animals, mostly goats and sheep in this area, selected by humans who, instead of eating or trading all of them, saved some for wool, hide, and milk production. People would choose to consume the animals that did not provide large yields of these products. This would have changed gene proportions in following generations, distinguishing domestic from wild populations. Domestication is considered to be the critical criterion for distinguishing Neolithic from Paleolithic societies. Early archeologists were able to distinguish fossil remains of domestic from wild plants even before understanding the genetics behind it.

Neolithic Lifestyle

However it happened, once early food production had begun, life changed in many ways. We can easily envision the consequences, and the well-documented archeological record provides ample evidence. In areas featuring intense use of resources, some settling into a less nomadic existence had already begun. Plant domestication would have furthered this transition from nomadic to semi-nomadic settlements and then to permanent villages in some areas. The reduced need to move frequently made food storage feasible, and surpluses could accumulate. In some areas, specific property rights for land and resources developed, and settled villages became sitting ducks for raids by more mobile hunters or early herders. While differences in leadership in egalitarian hunter-gatherer societies were based solely on personality or skill, accumulation of property allowed other types of social ranking, specialization, and division of labor to develop.

The hoe characterized this first, Neolithic phase of food production known as *horticulture* or gardening. Later invention of the plow marked a further advance, transforming horticulture into *agriculture*. The plow was more efficient in flatter and larger fields, especially when paired with a domesticated animal to pull this new invention.

Viewing land as property and using it more intensely, in contrast to viewing land as a shared resource, modified family and larger kinship groups. As we shall see in Chapter 6, ancestor-based kin groups are an ideal framework for transmitting property rights. Settling on the land and viewing it as property fostered a transition from the earlier use of a large variety of wild foods to a more limited set of domesticated plants and animals. In these ways, the built-in flexibility and resilience of the hunter-gatherer culture shifted to more rigid physical boundaries for human groups and greater rigidity in defining groups, eventually leading to an emerging class structure. Arlene M. Rosen and Isabel C. Rivera-Collazo propose a model of cyclical changes to explain this transformation.[32]

In wide fertile valleys with major rivers, the Neolithic phase was short-lived and transitional, leading to ranked social classes and the development of civilizations or state-based societies. Most ancient civilizations developed within so-called "lucky latitudes" whose climates made it easier for farmers to accumulate ever larger surpluses that could support larger populations. As populations increased, irrigation was organized, and communities expanded even further. By changing the characteristics of animals and plants and controlling their production, the seeds of culturally based inequality were also sown (pun intended), and with it increased motivation for war to extend or maintain land rights.

Neolithic Worldview

As noted previously, the worldview common to most egalitarian hunter-gatherer cultures emphasized the natural world as a giving, sometimes animated presence to which people were closely connected. Likewise, generosity and sharing were virtues, and egalitarianism was valued to the point of being called "militant" or "fierce" by observers. A contrasting worldview emerged in the Fertile Crescent after the Neolithic revolution. Anthropologist Ian Tattersall, following Niles Eldredge, quotes from Genesis 1:27 to describe this new view, which became the foundation for the three monotheistic religions that developed in that region: "God said ... be fruitful, and multiply, and replenish the earth, and subdue it; and have dominion ... over every living thing that moveth upon the earth."[33]

So this became the ideology of early food producers, declaring independence from the vagaries of the natural world. This contrasts markedly from Paleolithic ideology. As with any major transition, this one had tradeoffs: It brought new advantages for living, and, at the same time, introduced new challenges and problems. This is in line with the ongoing evolutionary dynamic of rising and falling species and rising and falling sociocultural systems: Each adaptation contains the seeds of its own destruction. Nothing lasts forever; all progress is relative (Red Queen idea).

The ideology of dominion over the earth, human control of nature itself, became a kind of mantra of Judaism, Christianity, and Islam. Steven Pinker remarked on this tradeoff to suggest that the demons of our human nature were abetted by laws and beliefs that became foundational for these religions. Specifically, he was referring to the extremes of patriarchy, hatred of outgroups and deviant individuals, and even the idea of children being born in sin.[34] Other tradeoffs with roots in the Neolithic, such as dietary changes and overuse of natural resources, are proving in the modern world to be adversely affecting human health and harmony in our multicultural, crowded world.[35]

Anthropologist Spencer Wells, in his book *Pandora's Seed,* describes the effects of the transition from gathering wild foods to producing food by changing the environment.[36] He depicts huntergatherers sitting around the fire at night, spinning tales, creating myths, changing each other's accounts and stories, in a kind of crucible for creativity. He views this activity as the original model for the brainstorming and focus groups that various organizations use today to encourage people to think creatively and collaboratively.

Wells speculates that this earlier mode was disabled by the workaholic nature of the Neolithic and was almost destroyed by the Neolithic's offshoots, class society and urbanization, and its later products, industrial and postindustrial society. Increased population, new but more standardized crops and foods, new contagious infections and other diseases of body and brain, new environmental challenges, and population explosion opened up a Pandora's box of surprises. While enabling us to dominate the world, they threaten our wellbeing also. Wells's book ends with a chapter that echoes a Paleolithic value that is regaining respect from some individuals living in postindustrial societies: Having and wanting fewer goods, less stuff, may help us to meet the challenges we face.

Some years ago, Marshall Sahlins spoke of similar changes wrought by the Neolithic Revolution, mainly that people worked harder and leisure time decreased. Economic changes enriched people materially while impoverishing them in other ways. He also referred to the effect of the additional behavior-controlling institutions necessary for pursuing a Neolithic lifestyle.[37] Again, we see that a given culture's ideology, its organization, and its technology are embedded in a large whole that includes the environment. Ideology plays an important role in defining who we are. It is a human invention that feels quite natural and obligatory to those who share it. We are what our culture tells us we are, at least before we subject it to extra thought and analysis.

Other observers of traditional cultures have been struck by other tradeoffs connected to major cultural transitions. Replacement of the complex and nuanced relationship with nature characteristic of hunter-gatherers with a totally different way of perceiving and living in the world that developed after the Neolithic and the birth of civilization was an important one. The advent of industrialization and our current ultra-rapid communication have had their own tradeoffs with profound effects.

The economic, technological, and political complexity that began around 6000 years ago and has continued to accelerate since then did not happen all at once, but it did introduce new challenges along with benefits that many of us enjoy today. The term *tradeoff* refers to the exchange of one set of benefits and challenges for a different set. Many humans have comforts today not dreamed of by hunter-gatherers or small-scale horticulturalists. Yet we have extracted and utilized earth's energy so efficiently and completely that we face new problems of considerable scope.

Transitions: From Kinship to State-based Society

Looking back at the archeological and historical records, we know that, as food-producing technology spread to other parts of the world from early centers, many small-scale societies retained a horticultural, locally centered lifestyle. These horticultural societies were based largely on household-based economies supplemented by a combination of trading and marriage exchanges with other local groups. Some had tribal networks coordinating some gatherings and activities without becoming centralized states. This domestic mode of production is geared largely for use, not gain; as such, it is self-limiting. Traditional Western economists would call this economic setup one of underproduction, featuring no surpluses and no progress toward complexity, but this adaptation produces far less degradation of the environment and far less waste of resources.

Settled or semi-settled nonranked tribal societies often had informal leadership of the "big man" variety that depends on a leader's personality. To further his status, the leader may begin to pressure his followers to increase gift-giving. Such a society may transition into a chiefdom as goods and prestige accumulate. This is expressed through ceremonial distribution of surpluses outward from the chief at the center, as in potlatch displays and even destruction of goods. The famous northwest American/Canadian harvesters of seasonal runs of salmon (surplus-producing hunter-gatherers) exemplify this model. The predictability of salmon runs provided the basis for a system of social ranking and a complex, centralized organization. Depending on conditions, chiefdoms such as these may dissolve into smaller tribal or band-level units again, or they may, under different conditions, undergo transition into state-based societies, as did Polynesian Hawaii, the ancient Kush Kingdom of eastern Africa, the Incas of Peru, and others. This brings us to the definition of "civilization."

Food Surpluses, Property Rights, and Inequality

From archeology, early *civilizations* were defined by their centralized or state-based political-religious organization. Central organization was inferred from artifacts these ancient societies left behind, including buildings, clothing, tombs, tools, ornaments, and more. Noted archeologist V. Gordon Childe, following Karl Marx, Friedrich Engels, and others, emphasized the importance of agricultural surplus following the Neolithic Revolution (a phrase he coined along with the phrase, "Urban Revolution").[38] Archeological remains demonstrated the following:

- Inequalities of property and power represented by social classes or castes
- Occupational specialization and wider division of labor
- Elitist political-religious authority and often a related hierarchal ideology
- Cities
- Writing
- Monumental art and architecture
- Different recognizable categories of people, such as peasants, slaves, or servants, supporting wealthy and powerful members of society.

The conditions that made centralization of authority possible also made it more necessary for keeping people in line through threat of force. This enabled the state to wage large-scale war and suppress individuals and powerless groups within the society. Central governments, in monopolizing the legitimate use of force, also featured combined religious and political authority.

For several centuries, historians, philosophers and anthropologists have offered hypotheses about how and why centrally organized, complex state societies developed in the first place, usually citing several key factors. These factors are interrelated and include food storage and surpluses as described above, land use and property rights, and population growth and concentration. We can specify several conditions under which civilizations and state-based societies did evolve.

Where food surpluses were produced in abundance, changes in the rest of culture followed, influencing economic relationships, organization of social institutions, and ideas about the world. Social inequality grew, originally in part through chance: As workable land became the property of families or other kin rather than being shared territory for an entire local or regional group, some land plots would be naturally more fertile and productive than others. Families would vary in size and composition, so some would produce more food per capita than others. After that, inequalities would tend to grow as those with surpluses would have a head start in generating further surpluses and wealth. Archeological records from the most fertile areas around the world show social inequality beginning around 5000 to 3500 years ago.

Adam Smith in the eighteenth century noted interconnections involving property rights, inequality, and the need for civil government. He also remarked on the role of government in providing public institutions necessary for defense, administering justice, and facilitating commerce and education, specifically citing roads, bridges, canals, and schools as examples. In line with subsequent archeological evidence, his notion that trade, markets, and early civilizations first developed along waterways was on target. Finally, he recognized the relationship between property and human relationships, and the tendency of land owners, particularly landlords, "to reap where they never sowed, and demand a rent even for its natural produce."[39]

Psychologist and philosopher Floyd W. Rudmin analyzed and compared data on property rights that he collected and coded from numerous cross-cultural studies over a number of years. He showed that the sharing norms typical of hunter-gatherers give rise to private property norms under particular conditions, most notably among agriculturalists who practice intensive labor for high returns (surpluses, beyond a domestic economy). He also showed that "private property is associated with a tight, controlling, and inward-turned, father-dominated social order." These societies tended to feature outgroup hostility and emphasize warfare.[40] He provided further confirmation in a later analysis of five different cross-cultural databases.[41]

Population growth and concentration most often happen when and where food resources are abundant enough to produce surpluses. And with population concentration comes a need for cooperation on a scale beyond that of personal relationships. Needs for large-scale irrigation or expansion of territory have been proposed historically as specific drivers of central organization and of war.

All early, state-based societies (civilizations, as defined by anthropologists) were *theocracies.* In these systems, political leaders and religious leaders are the same or are closely tied (note the same root for "theology" and "theocracy"). Theocracy existed until quite recently in Western Europe (e.g., "the divine right of kings") and still exists in many parts of the world. The potential for abuse with this kind of organization was an important reason that the founders of the United States agreed on separating church and state. The separation was designed to facilitate fair working of the newly minted democratic form of government (albeit for white, male landowners only). We can see how theocracy can easily give rise to an ideology that one way of thinking (one particular god in charge of the world) is the only way to think. A theocratic government with its legitimate monopoly on the use of force is incompatible with democratic decision making.

The emergence of inequality itself, like the beginnings of food production, had consequences for the health and well-being of individuals. Compared to persons in foraging societies, individuals in societies with agriculture on average experienced poorer nutrition, shorter life expectancy, smaller average height, faster reproductive rate, denser population, and more infectious disease, as evidenced by analysis of fossil skeletal and dental material. In the ancient world, these changes were accompanied by new ideas about the world of living things and the place of people in this world. As Neolithic societies developed, food production spread into many parts of the world. Then, as centralized, powerful, state-based societies expanded, hunter-gatherer societies became increasingly marginalized, as did those horticultural societies that did not produce surpluses.

Similar transitions would have occurred, of course, among the few hunter-gatherer populations in areas where natural resources were rich and concentrated enough to produce surpluses even without food production. These societies often resembled food producers more than egalitarian hunter-gatherers in their organization and ethos.[42] And the transformation from horticulture to plow agriculture and large-scale civilization did not occur everywhere. A number of horticultural societies continued to rely heavily on domestic economies into the last century.

Over time, during the years of Western colonialism, most traditional societies did become incorporated into larger state-based systems in which the original kin-based leadership mode became an avenue for colonial "indirect rule." Hunter-gatherer groups that were not incorporated in a similar way ended up marginalized within state societies, with variable retention of the old ways. Some anthropologists argue that existing hunter-gatherer societies are best understood as remnants of colonial domination and encroaching larger world economies. Domination took its toll on small-scale cultures everywhere, yet some individuals have chosen to hold on to portions of their lifestyle and values, at least seasonally, and we can learn from them and their histories.

Summary and Conclusions

Hunter-Gatherers and Human Nature

Early chapters of this book focused mainly on how we hominins evolved during the very long period during which we were subsisting on wild plants and animals. Ancient modern humans modified these products of nature only *after* they had extracted them, through cooking or using them to make tools, shelters, and body ornamentation. Thus, the human Paleolithic footprint was much smaller than that of modern humanity as we directly modify the air we breathe, the water we drink and use for manufacture, the content of our soil, and the plants and animals that we breed and eat. All human social behavior and cultural institutions build on the emotions and patterns that evolved in response to the conditions our ancient human ancestors faced. Cultural institutions and ideas, like biologically based behaviors, may be helpful or not so helpful in promoting harmonious living.

Many researchers of egalitarian hunter-gatherers have noted that this way of life has been extremely durable and fairly adaptable to varied conditions. Its persistence through centuries of post-Neolithic domination suggests that we can learn from those who practice this disappearing lifestyle. Calling it "the original affluent society" was an oversimplification but not totally arbitrary. No doubt it reflected a Rousseauian, excessively optimistic view of human nature, but one could argue that the Hobbesian view represents a biased, excessively pessimistic view of who we are. Reality may lie between these views, and we are shortsighted to judge one as a more accurate representation than the other. Lawrence H. Keeley suggests that perceiving either end of this dichotomy as typifying early people represents our failure as citizens of a different, fast-paced world to see hunter-gatherers as the complex and diverse human beings that they actually are.[43]

In describing the range of adaptations that hunter-gatherers have crafted, anthropologist Robert L. Kelly reminds his readers that "hunter-gatherer" is a human category rather than a causal variable. He prefers the phrase "foraging spectrum" that suggests the variety in patterns of land use, sharing, group size, female and male roles in subsistence work and child care, and degree of egalitarianism.[44]

Since the Neolithic revolution and the spread of food production to most ecosystems on the planet, all known hunter-gatherer societies have been decimated by disease, have taken up food production to supplement hunting and gathering, and have been incorporated in other ways into food-producing societies. Some supply wild foods, medicines, or information to markets, and others have been recruited to be servants or mercenary fighters for more powerful patron societies. Still others, with highly developed skills in noting details of the natural environment, are working to track and interpret fossil footprints and other signs. Attempts to reconstruct ancestral lifestyles remain speculative.

How Cultures Change

This chapter has focused on cultural variety, past and present. How can the range and distribution of worldwide cultural diversity be explained? Jared Diamond provided insight into this question in his popular book, *Guns, Germs, and Steel,* hypothesizing that "the striking differences between the long-term histories of peoples of the different continents have been due not to innate differences in the people themselves but to differences in their environments."[45] The plant and animal species available for domestication, geographical and climatic barriers that isolated human populations, population size, and size of available land were all important in influencing evolution of diverse societies.

Historian and archeologist Ian Morris, in his comprehensive and detailed work, *Why the West Rules—for Now,* notes the value of Diamond's work. He similarly utilizes geography, geology, biology, and social sciences to help him explain the human trajectory.[46] Morris updates Diamond's prehistoric detail, while limiting his own historical analysis to two cores of civilization, the Western core of hilly flanks surrounding the Tigris and Euphrates Rivers, and the Eastern core surrounding the Yellow and Yangtze Rivers in China. He credits biology with giving us "clever chimps" the ability to harness energy in unique ways, our curiosity and tinkering ability, and our common crowd behavior. Sociology, defined by Morris to include all social sciences, "tells us simultaneously what causes social change and what social change causes."

By this, he means that large geologic and climatic events and conditions in particular locations initiate changes in those places. These modifications of technology and organization, in turn, create new conditions and problems that require novel solutions. He utilizes his "index of social development" consisting of four measurable items: energy capture (consumption), organizational capacity (urbanization), information processing, and war-making ability. Under certain conditions, people come to extract energy more efficiently from the environment, enabling larger populations and requiring more social complexity and more resources. Changes spread outward, from a society's core to its margins. This spawns new (originally marginal) cores of development that, because of their newness, have more flexibility to innovate, so that population grows and the cycle repeats.

In the transition from Paleolithic food collecting to Neolithic food domestication to civilization, environmental and climatic conditions played a critical role, according to Morris, simply because we humans, like other animals, depend on resources; we are not free-flying, independent entities. In every society, as a population increases, its boundaries become more distant, and regulating what goes on at these edges becomes more challenging. His "paradox of social development," through which development sows the seeds of its eventual demise, is another formulation of the shifting "evolutionary potential" (phrase from Elman Service) that I introduced in Chapter 1 to describe the dynamic between adaptive specialization and adaptability.

This loosely resembles the thinking of others who proposed similar cycles (Edward Gibbon in the eighteenth century, Arnold J. Toynbee in the twentieth century); they too argued that societies and traditions undergo changes over time that are roughly analogous to changes that occur in biological organisms. Researchers of various stripes are currently exploring this notion by analyzing data from different fields of study. Archeologists Arlene Rosen and Isabelle C. Rivera-Collazo speak of cyclical changes driven by the collapse of one system; these result in reorganization, renewed innovation, and resilience, followed by consolidation and increased rigidity of responses.

Marx and Engels, in the nineteenth century, understood that socioeconomic systems develop and then create the seeds of their own destruction, but instead of repeating cycles, they predicted progress leading to a utopia of sorts. While failing to predict actual outcomes over time, their work was brilliant in providing a valuable analysis that drove improved understanding of economic and political forces and opened avenues for further work. French economist Thomas Piketty has revived and detailed that analysis, applying it to the growing inequality in today's world.[47] These several analyses are related to the notion of progress and controversy surrounding it, to be discussed more fully in Chapter 9.

Being Human and Continuing Biological Evolution

What is the significance of the checkered and complex collection of contrasting impulses that define who we current members of *Homo sapiens* are? Most of our evolution—our becoming fully human—happened when we were hunters and gatherers. Many writers have suggested that current societies are a poor match for our biological and emotional status as *Homo sapiens*. We evolved to live in small groups, to know most of the people in our locale, and to communicate face-to-face. But others think our hunter-gatherer past is not so relevant because human evolution continues today. Evidence for ongoing evolution comes from comparing genomes of different modern human populations. There have been measurable genetic changes since the agricultural revolution and perhaps even since the industrial revolution, and some occurred in response to the migration of ancestral populations around the world, carrying some variations with them and acquiring others along the way.

Genetic researchers find that particular traits are most often influenced by multiple interacting genes in combination with environmental conditions. No doubt, changes in human culture will continue to affect human genes and how they are expressed. The human epigenome is extraordinarily important as a kind of liaison between microenvironments and individual expression of genetic potentials. We are only beginning to understand how this takes place and how individual, cultural, and environmental circumstances play into it.

We might ask how equality and extreme inequality influence the human epigenome, and how a culture might develop institutions that make good use of the human potential to improve skills and thinking and, therefore, our capacity to fully utilize our prosocial features. I look at some of these issues in Chapter 9.

In the next chapter, I describe kinship as an important key to understanding the transition from egalitarian to hierarchal society, and the smaller transitions from bands to larger tribes, then to chiefdoms and finally, in some places, to state-based societies. Kinship can be used in different ways, to foster egalitarian values or to foster dominance of one group over others (*social hierarchy*). For human societies, we shall see how specific features of child care, women's status, and even warfare are correlated with how kinship is defined, how kin groups are composed, and how technology uses resources.

6

Holding People Together:
Kinship, Marriage, In-Laws, and Others

Both sexes [in prehistory] must have been able to care for young, protect themselves from predators, make and use tools, and freely move about the environment in order to exploit available resources widely distributed through space and time. It is this range of behaviors—the overall behavioral flexibility of both sexes—that may have been the primary ingredient of . . . success.

    —Adrienne L. Zihlman, 1981[1]

Literature is mostly about having sex and not much about having children. Life is the other way round.

    —David Lodge, 1989[2]

Kinship can be used to hold groups together or to pull groups apart. Both were basic to solidifying social ties within local bands or communities in nonstate societies and to making and maintaining ties of varying intensity among local groups. Eventually these ties also helped to consolidate early state-based societies, as demonstrated by kin succession of leaders (kings, pharaohs, priest-emperors). This chapter focuses primarily on the importance of kinship in pulling together and organizing people for cooperative ventures in nonstate or kinship-based societies. It covers female and male roles, intergroup relationships and kinship alliances, and how these are these related to peace and war.

Prehistorically, and for much of historical time that is accessible through written records, kinship was the organizing principle of societies. Kinship ties were the first way that caring for others and a sense of fairness were introduced into human society (described in Chapter 4). As hierarchy and inequality replaced relatively egalitarian relationships in human societies, kinship, or at least a kinship metaphor, continued to support centralized state-based organization. An example is a kin-based aristocracy with patrilineal succession rules that pass leadership from father to son.

Anthropologists have long been intrigued by kinship systems around the world. Many were more complex than modern, Western kinship systems, yet occurred in small-scale nonstate societies that were commonly viewed as more simply organized than those of the observers. As such, they stimulated curiosity, speculation, and attempts to make sense of the diverse ways of referring to and interacting with particular kinfolk. The much-studied original Australian kin-based section and subsection systems, for example, worked in complicated ways to define marriage, residence after marriage, group alliances, rituals, and stories about places where ancestors lived and wandered during the ancient "Dreamtime." Euro-American kinship categories and terms are only one pale version of the many ways of naming and grouping one's relatives.

Because of the wide variation in kin systems, many twentieth century cultural anthropologists viewed human sociocultural systems as practically independent of human biology. The complicated interpretations of kin-based alliances introduced by Claude Lévi-Strauss in his 1963 book, *Structural Anthropology*, ignited a lengthy debate regarding the relative importance of descent versus alliance in organizing cultures. This stimulated numerous articles and books by kinship-obsessed cultural anthropologists, who enjoyed spinning ideas and hypotheses about how these systems worked to organize people in different societies.

Since this mid-century heyday of kinship theorizing, some researchers have argued that the various analytical models had little bearing on reality. For example, patrilineality was often over-emphasized by Western anthropologists whose own societies had male-based institutions. More recent research, however, undoubtedly also reflects its times. Over the past half-century, huge historical changes in traditional societies and the different sensibilities and changes in perceptions of sex and gender influence what we study and how we represent it. We are again reminded that all research, even the most current, must be viewed with a skeptical eye.

Today, we recognize the interlocking roles of biology and culture in making sense of most things human. At the same time, we recognize that kinship ties continue to bind people together. The terms *sister* and *brother* are often used to refer to members of groups, as in fraternities or sororities, and even terrorist groups of different stripes. These use initiation rituals and the metaphor of kinship to cement bonds and create loyalty among members.

Kinship is integrally related to one's sex. The first human bond is between mother and child, and much follows from this kernel of kinship. No human being can escape the fact that her or his sex will be a significant fact of everyday life. The first division of labor in prehistory was probably between women and men and was related to reproduction and lengthy nurturance of infants and children. In all societies, sex has some bearing on lifestyle and work, and it influences one's relationship to and investment in children. Culturally defined gender roles are another issue, and they do not necessarily coincide with sex roles or biological sex differences. Family structure, child rearing, and organization of larger kinship groups make a difference in how people behave with each other. Relative status of women and men responds to and influences this connection.

Women and Men

A basic biological difference between males and females underlies kinship systems: Females produce a limited number of offspring during a lifetime, while males can father a very large number of offspring. For a woman to get her genes into the next generation, the challenge is to make sure that her limited number of children live long enough to reproduce themselves. This difference is based on the biological fact of long pregnancies, lactation periods, and childhoods that require nurturing and direct teaching.

From this point of view, women, to pass on their genes, must be more discriminating than men in choosing their mates, and they need to be sure that their offspring are well cared for. The male strategy of spreading genes frequently with multiple partners can conflict with the female strategy of careful mate choice combined with attention to caring for the offspring that result. But research is showing that among some animals thought to mate for life, the likelihood of actual female and male mating behaviors depends on the relative benefit to each sex within a particular population in a particular context.[3] It turns out that human behaviors respond to their natural and cultural environments in this way also. Ongoing research and time may clarify differences between male and female strategies. What seems clear is that mating behavior of females and males is more variable and less straightforward than originally thought.

A second, mostly hidden, struggle has been identified through genetic and epigenetic research—a rivalry between father and mother for expression of genes even in the developing embryo. Matt Ridley, using the Red Queen analogy in 1993, had suggested that this dynamic of competition between female and male reaches the genetic level.[4] At that time, understanding of epigenetics was in its infancy, and he knew little of how well-supported this notion of rival sets of genes would become as the field developed.

Biologists explain how all mammals begin life with a female body plan, to be modified during embryonic development. Errors can occur anywhere along the way, but typically a sequence of chemical events is initiated in an embryo possessing a Y chromosome to transform the "neutral" female embryo into a male embryo with all the requisite parts. Study of any accidental variation (inaccurate copy of a gene) of this normal sequence of events can provide information about development of the growing child and adolescent.

This chromosomal-chemical battle between the sexes that begins with the chromosomes continues during pregnancy.[5] Paternal genes favor increased utilization of maternal resources for that particular fetus, while maternal genes work toward anything that will preserve her health and that of the fetus, thereby preserving her potential for other healthy pregnancies and offspring. This apparently happens through epigenetic gene imprinting in which protein-producing genes may be "capped" and their expression silenced. A similar process works toward or against speed of growth and aggressiveness of the placenta in taking resources from the mother.[6]

If we accept that the mother-child bond is the basic kernel of human (and mammalian) sociality (see Chapter 4), then a question arises regarding how and why patrilineal and patriarchal institutions took such a strong and pervasive hold in many societies. This is related to the origins of pair bonding and male investment in offspring. In human evolution, *pair bonding* was a significant transition. Male investment in offspring differs among species. Chimpanzees and bonobos are sexually promiscuous with no long-term pair bonds. In contrast, the human male has fairly high parental investment. There are other mammals, including some primates, many birds, and even a few reptiles, amphibians, and fish in which male investment is larger.

Despite controversy surrounding the evolution of human pair bonding, monogamous marriage, the human institution associated with mating, probably describes most human relationships at a given time. However, "serial monogamy" might be a more accurate description in many cultures. The institution of marriage is universal but is defined variably. Polygyny (one husband, more than one wife) is considered ideal in some cultures, but demographically, even in cultures favoring it, not everyone practices it. Its counterpart, polyandry (one wife, more than one husband) is rare.

Some researchers suggest that the human male became less violent, more domesticated, and more bonded to a particular female and invested in her offspring during our evolution as hominins, perhaps beginning with some members of early *Homo*. One line of reasoning relies on observations of chimpanzee dominance and mating. I summarize this view here:

Dominance hierarchies among chimpanzees are contested by fighting, and they have a strong effect on mating: Top males usually monopolize mating and produce more offspring. But there are exceptions. In a field study of Tai Forest chimpanzees, some subdominant but enterprising males and females creatively worked out a means of getting around the normal chimpanzee pattern of dominant males hogging access to females.[7] These subdominant males began to offer meat to females in exchange for sex, and they were later found to mate twice as often as their peers who did not share food. Moreover, they continued to share their meat with favored females even through the infertile portion of the female cycle, mating again when those females returned to fertility.

Understanding this phenomenon requires modification of the long-standing notion that dominant males invariably produce larger numbers of offspring. If personality and mating strategy can influence sexual opportunities in chimpanzees, it surely could have worked this way among our ancestors. This notion is changing how we think about the origins of human societies.

Sergey Gavrilets used mathematical modeling to test the hypothesis that at some point in human evolution, low-ranking males began provisioning females with meat, and females began choosing these males as mates and, in turn, becoming faithful to them. He concludes that "the transition to pair-bonding can occur when female choice and faithfulness, among other factors, are included. The result is an increased emphasis on males provisioning females over male competition for mating." This hypothesis was supported by his study, which looked at several competing propositions.[8] C. Owen Lovejoy earlier proposed a similar hypothesis that was not accepted by many, but additional evidence is accumulating to support part of his understanding.[9] I also envision a connection between this development and the use of a kind of Machiavellian intelligence by female choosers as well as by male meat sharers.

Anthropologist Robin Dunbar with primatologist Dick Byrne demonstrated a correlation between the frequency of tactical deception (including Machiavellian intelligence) and neocortex size among primates. They later discovered that, among bigger-brained primate species, position on the male dominance hierarchy shows less correlation with mating than it does in smaller-brained primates; they suggest that a larger brain enables it to be used to overcome one's low position in the dominance hierarchy and increase reproductive success or, as Dunbar puts it, to "exploit loopholes" in the social system.[10] The biggest or most aggressive males weren't necessarily the smartest males, even in these nonhuman primates.

Many researchers have proposed that, in choosing mates, women look for generosity, trustworthiness, enduring commitment, and access to the particular resources that men tend to provide. After that, perhaps the sex hormones kick in and solidify the pair bond. But men and women have long provided food, so the idea that women look for what men can provide has become controversial. The specifics of food provision between men and women vary with the larger culture, and relative contributions of each sex in different cultures appear to be related to the resources available in particular environments and the technologies used to extract them. The roles of meat, fire, and cooking probably played a part in the evolution of mate choice also.

Evolution, Human Development, and Sex Differences

As we have seen, striking changes in individual development from infancy through adolescence were critical during our evolution into *Homo sapiens*. Melvin Konner, in *Evolution of Childhood*, reviews research on human developmental stages and the molding of sex differences, from prenatal through infancy and early childhood, middle childhood, puberty, and adolescence. In doing so, he covers genetic, epigenetic, and other biological influences; female and male parenting behaviors; and sociocultural influences.

His analysis, like that of Hrdy, draws from recent and ongoing work on brain plasticity and human flexibility, in part a function of the environment working on our many *facultative* traits (those that occur only under specific environmental conditions). These characteristics are influenced by biology but their specific expression depends on cultural learning (as opposed to instinctual or *obligate* traits). Konner and Hrdy cite data from developmental and broad cross-cultural studies to draw conclusions about how these multiple interacting factors influence almost everything from gender identity to parenting and other sex-based behaviors.[11]

The most consistently supported sex difference in behavior is the greater level of physical aggressiveness in males, perhaps related to larger amounts of testosterone. Greater female nurturance and affiliation was supported, but not as robustly. In newborns, differences between the sexes are seen in greater muscular strength in boys and greater skin-oral sensitivity and nonsocial smiling in girls. Differences in aggressiveness during play occur at age three and later on a cross-cultural basis.

Konner reviews clinical studies of disorders that modify the neuroendocrine system, or that change developing sex organs and perhaps brain structures connected to this. These support the idea that the difference in aggressiveness is at least in part biological. The most-cited studies are those of girls with congenital adrenal hyperplasia (CAH), in whom large amounts of androgens (male hormones) are produced during gestation. Even if treated at birth, these girls exhibit more typically male play behaviors than other girls. The caveat is that even the behaviors of normally developing girls and boys fall into overlapping ranges. Enough children with disorders have been studied, however, to conclude that the range of behavior for CAH girls is indistinguishable from the "normal boy" range.

Several other disorders result in ambiguous sex assignments and, in different societies, receive cultural designations as "a third sex" (for example, designation as "turnim man" or "becoming male" for Sambia of New Guinea).[12] He concludes that, contrary to a proposed connection between male aggressiveness and male hunting in our hominin past, aggressiveness and hunting are different neurologically and psychologically: Hunting has elements of problem-solving and play behavior, while aggressiveness relates to male fighting and sexual competition. Hunting and fighting, however, may both reflect greater risk-taking behaviors in males.

In addition to sex differences in aggressiveness, Konner reports that self-segregation of girls and boys during play is consistent and significant across cultures. In his dual role as anthropologist and physician, he explores cross-cultural comparative studies as well as data from medicine and biology. He notes that girls on average stay closer than boys to home base and to adult females, while boys have less adult contact, wander further, and congregate with other boys, particularly during adolescence when they frequently indulge in competitive and aggressive activities. Konner reports that, as formerly gentle hunter-gatherer groups move, or are moved into settled, denser population centers, they gravitate toward competitive, aggressive group action. Finally, he notes greater violent delinquency among male teenagers and young men than among young women.[13] He posits an indirect connection between male aggressiveness and war: Aggression is expressed through war under particular social, environmental, and demographic conditions that foster male groupings.

Neuroscientist Lise Eliot, like Konner, speaks of small differences in behaviors and skills during early childhood being enhanced by adolescent changes and social environmental differences that eventually result in larger differences between adult women and men.[14] Elizabeth S. Spelke's work, focusing largely on cognition in babies and young children, supports the notion that small differences in cognitive style become exaggerated during development; she attributes this to unconscious more than conscious perceptions, and to differing responses by others to girls and boys from infancy into adulthood.[15]

Our brains are plastic, flexible, and quite responsive to how we use them. Eliot puts it this way: "Obviously, boys and girls come into the world with a smattering of different genes and hormones. But actually growing a boy from those XY cells or a girl from XX cells requires constant interaction with the environment, which begins in the prenatal soup and continues through all the dance recitals, baseball games, middle-school science classes, and cafeteria dramas that ceaselessly reinforce our gender-divided society."[16] There is much more evidence for multiple, overlapping sources of influence on boys and girls during development, but further sorting of these strands of influence is beyond the scope of this book.

Eliot also reminds the reader that much of the evidence for sex differences in the brain comes from studying the brains of men and women, whose characteristics have already been shaped by experience and epigenetic factors that are not yet completely understood. Comparing sex differences between infants and adults, however, does not prove that increased adult differences represent only learning. Between infancy and adulthood is adolescence, with biological changes occurring in females and males. Adult behaviors would reflect these developments as well as an adolescent's experiences, which together influence the active pruning of neuronal connections that happens during that period.

The growing recognition of the influence of epigenetic factors for modifying DNA expression during development gives additional weight to the importance of environment. Even our individual physical characteristics that are most strongly inherited, such as height, can vary considerably based on changes that reflect nourishment of the fetus, infant, and child as well as other environmental factors. We might guess that other human traits, for example, personality, intelligence (however defined), and sex differences in behavior, which are harder to measure as accurately, are similarly modified during development.

Many cultures exaggerate or enhance biologically based sex differences by using dress, body painting, tattooing, and ornamentation. Differences in socializing and enculturating boys and girls can transform very small sex differences into much larger behavioral differences in adults. Some cultures set apart males or females by having separate "clubhouses," puberty rituals, taboos, or other restrictions around events such as pregnancy and childbirth. These practices would augment the effects of self-segregation that we see in children's play groups throughout the world. We might next ask *why* so many cultures enhance or exaggerate biological sex differences.

Back to Bonding: Babies and Parents

Given this background, I return to human bonds between women, men, and children. This is connected to the vulnerability of human babies and young children to predators, which goes back to the consequences of bipedalism and large brains for slowly maturing human offspring. The resources necessary to support their requirements provided impetus toward greater female-male cooperation and perhaps pair bonding and eventually the institution of marriage. These requirements also led to sharing of child care and teaching of youngsters. In most human societies, men as well as women do often have some role in caring for and helping to socialize children, particularly with boys as they move past toddlerhood. Pair bonding also may have helped prevent male infanticide and improve care of offspring, particularly important for very dependent human offspring.[17]

In Chapter 4, I reviewed the role of emotions as tools for managing life; these are mediated by neurochemicals and hormones that evolved in ancient times and were gradually modified as species differentiated. Testosterone is most closely associated with aggressiveness and violent behavior, while oxytocin and prolactin are associated with pregnancy, lactation, nurturance, and caring for the young (in females and males). Vasopressin appears to be especially important for males in pair-bonding and protection of their offspring, spurring aggressiveness toward outside intruders, and oxytocin stimulates this protective aggressive response in males also.

Both women and men make all of these signaling chemicals, but in different concentrations. Important for understanding human violence is that concentrations also respond to behavior. For example, levels of testosterone are reduced, and oxytocin and prolactin are increased, in men who are caring for young children. Women too produce more oxytocin while caring for children. Moreover, higher levels of prolactin are found in species in which both parents, rather than mothers alone, care for children; good mammalian exemplars of this are the nurturing male prairie voles.[18]

Finally, we are all individuals biologically and temperamentally. Individual variation depends on internal and external factors, including hormone levels, body build, personality or temperament, emotional and cultural environment, parents, peers, and a host of unknown specifics. No single category, such as maleness or femaleness, can predict individual behavior, although it may predict the likelihood of particular behaviors.

Given the demonstrated relationship between male sex and aggressiveness, and the probable relationship between female sex and nurturance, we see that both traits are related to hormonal levels, and behaviors and hormonal levels are variable and responsive to each other in a kind of circular feedback. If we superimposed two statistical curves representing female variation and male variation on either trait, we would see overlap, with some women, for example, showing more aggressiveness than some men. Individual differences and cultural role assignments matter. Human behavior is neither fixed in our biology nor totally explainable in terms of category. Instead it is variable and modifiable.

We can acknowledge that biology plays some part in sex differences for a few behaviors, while taking care not to exaggerate them and treat children as if they are destined to develop according to a particular pattern. Some researchers (e.g., Eliot, Spelke) worry that the eagerness to use biological tendencies to explain children's behavior may discourage children from developing a wide array of skills and interests.

This may call for a more balanced perspective. Perhaps our culture today has moved too far in pursuing a simple explanation. From Darwin's view of different temperaments in women and men (Herbert Spencer's "biology is destiny") to its backlash, of "environment is destiny," we now know that the nature versus nurture paradigm is far too simplistic for approaching human differences. I quote Konner again: "Genetic determinism died long ago, and now environmental determinism is dead too. Long live complex, measurable, and mainly deterministic interactionism."[19]

I turn now to the kinship foundations of society, related ultimately to the mostly biological features described above. It begins with the legacy of our ancient ape family.

Human Kinship and Our Primate Heritage

Primatologist Bernard Chapais, in his book *Primeval Kinship*, proposes that our variable human kinship institutions are the evolutionary products of our ape ancestry, which changed in definable steps. He assumes that the social groups of the most recent common ancestors of humans, chimpanzees, and bonobos resembled those of these two modern apes from genus *Pan*.

Chapais argues that the ancestral human group consisted of a core of related males (the "primal philopatric" core social group), with females moving into this group to mate and bear offspring.[20] He thinks that our coevolving human brains and culture-language complex eventually enabled recognition of fathers and other in-laws, hence opening the way for alliances between groups of in-laws. Later, as language and culture continued to evolve, local groups became more flexible, resulting in the variety of group composition observed among historical hunter-gatherers. Chapais holds that, during prehistory, females were usually the ones moving between local groups.

This claim, however, is not universally accepted. Anthropologist Joan Silk and others judge confirming evidence to be scarce, with more needed to warrant confidence in his model.[21] Yet Chapais does provide some valuable insights and evidence for several changes that probably were important in transforming groups of ancient apes into uniquely human societies. All agree that the variable and flexible kinship and residence patterns observed in well-documented modern human hunter-gatherer societies probably developed after modern *Homo sapiens* had emerged.

Specifically, Chapais attempts to trace the detailed steps through which earlier behaviors of these ancestral apes were modified, and several uniquely human features added, to form "the exogamy configuration" as the defining organizational principle of early human society. *Exogamy* refers simply to out-marriage, the practice of marrying outside one's own group. Edward B. Tylor famously said years ago: "Marry out or die out." With this, he was the first to recognize that marriage created social ties among groups; he was arguing against the commonly held notion that a repulsion against incest was the total basis for such rules.

Chapais goes beyond this formulation to name twelve building blocks of the human form of exogamy.[22] Of these, most are found in some other primates. Five are close to universal; others have been modified significantly in human societies. He considers only three of these to be uniquely human: (1) the tribe (defined as organization beyond the local group), (2) the brother-sister complex (not directly relevant here), and (3) matrimonial exchange. Of these, matrimonial exchange is particularly important here, and it refers to out-marriage as described above.

Matrimonial or in-law exchange became a tool for the organization and functioning of early human societies, in combination with female-male pair bonding. Our ancestors at some point began to recognize their fathers, and this led to acknowledging and building associations with father's relatives. What began as sexual pair bonding eventually became marriage exchange between different local groups and then a bridge between communities. These new *affinal* (in-law) ties were expressed through further marriages, gift-giving or trade, and sometimes extension of cooperation and peaceful contacts.

The system became more flexible and variable with time, enabled by language, social learning and the rapidity and ease of cultural change, in contrast to slower biological change. In this way, caring and altruism were extended, albeit imperfectly, to in-laws and their groups. Other researchers have updated this research and explain how, through using these uniquely human, novel aspects of kinship, local bands of hunter-gatherer societies would have become loosely connected, as was observed in the historical hunter-gatherer societies (described in Chapter 5).[23]

These loose connections are reflected even now through shared languages in regions larger than that occupied by a single or a few bands. The notion of marriage exchanges loosely holding together local bands is consistent with the hunter-gatherer ethic of generosity and egalitarianism that was an important adaptation for these small nomadic societies in an environment of fluctuating resources, and probably for our ancestors as well. Chapais argues that the development of tools and weapons was also critical in shifting chimpanzee-like, male-dominated, promiscuous societies into fairly monogamous, peaceful, and cooperative modern human groups.

Interestingly, recently reported archeological finds from the Balkan area show that women from early Neolithic groups had migrated *into* Mesolithic, advanced hunter-gatherer groups there, subsequently introducing cultivation. The inference is that the Neolithic women were modifying these groups, contrary to an earlier opposite hypothesis that hunter-gather women migrated and mated into groups that were already practicing food cultivation. This migration and modification appeared often to have been a peaceful process.[24] My guess is that some migration in both directions took place; evidence for this comes from genetic analysis and from tooth and bone nitrogen content determined for similar sites. This archeological and fossil evidence supports the notion of diverse organization developing out of ancestral groupings.

Michael Tomasello uses the term *mutualism* for the unique form of human cooperation associated with human kinship. He provides evidence that it differs from social behavior in other primates who, according to Joan Silk, function mostly through strong dominance and nepotism.[25] The ability of humans to extend kinship ties beyond the biological marks the uniqueness of our species, and it enables a mutualism that is not dependent on dominance. Another unique aspect is the flexible way that either women or men move at marriage, depending on circumstances. This flexibility is backed by archeological evidence and observation of modern hunter-gatherers. It contrasts with the earlier idea that the patrilocal band was the preferred pattern in early societies.

So, regarding the question of how a hypothesized ancestral male-based society was transformed into the militantly egalitarian, pair-bonded form that eventually developed, Chapais's sequence provides only a partial answer. An alternative possibility is suggested by conclusions of others regarding female choice of mates based on meat sharing behavior rather than on their high position on the dominance hierarchy. Another difficulty with Chapais's understanding is that, although he states that he is talking about the entire *Pan* species, the behavioral pattern he describes is that observed in common chimpanzees only. There is sparse reference to the quite different bonobo pattern, which some current researchers are positing as a more likely model for early human society.

From what we know of male dominance hierarchies and of male-female differences among primates, particularly our ape cousins, we might ask whether bonobo harmony results at least partly from the tight cohesion of females in suppressing male aggressiveness and perhaps from using sex as a peacemaking strategy.[26] It seems that bonobos, like common chimpanzees, practice patrilocal residence, yet females still form cooperative bonds through mutual grooming and sexual behavior. This enables them to sometimes unite and overcome male dominance and keep the peace.

Similarly, baboon social groups (these are monkeys, not apes) feature strong friendship bonds and dominance hierarchies among females. Here group females tend to be related in a roughly matrilocal, matrilineally based society, although there is a male grayback who seems to maintain overall control.[27] In calling these primates "discriminating nepotists," Joan Silk contrasts the use of actual kinship in monkeys and apes to the remarkable ability of humans to interact peacefully with total strangers and non-kin.

One clear contribution of primatology research to understanding human kinship is to highlight the transition by which our evolving ancestors came to recognize their fathers and father's relatives as kin, thus providing an avenue for them to connect with other human groups. These opportunities for further cooperation, trading, and marriage exchanges extended kinship ties to neighbors, and may have extended friendship and peace for at least some of the time. I argue later that this ability gives us humans the capacity to move beyond tribalism. We do cooperate in common pursuits almost anywhere on the globe without breaking into fights; this is quite remarkable.

Cultural Variation in Kinship-Based Societies

The last chapter compared hunter-gatherer bands with societies of food producers and outlined their different lifestyles and ideologies. Like modes of subsistence, kinship organization responds to and influences sex roles, group living, and the relative importance of conflict and cooperation in everyday life. Kinship has long been an organizer of social groups, and in mammals, the necessary mother-offspring bond formed its natural core.

I like the term *kinship-based* to describe societies that are not centralized into larger states. It more accurate and more neutral than Steven Pinker's term "anarchy," as borrowed from Hobbes, since disorder does not describe everyday life in these societies. For most people, most of the time, life was probably about searching for food, bearing and raising children, conversing, and making decisions. In lumping these societies together in most of his discussions, and by providing multiple anecdotes regarding violence in groups known particularly for that characteristic, Pinker oversimplifies kin-based societies without taking into account the institutions that did govern everyday life; not central governments, but interlocking, ordered groups nonetheless, some conducive to harmony, and others to conflict. My position is that the natural state of humanity was cultural from quite early in our evolution, and definitely by the emergence of *Homo sapiens* and the culture-language complex.

As *Homo sapiens* migrated into different areas, variations in organizing life would have developed in response to different ecological challenges, enabled by the cognitive flexibility and creativity that characterize our species. As time passed, some societies were forced into less hospitable territory, while others conquered and took over new areas. This was certainly the situation when hunter-gatherer societies were first described by Europeans.

Kinship as an Organizer of Economics and Politics

Ethnographic studies of contemporary nonstate peoples have shown that kinship forms the basis for economic and political as well as marriage and residential patterns. The word *economic* in anthropology refers broadly to the provisioning of people with goods, not to a particular mode of economic exchange. Likewise, the word *political* refers to any social arrangement for getting group jobs done. We see remnants of kinship organization in modern industrial and post-industrial state-organized societies in the inheritance of property along kinship lines, and in succession of leaders in some of them.

In his classic 1972 book, *Stone Age Economics*, anthropologist Marshall Sahlins describes the domestic or household economies of kinship-based societies. In these, distribution as well as production of goods took place largely through kinship ties. In more recent publications, Sahlins has turned to the interpersonal understandings, power dynamics, and ambiguities involved in kin-based gift exchange and reciprocity.[28] Yet his earlier analyses offered lasting insights into economic and political relationships in small-scale societies and stimulated considerable research.

He originally identified three levels of exchange in these societies based on their degree of "sociality," viewing reciprocity as a continuum.[29] On one end, generalized reciprocity was represented by free giving with no return expected, as applied to close family members (his "golden rule"). In the middle of the continuum was balanced reciprocity, gift-giving with the expectation of equal return that might be immediate or delayed. Balanced reciprocity characterized the next level of intimacy within local groups, and among kin (his "silver rule"). Finally, at the least social end of the continuum was negative reciprocity, which applies to intergroup and even intertribal exchanges with strangers and contains the idea of giving little to gain much (his "brass rule").

The continuum represents relationships ranging from the most social to the least social and is very often defined by kinship or its lack. Emphasis at the most social or domestic end of the continuum is on provisioning the family and the local group, which Sahlins described as underusing both resources and labor. Modern market relationships would fall mostly at the other end of the continuum, based mostly on his brass rule, with emphasis on overuse and overproduction.

Sahlins credited French sociologist Marcel Mauss, whose small book is entitled (translated) *The Gift*, with calling attention to the economic importance of gift giving in kin-based societies.[30] With a gift, one initiates a contract of reciprocity that involves giving, receiving, obligations; and friendship among groups. Generosity is a key in this. Referring specifically to kinship-based traditional Melanesian (Pacific) islanders, Mauss describes their "highly developed exchange system ... that cuts across geographical and linguistic boundaries. They replace our system of sale and purchase" with one of gift exchange.[31]

Sahlins noted that reciprocal gift giving was an important mechanism for keeping the peace in many societies around the world. In his more recent analysis, Robert L. Kelly details working reciprocity among some contemporary hunter-gatherers that is responsive to a complex set of social variables and individual choices. In recent years, this reciprocity has been analyzed through several mathematical models (for example, tit-for-tat). Despite changes that partially incorporated the people into modern economies, reciprocity norms still provide a kind of social security network for members of those societies.[32]

Alliances between groups made through exchanges of gifts and people (framed as men exchanging women at the time) became an important and controversial theme in twentieth century anthropology. Descent ("blood" or *consanguineal* kinship) and alliance (with affines) provided two means for extending family kin bonds to a larger community. And they did, however imperfectly, extend family sentiment and peaceful relationships among groups some of the time. This works differently at different levels of organization (as described in Chapter 5) for bands, tribes, and chiefdoms. In early civilizations, the first state-based societies, kinship and religion often combined into a theocratic hierarchy with a ruling kin group or family member as a kind of priest-ruler.

In reality, marriage and births of children extend kinship outward from the immediate family, as long as people from local groups marry out of their groups. Because people have relatives living in different local groups, varying degrees of family sentiment in many cases may motivate groups to keep the peace. Through interacting birth and marriage ties, kinship bridges groups and creates larger social networks.

Kinship Variety, Flexibility, and Change

Organization through kinship works differently in different societies, and it varies with other features. These include (1) natural and cultural environments, (2) subsistence base, (3) organizational level, (4) permanence of settlement, and (5) specific forms that kin groups take. Given our human capacity for defining situations, there is plenty of flexibility in engineering ideology and social organization along one ancestral line or another (patrilineal, matrilineal, or bilaterally through both). Many societies also augment this flexibility with fictive kinship, in which individuals are creatively assigned to roles or groups to which they would not belong through biological kinship.

Although nonstate or kinship-based cultures are thought to be intrinsically more tradition-bound than cultures based on modern technologies, they have more flexibility than is normally thought. Current students of kinship stress the idea that, in the real world, the elaborate systems that were previously described, debated, and analyzed do not reflect the flexibility of actual human behavior, which often uses its culture's institutions in new ways as conditions change, exploiting various loopholes within whatever system is in place.

Historically, ethnographers did acknowledge and describe variation and flexibility, identifying adoption of children, borrowing of males or females from other lineages when they are needed, and even altering usual sex roles in response to individual differences or preferences. A well-known example from some North American Indian tribal societies is the institutionalized alternative "berdache" role for men who choose to live, work, and dress as women. Other forms of alternative role choices did not involve total identity shifts. But flexibility was achieved in most societies by use of inventive means of redefining individuals and kin categories.

With today's accelerating rate of cultural evolution, this kind of response probably has become more common. All world societies have undergone large and rapid changes over the last century; few original forms remain intact. The concepts presented here illustrate the versatility of the kinship idiom for organizing small-scale societies in the past. Anthropology itself has changed and some practitioners argue that earlier-reported kin patterns were products of the observers as much as the observed. Today, ethnographers place greater reliance on how individuals in particular cultures describe their own worlds than on analysis by outsiders.

Anthropologist Janet Carsten suggests that we go further and substitute the concept of "relatedness" for "kinship" because of the variable ways that human cultures and individuals have transformed its meaning past the common understanding of kin as biologically connected.[33] Alternative forms of human engagement, such as reproduction using sperm from donors, surrogate motherhood, adoption of children by gay couples, and other ways of creating families need to be added to the equation. Fictive kinship might be incorporated into her concept of relatedness.

The main point here is that social kinship and social roles are not equivalent to biological roles. This creates difficulty for sorting out influences of biology and culture on human behavior, and for determining the effects of individual selection, kin selection, and group selection on the evolution of human behavior.

Next we turn to the connection of kinship to peace, war, women, and men, and our future as *Homo sapiens*. Individual violence and war are part of our legacy, just as are talking through issues, caring for others, and cooperating in getting food and building homes. I suggest that how kin groups are defined and organized can make a difference in the emphasis on and the prevalence of peace and war. These definitions can be associated with the well-being of individuals in a society.

Kinship, War, and Peace

Were our ancestors more peaceful or more aggressive and prone to engaging in war than modern humans? Evolutionary psychologist and popular science writer Stephen Pinker, following researchers Lawrence H. Keeley, Azar Gat, and other sources, concludes that today's world is more peaceful, overall, than it was in the past. He bases this on the proportion of deaths from wars and other forms of physical violence from prehistory through recorded history to the present. He argues that central, formal governments do a better job than pre-state societies in curbing our human impulses toward violence. He suggests that the expansion of literacy and human rights movements that began in the Enlightenment added to this trend toward a more peaceful world.

Many other investigators agree that this trend is supported by sufficient evidence, although it seems counterintuitive to many of us as we are bombarded by news of violent deaths and other atrocities on a daily basis. Also, we are moved by the sheer numbers of victims of modern acts of violence and war more than by statistics, such as percentages of the population. These numbers become overwhelming when we realize that each victim was a living person with hopes and dreams not unlike our own.

Two preliminary points are relevant to this discussion of war and peace. First, the fact that the average man has greater propensity for violent behavior than the average woman has little explanatory value for understanding why war varies in importance from one human society to another. All societies, after all, have and need both sexes. But how sex differences are defined and how they are supported by social institutions and ideologies do make a difference. For example, the value placed on stereotypical tough male behaviors may explain some of the differences among societies. Other sociocultural or environmental features can influence war either directly or indirectly through their influence on cultural sex role differences.

A second point is that although the biological basis for violence or aggressiveness cannot explain variation between societies, it can provide insight into the origins of war. Our emotions, like the impulses or instincts of other animals, motivate us to pursue the life goals of survival and reproduction through seeking food, water, shelter, and sexual opportunity. Animals compete for resources; additionally, social animals cooperate in obtaining them. In one sense, the human story of war reflects attempts to gain resources and to extend cooperation beyond small groups. In this, our species has had mixed success.

Political scientist Azar Gat distinguishes *basic drives,* such as those directly connected to survival and reproduction (hunger, thirst, sex) from violence, which he calls a *secondary drive,* in that it is "both innate and optional." It is switched on or off in response to external conditions such as resource availability, competition, and perhaps other sociocultural and demographic factors. He points out that while no one can survive without food or water, or reproduce without sex, most individuals can survive very well without acting out in violence.[34] In humans, men do not need to fight physically in order to mate, and even in our ape relatives, options other than physical violence enable subdominant males to mate. So, human violence is not a mandatory activity, even for males.

Human competition and violence are products of evolution from other creatures and part of how life has evolved. But cooperation and peacemaking are as much a part of how we evolved. Moreover, human war is as much a product of culture as biology. Its frequency varies among cultures and seems to increase with greater competition for resources, with growing populations, and in conditions of resource scarcity and perhaps crowding.

Gat suggests that war and conquest enabled the establishment of state organization. Once established, a state holds authority to use force legitimately to prevent armed conflict within it, hence generating peace. Like Melvin Konner, he concludes that although modern war and modern politics are ultimately about competition for resources, other complex cultural motives are at work. Human reproduction no longer needs to be tied to resource acquisition. By this standard, war and aggression should be eliminated.[35] Gat suggests that our psyches have not yet caught up with the new realities of global interdependence and global environmental challenges. But our psyches also seem responsive to reasoned consideration of other options. (We return to this in Chapters 8 and 9).

Most researchers of kin-based societies also acknowledge that multiple factors interact to encourage war or relative harmony among groups. These include kinship, family, forms of exchange or trade, and distribution and use of land and other property. Lawrence H. Keeley suggests that trade, like marriage bonds, can encourage war or peace, and that trade of unlike goods has a greater chance of encouraging peace than trade of similar goods.[36] Anthropologists who study kin-based societies recognize that the frequency of war and other forms of violence are variable cross-culturally. Cultural differences provide insights into conditions that foster cooperation even without state organization.

Kin Group Organization and Prevalence of War

There is a broad connection between kinship and war in human populations. Egalitarian, nomadic hunter-gatherer bands often are composed of a few extended families that form a loose group of bilaterally related kin. No matter how the kinship composition of bands originated, the typical band is a pragmatically formed group that splits and merges with changes in resources and seasons, and its members readily move from one band to another.

In speaking of these societies in Chapter 5, I suggested that although they were not free of violence, as a category they did appear to demonstrate less warfare than many nonstate food producers. In discussing the transition from a Paleolithic to a Neolithic way of life, I reviewed how changes wrought by that transition increased incentives for war, resulted in institutions with greater capacity to organize and pursue war, and eventually led to surpluses that gave economic support to and incentives for war. The institutions and surpluses also created differences in power, property, and wealth that could not only encourage but force individuals to fight.

Many examples picked by scholars of war to illustrate primitive, non-state based warfare are from societies that produce food rather than those relying solely on wild food sources. These societies usually have settled villages rather than nomadic bands, some food storage, and property in land, and they do not represent the Paleolithic, egalitarian, nomadic hunter-gatherer lifestyle. The Yanomamo of South America and most New Guinea tribal people are typically cited as examples of primitive fighters, but they practice horticulture, supplemented by hunting.

Using a different approach to analyzing warfare, anthropologist Raymond C. Kelly in *Warless Societies and the Origins of War* begins by identifying a sample of relatively warless societies, without regard to subsistence base, and looks for commonalities among them.[37] Although his sample is small, he shows that the common ground is the absence of corporate group responsibility for individual infractions of social behavior, such as homicide. All cultures have groups, but not all human groups have the notion that the entire group can be held accountable for a homicide committed by one of its members. Group accountability is the defining trait of *corporate* groups, and is sometimes called *corporate responsibility*.

Individual nuclear families, even bilateral extended families that include a variety of relatives, often occur as temporary groups only. This description most often fits egalitarian, nomadic hunter-gatherers that do not have more formal groups; Raymond C. Kelly also uses the term *nonsegmental* to characterize societies that have loosely-defined kin groups that are not corporate. Such societies seem to be the closest to being relatively warless, while not necessarily peaceful, as they still demonstrate violence between individuals. In these societies, however, a wrong to an individual does not usually engage the kind of group responsibility for revenge that can be seen in societies that are more tightly organized (Kelly's *segmental* societies).

In contrast, *unilineal descent groups* (one line of ancestors of the same sex), create a different situation. The *patrilineal* variety features a line or branch of related men; fathers, sons, grandsons, and on through the generations; this built-in structure is continuous over time. These more permanent and more cohesive groups can easily become a core for making war, finding spouses, and inheriting property from father to son. Marriages that unite two unilineal descent groups are often accompanied by material exchanges that reinforce larger group alliances. Even *matrilineal* groups can sometimes work this way, with women creating a line of related mother's brothers, but this kind of group often has a different authority structure and flavor to it.

Kelly found strong support for war being important in segmental societies. On this basis, he proposed that such societies, featuring corporate, ancestor-based kin groups, coevolved with war in nonstate societies.

Societies with tribal or chiefdom organization, in contrast to egalitarian hunter-gatherer bands, usually feature these descent groups in which membership is determined through a patrilineal or matrilineal line. These groups are exogamous. Individuals must marry into a different group, and sometimes a specific group is preferred. If this pattern is followed, and if there are more than two groups, a circular marriage pattern can result (traditionally viewed as groups of men exchanging women). This is the type of exchange Chapais was referring to by the phrase "matrimonial exchange." It is seen only in humans, not in other animals.

Some have suggested that this kind of analysis is oversimplified. Perhaps the strict patrilineality that Euro-American anthropologists ascribed to many African and Near Eastern kinship systems of the past were exaggerated, and more subtle matrilineal and bilateral family ties were neglected. Colonial powers, particularly the British, did make use of the existing formal patrilineal framework for administering indirect control during colonial times, recruiting native men who were chiefs of their patrilineages.[38]

Nevertheless, marriage and the flow of gifts do make new relatives and create alliances, which extend reciprocity but also create new conditions for conflict. The new relatives (affines, based on marriage) can become larger cohesive groups that have greater potential for organizing either raiding groups or peacemaking efforts. This is one way that marriage ties can make friends and potential allies, but can also make potential enemies, as has been noted frequently in the anthropological literature (see Marshall Sahlins, for example).[39] Kin ties can enable or stabilize relationships but they can also divide people (think of in-law humor). Often there is an uneasy combination of both; in-laws can be friends or enemies, or both at different times.

The best-known examples of common-ancestor–based kin groups as vehicles of both stability and change in tribal and chiefdom societies may be the African segmentary lineage systems. In a much-cited study, Sahlins drew from earlier detailed fieldwork by social anthropologists who studied several African herder/horticulturalists (Nuer and Tallensi societies are two examples).[40] He, following the work of E. E. Evans-Pritchard, Meyer Fortes, and others, proposed that the structure of these patrilineal groups made them excellent instruments of organizing war for "predatory expansion" in nonstate societies because of the lineage's multiple branching, tree-like structure.

In these, nodes of branching provide built-in points for the merging or division of segments in relation to size of the challenge from a rival. How this works is reflected in the following quip, often called a traditional Bedouin proverb: "I against my brother. My brother and I against my cousin. My cousin, my brother, and I against the world." This structure can function similarly, of course, for cooperative ventures of any kind, not just for wars of expansion.

In contrast, the loosely organized groups of most nomadic, egalitarian, hunter-gatherer bands are not very efficient for making war. With this understanding, we can compare these egalitarian hunter-gatherer bands to original Australian hunter-gatherer societies that Azar Gat used in his analysis of war; the rate of war was high there in some regions. Gat selected these societies to study because they were isolated for a lengthy period before the encroachment of food-producing and then industrialized societies, and because Australia has a wide range of ecological niches that they occupied.[41] But they were organized around ancestor-based patrilineal kin groups, in this way resembling the eastern African pastoralist societies more than other egalitarian hunter-gatherer societies.

Other Probable Associations between Kinship and War

I now address a set of rough associations that have some support and seem plausible, but that need further study to be confirmed or disconfirmed them. As described in Chapter 5, subsistence patterns, technology, and natural resources are significant correlates of warfare.

Here the focus is on family structure and kinship institutions, which also influence and are influenced by warfare as described here.

Features of *subsistence efforts* make a difference and influence how food is gathered and divided between women, men, and children. This interacts with typical *family structure*, the number of wives (or husbands very occasionally) and children, the amount of contact between father and mother and between father and children, and the time men devote to defending their group. *Property* is another factor; egalitarian hunter-gatherers usually share rights to territory, and sometimes to water holes, always within bands and often also with other local bands, particularly those that share a language.

So, in these societies where land is used as group territory, even shared territory, and hunter-gatherer bands move regularly through it, mobility would have itself constrained property accumulation and the ability to wage war. These factors would have varied through time also, with periods of increasing and decreasing scarcity coinciding with changes in temperature, rainfall, and other climatic factors. Hunter-gatherer bands often responded to sociocultural and population pressures from more powerful societies by retreating to less hospitable environments. The loose kin composition of these nomadic bands helped them to remain flexible as conditions changed.

A large-scale, multidisciplinary approach to understanding these connections in all human societies has yielded comparable conclusions. This recent study by Michelle J. Gelfand and others distinguishes *tight* and *loose* societies.[42] The distinction in strictness of adherence to cultural norms was originally identified in the 1960s by cultural anthropologists describing nonstate cultural variation. This newer study applies the notion to nation-states and operationalizes it as a hypothesis by utilizing measurable criteria in the broad areas of (1) ecological and historical threats, (2) sociopolitical institutions, (3) recurrent episodes of everyday experience in different societies, and (4) psychological adaptations. The research team gathered data from multiple databases, including historical documents and surveys of individuals representing a range of occupations.

Their results suggest that the tight and loose distinction is a useful way to understand cultural differences. The authors acknowledge the need for additional research to determine cause-and-effect relationships among variables and to aid practical application of the model, but I find that this model fits the evolutionary dynamic between adaptedness and adaptation, as well as other concepts presented throughout this book.

We next look at kinship organization, this contrast between tight and loose adherence to cultural norms, and war. The unilineal, ancestor-based, corporate kin groups described above are typical of cultures organized as tribes and chiefdoms. These have more permanent settlements and a conception of property rights in particular plots of land or herds of animals, conditions conducive to development of such groups. The most common variant is patrilineal, with rights passing from father to son and often with a woman moving into her husband's group upon marriage, forming an extended family with a core of fathers, sons, grandsons that makes an effective corporate group associated with revenge and war.

In mostly nonsegmental egalitarian hunter-gatherer bands with loose kin ties, organized war is less likely, but individual violence and homicide do occur, sometimes frequently and sometimes less often. Perhaps the characteristic fierce egalitarianism comes at a cost. Individual stress can come from maintaining balance between caring for one's family and providing for self and all others in the local group. High rates of homicide and individual violence are reported for some of these societies, while more peaceful relations are described for others. Given little personal property, no animals of burden to carry supplies of food, tools, weapons, and equipment, however, waging organized war is simply not feasible for societies occupying wide territories with scattered resources.

Part of the disagreement about the importance of violence and war in different societies depends on how they are defined. At what point does individual violence become war?

Socialization and Enculturation of Girls and Boys

Specific features of child care, women's status, and degree of violence are associated with a society's use of resources and its set of cultural values, and with how kin groups are organized. How violence and war are perceived and framed in different cultures plays a role also. These factors interact to influence how children are cared for and taught.

A father's role in child care and closeness to his children vary in relation to these factors: Males generally do not spend as much time caring for and being with babies and young children in societies with strong patrilineal fighting groups. In contrast, fathers who spend time caring for young children show increases in levels of oxytocin and decreased levels of testosterone, which correlates with decreases in male violence. This oversimplifies a complex relationship, but it cuts to the core of how group organization and male biology can interact to influence levels of violence and even warfare.

Melvin Konner, in *The Evolution of Childhood*, reviews anthropological studies of fathers and children and examines variation in the amount of time spent together and the closeness between them. In almost all human cultures, mothers and other females do much of the baby and child care. After this early period, child care becomes more variable, and it is somewhat predictable in relation to other sociocultural features. Several generalizations can be made about associations between warfare on the one hand and child care on the other. I supplement Konner's summary[43] with a few additional studies of kinship, sex roles, and war. The goal is to suggest areas for further study, not to declare that these generalizations or interpretations are definitive.

Unlike the involvement of mothers in child care, which is essential in traditional societies, father involvement varies. Compared to other mammals, human male investment in children is high and often involves protection, provision of some food, and some direct child care. Contributions by others in caring for infants and children and mentoring the young (fathers, friends, grandparents, older children) has resulted in childhood mortality rates that are lower in *Homo sapiens* than in other primates, probably because it really does take a village to raise and educate a child.

During our evolution, meat was probably the most critically needed item that was often provided by men. Now, in some modern state-based societies, men can replace women for many child care tasks. Sarah Hrdy and Melvin Konner cite research suggesting that in some situations, including some modern urban societies with large pockets of poverty and in other situations where fathers are not readily available, it makes sense for women to mate when they are young. This enables family cooperation in child care; in these situations, young women with children have more older women to help them, to be alloparents, than they would later in life. Under these circumstances, having multiple mates can increase a man's or a woman's chances of reproducing.[44]

How subsistence work is divided between men and women is critical for female status and for how societies are organized. What the work is like and how close it is to home base or camp will influence how it is divided between women and men in traditional cultures. Particular kinship structures mesh better with particular adaptations to the natural and sociocultural environment. In many tribes and chiefdoms, in contrast to mobile bands, patrilocal residence rules create groups of men; the resulting structure then reinforces the patrilineal and patriarchal (men in control) bias.

A 1913 study of Rwala Bedouins exemplifies this pattern; their traditional subsistence depended primarily on herding large animals, a job usually performed by males. Konner reports that "frequent warfare, strong male authority, and cultivated fierceness made fathers very distant." Kin groups were patrilineal, residence patrilocal, authority patriarchal, and marriage polygynous. Each father stayed in a separate compartment of the family tent.[45]

In such societies, the emphasis for men is on hypermasculinity, violence, distance from women and children, tough initiations, warfare or raiding, and strong division of labor between the sexes. Konner's work summarizes these connections, which were documented in several comparative, cross-cultural studies. We might view this as the extreme of male corporate grouping or segmental, patriarchal, tight organization.

Konner compares these hypermasculine behaviors to those of some other animals, remarking that "associations of aggressive activities with male acquisition, mate guarding, and polygyny somewhat resemble the cross-species continuum, which links male competition to greater male size, strength, and metabolic rate." He places polygynous or patrilocal cultures that must defend accumulated resources without specialized armed forces at the "distant" end of the continuum of human fatherhood.[46] He also connects these male-based kin groups to military interest and activity.

We might think that matrilineal descent, particularly when combined with matrilocal residence (a married couple lives near the wife's family) would make it a bit more difficult but not impossible for male corporate groups to become strong or cohesive. It has also often been suggested that such female-centered societies are more conducive to peaceful relationships between groups. But this connection to peaceful relationships is not always the case, and groups of men associated through a line of women (their mothers and sisters) have and sometimes do form fighting groups.[47]

In contrast, most egalitarian hunter-gatherers without significant intergroup violence almost certainly had a closer parenting style (summarized in Chapter 5). Konner ties this to sex roles also, suggesting that where women contribute more to subsistence, men tend to share child care. Women tend to contribute less to subsistence in societies that depend on plow agriculture and large animal herding.

Mary West Katz (now Mary Maxwell West) and Konner concluded that gathering and gardening *without* polygyny, patrilocality, male-dominant division of labor, or patrilineal extended families, tend to be better for women and girls. Gathering and gardening cultures tend not to foster violence and war to the degree found in those based on distant fathers and strong male-based organizations.

These findings are consistent with other cross-cultural studies, and my own work demonstrates that the notion of female impurity is often found in societies in which women have little sociopolitical authority or status,[48] perhaps supporting this power arrangement. Floyd Rudmin's research relating private property in land and grain to patriarchal institutions also strengthens this notion.

Finally, specific institutions seem to encourage group thinking and corporate identity, or tightness. These include rigorous rites of passage that incorporate painful and stressful experiences that are followed by symbolic rebirth into a new identity. Institutionalized age-group and men's houses reinforce the self-segregation of sexes often found in voluntary child play groups. Cultural exaggeration of biological sex differences and different parenting of girls and boys foster greater adult separation. These features may also be reinforced through religious rituals and taboos.

Sharing of work and family roles by women and men may help to de-emphasize sex differences and discourage the rigidity that is associated with war. The Gelfand article featuring the tight versus loose contrast seems to suggest this possibility and encourage this kind of comprehensive scenario. My guess is that egalitarian hunter-gatherers are good early examples of loose societies.

Summary and Conclusions

Kinship ties were powerful organizers of small-scale societies and, like other biological and cultural evolutionary products, they continue to retain the potential to bring people together or to pull people apart, depending on how they are defined and used. How these work in the real world depends roughly on perceptions of the relative benefits of cooperation or conflict in given situations.[49] Kinship can foster cooperation, trust, reciprocity, caring, and concepts of fairness among kin. These institutions can also foster intergroup differences and violence. As such, they have implications for human relations within and outside one's own sociocultural group.

Woven through this material about *Homo sapiens* in groups are several specific themes: One is that the relationship of a human group to its environmental context (natural features and surrounding sociocultural groups) is critical to all events, institutions, and values of that sociocultural unit. A second is that human societies, like biological organisms, most often change through tinkering with structures that already exist, rather than by beginning anew (although the latter option is possible and more likely with sociocultural change). It is becoming clear that we cannot accurately predict the type of kinship organization or the type of ethos from a particular mode of subsistence alone. Just as the several phases of the evolving human animal featured specific fossils with a mosaic of traits, cultural evolution has been at least as messy, and probably messier, with some trials of group living not making it into subsequent generations.

Researchers of human sociocultural behavior will need to continue focusing on the complexity of interconnections between biology and culture. We cannot understand the relative status of women and men, political relations between modern nation-states, economic relations within and between countries, or ideological differences without looking at who we are, what we need as animals, and what forces motivate us to behave as we do.

Regarding women and men, peace and war, loose and tight, adaptability and adaptedness, a number of investigators have proposed that our world might be more harmonious and peaceful if women were in charge. Even Bernard Chapais ties peacemaking to the reduction of sexual dimorphism, male pacification, and relations with affines.[50] Any hypothesis about a world run by women is not testable at this point, but it is an empirical question. Perhaps women on average are a bit better at avoiding violent behavior and empathizing with others and using language to negotiate or compromise. Pinker too called feminization of Western society one of "the better angels of our nature," meaning an influence away from war and toward peace in societies and even internationally.[51] Izzeldin Abuelaish argues that adopting "female values" concerned with producing life would help us all in pursuing peace.[52] How particular cultural institutions are organized and how they are run can contribute to either merging or sharply dividing female and male roles, and this may make a difference.

In this chapter, I have suggested that how kinship is organized influences how people behave toward each other. As our many cultures evolved, long before the origin of civilization and state-based central governments, these diverse kin arrangements gave rise to differing degrees of human violence and war. Small-scale, nonstate societies have kin groups that vary in their degree of corporateness, which itself is related to external and internal forces. Early societies of *Homo sapiens* may have been fiercely egalitarian, but they had to work at it. They also had to work at keeping the peace. These early groups were probably loosely and informally organized, in keeping with their small size and frequent moves.

Climate change and intense use of resources ushered in the Neolithic Revolution, whose consequences eventually undid the more relaxed Paleolithic lifestyle. Particularly in Ian Morris's "lucky latitudes" with abundant concentrated resources, conditions helped to spread a new form of ranking people; a new kind of hierarchy, culturally based but otherwise reminiscent of the dominance hierarchies practiced by our primate relatives. These same developments set the stage for ever more efficient ways of harnessing and using up our earth's resources.

In Chapter 7 I review religion as an institution comparable to kinship in its influence on how we think about other individuals and other groups. Chapter 8 then addresses the phenomenon that I call *tribalism*. This leads into the book's concluding section whose aim is to sort out how we might move beyond the negative aspects of bonding with our small groups, beyond tribalism, and to offer one perspective on making sense of our place in nature.

Holding People Together:
Religion

The brain is a belief engine.

　　—Michael Shermer, 2011[1]

Is man one of God's blunders? Or is God one of man's blunders?

　　—Friedrich Nietzsche, 1889[2]

Is *Homo sapiens* a religious animal? And what would an answer to this question mean for our chances of overcoming tribalism and moving into the future as a species? In this chapter, I look at the human institution of religion from an evolutionary perspective, focusing on the question of its adaptiveness from the past to today.

Although we moderns view and define religion as a recognizable entity, and although every known human society has components that make up this entity, not all cultures have a word for "religion" as such. They may have spirits, or gods, or totems, or ancestor souls, or particular natural features that are considered sacred, or a god that stands alone. And every culture has stories about how things came to be. All societies have rituals, and many are accompanied by music, dancing, and visual arts (engraving, painting, sculpting). All societies have ideas about how people ought to live. These components— ritual, myth, and morality—comprise a triad that is seen across cultures and through time. In most small-scale societies these components are integrated into everyday life rather than existing as a separate institution like the one that many people today call *religion*.

Clifford Geertz provided anthropology with a comprehensive definition of religion that covers the cultural variations: "(1) a system of symbols which act to (2) establish powerful, pervasive, and long-lasting moods and motivations in men (3) by formulating conceptions of a general order of existence and (4) clothing these conceptions with such an aura of factuality that (5) the moods and motivations seem uniquely realistic."[3] In this definition, he recognizes that religion has to do with human cognition and symbol-based language, with the human attempt to make sense of the world, and with human emotion and motivation. Through its history, anthropology has sought to understand not only how and why these practices came to be, but also how to make sense of religious diversity.

Morality is probably the most ancient part of the religious triad, in that it most directly arises from our being social animals, and it exists in the absence of religious myth and ritual. As outlined in Chapter 4, social mammals typically demonstrate two key behavioral features regarding the treatment of others: caring and a sense of fairness. Impulses toward social behavior are even more ancient.

Not everyone agrees about where in the sequence those features become pre-morality or morality. I defined ethics in Chapter 4 as the human variety of morality that adds language-based reasoning to the earlier core of sentiments that evolved in our mammalian ancestors. Particular versions of human morality and ethics are influenced by cultural definition, organization of social groups, and environmental challenges. From small-scale, egalitarian hunter-gatherers whose behaviors toward each other are mostly regulated informally to large-scale, hierarchical societies with elaborate ethical codes and abstract ideas of justice, all religious variations are tied to the ancient emotions of caring and fairness. Other ancient emotions also influence human behavior everywhere.

Why Religion? Origins and Functions

Religion is a social phenomenon whose features evolved as part of the human culture-language complex. Its presence is supported by evidence from prehistory that includes engravings, paintings, drawings, musical instruments, use of color and design on tools, body ornaments, and burial sites that feature artifacts along with human remains. These indicators of symbolism and burials are also interpreted as indicators of fully human language, culture, and behavior. We saw in Chapter 3 that the presence of language itself is inferred from combined evidence from skull endocasts and imaging that that indicate brain size and shape, tools and other artifacts, modifications of DNA, and changes in placement of the larynx (voice box) in the neck.[4]

There is no simple answer to why *Homo sapiens* has religion. There are two different ways of answering "why" questions empirically. One looks for origins, another for functions. In an evolutionary perspective, these are related: A feature that originates (often by accident) is more likely to persist through natural selection if it serves a function, i.e., if it does something that enhances the survival of an organism. Assuming multilevel selection, a feature may persist if it enhances survival and reproductive chances for a kin group, a local group, or a larger population under particular conditions. One recurring debate regarding religion's origin is whether it is an adaptation, an accidental product of other human adaptations (a spandrel), or a maladaptation (an outmoded way of viewing the world).

My view is that religion evolved as a human adaptation, albeit a flawed one, and like all adaptations it arose in response to specific conditions that our ancestors faced. The adaptation that we moderns call religion, however, is in reality a collection of ideas and behaviors that did not all evolve together. Like other aspects of human behavior already described, these components are rooted in our evolutionary heritage. Some suggest that scientific and religious ideas spring from the same roots. They have in common an effort to make sense of the world, to solve its mysteries, and to come to terms with our fragile existence as rather peculiar life forms.[5]

Historically, the universality of religion has often been explained by its purported function. First, it may help individuals to understand events ranging from dreams to environmental phenomena; to cope with uncertainty, illness, and death; and to achieve psychological well-being. A second functional explanatory frame is that it creates common group sentiment and fosters cooperation that benefits society as a whole. Emile Durkheim outlined the latter aspect a century ago in his brilliant analysis based on accounts of religious expression in original Australian cultures, *The Elementary Forms of the Religious Life.*[6]

Under some circumstances, religion can work as an instrument of sociocultural change, as documented by analyses of millennial movements that became political in response to colonialism. These have been labeled differently, as nativistic (Linton), revitalization (Wallace), messianic or millennial (Barber, Worsley et al.) movements.[7] A more recent and familiar example of religion's role in social and political change in the United States was Reverend Martin Luther King, Jr's leadership in the African-American community through organizing people, pushing changes, and increasing awareness among all Americans of economic and political justice as moral issues. Eventually, the effects on Jim Crow practices, voting rights, and education were profound, although many observers feel that we are currently sliding backward.

Religion can have a dark side as well, which this sliding backward may represent. Some critics of religion argue that it has caused more negative than positive effects on the human psyche, on human society, or even on humanity as a whole. For example, religious doctrines have created new fears, increased anxiety, and led to dissension and war. Some fear that warring religious factions will eventually destroy all of us.

Anthropological analysis of religion seeks to study religious groups as we study other products of nature, to derive empirically based con-

clusions regarding how religious ideology and practices influence behavior in today's world and in past societies. Drawing from Emile
Durkheim and from evolutionary biology and psychology, two American anthropologists, David S. Wilson and T. M. Luhrmann, apply
this to contemporary U. S. society. I summarize their work in the
next paragraphs.

D.S. Wilson identifies religion as an adaptation.[8] He revives Durkheim's analogy of society as an organism, and examines the built-in
conflict between individual selection (competing individuals in a society) and group selection (groups competing with each other), utilizing
the notion of multilevel selection. He reminds his readers that all of
us behave nonadaptively on a regular basis and that our impulses often move us in opposing directions. Every society, like a species,
evolves as a compromise between individual and group goals.

He takes the position, as I do, that understanding the egalitarian
hunter-gatherer way of life and its strong ethic of sharing is critical
for understanding why we humans developed religion in the first
place. In these small-scale societies, moral communities are united in
part by ritual behaviors and shared stories (mythology) through
which people make sense of nature and their place in the world. In
the sense that humanity, by definition, faces life through a sociocultural screen, no human societies represent what philosopher Thomas
Hobbes described as a "state of nature"(I will return to this point
later).

Wilson describes the brain as an evolved mechanism for directing
behavior. As an adaptive tool, it comes up with ideas and stories that
are not necessarily empirically valid, but that function to hold groups
together or explain the unexplainable so that people can go about the
daily business of living. He uses the phrase "adaptive fiction" for
such ideas and stories, referring to religious myth and other such
propositions.

Of course, differentiating fantasy from reality is critical to science
and to how we approach the future. In this regard, Wilson points out

that any of us, including scientists, can fall into the trap of becoming too fond of a particular point of view and rejecting other plausible solutions to problems.

I turn now to cultural anthropologist T. M. Luhrmann, who studied two American Christian evangelical congregations (Vineyard congregations) in Chicago and in California, during four years of participant observation.[9] The religious movement she studied developed from a merging of fundamentalism, experiential Pentecostalism, and the remnants of so-called "hippie" Christianity. The stated goal of members of the self-labeled new evangelicals is to achieve "personal relationships with God."[10]

She designed an experiment to determine how some individuals are able to learn, through training and practice, to experience the presence of "god" by using their brains in a particular way. She compares her experimental group trained in this method, a type of Christian prayer (*kataphatic prayer*), with two control groups. Preparing for the experiment, participants in all three groups completed in-depth interviews and were rated on the Tellegen absorption scale, which was designed originally to measure one's susceptibility to hypnosis.

The probability of achieving this type of sensory experience was significantly greater for those subjects who had ranked high for susceptibility to hypnosis on the Tellegen scale and had been part of the experimental, kataphatic prayer training group. Luhrmann concludes that this particular form of training, in how to employ mental imagery in seeking a sensory experience of a supernatural presence, enabled susceptible individuals to acquire and maintain their conviction that they had been touched by god.[11] Although some in the mental health field would judge such perceptions as indicating mental illness, there is growing recognition that these experiences, and other transient hallucinations, are rather common.[12]

She compares this training to methods of inducing "mystical" experiences in diverse cultures, such as solitary vision quests. I wonder if individual differences in receptivity may help to explain differences in religiosity or spirituality generally. Perhaps mystical experiences exemplify a pervasive but not universal human phenomenon that is readily incorporated into religious practices.[13]

These human experiences seem to result from a complex interaction between built-in and acquired patterns of neural connections, and internal and external conditions. There are differences in individual susceptibility to suggestion; to hypnosis, to flights of imagination, to vivid dreaming and daydreaming, and to other unusual sensory experiences. These may be important for understanding various idiosyncratic perceptions and behaviors that appear in societies around the world. Perceptions and emotions connected to such experiences are regularly being deciphered by biological and social scientists through advances in research techniques and brain imaging. Exposure to one's culture and language influences the form that a particular expression takes. All of our cultural narratives, fiction and nonfiction, inform our experiences and how we interpret them.

As a second goal, Luhrmann attempts to explain why this evangelical form of religion appeals to individuals who are citizens of a complex, modern society. Her subjects were aware that they use their minds imaginatively in a special way in this context, in contrast to everyday work and interactions. She drew two conclusions. First, she related the element of play in this practice to the regular engagement of adults with fiction in everyday life through stories, online games, and digitally mediated relationships. In Western cultures, pretend play is not restricted to children as it is in some other cultures. Second, she concluded that a sense of attachment to a personal god may ease the pain of isolation that some people feel in the midst of our rapidly changing, increasingly impersonal society.

In her view, this helps to explain the increasing popularity of evangelical religions around the world, in contrast to the reduced participation in more liberal religious institutions, or the predicted fading away of religion and secularization of society proposed by twentieth century philosopher of science Karl Popper. He viewed a more open society as conducive to the creative, unrestricted problem solving on which scientific progress, and our future, depend.[14]

I wonder if the closeness to a spiritual being that Luhrmann describes is a kind of "fictive friendship" analogous to fictive kinship. Perhaps online-only relationships are another example of this, and may have become popular for similar reasons: They reduce the sense of social isolation, foster health, and organize people for joint action. This "flight to fiction"(my phrase) may also stem from interpersonal relationships being less immediate, more indirect, and more distant, in striking contrast to life during human prehistory and much of historical time.

During our evolution, we human apes gradually replaced grooming with talking (Sarah Hrdy's "grooming at a distance"). Today we still talk face-to-face but our close personal and social contacts are often mediated through devices that create greater distance and isolation. Written communication, printed communication (especially after invention of the printing press) and, today, accelerated digital communication have replaced earlier modes. Texting is one example of communication that can create isolation: Friends or parents with children sitting in a cafe together can be observed texting instead of interacting directly with those they are with.

Anthropologist Robin Dunbar (known for connecting brain size with group size in primates) also notes the discordance of current lifestyles with most of our past. He describes the ease with which moderns get caught up in fictional scenarios (e.g., novels, movies, soap operas, electronic relationships) and wonders about the eventual outcome for our species. Hrdy expresses concern about consequences for our capacity for empathy, which evolved with "mind reading" in our ancestors living in face-to-face groups. These abilities made us human. Of course, people have worried about social isolation whenever new technology has emerged. We may simply be in transition right now, and people are trying hard to find their way through the maze.

Rapid cultural changes have produced books such as *The Lonely Crowd* (David Riesman et al., 1950), *Things Fall Apart* (Chinua Achebe, 1955), as well as *Future Shock* (Alvin Toffler, 1970), and *Present Shock* (Douglas Rushkoff, 2013), as attempts to make sense of our changing world.

These remarks remind us of a perspective that views religion an all-purpose institution or cultural tool which can function to meet varied needs of individuals or the society as a whole. In the past, this tool was used to explain phenomena that science now explains. Today, perhaps it is used to meet a different set of unmet needs from those of people in earlier societies. Perhaps it is a stopgap tool that takes over when times are difficult and recedes when times are good (god of the gaps). The challenges we moderns face are certainly different from those of our ancestors, but they are big challenges nonetheless.

Maybe the contradictory nature of our humanity itself calls out for understanding and solutions, and our brains, liking solutions, come up with them, rationally improbable as they may be. Many of us take seriously a quest to understand the world around us and to make sense of our place in it, through either perceiving or constructing meaning as part of processing events and our individual lives.

Setting these speculations aside for now, I turn next to ritual (religious behavior) and then to myth (religious stories and concepts). Performance of a ritual often involves incorporation of the story involved, so that ritual and mythic aspects occur together. Some cultures emphasize ritual to a greater extent, while others emphasize narratives, creeds, or propositions. Music, dancing, and visual arts are part of this configuration. We see combinations of ritual, myth, and the arts around the world, from the elaborate Dreamtime stories and enactments of original Australian cultures to J. S. Bach's *Mass in B Minor* from Western European culture. Both ritual and myth are related to narrative and symbolic language, with prayers, sacraments, and other patterned behavioral sets.

Ritual

Ritual behaviors are evident in other animals; best known are the mating rituals of various creatures. A *ritual* is a repeated set of actions that occur regularly and stereotypically in response to particular events. For example, mating or marriage, seasonal changes, and life-cycle transitions often have associated rituals. The word "ritual" is also used to describe any obsessive or compulsive action that fulfils a biological or psychological imperative. Human ritual in its several guises often attempts to foster a particular state of mind, attitude and emotion, or sense of order. Most of us have a few personal rituals or routines of this type.

Social rituals often convey messages about the participants or about our way of understanding life transitions, as Arnold van Gennep described in his classic 1908 work, *Rites of Passage*. They may communicate information about the special group of *Homo sapiens* that is participating together. Besides marking transitions or marking a group as unique, they promote a feeling of oneness within the group. Mating and courtship rituals in other animals might be viewed as precursors of human rituals. In humans, dancing, music, and other artistic expressions add much to the human ritual complex.

Anthropologist Pascal Boyer calls religious group rituals "cognitive gadgets" because they influence how we think and easily capture our thoughts, helping them to spread (they are highly contagious in this respect).[15] Emile Durkheim provides insight into how these gadgets may have evolved. He was a pioneer in viewing ritual and myth as products of social living, noting that much human religious expression happens when people come together into larger than everyday assemblages. His thinking became important for informing later understanding of religion.

When reviewing evolution of the human brain and the culture-language complex in Chapter 3, I spoke of human symbolic behavior and arbitrary symbols as the building blocks for language. I now turn briefly to the increase in potential for lying and tactical deceit that this enables. Chimpanzees, bonobos, and other animals practice simple deception, but language gives *Homo sapiens* the capacity to be the most deceptive of all animals: We can talk about anything, anywhere, anytime (present, past, future) because we use symbols (words) that have only an arbitrary connection to what they represent. Self-deception is common; the hidden, unconscious brain is at work, fooling even its owner.

Anthropologist Roy A. Rappaport's analysis of religion emphasizes the centrality of ritual in negotiating these problematic features of human communication. Based on his field research among the Maring Tsembaga of Highland New Guinea, he originally (1968) proposed that human religious ritual evolved as a defense against lying and deceitful freeloading, a side effect of having a language that so readily can disrupt trust within a group. Group ritual visually demonstrates to onlookers and neighboring groups, often through dance and performance, the group's strength and fitness. In this way, it verifies or sanctifies verbal propositions about the group, serving as a mechanism for regulating the dynamic relationship between human populations and their ecosystems.[16]

Through his life, Rappaport came to assign an even larger role to ritual, proposing that it not only created the other components of religion but that it coevolved with language and with humanity to make us who we are today. The emotions associated with social ritual, first described by Durkheim as feeling oneself as part of a larger whole, are what Rappaport called the "numinous" and viewed as a product of the ritual experience. At the same time, Rappaport viewed the "sacred" as a product of the *language* of ritual." He credits Leslie A. White with recognizing the critical role of symbolic language and noting a connection between "Word" and "God."[17]

Rappaport considered religion to be an adaptation in its role of managing or self-regulating an organism or population in its particular context. He explained that *self-regulation* (homeostasis) and *self-organization* do not oppose each other as some have argued, but are two aspects of the same function. Self-regulation happens in context, and as contexts (environments) change, so do regulatory systems need to change.

My understanding is that the action of ritual can produce feelings of awe, wonder, and unity of self and society in some individuals. These are often called mystical experiences. They can lend a sense of sacredness to even arbitrary (symbolic) postulates or stories. In this way, such stories and propositions become unquestionable, or immune to being logically falsified when embodied in this ritual, emotional experience. Sacred narratives are often about how people "ought to" be, defining worthiness, virtue, or value. The rituals and postulates vary with their particular environmental and cultural contexts: In tribal societies people should be generous and brave; in state societies, in contrast, people ought to be meek, loyal, and dutiful citizens.[18]

A major trend in hominin evolution was increasing adaptability—increasing behavioral flexibility—and it was culture, based on symbolic language, that enabled this human versatility. But it is also language that enables the chaos resulting from deceit. Shared sacred propositions help to restore order and maintain sociocultural meaning. In real societies, as conditions change, disconnects occur. A given system develops glitches and needs to be recalibrated. What once was adaptive no longer is in its new context. Rappaport applies this to our human present with implications for the future. In Chapter 9, I return to this idea.

For Durkheim, Rappaport, and Wilson, then, religion is about community; the dancing, music-making and physical action of the ritual itself reinforce, or in a sense make sacred, the language that goes with it. The religious celebrations we see around the world, and even patriotic celebrations, carry messages regarding the group's strength, intentions, and sometimes the fitness of the individuals involved.

Those who view religion as an adaptation view it as a means of understanding our place in nature and helping our beleaguered species weather and survive changing times. The analysis by Ara Norenzayan (discussed later in this chapter) regarding reputation and religious prosociality is consistent with portions of Rappaport's work.

Rituals often regulate boundaries between groups, between nation-states, political parties, males and females, ingroups and outgroups, different stages of life, and seasons of the year. Perhaps all human cultures celebrate boundaries in one way or another. Even personal rituals during illness have to do with the boundary between sickness and health. Arnold van Gennep's classic book from 1908, *The Rites of Passage,* and Mary Douglas's *Purity and Danger* explore various boundaries and the rituals and taboos surrounding them.

In Chapter 8, I describe our tendency to classify ourselves into social groups, and then to assume that there are natural differences between them even when they are arbitrary in origin. Boundary-building is part of this human propensity to categorize, and this is closely related to the subject of tribalism.

The Arts (with emphasis on music)

Much research has focused on the origins of music, dance, and visual arts. These activities in most cultures of the world take place as part of socioreligious rituals or celebrations. In this section, I outline general ideas regarding their evolution and note connections among them. The arts express ritual and mythic portions of the religious experience. But they also express universal human emotions regardless of religion. I see the arts as a means of emotional communication and other-feeling, a secular experience of awe, wonder, and sense of unity with nature and humanity without requiring reference to a belief system at all. I emphasize music in the following paragraphs only because I am personally more familiar with it than with other art forms.

Music is ancient and seems to have deep biological roots that may be related to language. For most of prehistory, from the emergence of *Homo sapiens* and through historical times, music, like religion itself, was part of everyday life. A bone flute unearthed in Germany has been dated to 42,000 years ago,[19] and most certainly percussion instruments predate this find. Later, with economic specialization arising after the birth of food production and with settled life, music and musicians begin to specialize. Only in recent centuries did they become part of specialized arts activities that characterize the modern music scene.

How did this amazing part of all human cultures begin? Our ancient ancestors, several million years ago, were surrounded by nature's rhythms and melodies; wind, rain, storms, quakes, eruptions, the buzzes of insects, songs of birds, and the howling, growling, and calling of various animals. These perhaps stimulated a fondness for rhythms and melodies and attempts at music-making. Music and language may even have evolved together. The very earliest environment for each of us individually is quite noisy, with the sounds of our mother's bodily fluids, movements, and, above all, the rhythmic beat of her heart. After birth, the act of nursing keeps mother's heartbeat close, and the universal activities of rocking and crooning help to soothe cries of discomfort. Perhaps our rhythmic and musical sense originated, like so much else, with the mother-child bond.

Musician and neuroscientist Daniel J. Levitin attempts to discover why most of us are drawn to music, calling it an obsession of humanity.[20] In his book, *This is Your Brain on Music*, he reviews competing views of its origin. One made popular by Stephen Jay Gould and then Steven Pinker is that music is a spandrel (Pinker: *auditory cheesecake*), a pleasant by-product of language evolution. This conclusion surprised many and inspired further investigation. Levitin suggests that the spandrel hypothesis may reflect today's musical scene of specialists, criticism, and concert halls, but that it is inadequate for explaining the ubiquity of music and the universal participation in music and dance in traditional cultures around the world.

Aniruddh Patel offers an alternative view that he calls trans-formative technology of the mind (TTM), proposing that music is neither spandrel nor adaptation, but something in between, an invention comparable to reading or to the control of fire.[21] He argues that this kind of cultural invention can be biologically powerful in its capacity to modify the brains of participants without being an adaptation itself. In his view, music has such a wide range of functions and is so broadly distributed in the brain that it cannot have been a direct product of natural selection. Every brain modification that supports music evolved in response to a nonmusical function. To me, this resembles the concept of *exaptation* (See Chapter 1). And natural selection works on phenotypes, whole organisms with their genes, not with isolated genes. The interested reader might consult Patel's larger body of work.

Levitin, in contrast, sees music's universality, ancient origin, use of specialized brain structures that can take over if other "memory systems fail," and its presence in other animals; particularly birds, whales, and gibbons (lesser apes), as evidence for its being an adaptation. He argues that music's ability to promote cognitive and language development and its role as a memory aid make it a good candidate for having arisen through natural selection.[22]

We enjoy music partly because it awakens our emotions. This speaks to the role of repetitiveness, anticipation, and surprise that musicologists consider basic to our enjoyment. Music elicits emotions that can be measured by brain scans; upbeat music increases brain dopamine and improves verbal fluency and activity level and interest in tasks.[23] Music and language share some areas of the brain, although music apparently is less localized. Even spoken language is not as localized as past research indicated.

My guess is that music evolved because it enhanced survival and reproductive chances in our early ancestors. Since musical participation involves physical movement (singing, dancing, playing an instrument), it uses the motor cortex and other brain areas whether we participate as performers or an audience. Music is moving in this physical sense. Likewise, music awakens and perhaps enhances emotional responses, so it is emotionally moving as well. Perhaps it bridges the ancient emotional nuclei and reward centers of our brain and our more recently acquired and enlarged cerebral cortex. Humans everywhere may be fond of music because it moves us.

Evolutionary anthropologist Steven Mithen shows that the same music elicits similar emotions across diverse cultures, hence transcending these boundaries. In conveying emotional information to a listener, responses by the brain's amygdala seem to be critical. Apparently, some individuals with damage to this structure can no longer feel sad when hearing "sad" music. The fact that infants respond to music indicates our innate readiness to react, which Mithen uses to bolster his contention that language and music evolved from a rhythmic, melodic protolanguage.[24]

Ever since Darwin, students of evolution have talked about ties between music and language.[25] Darwin suggested that music, gesture, and dance may all have evolved from earlier forms of communication that utilized gestures, rhythm, and calls. Many other animals use calls and other sounds, and some even use melody or different tones to communicate. He also proposed that music evolved through sexual selection as a kind of "primordial love song," noting that many animals vocalize during courting and that all animals react to musical rhythms or cadences.

A striking example can be seen in the siamangs, lesser apes in the gibbon family, who sing in melodious sequences using expandable throat sacs. By practicing singing together, they coordinate melodies and eventually move from unison to harmony. Frans de Waal reports that "Siamang couples that sang together a lot also spent more time together and synchronized their activities better."[26]

British neuroscientist Geoffrey Miller[27] updated and added to Darwin's hypothesis. Sexual selection is based on the idea that people choose mates based on fondness for particular secondary sex characteristics. These serve as indicators of overall fitness, and female choice results in enhancement of those characteristics. Citing the role of language (e.g., poetry, song) in human courtship, he suggested that flowery language and music in human males has the same appeal to women that the peacock's tail has to peacock females, with some important differences. That women and men can be equally musical seems to be an obstacle for this hypothesis. Mate selection in *Homo sapiens* no doubt is more complex and culturally based than in other animals, and it also may be more dependent on bilaterally distributed brain features.

Other investigators also view music as an adaptive trait. Robin Dunbar suggests that language and its musical components replaced grooming as a mechanism of social bonding in our ancestors. He also highlights connections between music, dance, group rituals, social emotions, bonding, and alliance-building.[28] Others note the role of rhythm and melody of language, especially in the word play that characterizes its development in children. Precursors to vocal language can be seen in Old World monkeys and other apes who communicate using sounds, gestures, and facial expressions. I wonder if music and spoken language may have separated gradually as reflective thinking and language came to replace the reflexive responses that characterized our ancestors.

Neuroscientists Michael Gazzaniga and Oliver Sacks note the effects of music on human emotions, behavior, and even cognition under some conditions. We experience pleasure in singing, playing, and simply listening to music. The observed increase in neurochemicals oxytocin and dopamine corroborate this. Rhythm and melody influence various human endeavors, including healing. Sacks reports that rhythm and music can facilitate movement in patients with certain brain lesions, and can facilitate retrieval of memories and language in some patients. Finally, persons with memory loss often retain memory for melody, and for words that accompany familiar melodies.

Songs and rhymes facilitate learning in children (e.g., the alphabet song). Learning how to perform music requires focused attention and thinking about sequencing, which may prepare children for other learning experiences. The use of rhythm, gesture, and song may have helped people in the earliest fully human societies to recite and remember oral traditions and stories, in this way building cultural knowledge. Sacks proposes that this may have been one of the early uses of language.[29]

Many traditional folktales and myths, accompanied by song and dance, reinforce group sentiments, clarify ideas about the world, and pass on religious tradition. Through these physical activities, cultural memories become motor memories, further reinforcing them. We can enjoy music whether we are alone or in a group, although human song and dance are traditionally social. Music can synchronize and energize large groups, in line with Durkheim's original proposition that religions originated in this way, promoting social solidarity in societies without specialization or centralized government to hold them together.[30]

Crooning and lullabies with simple, regular rhythm and melody are universal, and infants everywhere react by smiling and cooing. Human infants and mothers (and other caregivers) interact using rhythmic vocal play accompanied by verbal turn-taking. The lyrics for the traditional "Rock-a-bye baby, in the tree top ..." are interesting in light of our earliest ancestors (the australopithecines) having probably rested in tree nests for safety and nighttime sleep.[31] Conversation and music became pleasurable activities that helped humans maintain bonds with others throughout life, again "staying in touch without touch."[32] Perhaps some of us even self-regulate our emotions musically, at least some of the time.

Ideas about the origins of music merge with hypotheses regarding the origin of human language, described briefly in Chapter 3. In that chapter, I described mother-infant exchanges evolving over time in the direction of melodious crooning. High-pitched, rhythmic *motherese* may have been a precursor to ordinary spoken language, as posited variously in the hypotheses of Falk, Hrdy, and Dissanayake.[33]

Elizabeth Spelke's research adds to this idea by demonstrating that at three months, an infant is already tuned into the melody and intonation of its mother's language. In experiments, intonation trumps the visual appearance of the speaker, indicating that melody and intonation are basic to language, just as they are to music.[34] Demonstrated to increase dopamine levels in the brain, rhythm and melody would have become connected to the pleasure-reward system, performing adaptive functions.

Most of us recognize that some features of ordinary spoken language are rhythmic and musical. We distinguish different meanings from the same string of words by relying on intonation patterns and soft-loud contrast, and we use rhythmic elements in speaking. Alterations in tone differentiate meaning in some Asian languages.

The connection in the brain between hand movements and movements of the oral mechanism tied in with the notion that early language may have combined vocalizing with gestures. And we can see the connection to ritual, which might be called the motor aspect of religion. This leads to another of the arts, dance.

Steven Brown and Lawrence M. Parsons.[35] summarize neuroscientific research in this area. They describe our natural and unique capacity for this activity and the extraordinary coordination that it requires, involving spatial awareness, balance, intention, sequencing, and timing. These capabilities use many different areas of our brain. These authors suggest that percussion may have evolved from storytelling accompanied by synchronized movement that would have fostered group sentiment.

It turns out that neurons themselves have rhythms; they regularly oscillate; the electric potential of the cell membrane changes back and forth, and when movements are coordinated, cells oscillate together in a kind of harmony. According to neuroscientist Rodolfo Llinás, the thalamus and cortex must work together for coordinated thinking or movement to take place. He thinks that disruptions of brain rhythms (thalamocortical dysrhythmias) are the root of many brain illnesses.[36]

Perhaps music continues to thrive, while changing as cultures change, because of this motivating effect: It moves us physically and emotionally. Biologically, emotions activate us and therefore have great survival value because action is how all animals get food, escape from predators, and reproduce themselves. I wonder if we express thoughts, particularly propositional statements, primarily through spoken language, while we often express global or integrative emotions through music and dance. Maybe music with words, or rhythmic poetry, bring thoughts and emotions together. In using language and music together, might we be helping to integrate reflexive brain system 1 and reflective brain system 2? (See Chapter 8, page 232.)

Ellen Dissanayake, Michael Gazzaniga, V. S. Ramachandran, and others have applied similar reasoning to expressions of visual arts, seeing them as adaptations. One suggestion from neuroscience is that we perceive shapes and forms as beautiful when our brains process them easily. This depends on our brains responding the things we see. Some experiences give us positive feelings, which lead us to value those experiences (for example, a given painting or sculpture) and call them "beautiful." We like vegetation, trees that spread, savannah scenes, the human form, symmetrical shapes, and repeated designs. Even infants seem to prefer faces, symmetry, and curved objects, and other animals appear also to prefer regular patterns and geometric shapes. Yet as we expose our brains to less common images (or less familiar musical compositions), we learn to perceive beauty in them.

Ramachandran, in *The Tell-Tale Brain*, identifies and discusses nine attributes of aesthetics (symmetry, grouping, contrast, etc.), viewing the internal logic, evolutionary function, and neural mechanics of each. He emphasizes that specific art forms, like language, are culturally influenced, disagreeing with Gould and Pinker's spandrel idea and Geoffrey Miller's sexual selection hypothesis.[37]

Dissanayake emphasizes that the behavior of "artifying" or "making special" carries the adaptive functions of art. These verbs refer to what the activity does for the individual (reducing stress and providing meaning), and how making art reinforces group values, for example, as part of initiation rituals. Its adaptiveness is indicated by its universality, its presence in children, its motivating effects, and its presence during important life events.[38] This is consistent with Levitin's view of music making, Rappaport's understanding of ritual, and Pascal Boyer's contention that ritual, in marking important occasions, at the same time creates them.[39]

In summary, we are simultaneously biological and symbolic animals who give significance to events that matter to us. Symbolic statements define who we are regardless of particular religious or nonreligious orientation. This may be why some have equated *word* with *god* and defined humanity by the ability to symbol, i.e., to make and use language. This mode of complex symbolic communication is our species' most important tool.

Religious Narrative: Myths and Propositions

The only uniquely human component of religion, and an outgrowth of language itself, is narrative. Precursors of morality and ritual, or at least hints of it, are found in other animals. Yet only we create narratives; every culture has a story about its beginning and its place in the overall scheme of things, including the relationship of humans to other living creatures. Most myths place the particular people from which they arise at the center of things, as *the* people, or the chosen people, the saved, or God's children.

Myth is embedded in our human propensity to look for cause-effect, tell stories, imagine past and future, and create meaning for ourselves. It also depends on our having self-consciousness beyond that of any other animal that we know. Myths explain why things happened as they did and offer speculations or prophecies about why and how events are expected to unfold. Myth-making is part of the evolution of language, narrative, storytelling, and perhaps creativity itself.

Human brain evolution, as outlined in Chapter 4, was a very large part of how we humans adapted to changing conditions over the several million years of becoming fully human. Religious ideology, stories, and theology are products of human thinking, and they rely on specific features of human cognition. Strategies of our ancestors for negotiating their changing world may explain some of the common characteristics of the beings and cosmologies that developed into what we call religion.

I summarize here five related features of human brain functioning pertaining to religious universals, as discussed by several neuroscientists and anthropologists, including Pascal Boyer, Michael Gazzaniga, and Michael Shermer, among others.

First is the notion of dualism. This seems very natural to many of us. Philosophical dualism is the idea that each of us is more than just a body. Even people who do not accept the idea of dualism, who view human behavior to be reducible to brain chemistry, act as if they have a kind of essence or self separate from their bodies. We all feel as if we make choices and respond to events as a whole person, and we talk about our bodies (which of course include our brains) as if they were a separate part of who we are.

As biological organisms, we have many bits of information and sensations coming in all the time and thousands of bodily reactions to them. Our brains are constantly processing this input, although we are aware of only a tiny bit of the immense volume of data. We have less awareness of the ongoing work engaging our brains. We feel like whole beings with intention and purpose, and we act as if we have an essence, or soul, or unembodied mind. All human languages have a pronoun or special noun for referring to oneself.

A second feature is the theory of mind (ToM), described in Chapter 4 as the cognitive "twin" of empathy through which we are able to infer feelings and intentions of others as we observe and interact with them. Nonhuman apes, like bonobos and chimpanzees, may have a rudimentary form of this. We share "mirror neurons" with a number of other animals; these are active when we unknowingly mimic postures and facial expressions in interactions with others and when we attribute feelings and thoughts to them.

Third is our propensity to recognize patterns and categorize incoming data, even when the data are random (e.g., dots on a page, or Rorschach inkblots). This apparently begins early in our lives; even infants can distinguish animate from inanimate objects and soon begin to make other distinctions. At the same time we constantly and automatically draw inferences when we identify and categorize; a small, moving, four-legged, furry creature becomes "cat," or "dog," or "mouse" without our thinking about its separate characteristics. Very young children do confuse or overgeneralize such categories as their language develops.

Thinking back to our evolution, we can see how natural selection would have favored individuals who quickly noted and interpreted a moving shadow or movement of grass as a possible predator. Even individuals who overreacted would live to reproduce their genes with greater frequency than those individuals who failed to see patterns quickly. We can infer characteristics from a small bit of information, as inferring "cat" from a single meow because we have the "cat" template already in our brains. These inference-making, pattern-seeing, categorizing abilities evolved from our evolutionary past as hunters and gatherers, as scavengers, and as prey of fiercer animals.

The ability to automatically interpret bits of incoming data as having meaning has mixed consequences: We easily over-interpret stimuli and imagine not only other beings, but also threats that are not real. This super-sensitivity, which Gazzaniga calls part of intuitive psychology, can create problems for individuals and for groups.

A fourth important capacity of our species is sequencing. We do this whenever we take action, imitate a behavior, or initiate or execute a plan. Other intelligent animals sequence to a lesser degree than humans. But it is a highly developed ability of human brains, and much conscious thought is linear, as is language itself. We sequence sounds into words, words into phrases, and phrases into sentences. We are unique in further sequencing events into stories and complex ideas into narratives. Moreover, human language, with its arbitrary symbols, enables us to make up stories about creatures and events that don't exist.

A fifth trait is our mental attribute of agency, sometimes called agenticity; this refers to perceiving that things and events have causes. Its consequences are mixed. In most areas of living, it is helpful to look for causes, but this ability also makes it easy to invent them when we do not understand something. Causes can be intentional, unintentional, and even random, and the latter are often interpreted as intended. People often say, "It was meant to be," or "It was God's will," about events beyond their control. We are so fond of causes that we attribute chance events to an agent. Pascal Boyer writes in considerable detail about agency and its importance in the development of religious ideas and narratives.

Of course, these five features work together and might be combined or split in alternative ways to form different lists. All probably play a part in nudging *Homo sapiens* toward developing ideas and populating stories with beings beyond everyday experience in the form of human, other animals, and forces of nature. Imagination is a component of these ideas and stories, and it is connected to self-consciousness. It is the root of storytelling, books of fiction, movies, and games. Luhrmann's study (discussed earlier in this chapter) illustrated use of the imagination in the context of religion.

Sequencing and narrative-making are the crux of myth. Early people, combining imagination and real life, would have developed stories that came eventually to represent "remembered facts" that become integrated into religious postulates. Narratives capture our emotions, especially when characters' interactions are believable and the emotions recognizable. Even young children invent characters to whom they attribute emotions and thoughts (imaginary friends). The use of narratives in teaching and learning may be rooted in the evolution of social cognition itself. Many folktales have messages about how others ought to be treated or about what makes a hero or a villain. Tales tend to have repeated themes across cultures, such as romantic love, statements about ideal men and women, descriptions of tricksters (Brer Rabbit, with precursors in African and native American folklore), pursuit of goals, and heroic sequences. It may be easier for most of us to remember concepts when they are embedded in stories or narratives. Advertisers make effective use of the power of narratives to sell almost any product, regardless of its value.

When we combine narrative with the notion of agency, we can and do often end up with supernatural beings, according to Pascal Boyer.[40] Concepts of supernatural beings—gods and goddesses, nature spirits, ancestor spirits, ghosts—have similar characteristics wherever they are found. They are reportedly capable of doing things for or against people even though they are usually invisible. They have some powers that regular people do not possess, yet they are often anthropomorphic. They move around, they have feelings, they can see us and know what we are thinking and doing. Some of them have ideas about how we ought to act. These characteristics are all patterned, not randomly imagined, and relate to how our brains work and to the combined cognitive and emotional content of our perceptions and thinking.

Boyer says that this kind of supernatural being triggers emotions in us that makes the concept "click" in our brains, while competing concepts that do not fit as well into this groove are less likely to occur to us and do not stick around for as long in the culture. He has compared religious concept acquisition to language acquisition, and he contends that our brains are ready to latch on easily to particular kinds of concepts. Concepts that take tend to (1) connect to one of our brain inference systems, (2) trigger emotional responses, (3) relate to our social impulses, or (4) direct our behavior. We don't have a "God gene" as a few people have argued, but we do have brain mechanisms that make it very easy for us to conceive of and hang on to concepts of the supernatural.

An interesting point about theism is that a belief in one god, or a main god, doesn't eliminate belief in other minor supernatural agents, such as ghosts, a holy ghost, angels, devils, or saints. Many traditional cultures have incorporated one of the major monotheistic religions into their own conceptions while keeping their own culture's spirits as well. Boyer summarizes his work by noting that we humans have in common brains that function according to a uniform, neurologically based scheme that makes particular kinds of ideas likely.[41]

Yet there are individual differences between brains and developmental circumstances as well as particular cultural influences. Individual variation helps to explain why religion is universal to cultures, but not to individuals. Cultures differ in the intensity of typical religious expression, the percentage of population for whom religion is important, and the flexibility allowed to individual practitioners. No one knows whether or to what degree religion as an institution will persist into the future.

The attributes of our brains that make *Homo sapiens* receptive to religious narrative are influenced by specific conditions and cultural histories. It may be that many persons cling to religious beliefs because they are reassured of their importance in the universe as individuals, as members of a particular group of people, or as a species. We return to the notion of individual meaning-construction in the final chapter.

Religion and Cultural Variety

Anthropologists have long hypothesized that the specific forms that spirits take in a given society are related to the way a particular society is organized or how it relates to its environment. Numerous studies have explored these connections. I offer a few examples here, some suggested, some partially confirmed. Small-scale egalitarian societies in which authority is dispersed often have spirits associated with natural environmental features that are themselves dispersed (e.g., native Australian totem animals and plants). Societies organized through unilineal kinship ties often feature ancestor spirits and associated rituals. Centralized societies such as chiefdoms and state societies often feature one god, or one main god with subsidiary spirits. In these examples, the spirit world mirrors the environmental context and social organization and perhaps reinforces it.

A related finding associates the presence of big, morally concerned gods with large, post-Neolithic societies. This can be understood from what we know about group size and individual connections within groups, as proposed and documented by Robin Dunbar. He estimated approximately 150 individuals to be the maximum for *Homo sapiens* to manage. This is called Dunbar's number. We can keep track of the reputations of individuals in a group of this size, which allows informal social control to be fairly effective. Beyond this size, something else is needed. The idea that someone, a person or a deity of some kind, can see how we are behaving helps most of us to behave well toward others, i.e., to act prosocially. For example, the addition of a picture of an eye above a coffeemaker increases the total contributions made to a voluntary and shared coffee fund.[42]

The work of social psychologist Ara Norenzayan resulted in a book about the relationship between big gods and big societies. In this, he also attempts to explain that under some conditions of fairly high trust related to social structure and norms and conditions, the role of "big gods" can and does fade away.[43]

Connected to this function of religion, we recall that early civilizations (state-based societies) were theocracies, with the priest or priest-ruler-god having absolute power, not only to extract tribute from the population but to sacrifice people to the deity or to murder people on a mass scale. Many cultures, regardless of type, have some notion of supernatural sanctions by which external sources or beings can punish individuals who get out of line.[44]

Adam Smith wrote of the relationship between social organization and religion, pointing to the power of these institutions in state-based societies. Here sovereigns promote views through religious education, punishing clergy who expound alternative views, and propagating fears and expectations based on beliefs. Likewise, clergy with power can control politics directly, as happened during the tenth through thirteenth centuries in Europe through the Roman Catholic Church, with some change following the Protestant Reformation.[45]

Robert M. Sapolsky, in "The Cultural Desert," reviewed several compilations of worldwide data designed to aid researchers in discovering patterns of interconnections among various cultural and environmental features.[46] The object of this type of study is to discover whether particular cultural traits occur at random or in a patterned way. If correlations are found regularly, then there is more reason to investigate why that might be so.

In his essay, Sapolsky looked at several large studies and identified a prominent pattern, strengthened by its appearance in studies designed for different purposes. He identified a "basic dichotomy" between rain forest cultures and desert cultures in their constructions of religion. Rain forest religions often feature a "proliferation of spirits and gods," while desert-based religions tend to be monotheistic, with a powerful deity and strict rules regarding how people should behave and think.

Desert cultures tend to have poor opinions of women and strict rules about sexuality and nudity. Hierarchy (social ranking) is another feature of desert societies, supported by military organization and high status for men who excel in military activities. Rain forest morality tends to be looser, with greater acceptance of individual differences and more flexibility in who takes charge when leadership is needed for a particular task. This seems to fit the diverse environment that defines the rain forest itself. Historically, desert cultures spread readily and came to dominate rain forest people. The latter have the greatest linguistic diversity, less staying power, and less resistance to being taken over and changed (just like the rain forests themselves, which are fast disappearing).

We do not know exactly how this pattern of religious diversity came to be; we do know that the relationship is an association, a statistical correlation and not a description of every rain forest or desert society. It is consistent with the distinction made in Chapters 5 and 6 between tight and loose societies, notions of which were also based on large-scale, cross-cultural data. Tight societies were described there as having strong norms and low tolerance for deviance while loose societies have weaker norms and greater tolerance for deviance.

Perhaps cultures with strong monotheistic religions are less open to individual and cultural differences than cultures with a variety of spirits or gods, each with a different personality and set of skills. Robert Wright also emphasizes the variety of spirits among people in nonstate cultures that do not have a label for the abstract overall category that we call religion.[47] Frans de Waal reminds us that rain forest cultures, unlike desert cultures, invariably view themselves as part of the natural world, not separate from or above it.[48]

This may be analogous to a contrast between "literal" and "liberal" religious traditions, as presented informally by Kate Lovelady.[49] The liberal religious traditions utilize multiple texts, multiple interpretations, and discoveries of science and experience as sources of ideas. The literal traditions, in contrast, utilize one source, one authority, and one interpretation.

I wonder if this same contrast is associated with the extremes of a purity-danger continuum introduced by anthropologist Mary Douglas some years ago, and more recently highlighted in the technical and popular writings of social psychologist Jonathan Haidt.[50]

A final aspect of religious variety concerns mystical experiences. These are near-universal features of religions, as described in individual accounts from many different cultures, and are accompanied by physiological changes that are measurable with brain imaging. Not all individuals have such experiences, but some individuals from many cultures describe them. Despite cultural variety, these descriptions are similar throughout the world, whether the experiences are induced by ritual, privation, music, meditation, isolation, drugs, or near-death states. Often, an individual will express elements of the religious ideas of his culture even when the experience is induced by drugs and lacks religious intent.

Luhrmann's study utilizing the Tellegen scale ratings noted individual differences in susceptibility to mystical experience, although training was shown to improve a participant's ability to experience it. I wonder if this kind of experience might present a very intense expression of the more common but still striking and memorable sense of awe, wonder, or "aha" moment of insight. Another question concerns how the excitable variety of mystical experience is related to the sense of inner calm that can be induced by meditation, deep breathing, self-hypnosis, drugs, or even aerobic exercise. Perhaps there are gradations of intensity that relate to personality as well as to culture. Some cultures may value intense experiences more than others. Pursuit of these issues would be enlightening but is beyond the scope of this book.

It has often been suggested, beginning with Paul Radin's 1937 book, *Primitive Religion*, that religious practitioners invented and used trances and other mystical experiences to exploit individuals. I would agree that it has been used this way in some societies and in some periods, but it isn't always used in this way, particularly not in small-scale egalitarian societies. In societies with hierarchy, it can be a convenient way for freeloaders to control the behavior of others, and some shamans and priests can and do take advantage.

Summary and Conclusions

Here I attempt to combine some ideas about religion to consider their connection to tribalism in preparation for the next chapter.

Play, Creativity, and Religion

Robert N. Bellah suggests that in *Homo sapiens* the freedom and the capacity to play enhance creativity and, with language, enable the development and elaboration of new ideas and solutions for problems. We speak of having to play with a new idea, and we like playing with words and manipulating words and ideas. Many of us like solving mysteries and puzzles of all kinds. Perhaps Bellah is onto something when he concludes that religious ritual, myth, music, and art evolve from mammalian play and that both religion and science are kinds of patterned play.[51]

Noting Luhrmann's observation of a play element in her research subjects' perceived relationship with their god, I wonder if this is relevant to the role of imagination and insight in human creativity. Several other researchers (see Chapter 9) have noted the importance of play and imagination for individual development and social change. If the play element is relevant to all imaginative endeavors, then it may help us to find a way out of the complex dilemmas that face our species.

Child development researchers Stanley I. Greenspan and Stuart G. Shanker also make a connection between ritual and play and emphasize their importance to human development. In describing child-parent play, they note the importance of rhythm, timing, turn-taking, and flow of communication. These patterns transfer later to a child's play with peers.

Connections between music, crooning, motherese, language development, and rhythm also come into the mix. They argue that increased exposure to variable human behavior shapes and increases a child's repertoire of responses. The interactions foster development of children who are better able to learn, are more responsive to others, and who are likely to come up with novel responses to challenges.[52] Their work places the emotional roots of human intelligence and human language in specific bonding experiences between caregiver and child, suggesting that these interactions enable language learning.

Certainly early bonding experiences stimulate and reinforce language development and influence the development of other behaviors that mark us as human. But considerable evidence supports the idea that these experiences trigger and build on an existing biological, genetically based framework (specifically Noam Chomsky's language acquisition device (LAD), popularized by Steven Pinker in *The Language Instinct*). The flavor of the interactions and the particular language and culture influence the specific content that a child acquires.

It is also difficult to determine which appears first, language or a core knowledge system. Both develop in the context of interactions; what is built-in and what is acquired is too complex of a web to isolate the strands, at least at present.[53]

To summarize this connection between child development, play, and creativity, we saw in Chapter 4 that play interactions require the relaxation of normal constraints, such as ordinary dominance and submission behaviors. This happens regularly as young mammals play, and human children are exceedingly playful and creative. They come up with unexpected notions because these have not yet been inhibited, curtailed, or made rigid by cultural expectations. Childhood represents the most important relaxed field that we have, a hotbed for creativity, certainly a reason for generously nurturing children everywhere. Adults must work harder to achieve that freedom from constraint in thinking. Neuronal pruning, after all, has been mostly completed by adulthood.

In a different meaning of play, enacted drama, actors shed their normal roles and become different people. In a very common form of role-reversal ritual seen in a number of cultures, people deliberately exchange roles (women dramatizing dominance behaviors or normally-male activities; men dramatizing women; commoners exchanging places with aristocracy) temporarily. Halloween night may represent a remnant of this, with children in costume punishing adults with tricks for not doling out treats. In these examples, individuals temporarily experience freedom to act in a different way (a relaxed field). William Shakespeare described it in "As You Like It:"[54]

> All the world's a stage,
> And all the men and women merely players:
> They have their exits and their entrances;
> And one man in his time plays many parts . . .

Keeping this in mind, I review a possible connection between individual creativity and social organization. In Chapter 6, I discussed one view of the evolutionary transition from ape dominance hierarchies to egalitarian hunter-gatherer bands and described the sharing ethos considered to be ideal in those cultures. Secondly, I noted the freedom of children to play and explore and the permissive parenting that Melvin Konner, Sarah B. Hrdy, and others documented for some of these societies. Bellah, whose research interest is religion, suggests that this type of "moral community," with face-to-face connections, fosters the kind of patterned ritualized play that encourages creativity and imagination.

It may be that the loose kinship and social organization in these nomadic bands fosters this freedom to a greater extent than in those settled food producers with fixed tasks and segmental, ancestor-based kin groups. This is certainly speculative and may be off the mark but might be worth pursuing further. On this point, educators in today's world are beginning to recognize that over-programming of modern children into group athletics and other structured activities at young ages may be limiting opportunities for informal play. When children play spontaneously, they create games, rules, drama, and even objects to be used, fostering growth of imagination and invention.

So, although Bellah may be stretching a point to propose that religion emerged from play, his understanding that play and creativity are connected may be important indeed. The association of this to the looseness versus tightness distinction between societies may also be significant.

The world of hunter-gatherers is mostly gone. Prehistorically, it was superseded by transition to a new form of human hierarchy after the Neolithic Revolution, as outlined in Chapter 5, eventually evolving to include distant rulers (frequently religiously based) who combined dominance with an ideology of controlling nature's bounty and attributing what could not be controlled to a new kind of supernatural being. The idea of a sometimes loving and sometimes angry distant father became part of this understanding and part of a monotheistic world view. The notion of one god or a major god characterized archaic civilizations and small states. Bellah speaks of a pattern of regular and frequent wars among these ancient states. Perhaps post-Neolithic societies transitioned from a looser to a tighter form.

Perhaps there was some suppression of individual creativity in the general population associated with the Neolithic as work became more routine. Later, however, as greater specialization evolved, some people had considerable freedom to create, innovate, and invent, but others did not. Experiencing a relaxed field may have become confined to the youngest of children and to adults of leisure.

Religion, Science, and Human Imagination

We have seen that a religious (or humanistic) impulse probably originated as part of our sociality combined with the particular cognitive tasks that our brains evolved to do. Since we are symbolic animals who like to sort and label things, particular religions often feature beings that fit the social organization of particular cultures people have. People in state-based societies define religion as an entity, while it is perhaps more accurately described as a collection of sentiments, concepts, and behaviors.

As science continues to teach us more about the universe, our earth and its biome, and our brains and human consciousness, religious propositions about who we are, like early propositions about the universe and static species, are replaced by new understandings. The mythological or traditional explanations for natural phenomena become positions that are in line for becoming overruled by evidence-based conclusions. As E.O. Wilson puts it: "There is a real creation story of humanity, and one only, and it is not a myth. It is being worked out and tested, and enriched and strengthened, step by step."[55] Like any scientific narrative, it changes as new information is obtained through ongoing, empirically based study.

Religious beliefs and practices that foster fixed "truths" about the world we live in can blind people to discoveries that can help us solve problems we face today. Fixed notions of truth can also inhibit creativity and imagination. Not amenable to new empirical data, they easily foster a sense of superiority toward those with different ideas. Immersed in a particular ritual and belief system that *sanctifies* their point of view, they become less willing to consider alternative views and solutions. This is part of what tribalism is about, as described in the next chapter.

Religious institutions, like kin institutions, carry the potential to unite or divide people; they have bright and dark sides. Over many centuries around the globe, religion has united small groups and furthered peace efforts in some areas. Shared ritual and myth can seem to validate group claims; certify sacred statements, myths, and group histories as true; and create strong bonds within that group. Music's ability to move us and enhance a sense of unity can bring individuals together to get jobs done. But it also has the capacity to nudge disparate groups toward a larger sense of commonality and unity. It can influence group sentiments toward exclusion or inclusion, and it can move people toward making war or making peace.

In professing an ideology that enforces group solidarity, religion has been used to justify pillage, plunder, slavery, pogroms, inquisitions, and massacres wherever the command of resources enabled surpluses to support such ventures. This happens when people become convinced that their accustomed way of being human is the only right way to believe or to act, and when they view alternatives as unacceptable or even evil. Alternatives are then framed so that people feel justified and even heroic in stamping them out, sometimes to the extent of killing those who think differently.

Because of this potential and this history, we might wonder if religion can ever help us to move toward peace. To the extent that it emphasizes parochial concerns and creates solidarity around those or around a myth of superiority, it encourages conflict and war. On the other hand, to the extent that it emphasizes common humanity, universal love, acceptance of diversity, and pursuit of knowledge, it has the potential to move people toward harmony.

Biologist Ursula Goodenough describes a version of naturalistic religion[56] that promotes a "global ethos," reminding us that the beautiful, awe-inspiring story of the evolution of all living things provides a core narrative of our human heritage that emphasizes our common humanity. Individuals and cultures can add beauty to this epic by embroidering into it their side narratives, interpretations, practices, and artistic creations.

It seems to me that the features that emphasize our shared humanity could be part of either a religious humanist or a secular humanist point of view, depending on one's particular frame. In this regard, Bellah points out that each of the four ancient, pre-Christian religious traditions (ancient Israel, classical Greece, Confucius China, and Buddhist India) cycled, in different periods, between a sectarian emphasis and an emphasis on humanity as a whole.[57] The same historical variation has happened since that time to each major religious tradition. So, the capacity for extending ties outward is lurking in the background. We need only to recognize and nurture this capacity to broaden our ties, to bring out the best instead of the worst of human nature.

Interpreting the various creative expressions of group sentiments as products of a general religious or a humanistic impulse can nudge us toward appreciating our common humanity. Participating with others by beating drums, playing flutes, or singing and dancing creates a sense of solidarity or social bonding. Emile Durkheim proposed a century ago (1912) that this produced the sense of excitement and sense of oneness or unity greater than any single individual, which we understand today to be related to our built-in reward systems. Durkheim attributed the idea of the sacred to this kind of experience.

Imagination and creativity are legacies of our evolution as intelligent, self-conscious creatures that resulted in attempts to understand our world. Early on, explanations and activities took the form that we today call religion. Later, other tools for understanding were developed, namely, the tools of science. Yet the germ (the primordial soup, so to speak) of both developments was awareness of ourselves as organisms, coupled with imagination and creativity. This, in turn, built on our mammalian playfulness that moves us to relax everyday restraints, get beyond the ordinary, and "make special."

Today, this enables us to think universally, to get beyond ordinary and petty jealousies and hatreds. We are playful, imaginative, and creative animals, whether we couch these traits in a religious or a secular frame. Such experiences can inspire music and stories and art that bring out the best in us, and it can produce symbols and songs that represent hatred and bring out our most destructive and selfish impulses. What matters is how we use these human talents.

In the best sense of religion, we can glean aesthetic value and inspiration from many of the religious narratives and related art and music without viewing them as scientific accounts of the world or even of human nature. This would allow us to preserve the beauty of these products of human traditions, while basing our understanding of the natural world firmly on scientific evidence-based knowledge. Inquiry, scientific quest, and attempts to construct meaning utilize human creativity and insight that integrate bits from different parts of our brain into "aha" moments.

Ancient myths and stories, even those from the earliest years of humanity before writing was invented, contain grains of truth about who we are as people, with examples of beings who exemplified the best and the worst of our species, in guiding us through everyday life. Stories and myths about the larger world have this kind of value without being scientific accounts. Most of us gravitate to stories about real and imaginary characters and identify with some of these characters even when their feats are beyond normal belief.

There may come a time when humanity as a whole will celebrate all of nature, all life as interconnected in the beautiful evolutionary narrative of how it came about. With this, we can use our considerable imaginative capacities to move people together in this celebration. It can only be good that our many differences produce a diversity of ideas, stories, and art that can inspire us to move forward.

In the next chapter, I explore the dark side of these positive sentiments: tribalism in its many guises, not as a particular variety of human society but as a particular attitude toward one's own group in contrast to outside groups. We look at how this particular group sentiment develops and can strengthen even in totally contrived human groups.

8

Pulling People Apart:
Tribalism—
Ethnocentrism, Racism, and More

There's never been a true war that wasn't fought between two sets of people who were certain they were in the right. The really dangerous people believe that they are doing whatever they are doing solely and only because it is without question the right thing to do. And that is what makes them dangerous.

—Neil Gaiman, 2011[1]

The last two chapters focused on two major means of holding people together in societies: kinship and religion. We saw that in small-scale societies, these ancient institutions would have improved the survival and reproductive chances of members by fostering ingroup cooperation, care of the young, acquisition of food, and defense. But this group solidarity and ingroup sentiment, supported by our brain's circuitry and neurotransmitters, has a dark side.

This chapter is about the dark side of bonding, which I call *tribalism*. In the context of our global economy, rapid communication, and the enormous worldwide supply of highly destructive military technology, tribal ideologies have become ever more problematic for our species and others as we navigate our rapidly changing, shared environment. We are in this sense a beleaguered species.

What Is Tribalism?

I define *tribalism* as a particular orientation or bias that favors one's own group (ingroup) while devaluing members of other groups (outgroups). Its underlying assumption is that members of one's own group are of greater value than those from other groups. As such, it encompasses impulses, thoughts, feelings, and actions toward members of outgroups that are expressed through spoken, facial, and gestural communication as well as overt behaviors. Because of the often subtle and unrecognized ways that our human brains work, we often do not acknowledge our own tribalistic biases. Yet tribalism is often legitimized and reinforced by larger social institutions and ideologies.

This definition of tribalism is generic, applicable to any human group whose members display this set of attitudes and behaviors, regardless of how that group is organized. It is not meant to designate individuals who belong to societies organized as tribes. Instead it refers to any society or group whose members carry the attitudes and behaviors described here. Tribalism refers to group bias; any group can take on a tribalistic orientation.

I refer later to a tribalistic attitude attached to social class. This may be a bit confusing because social classes crosscut other groups, for example, religious and ethnic groups. Yet members of particular classes can and do develop tribalistic notions that at times have been interpreted as reflecting biological differences. This notion then is used to support a social system in which an "upper class" views itself or is viewed as naturally superior and hence entitled to special privileges. As mobility between classes is reduced, this kind of explanation becomes more common.

Neuroscience has demonstrated that all of us perceive people and events in a biased fashion; one example is our ability to distinguish human faces. We more easily distinguish individual faces of members of our own groups than those from a different group. This illustrates our tendency to be deceived by appearances. Optical illusions reflect a different issue with perception and interpretation, but both illustrate the importance of our visual sense in forming perceptions and influencing thinking.

Group membership influences how members perceive, think about, and talk about outsiders as well as how those individuals are treated. When we embrace tribalistic attitudes, our perceptions of others often come to feel natural or almost biological. Members of one's own group, in contrast, often come to feel like kin and evoke a strong sense of group identity and belongingness. Much of this happens underneath our full awareness. Many of us have good intentions and do not realize the degree to which biases influence our perceptions, thoughts, and behavior.

Evolution of Tribalism

The evolutionary roots of human tribalism most likely go back to our very long Paleolithic phase. Within these small, scattered groups, informal ties of kinship, shared stories and rituals, and face-to-face contact would have held individuals together and enabled these relatively weak, fangless, clawless human animals to survive. A sense of strong group solidarity, boosted by heroic stories of overcoming outside obstacles, would also have enhanced survival. Group sentiment utilized the ancient neurochemicals associated with attachment and threat. In this sense, tribalistic sentiments are probably endemic to our species. They are related to the fact that we most easily bond within small groups of 150 or fewer people.

Our chimpanzee cousins also appear to have a strong tribal orientation. This seems weaker in bonobos (described in Chapter 6), but the common chimpanzees have been observed for more years and by more observers than the bonobos, so we have less information about the latter. Bonobos have stronger bonding among females, and sexual bonding has been observed also between bonobos of different groups, suggesting an alternative.[2] The tendency to extend caring outward, to expand our circles, is also a well-developed human trait.

E.O. Wilson in *The Social Conquest of Earth* uses "tribalism" in the way I use it here, speaking of the pleasure we derive from belonging to "tribes" as an essential piece of our humanity. Think of the role of emotions in talking with and being with like-minded people. The sense of being understood, of being known and loved for who one is, may be a basic human need that fosters tribalism. The dark side of this human need is expressed by the ease with which we reject or de-value outsiders.

I use the phrase *dark side* with some trepidation because our no-tions of dark and light, originally probably derived from perceptions of night and day, are reflected in notions and attitudes regarding skin color, a common marker for tribalistic attitudes. Yet the evolved flex ibility of human thinking and behavior is as much a product of our biological legacy, and it distinguishes us as humans. All of us, regard-less of skin color or other differences, must work to override auto-matic responses that arise from these associations. Our human brains enable us to accomplish this.

In the past, many evolved traits of once-successful organisms eventually became maladaptive and led to their extinction. Our pro-pensity toward tribalism may turn out to be one of those traits. We know that other evolved features of *Homo sapiens*, important to our survival in the past, have become maladaptive. For example, our abil-ity to store fat readily and our strong cravings for sugar and fat are endangering the health and lives of many individuals today. These traits and our tendency to take on tribalistic attitudes are two exam-ples of once-helpful features that serve us poorly today.

Tribalism has perhaps been around since human prehistory, but it has taken new forms while retaining some ancient ones. A partial list of its many "flavors" includes ethnocentrism, racism, religious sectar-ianism (religion run amok), sexism, heterosexism, national chauvin-ism, political party-ism, and "American exceptionalism." Formal ex-periments and informal observations demonstrate the ease with which we slide into this pattern. Tribalism is group bias; viewing one's own group or "tribe" as special or especially accomplished in contrast to others. It can apply to almost any type of human group.

Moreover, almost any characteristic will work, including a contrived feature such as different clothing, to stimulate tribalistic sentiments and thinking. The strength and intensity of emotions and group loyalty expressed by players and fans during sporting events provide a trivial example. But tribalistic impulses can be modified and redirected; this is the beauty of human plasticity. We have many biologically based impulses, but their expression can be influenced by how we frame them and the degree to which our institutions and cultural values support them.

How Tribalism Works: Psychosocial Bias

A classic account of the psychology of tribalism can be found in social psychologist Gordon Allport's 1954 book entitled *The Nature of Prejudice*.[3] In it he describes ethnic and racial stereotyping and how it influences perceptions, thoughts, and behaviors toward members of stereotyped groups, and outlines a process by which young children acquire prejudice. Since then, considerable research has augmented and clarified emotional and cognitive development during childhood and refuted some of Allport's suggested connections, but he deserves credit for initiating conversation and experimental study in this area. One of his important ideas, supported by a number of studies, is the *contact hypothesis*, which states that contact between members of different groups can reduce anxiety regarding differences and encourage positive attitudes. The exception to this occurs when interacting groups are experiencing extreme stress, as in times of war or famine.[4]

Lyricist and social activist Oscar Hammerstein expressed a similar understanding around the same time in his lyrics from the musical *South Pacific* entitled "You've Got to be Carefully Taught," referring to fear and hate toward outsiders. George Orwell's dystopian novel entitled *1984*, published originally in 1949, already had powerfully illustrated the acquisition of negative attitudes and the tendency to acquire stereotypes of outsiders. That novel also featured a setting of endless war.

In addition to describing prejudice, Allport contrasted the social psychological authoritarian stance with a more open frame of reference, proposing that prejudice is more commonly found in persons and groups with an authoritarian stance. He found some correlations between these and other social indicators, including education and religious attitudes. We might compare his patterns to the distinction between tight and loose societies and between literal and liberal religious traditions (described in Chapter 7).

In recent years, neuroscientists and social psychologists have added significantly to research by applying technology that enables analysis of large bodies of data. A wealth of experimental evidence demonstrates that our stated values and our behaviors often do not match, and that all of us are more biased than we imagine. From infancy onward, we make inferences in response to our social environments. Later in life, these early experiences influence perceptions and decisions, such as suspecting individuals of crimes, identifying persons in police lineups, and sentencing convicted criminals.[5] Techniques are available online to personally assess one's unconscious, or implicit, associations (subtle hidden biases) toward different categories of people (ethnic, religious, female, male).[6] This tool provides a valuable means of increasing one's awareness of these associations.

Developing and Maintaining Tribalism

Psychologist Drew Nesdale of Griffith University in Australia outlines four stages in the development of prejudice in children,[7] beginning with an undifferentiated period between years 2 and 3 during which a child begins to perceive others' attitudes. Ethnic awareness appears around age three. This is followed by ethnic preference, which a child picks up when group membership becomes important.

After age 12, he argues, this kind of group tends to solidify and become a hardened, more hateful entity

Other studies suggest that children subject to negative stereotypes regarding their *own* group incorporate these into their views of self between ages 6 and 10.[8] Internalizing negative stereotypes can make a huge difference in one's achievement, success, and test-taking performance. Evidence for this effect is overwhelming. Some researchers and educators are developing strategies to reduce self-stereotypes and the anxieties arising from them to ease test-taking and learning experiences. Ed Yong summarizes the outcomes of some of these strategies in a *Scientific American* article.[9]

All these aspects of prejudice and tribalism underscore the value of maintaining a skeptical stance toward one's own perceptions and ideas about others, and the value of acknowledging our human tendency to misinterpret incoming information. Many double-blind experiments demonstrate that we see, hear, feel, and even taste and smell differently depending on our biases, preconceptions, and current circumstances. Eyewitness reports of events are particularly unreliable, especially those involving people from groups other than our own. Science journalist Shankar Vedantam in *The Hidden Brain* presents many examples and experiments that demonstrate biased perception and thinking.[10] We are readily fooled by our own biases connected to gender, ethnicity, religion, and other differences, even when we work at being unbiased. In noting the strength of human bias, he describes how easily persons can be seduced into becoming terrorists under the right set of circumstances.

So our hidden brains play innumerable tricks on us, and no one is immune. Apparently, children acquire biases simply from what patterns they see around them. This adds to and sometimes contradicts what parents, teachers, and other adults teach or model. These biases come from the child's own social inference system. Children unconsciously draw conclusions from observing how individuals are treated and what jobs they do in the real world.[11]

A distinction related to this is between automatic and reflexive "fast thinking," and effortful and more tiring "slow thinking," which involves careful reflection. Neuroscientist Daniel Kahneman employs the shortcut designations of brain system 1 (fast) and system 2 (slow), first coined by psychologists Keith Stanovich and Richard West in 2000. Kahneman advocates training ourselves to recognize the high-stake situations that are most likely to trigger automatic responses. In his view, training works better than continuous hypervigilance, which can reduce efficiency and speed of thinking too much. People tend to do what is easier cognitively. Fast responses require less energy and are typical in stressful situations. In reality, all of us employ both kinds of thinking in managing our lives. Kahneman describes *priming* as an important way our brains use our most recent experiences to automatically draw conclusions and make choices, without our recognizing that this is happening.[12]

David Eagleman, in *Incognito,* adds historical detail to these concepts and discusses the complex interaction taking place within the brain between emotion and cognition, calling the whole a "two-party system." In this system, deeper brain centers monitor internal states (Sigmund Freud's "unconscious"), while higher brain centers monitor external and more conscious events. Eagleman emphasizes an ongoing "civil war" and "ceaseless reinvention" taking place in our brains as we react to this complexity.[13]

Noting this complexity, evolutionary psychologist Joshua Greene describes it as "the tragedy of commonsense morality." He uses the metaphor of a dual-mode camera with settings for automatic (fast, reflexive, emotional) and manual (slow, reflective, cognitive) to denote the sometimes conflicting responses. He give credit for the manual mode to the work of the brain's prefrontal cortex.[14]

Michael Shermer in *The Believing Brain* provides a summary of the many ways our brains trick us into bias, identifying *confirmation bias* "the mother of all" biases.[15] This influences individuals to seek and attend mainly to evidence that supports their own view, as expressed in behaviors, history, interests, or simply the status quo. This narrow focus is related to "bias blindness," such that we more easily notice biases in others than in ourselves. Some of our biases result from how information is presented (framing) or how recently or frequently we have heard or seen it (availability). We generalize widely from our particular life experiences, often neglecting to notice or attend to information that is outside our current focus of attention. Shermer agrees with other investigators that science provides the most reliable approach to detecting and reducing our susceptibility to biased thinking and behavior.

Neuroscientist Michael Gazzaniga applies understanding of common biases to describing how our brains register members of groups or "tribes" other than our own.[16] The ease with which we dehumanize members of outgroups has been demonstrated by various experiments. One looked at people's neural responses to photographs of individuals. The medial prefrontal cortex is normally activated as we experience positive emotions and as we respond to other persons. But this failed to happen in an experiment, in which individuals viewed photographs of persons from a "racial" group other than their own. Instead, the cortex remained dormant, as if it were responding to an inanimate object.

This response exemplifies the dehumanizing of outgroup members in contrast to responses to members of one's own group. This particular form of bias (own race bias or ORB) is commonly on display in courtrooms even from persons who feel and think that they are not biased.

Variation in brain responses of different individuals also relates to emotional predispositions and personality. Moreover, a given individual's brain responses vary over time. Although this makes life difficult at times, it suggests that such responses are amenable to change. Perhaps the resulting inner conflict can enhance flexibility and contribute to creativity, another hopeful possibility.

The Words We Use

We humans are natural classifiers: We invent words and categories and impose them on reality to make sense of nature and the rest of the world. We like classifying because it makes life simpler and thereby saves thinking energy for other problems and events. But like the fuzziness of the distinction between nonlife and life, most categories have fuzzy boundaries. Differences of opinion often have to do with this fuzziness, with how we define boundaries. This manifests itself in diagnosing illnesses in medicine and identifying learning difficulties in children, two familiar examples. Although we need categories to investigate the world, they do have a downside.

To relate this to tribalism, I take a brief detour to contrast two philosophical and scientific views of concepts. *Essentialists* argue for there being real, natural categories, harking back to Plato's ideal "forms." *Social constructionists* (*constructivists*), on the other hand, see categories as products of reasoning within particular social contexts, often without the inventor's awareness of the degree to which the context informs the categories. This brings up the question of whether we humans are biased toward either view.

Michael Shermer explores the human tendency "to infuse patterns with meaning, intention, and agency."[17] He sees this as an essentialist bias that feeds into notion that *race* is a natural category. Philosopher Paul Bloom, summarizing the results of what have become classic experiments that separate people into groups based on completely arbitrary criteria, describes it this way: "People will not only favor their own group but will also believe that there are significant differences between the groups, and that their group is, in an objective sense, superior. The essentialist bias leads us to see deep commonalities even when none exist."[18] Bloom goes on to report experiments showing that infants and toddlers demonstrate the beginnings of essentialist perceptions. Social contexts makes a difference in how we construct and view categories.

Essentialism and constructivism might be envisioned as sitting at the opposite ends of a spectrum, similar to the spectrum between nature and nurture; essentialism corresponds to the nature end and constructivism to the nurture end. Melvin Konner, who emphasizes complex interactions in his work, borrows the term "pseudospeciation" from twentieth century developmental psychiatrist Erik Erikson, who noted our fondness for dichotomies and the power of the group over individual behavior. We humans sometimes act toward other humans as if we belong to different species, which is why we have this term. Konner also reminds us that, with knowledge and effort, we can modify how we think and act.[19]

Language is powerful and can be laden with value. It can be used in other ways either to support or to help defuse tribalism. The phrase "ethnic cleansing" is one example of value-laden language. It is also a good example of "doublethink," coined by George Orwell, and of "doublespeak," a word derived from his thinking about words and how their meanings can be distorted to support political agendas. Special words or phrases are often used when sensitive issues are reported. Doublespeak refers to saying one thing while meaning its opposite, and oversimplifying language and thought accordingly. These concepts were part of the dystopian future that Orwell feared and described in *1984*.[20]

Ethnic cleansing refers to the genocide of members of an ethnic or religious group simply because they belong to that group. The act of genocide is old, but this phrase for it became part of regular usage in news stories about the genocide of Bosnian Muslims and Croats in former Yugoslavia in the early 1990s. Employed in news items, it seems to imply that "cleansing" is somehow descriptive of what was really happening, as if ethnic "purity" were a reality instead of a fiction created by tribal ideology.

The reality is that people have historically been and still are persecuted and murdered solely because they belong to particular groups. The word *cleansing* was used by German Nazis, who added another similar phrase, *racial hygiene,* to their attempts to justify the mass murders of Jews, Gypsies, and others they had marked as outsiders.

The issue of cleanliness or purity has an interesting history in the study of religions around the world, as described and analyzed by anthropologist Mary Douglas in her 1966 book *Purity and Danger.*[21] The notion of female "impurity" is familiar, associated with menstruation and childbirth in many cultures, including the Judeo-Christian tradition. Then, as now, the notion of cleanliness or purity is used to stigmatize a category of human beings. This relates to a tribalistic attitude that can be applied to almost any kind of human group. Historical persecution of presumed "witches" and historical mistreatment of women in many societies may be related to this form of tribalism.

The concept of purity has been revived and discussed extensively by psychologist Jonathan Haidt as a feature of various systems of morality; he relates it to group loyalty.[22] My interpretation is that the widespread concept of loyalty refers to a human sentiment to which most of us do assign some value. If I were forced to choose between saving one of my children or another person in distress, I would save my child first. But I question this behavior's connection to "purity" or any meaning of the word that goes beyond describing whether an item of food contains a toxic chemical. It is when loyalty to a particular group (such as family or nation) is infected with the notion of purity that it becomes a dangerous, tribalistic stance.

An emphasis on loyalty above all seems to coincide with the distinction between "tight" and "loose" societies and other institutions that influence how we think about the world. Gordon Allport's distinction between authoritarian and democratic perspectives, Haidt's distinction between forms and emphases of morality, and the contrast between literal and liberal religious perspectives also exemplify this distinction.

Around the world today, we see intergroup conflicts that use tribalistic concepts and associated language. Many instances of interpersonal violence and armed group conflict represent tribalism at work, and they are often framed as if there were intrinsic, immutable, biological differences between the two groups.[23] Steven Pinker covers this territory in his discussion of genocide in *The Better Angels of Our Nature*, noting that it is a form of "killing by category." It is invariably associated with moralizing a particular ideology, demonizing outgroups, and utilizing a notion such as "uncleanness" or impurity.[24] We are speaking too of Joshua Greene's moral tribes.

In thinking of morality, I follow philosopher Sam Harris, who describes behaviors and notions as moral when they increase the well-being of conscious creatures,[25] noting that use of the word "moral" to describe an action or idea does not necessarily represent this criterion of increasing well-being. It seems to me that ideas associated with purity and loyalty by definition favor a particular group at the expense of other human groups; loyalty easily merges into tribalism. When powered with guns and combined with the medieval notion of defending one's castle or standing one's ground, this tribalism is toxic to our chances of moving toward a positive future or toward any future at all.

The take-home point is that effort is required to stretch one's circle of caring, but it is also required to restrict one's caring to a particular group. People must be *taught* not to associate, or not to fall in love, with outsiders. Adolf Hitler had to work to find real differences between Jews and Aryans, and he did not succeed in that endeavor, while succeeding in his genocidal intent. Religious groups or parents have to work to restrict young people from marrying into other "tribes." The contrasting impulses, to restrict social circles and to widen them, are both part of being human.

Sociocultural Supports for Tribalism

Are group sentiments always tribal and toxic to outsiders? The answer depends partly on the degree of support for these sentiments from existing economic, political, and ideological institutions; differences in power may also play a critical role. Knowing this, we might try to understand and avoid forms of *institutional* tribalism. Some approaches for doing this will be described in Chapter 9.

Human Diversity, Race, and Racism

What do we mean when we talk about human "races"? This question prompts three others: (1) How do biologists define "races" in other organisms? (2) In what ways does human variation differ from that of other creatures? (3) How have we humans classified ourselves historically?

Approaching these questions requires looking at human society and culture as well as biology. What most of us refer to as races are in reality sociocultural groups more than they are biological groups. This is so even given the clustering of genetically based variation in a visible trait, such as skin color, which in fact ranges from very dark to very light in relation to geography and ancient human migration patterns. I will begin the discussion with an overview.

The word *race* was historically used by taxonomists to refer to subgroups within a given species that could be distinguished by a physical trait, such as beak shape or pattern of feather coloration in birds. The words *subspecies* and *variant* were also used for this. Many attempts were made to classify different groups of people this way, and speculative stereotypes based on physical variations were developed and assigned moral value even during antiquity. However, some individuals from these early times recognized the role of bias. The following is attributed to Greek philosopher Xenophanes (approximately 570–478 BCE):

> But mortals suppose that gods are born,
> wear their own clothes and have a voice and body.
> Ethiopians say that their gods are snub-nosed and black;
> Thracians that theirs are blue-eyed and red-haired.
> But if horses or oxen or lions had hands
> or could draw with their hands and accomplish such works as
>   men,

horses would draw the figures of the gods as similar to horses,
and the oxen as similar to oxen,
and they would make the bodies
of the sort which each of them had.[26]

Others looked at human variety differently. From ancient Mediterranean cultures came the idea that climate differences were responsible for both human appearance and character. Anthropologist Marvin Harris quotes first century BCE Roman architect Marcus Vitruvius Pollio: "Southern peoples have a keen intelligence, owing to the rarity of the atmosphere and the heat, while northern nations, being enveloped in a dense atmosphere, and chilled by moisture from the obstructing air, have but a sluggish intelligence." Moving forward to the Enlightenment era, some European scholars offered a roughly opposite point of view regarding climatic influences.[27]

Imperial Chinese leaders a few thousand years ago contrasted themselves with outsiders, referring to both white-skinned and black-skinned "barbarians." And on the subcontinent of India, variations in skin color were used to indicate status. There, conquest of less militant southern peoples by lighter-skinned northern Indus River civilizations led to color-based social hierarchy.[28] As can be expected, each description was an essentialist concept, yet each reflected social constructivism in that sociocultural judgments informed the descriptions.

Some researchers and philosophers did recognize human commonalities. Nineteenth century British founder of the field of anthropology, Edward B. Tylor, spoke of the "psychic unity of mankind" and Charles Darwin declared human races to be of little importance, "for, had they been important, they would long ago have been either fixed and preserved, or eliminated."[29] He also predicted accurately that the common ancestor of us all would be found on the African continent.

Human Migrations and Human Differences

In describing the biological concept of race, Ian Tattersall and Rob DeSalle follow Darwin, while updating his science.[30] Within species, variants (subspecies, races) that remain separated or isolated for long enough can become different species through random changes (drift) or through natural selection; this is called speciation. This did not happen in *Homo sapiens*. For thousands of years, we have all been one species, and our biological unity increases daily through rapid globalization, migration, communication, war, and trade.

We saw earlier that even the well-recognized concept of species is a work in progress; it is imprecise. And categories within species are even less clearly defined by biologists. Moreover, the older Linnaean classifications are being replaced by genetically based analyses. Sequencing of the genomes of nonhuman primates (for example, baboons or bonobos) and archaic species within our genus *Homo* has provided evidence for interbreeding among closely related archaic species during early human migrations. We know today that many of us carry a few genes that came to us through one or more of our fellow archaic species.

We know, too, that every local population of organisms differs somewhat from every other local population. For example, there will be some differences between groups of mice and between groups of people living in two different regions of a state or country, based simply on the fact of propinquity. All animals, including human animals, tend to mate with individuals who are geographically close. But in our wide-ranging species, whenever and wherever there has been exploration, migration, trade, or war, mating has taken place.

Understanding human diversity is particularly difficult for two reasons. First, we are unique in our ability to live in almost any environment on earth, so that our prehistory and history is a story of numerous migrations, divisions, and mergers of populations. Secondly, we humans are both the authors and the subjects of our classifications. This means that each of us belongs to a specific sociocultural group, thus inevitably acquiring a degree of ingroup sentiment. Hard as we work to objectively observe ourselves, we do fall short, and our history of classifying ourselves reflects group biases. Hence, the concept of human race has been fraught with controversy and misconceptions over the years.

This situation led physical anthropologist Frank Livingstone to pen an article in 1962, "On the Nonexistence of Human Races."[31] The term *race* has been used variously and inaccurately to refer to and to discriminate against various ethnic, religious, linguistic, national, and other groups as identified by perceived variations that often had little or no resemblance to objective biological subcategories. This kind of thinking had reached dangerous levels in the period surrounding World War II.

Livingstone pointed out that the biological differences between groups usually viewed as human races, persons who look like they have African or European or Asian ancestors, represent continuous rather than discrete variation. If we could line people up according to particular biological traits, we would need to make almost as many different lines as the number of traits, and most of these lines would not coincide. This would be true for clearly biological traits, such as hair form, height, and skin color, and for behavioral traits with genetic components, such as shyness, intelligence, aggressiveness, or nurturance. We also know that the expression of even physical traits depends on environment. Height is a good example because it is known to be highly heritable, dependent on one's genes, yet it responds strongly to the environment from fetal development (including nutritive support of mother) through late adolescence.

Our recent origin as a species is reflected in the smaller proportion of genetic (nucleotide) differences between randomly chosen human individuals than for many other species, such as chimpanzees or domestic dogs. Spencer Wells traces this to a somewhat speculative human population bottleneck approximately 70,000 years ago, during which the human population may have been reduced to about 2,000 individuals. This event would have reduced not just population size but also its genetic diversity.[32]

Comparing human DNA variability in general to variation between the three traditional continental clusters reveals greater genetic diversity within each cluster (historical races) than between clusters. Moreover, human biological variation today is only loosely related to geography and origin of populations.[33] Boundaries have become increasingly fuzzy through rapid travel. People fly quickly around the world, meeting others routinely from distant locations for work, study, and recreation, no longer confined to encountering each other in adjoining regions.

Geographic populations of modern *Homo sapiens* originally came to possess identifiable differences in appearance as they migrated and settled in different environments around the world, but our species is unique for continuing to trade, fight, migrate, and mate with people we meet no matter where they live. Occasionally, early members of our species managed to mate with persons from more archaic human groups (Neanderthal, Denisovan, and perhaps others). Over time, it has become increasingly difficult, and impossible in many cases, to define, describe, or assign a given human being to a particular "racial" category or even a nation or continent.

Evolutionary anthropologists and geneticists continue to be surprised about how very complicated and intertwined ancient human migrations and matings were. This reinforces the understanding that varied human populations are not discrete categories and often not meaningful categories by any criterion. It was recently determined, for example, that a group of ancient South African Khoisan people had migrated out of Africa into Asia during prehistory, and that some of their descendants migrated back into the African continent several thousand years later, between 5,000 and 1,000 years before the present era.[34]

To further complicate the picture, scientists understand that for any trait having to do with human behavior, such as temperament or intelligence, analyzing its distribution would be more challenging, perhaps impossible, because of the pervasive, complex web of sociocultural and biological-genetic-epigenetic interactions that determine who each of us becomes.

More important, there is little point to such an endeavor. All of us *Homo sapiens* are conscious creatures whose well-being should have nothing to do with our height, our ability to do calculus, the kind of work we do, our religious or nonreligious persuasion, our skin color, our verbal skills, our athletic abilities, or anything but our common humanity. I propose in the next chapter that it is cultural and behavioral variety that gives our species its potential for solving today's problems.

Chris Stringer makes another point about human differences: Some of the visible features used historically to classify people into races turn out to have resulted from chance alone, having no adaptive significance or relevance. Random "spelling" mistakes in DNA copying resulted in a few quirky features, such as the shovel-shaped incisors of some Asian populations that had been used in the past to sort people into races. This trait appeared to have originated as various populations were crossing the important Asian steppe, a migration route used by many of our *Homo sapiens* ancestors as they spread around the world.[35]

While other animals usually have natural barriers of geography or ecological niche to keep populations apart, human mingling and melding has complicated distributions of traits. Recent attempts to determine splits within human populations have been based on evolutionary, tree-style, cladistic analysis that utilizes genetic markers. Yet, these do not resolve the fact that most individuals use sociocultural definitions when defining their own group membership, using one or two traits, perhaps skin color, or as likely, a cultural trait like religious affiliation or nationality.

Although Darwin was a product of his own time, he studied those classifications and applied his insights, concluding that differences reflected gradual transitions in specific traits, that all humans shared a common ancestor, and that cultural rather than biological human variation determined success in geographical spread, war, and conquest. He came up with the notion of sexual selection (for desired traits in a mate) as a possible cause of some of the visible differences in different populations; this, he reasoned, would reflect different cultural ideals of beauty.[36] British geneticist Geoffrey Miller updated this notion of sexual selection (See Chapter 7).

Skin Color

With our fondness for labeling and classifying everything in our world, and with our brain's affinity for vision as a key sense, we often respond to people in terms of visual differences. Physical appearance was the basis for early race designations; the historic clusters of people associated with Africa, Asia, and Europe were identified this way. There have been numerous other schemes based on skin color gradations, varying with culture and historical period. Yet it makes as much sense to use the term "fictive" for race as to refer to fictive kinship. One's assignment to a particular race is largely defined by sociocultural boundaries.

In all cultures, individuals modify their visual appearance by adorning their bodies with paint, scarification, clothing, jewelry, and hair styling. These add-ons contribute significantly to one's appearance and identity as viewed by self and others. People also modify skin color, attempting to darken it through tanning or chemicals, or to lighten it by complete coverage with clothing, or by using bleach and other chemicals. We are indeed a strange species!

We saw in Chapter 2 that the skin of our ancestors darkened between 3 and 2 million years ago. This coincided with the loss of most of our body hair in response to the intense African sun as we became daytime, long-distance runners, chasing prey in an increasingly treeless environment. As summarized there, strong selection worked on the ability to preserve folate, a B-vitamin that comes from fruits and green leafy vegetables and is critical to DNA replication and thereby to embryological development. Without sufficient amounts of this vitamin, defects of the neural tube are more likely; this tube develops into the brain and spinal cord in vertebrates.

Folate is unstable, breaking down in response to penetrating ultraviolet A (UVA) and ultraviolet B (UVB) radiation from sunlight. Melanin in the skin protects our folate reserves, which gave dark skin its advantage in tropical areas. Epidemiological studies support the hypothesis that folate preservation was the significant selective factor. Because folate is critical for preventing neural tube defects, physicians regularly prescribe folic acid to pregnant women.[37] Dark skin, then, was an evolved adaptation, not a mark of an imaginary "essence."

Light skin evolved only later in those human populations that migrated to northern climates characterized by sparse sunlight. These populations failed to get enough sunlight for the skin to manufacture vitamin D, which is critical for bone development and health.[38] Jablonski describes different genes that result in the several types of melanin (skin pigment) found in different areas, and the later role of clothing and shelter to further block the sun's rays in colder climates. Although the general idea about skin color and climate has been around for a long time, Nina Jablonski, her biogeographer husband George Chaplin, and their research team present a wealth of evidence for how and when these changes happened. It turns out that our bodies must strike a balance between too much and too little sunlight.

Jablonski describes the historical uses of skin color as justification for numerous discriminatory policies and institutions. She outlines various sociocultural meanings associated with skin color, the ease with which we acquire stereotypes, and the difficulty of changing them once established, concluding: "Skin color is a biological reality; race is not."[39] In today's world of rapid travel and communication, we can hope that eventually our ideas and emotions will move closer toward this view and to the kind of spectrum envisioned in the late folk singer Pete Seeger's "Our Rainbow Race."

The Difference "Race" Makes in the Real World

Assignment of humans to different biological races engenders the same ingroup and outgroup sentiments and thinking as other forms of tribalism, but easily visible differences can strengthen these attitudes, particularly if differences cannot be modified. It is easier to change shirt color than skin color, although *Homo sapiens* have attempted the latter. To complicate matters more, an individual may be assigned to different races in different cultures. The difference in attitudes between U.S. and Brazilian populations is a classic example of this. The United States historically embraced the idea that "one drop" of African ancestry makes one "black." Brazil used a range of shades to identify and name categories of people. There, and in some other countries, for example, Cuba and India, shades of skin color also influence perceptions and behaviors toward others.

We can blame some of this on our brains, which tend to exaggerate particular features and interpret them as part of a package of other, sometimes fictional, features. This is part of our craze for categorizing. It is also partly a product of the complex visual cortex and keen color and binocular vision that we share with other primates. We pay particular attention to faces and have a brain area (the fusiform gyrus of the temporal lobe) dedicated to it; we even have a neurological disorder (prosopagnosia) defined by one's inability to recognize faces.

Anthropologist Ashley Montagu in a classic book published in 1942 explained how during the pre-World War II and Nazi era the social concept of race was given exaggerated, "scientific" importance in determining who people were.[40] This scientific racism was used to justify public policies that harmed people, and it was found in many societies, not just in Nazi-ruled countries. In the United States, the infamous studies of untreated syphilis in men of African descent exemplify this sorry phase.

Such policies reflected biases in perceiving, defining, describing, and understanding differences among people. Jablonski describes how, during much of the twentieth century, the high frequency of rickets in inner city African Americans was blamed on behavior and lifestyles. Only later was it determined that reduced production of Vitamin D in the body resulting from darker skin color, combined with insufficient sunlight in urban environments, was the cause of rickets.[41] This is another example of how bias has influenced even disciplines that attempt to be scientific.

Adam Smith wrote about perceptions of group differences generations ago: "the very different genius which appears to distinguish men of different professions ... is not upon many occasions so much the cause, as the effect of the division of labour." This "seems to arise not so much from nature, as from habit, custom, and education."[42] He also observed that such differences widen and solidify with time and experience.

European Enlightenment, Tribalism, and Race

Noting that state-based societies come in different varieties, from brutal to fair and democratically based, Steven Pinker gives credit to the Enlightenment period in Europe for eventually transforming brutal state regimes into societies with wiser, more enlightened governments. As an instrument of peacemaking, he depicts the "logic of the Leviathan" as a triangle with combatants at two of the angles and a bystander representing Leviathan as a peacemaker. He describes the European imposition of a kinder form of government as a process with three steps, beginning with "pacification" of nonstate societies, followed by a "civilizing" process, and finally resulting in a humanitarian or "rights revolution."[43]

Imposing Leviathan on weaker societies, however, was hardly benign. And the Leviathan in question was neither non-sectarian nor a third-party. Through the colonial period, violent means were regularly used to "pacify" and "civilize" non-Westerners in a Eurocentric version of tribalism. Primary beneficiaries were European and then Euro-American nations. The brutal slave trade resulted in millions of violent deaths during the Atlantic passage and during slavery itself, to a degree not seen in earlier forms of slavery.

Another product of this history was the "scientific racism" mentioned above, a complicated rationale for ideas about racial inferiority that continues to be part of tribalistic thinking today. Finally, democratic ideas and personal freedoms from the Enlightenment did not extend to women or to individuals from non-Western cultures. The word universal applied only to white males, as Jablonski and others have amply documented.[44]

Specifically, in applying the Enlightenment notion of "white man's burden," the tribalistic concept of European superiority was formulated as morally motivated, while in reality it justified the use of violence against fellow humans from other traditions, followed by domination through colonialism and imperialism. Persons of non-European descent were regularly treated as "less than human" and were depicted as particularly suited to serving lighter-skinned "masters."

Jablonski reports the renowned philosopher Immanuel Kant to have dismissed a commentary written by African scholar and artist Anton Wilhelm Amo, simply because its author "was quite black from head to toe, a clear proof that what he said was stupid." In a 2013 commentary on current issues, journalist Justin Smith writes: "We are allowing the 18th-century legacy of Kant and Hume, which was never really anything more than an ad hoc rationalization of slavery, to define our terms for us. We are turning our back on the legacy of Anton Wilhelm Amo, and of his European contemporaries who were prepared to judge him on his merits."[45]

Steven Pinker cited the growing literacy that characterized the European Enlightenment as critical to beginning the spread of ideas about human rights. Yet during this long period and its aftermath, millions of lives were lost, societies were geographically divided, resources were extracted, and profits were gained through economic and political domination that included war and other forms of violence, primarily against people of color. Suppression of violent local conflicts reduced local war in some areas, yet the same people were often later recruited to fight in wars of those dominant powers, external to their own societies.

Human rights were not extended beyond white males for several more centuries. Nevertheless, the use of indirect rule, the spread of literacy, and the imposition of peace over some areas of former regular lethal wars were positive developments. And we have seen peacemaking attempts following some wars that did use more neutral bystanders than a single country. NATO is one example, and the United Nations is another.

Institutional and Insidious Racism

When institutions themselves, including government, incorporate tribalistic or race-based biases into policy, the result is called *institutional racism*. While individual racism or prejudice can exist without institutional support, it becomes more powerful, pervasive, and harder to modify when it is combined with regulations and restrictions. With reduced opportunities for housing, education, work, access to health or legal professionals, or voting, racism becomes more entrenched even if it is not targeted directly as policy connected to "race." Through these means, institutional racism adds "fangs" to the indignity and emotional pain of personal racist attitudes.

What, then, does racism have to do with race? *Racist* thinking is a specific variety of tribalistic thinking that presumes to be about built-in biological differences that influence behavior. In fact, it is not about meaningful biological traits. When racist practices are employed, people from outgroups may be forced to wear a visible sign of their difference, such as the armband or badge used to identify Jews in Germany and the countries it occupied prior to and during World War II. Since one's category was not easily visible, a cultural sign was used to make it so. Experimental studies have confirmed the ease with which even completely contrived groups (green shirt, yellow shirt) easily develop ingroup and outgroup sentiments.[46]

The idea of "race," of biological differences between groups, remains powerful: If we can convince ourselves that other human beings are so different from members of our own group that they can be treated without respect and are less than human, then we can justify almost any brutal or demeaning treatment of them.

Name-calling, reframing, and redefining outgroups discourages others from identifying and empathizing with individual members of that group. These actions create greater distance between individuals, work against intergroup tolerance, and encourage support for discriminatory policies. In these various ways, racist thinking is a particularly vicious variety of tribalistic thinking. It has been used to motivate people to fight wars, commit genocide, and inflict other atrocities on fellow human beings who belong to specific groups. These atrocities have taken many forms: lynching, beheading, burning at the stake, torturing, and dragging persons behind moving vehicles.

Current Examples in the United States

Concepts of race continue to occupy a large place in public behavior, and they are often not understood or even recognized. Despite the ease with which members of one group stereotype members of another, the same individuals often ignore events and behaviors perpetrated by members of their own "tribe" that could be used to stereotype it.

One example comes from the 1995 bombing of an Oklahoma federal building. Initial speculation, and the early arrest of a person of Middle Eastern descent, led to media statements decrying foreign terrorists. When the culprits turned out to be two American-born white males, no generalizations were made about other white males, and no public alerts were put out to warn of the dangers posed by this group. Similarly, recent mass murders in numerous public places, also primarily the work of white males, did not result in attributing the behavior to their white identity or their (usually) Christian backgrounds. Media discussions did focus on male violence.

The American experience before and during President Barack Obama's terms of office provides a second illustration of the pervasiveness of hidden and not-so-hidden racist bias today. The degree of obstructionism toward his ideas, unwillingness to accept his credentials, his valiant but often unsuccessful attempts to reach compromises and unite obstreperous factions, and the enormity of all-out fabrications regarding his religion, political ideology, and even his birth and citizenship, are only a few of the obvious distortions of reality that have surfaced. Unable to find real personal or political scandals with which to discredit President Obama, his opponents resorted to these and other tactics, including denouncing initiatives that were in some cases substantially the same as positions these same opponents supported during other administrations.

Historically and today, the concept of race has been loaded with notions of superiority and inferiority. The so-called "science" of race was no exception, and worse, it gave a sense of legitimacy to stereotypes. The term *race* has been used to discriminate against various groups. That different cultures perceive and define races differently indicates that they are largely sociocultural inventions.

Racism, Medicine, and Education

Strides are being made in the field of medicine to understand the distribution of diseases among humans, and several methods of sorting variables have been developed, each with problems of its own. Although understanding human differences is important in personalizing diagnosis and treatment of human disease, using racial categories alone increases the chance of missing diagnoses and applying treatments inaccurately. With our increasingly interconnected world population, genetically based diseases are not confined to local populations. As people travel, mate, and communicate across boundaries, diverse populations become closer to each other biologically. Because one's racial identity is based on sociocultural classification and on superficial appearance, the correlation with disease is only rough. Given this, a debate in medicine revolves around the value of using these categories. Ian Tattersall and Rob DeSalle suggest that as genome sequencing becomes less expensive, it may be a more practical and more accurate diagnostic tool.[47]

A more dangerous practice is to attribute behaviors to an individual's racial category. In reality, much human behavior is influenced by one's individual genome, but an individual's behavioral phenotype (actual behavior) results from complex interactions among numerous genes, some of which have multiple effects. Moreover, environmental conditions inside and outside an individual's body at different stages of development and different stages of life influence the expression of genes, as do interpersonal encounters and cultural patterns. So, if the physical and behavioral differences among humans cannot reliably be used to assign individuals to a "race," then using this identity as a basis for targeting particular educational or legal policy initiatives clearly makes no sense.[48]

For these reasons, I find Gregory Cochran and Henry Harpending's analysis of group behavioral differences and suggestions regarding education to be problematic.[49] An individual's performance on academic tests depends on his or her own bias, what she is told prior to the test, her experience with test tasks, and the biases of test givers and makers. Much of this priming is unconscious. It also depends on sociocultural and environmental conditions during a child's developmental years, such as diet, sleep, nurturance, family, and safety. The entire issue of group intelligence quotient (IQ) differences, even given high heritability, is suspect based on these considerations. As long as human beings are embedded in societies in which people experience drastically different opportunities and life experiences, and as long as children are given different messages about their abilities and attend schools with vastly different resources, how can we make valid inferences about a biological basis for group differences in learning?[50]

And with this too, intragroup differences trump intergroup differences.

Nonetheless, bias is real, and we human beings categorize people and act according to whatever criterion we hear about or invent, whether it is based on real or unreal differences. Our brains easily form essentialist categories that focus on commonalities or presumed commonalities, while ignoring variation among individuals assigned to that category.

In medicine and education, distinguishing individual differences from generalizations about groups is critical. Knowledge of group risks can be helpful in the diagnosis and treatment of disease, but the problem is in defining the relevant group. Within families shown to carry a genetic marker for serious illness, screening members of the extended family group makes sense. In the field of education too, learning problems need to be identified in individuals without making assumptions based on group membership. My guess is that learning abilities and learning styles are influenced by the environment to a greater extent than human disease. To be effective, educational tests and techniques must be tailored to the individual. The fact that one's race designation is more often sociocultural than biological reinforces the importance of separating education and medicine from race.

Melvin Konner has intensively and extensively reviewed perspectives on individual and group differences to reach this conclusion:

> We have in general understated intrinsic individuality, ... [while exaggerating] genetic explanations for group differences. But we now know that the two main thrusts of genetic analysis are to help explain human universals and individual differences, while group differences are overwhelmingly cultural. Ongoing progress in behavioral genetics and in other biological explanations of behavior will benefit individuals and enhance our understanding of universals but ... we have to look elsewhere to explain group differences.[51]

In short, human diversity is not distributed into discrete packages. Even if ancestral and early isolated human populations were more distinct than today's populations, the massive migrations, long-distant trading, resource extraction, and wars have transformed that picture. The Neolithic, followed by urban civilization, industrialization, and revolutions in travel and communication, accelerated the rate of mating, marriage, warfare, and trading among diverse people. The frequency of genetic and cultural exchange in twenty-first century people is many times greater than it was in the past.

Understanding racism helps us to understand tribalism in general. Our pattern-seeking brains play a key role in our perceptions of others, moving into high gear to note differences, to categorize, and to draw conclusions. When there are no visible differences among groups, we often construct differences through distinctive dress, decoration, language, ritual, and music. Caution is in order whenever we are tempted to generalize about persons from particular groups.

In the remainder of this chapter, I look at human war as an endpoint of tribalism, or, tribalism gone amok.

Violence, Tribalism, and War

What is the relationship between tribalism and war? All animals, all mammals, all humans have the capacity to act violently toward others. The emotion of fear is basic to survival and readily sparks a fight or flight reaction. Animals can acquire fear responses in association with almost any stimulus. In attempting to understand the origins of war, some researchers have considered the biological and psychological roots of violence. For humans, sociocultural institutions and values influence how we think and behave. They can increase or decrease our tendency to respond impulsively when fearful or angry (brain system 1). The cultural overlay can also encourage and enable us to override impulsive responses by deliberately using reasoning (brain system 2).

In earlier chapters, we saw that different ways of organizing society influence how people perceive societies surrounding them and the larger world. People organized into loose local groups consisting of varied kin ties and carrying a strong ethos of sharing are less likely and less able to organize raiding parties designed to grab land or other possessions.

Frans de Waal reminds us, too, that modern warfare is usually fought by specialists who have not been personally wronged or in danger, but who have been trained as fighters. Moreover, wars today are usually based on power and profit. In many cases these specialist fighters have been taught to despise an enemy to make them more effective fighters.[52] Stimulating and exaggerating fear of, and demonizing the enemy are used also to nudge citizens toward supporting wars. Adam Smith warned about governmental use of this fear strategy over two centuries ago, calling fear "a wretched instrument of government, ... [that ought] never to be employed against any order of men who have the smallest pretensions to independency."[53]

Modern war can be executed impersonally from a leader's point of view. Physical distance from the enemy and methods of carrying out war foster emotional detachment. Many decisions are made by persons far from a war zone, and unmanned drones and bombs can be launched and targeted with no direct enemy contact. We do not yet know how these technologies will influence who we are as a species or how they may change our emotional capacities and those of later generations.

One thing is certain: These modern expansions to warfare will profoundly affect those who directly participate in it and have consequences for the rest of humanity.

Sociocultural Correlates of War

In Chapter 6, we saw that the connection between biologically influenced male aggressiveness (and thus war) can be strengthened or weakened by differing cultural definitions of ideal roles for males and females. Melvin Konner points out that war is just one possible expression of male aggressiveness that tends to occur under specific social and environmental conditions.

Cultures with patrilocal, patrilineal, patriarchal corporate groups tend to emphasize war and aggressive norms for men. Muzafer Sherif's well-documented Robbers Cave experiment with groups of 11-year-old boys demonstrated the ease with which this kind of mindset can develop. Konner refers to Stanley Milgram's experiments, which demonstrate the capacity of ordinary male subjects (students) to torture others based on orders to do so from an authority figure. He suggests that an army in the midst of war is a real-life setup for the kind of mass psychology that causes people to behave violently.[54] Erich Fromm made a similar argument regarding the pull of group membership in his classic book, *Escape from Freedom*.[55]

Shankar Vedantam, in Chapter 7 of *The Hidden Brain*, describes this dynamic in the recruitment of members to terrorist groups. Group membership may appeal to young men who are searching for approval and meaning by focusing on a cause that is larger than life. Becoming part of a group with stringent membership requirements encourages a sense of specialness and elitism. Such groups develop under particular conditions and are not found in all societies or at all times in history. Knowing this offers hope for reducing terrorism by working to prevent conditions that encourage its development.

Steven Pinker on War and Violence

Drawing from many primary and secondary sources, Pinker summarizes evidence to show that, although the total number of deaths by human violence has increased as world population has increased, the rate of deaths from violence has decreased worldwide over time. Pinker relied heavily on compilations of data in Azar Gat's 2006 *War in Human Civilization*, archeologist Lawrence Keeley's research data and analysis as presented in *War Before Civilization*, and several pieces by economist Samuel Bowles. He supported his conclusions with tables based on these and similar primary sources. The sources documenting war that happened before written records were kept, however, came from archeological sites almost exclusively representing the post-Neolithic world, the past 10,000 years of modern human existence. This period represents less than 10 percent of the tenure of *Homo sapiens* on our planet.

Pinker begins with a Hobbesian framework for understanding our human propensity for war and our difficulties keeping the peace. He argues that the development of *leviathans*, Hobbes's word for state-based societies that hold a monopoly over the use of force, eventually altered the human trend to one of less violence. His work stimulated a combination of surprise, joy, and disbelief; the topic is clearly an important and timely one, and reviewers have responded accordingly.

In his view, the primary contrast in rate of violence is between nonstate (Pinker calls these "anarchies") and state-based societies. He takes the position of Hobbes that without strong central governments, human lives are "nasty, brutal, and short." Yet, like all of us, Hobbes was a product of his own time, which was a period of great economic, political, and religious upheaval and unrest in England. This period may have resembled the anarchy that he described in his major work, *The Leviathan*. From his birth in 1588 until his death in 1679, Thomas Hobbes, a poor man by birth with extraordinary abilities that were recognized and nurtured, was buffeted by the ongoing upheaval. He earned a reputation of relishing verbal combat.[56]

Pinker describes Hobbes and Rousseau, whose views about early people were polar opposites, as being fairly ignorant about the societies they tried to describe. Yet Pinker takes the position that Hobbes was basically correct in his view that "human nature" was without order (anarchic) without a centralized state. Pinker's stated aim is to "zero in on the contrast between foraging bands and tribes who live in a state of anarchy and peoples who live in settled states with some form of governance."[57] Unfortunately, this statement contains assumptions that are problematic., which I address next.

In presenting evidence, Pinker acknowledges that the trend toward a reduced frequency of deaths through violence has not been straight. Instead, it has moved up and down along the way. As an anthropologist, I am interested in the lumpiness in this trend, which contains information regarding specific conditions that foster peace or war, harmony or conflict. Rates of lethal warfare and emphasis on violence and war vary within state-based societies, as he notes and discusses. But they also vary within the kinship-based, nonstate societies that he calls anarchies.

Providing an alternative view, anthropologist Robert W. Sussman addresses the persistence of the "legend of the killer ape,"[58] arguing that it developed out of a Western European world view and history beginning with Hobbes and continuing its thread into the present, as expressed in Richard Wrangham and Dale Peterson's *Demonic Males* (1996). Sussman counters this point of view by referring to the many studies of the evolution of cooperative sentiments and practices that are built into social animals in addition to the competitiveness and aggressiveness featured so heavily in that model. He applauds the work of researchers in the biological and social sciences who have documented other aspects of our humanity.

With a traditional anthropological perspective and focus on small, kinship-based societies, researchers have provided considerable evidence for sociocultural factors associated with higher and lower frequencies of war and violence (summarized in Chapters 5, 6, and 7). We saw that size and permanence of local groups, relative status of women and men, type of leadership, kin group composition, religious views, and the ethos governing relationships were important sociocultural variables.

I propose that these factors are associated with the importance of tribalistic sentiment within particular societies, and the importance of war as a solution to human conflict. Not accounting for variation within nonstate, kin-based societies creates an impression that past violence was based solely on the absence of central government. The reality was considerably more complex.

Given this diversity, I agree with Pinker and others that such societies were not necessarily peaceful or free of violence, even the egalitarian hunter-gatherer societies. Some experienced more individual violence than indicated by many mid-twentieth-century characterizations. And for some, the imposition of state-based rule helped to reduce incidents of violence. The Rousseauian view of these cultures as peaceful and nonviolent was as utopian as Hobbes's view was dystopian, and both were inaccurate portraits of early societies or contemporary hunter-gatherers. The emphasis on nurture over nature, or "blank slate" thinking of that period resulted in some exaggeration of the degree of peace and harmony among people without central governments.

Individuals may fare better, especially in a crowded world, when coerced into behaving harmoniously through the authority of central government, at least if the authority acts efficiently and fairly. But this is not the only effective influence for decreasing war. One source of confusion in studies of war and peace has been a limited understanding of the degree of organizational and ideological diversity within kin-based societies. Equating egalitarian hunter-gatherer societies with those who combine horticulture or herding with some hunting results in an inaccurate image of band-level hunter-gatherers.

In reviewing changes wrought by the Neolithic in Chapter 5, we saw that people with farming and herding developed quite different views of their place in the natural world than those of people subsisting on wild foods alone (a Paleolithic lifestyle). The change of lifestyle transformed the relationship of people to nature, influencing the reasons and means for engaging in war.

Obstacles to Understanding War and Peace

Collecting and interpreting evidence from prehistoric sources and ethnographic material purported to depict small, nonstate societies, and attempting to define "primitive warfare" are difficult enterprises.

Evidence for war deaths among prehistoric people must be inferred from archeological and fossil remains. Problems include (1) representativeness of fossils in relation to population, (2) distinguishing deaths by predators from deaths from human violence, (3) overlapping or duplication of data in tabulations, resulting in inaccurate counting of deaths, (4) and estimating overall population sizes. Archeological sites do not necessarily represent the whole of a population; using the sites of massacres or battles to count deaths and determine rates of violence can inflate percentages for the society or language group as a whole. Samuel Bowles suggests that the fascination of researchers with finding and reporting evidence of spearheads embedded in human tissue probably biased sampling in favor of those reporting warfare.[59]

Bowles also recognizes selection bias in studies of pre-modern war that over-utilize living societies with reputations for violence; the Yanomamo of Venezuela and Brazil are almost invariably selected to illustrate "primitive warfare."[60] These people, however, have a reputation for being one of the fiercest nonstate societies ever observed, along with tribal people from the New Guinea Highlands, who are also over-represented in lists and statistics on violence. Additionally, these post-Neolithic societies practice horticulture, so are not representative of either ancestral or modern hunter-gatherers as described by ethnographers specializing in that area.

In reviewing Pinker's book, anthropologist Douglas P. Fry points out that evidence for organized war does not appear in the archeological record until the 10,000–12,000 year mark, around the time of the beginning of food production. Before that time, before food production and storage of food and other materials, and during our nomadic Paleolithic past, low population density often precluded the social organization needed for war and definitely for oppression of one group of humans over another.[61]

Dating of the one earlier African archeological site (Nubia) used in Pinker's data base was speculative because it was based on indirect dating of rock layers, not direct dating of fossils or artifacts. Anthropologist R. Brian Ferguson compiled evidence that Pinker's charts and lists of archeological prehistoric sites, derived from others' research, contained errors, including duplications, that cast doubt on the conclusions Pinker drew for the prehistoric portion of the data used to compile rates of violent death.[62]

Firsthand studies of the hunter-gatherer lifestyle support the conclusion that evidence is spotty at best for war during our Paleolithic past, at least for the more typical, scattered nomadic groups. Most shared a core of typical moral values emphasizing egalitarianism, tight control over "alpha male" tendencies, and flexible group composition. Other predominant features were nomadism, variable female status, and group size that was typically between twenty and thirty individuals during most of the year with larger gatherings on special occasions.

Anthropologist Christopher Boehm, whose carefully derived hunter-gatherer sample was an attempt to approximate earlier lifestyles, recently concluded that about 50 percent of these societies did have notable violent encounters between members of local groups, some between individuals from those groups, but others involving coalitions with revenge as a motive. The other 50 percent were mostly peaceful. We saw earlier that storytelling, gossip, humor, and song would have been fairly effective means of social control. We can add specific peacemaking efforts to this list. These efforts were less effective between groups than within groups. But it was only when *Homo sapiens* developed a new kind of hierarchy and dominance based on cultural inequality, that modes of behavior shifted to something more recognizable as war.[63]

Most evidence indicates that war, as organized group violence, increased with significant population pressure, domestication of plants and animals, storage of food and goods, private or family ownership of plots of land, and settled villages. Organized warfare, oppression of specific groups, and culturally based hierarchy developed in synchrony. Yet we *Homo sapiens* had already developed means of talking, listening, empathizing, discussing options, and making group decisions cooperatively. This conclusion is in line with the abundant evidence regarding human relationships in the egalitarian variety of hunter-gatherer societies. Firsthand observers consistently emphasize the critical role that cooperation and deliberate suppression of aggressive and competitive tendencies play among those people. Most likely these were important during the longest portion of our tenure on earth, when the ancestors of all of us all were hunter-gatherers.

Multilevel Selection and the Paradox of War

War seemed to have coevolved with the settled village life that had begun with the resource-rich complex hunter-gatherers and spread quickly after the Neolithic adaptation. The form of tribalism that I call *classism* became important in association with food production and storage, property in land, and accumulation of wealth. Human societies have struggled with it since that time. Samuel Bowles and Herbert Gintis hypothesize that war *enabled* state formation, complex societies with hierarchy, and in some areas, the imposition of peace within the state.[64] This argument is based on the notion of multilevel selection, the simultaneous working of individual and group selection, and is certain to be followed with further research.

Using his knowledge as an archeologist as well as a historian, Morris assigns a large role to the environment and its changes through time, emphasizing that as cultures evolve, they perceive and therefore use their environments in new ways. Events happening outside an organism or a society, which form its natural and sociocultural environment, influence the range of responses available.

Morris applies anthropologist Robert Carneiro's *circumscription hypothesis* here: At some point, smaller societies have no place to retreat, being restricted or walled off by surrounding powers, which then incorporate these small groups, often on a lower rung of the sociocultural hierarchy. The paradox of war is that, as societies become larger after defeating outside groups and incorporating them into their hierarchal structure, they can and sometimes do become more peaceful and wealthier internally. Peace within, however, does not necessarily translate into just laws for incorporated peoples. Morris agrees with Bowles and Gintis that this kind of war can reduce the overall level of violence within the complex society. But this is not a necessary outcome; it does not invariably happen.

These researchers distinguish *productive* from *unproductive* or *counterproductive* war. The distinction does not deny the destructiveness of war; it simply states that some wars (the productive ones) result in extending peace to a larger population that previously engaged in regular violence.

To support his analysis, Bowles uses a game-theory-based mathematical model of conflict between groups and a combination of cultural and biological selection for altruistic behaviors within groups. He argues that, in areas of relatively high population densities and competition for resources, selection may have favored human groups that were able to coax or force individuals to fight. He and Gintis argue that humans evolved to be cooperative, and that war played an important role in this process. This "paradoxical role of war" in human evolution is consistent with Pinker's hypothesis relating Leviathan to peacekeeping.

My sense, based on the more ancient needs for cooperation during the long duration of our hunter-gatherer existence, is that becoming cooperative evolved much earlier. Coerced cooperation was an add-on to that cooperative substrate.

Morris describes the growth and fall of empires over the very long time span from post-Neolithic prehistory into the present. He agrees with Pinker that, since World War II, major world powers have come to view the prospect of another world war as so devastating that the chance of its happening seems to have lessened, enabling the transformation of military competition into economic competition. Both agree that such a transformation, substituting competition through trade for competition through war, is key to reducing violence and promoting peace.[65] But with the degree of current economic and political uncertainty, both are cautious about predicting the future.[66] And as I complete this book, nonproductive or counterproductive wars continue to create new divisions and new conflicts without reducing war death rates or extending peace.

Pinker and others call the span of time since World War II *the long peace*, attributing it to the shared fear of "mutual assured destruction." A third world war has been avoided so far. Morris notes aptly that while avoiding this, we have instead "made do with war in the Third World." These smaller but substantial wars have been supported and sometimes instigated by Western powers, and resulted in the loss of approximately ten million people from 1946 to 1989. Both Morris and Pinker agree that these numbers are fewer than would have died in a World War III.[67] Yet economic and political instability have been encouraged by importing lethal weapons and military gear into these warring countries. Instability has also been abetted by recruiting and training fighters from various other societies to serve in these small wars.

For the United States, recruited individuals often work for security companies and private militias that get government contracts to provide fighters.[68] We can only speculate about the long-term consequences of this policy for individual recruits, and for the reputation of the United States. Recruiting, training, and arming fighters around the world is producing unintended consequences for us all that we are seeing in this second decade of the twenty-first century. There seems to be limited consensus regarding the number of deaths from ongoing conflicts. An online news source, *World Post*, reported 70 percent of Iraqi deaths from 2003 to 2011 to be from direct violence.[69] Other war-related Iraqi deaths would increase that rate.

Many questions remain unanswered. Pinker in 2010 identified three types of conflict to be the greatest threats to peace in this century: (1) civil wars, (2) ethnic and religious conflicts, and (3) terrorist attacks.[70] All seem to be prototypical examples of counterproductive wars.

I would be quite disheartened if creating larger political units through the paradox of "productive war" were the only means for promoting and extending peace. There is some evidence that peaceful relationships among groups can and do develop through means other than war. I next review some of these ideas.

Other Strategies for Promoting Peace

One alternative was summarized above, replacement of armed conflict with other forms of competition, particularly trade. Morris considers economic competition to be a new kind of nonmilitary productive war, while Pinker uses the phrase "gentle commerce" for the same thing. Lawrence Keeley's similar understanding of the role of trade was explored earlier. Intergroup trade is quite ancient, dated by archeologists to the earliest *Homo sapiens* communities between 200,000 and 100,000 years ago. This dating comes from discovery of artifacts and material originating in South African coastal sites, but widely distributed into other parts of that continent and into the eastern Mediterranean (see Chapter 3).

Avoidance is a second alternative to violent conflict; humans and other animals regularly make use of this technique. In using a common water source, an animal or group arriving first takes priority over latecomers, who wait or come back at another time. Animals begin by carefully observing the scene before acting to join or to retreat and wait, and this reduces the likelihood of violent conflict. A

similar but longer-term strategy of avoidance was commonly employed by egalitarian hunter-gatherers confronted with herders or
agricultural people with more material resources.

Observation is a component of a third alternative to violent conflict: ritual displays of strength. Animal displays were discussed in
Chapter 7 as precursors to human rituals; peace-loving gorillas pound
their chests in a ritualized display, creating fear in others but rarely
fighting themselves. Social rituals of human groups that involve
dance also provide a chance for outside individuals to assess group
strength before acting, as described by Roy A. Rappaport in his classic study of human ritual.

Finally, extension of social bonds among kin into friendships that
bridge geographical divides and enable sharing of wild resources and
water sources for mutual benefit is probably ancient. Other species
demonstrate different patterns. In elephants, the matriarch of a group
is often a peacemaker who maintains close social ties with other
group members.[71] In many species, grooming, play, and vocalizing
are part of maintaining social bonds. We might conclude that gentler
options often trump violence when there is a chance of them working.

Limiting the degree of harm, reducing the consequences of violent conflict, is a different kind of strategy. This occurs when animals
sheath their claws or bite gently (seen mostly in play activities). Male
kangaroos use their much smaller forelimbs to box each other com-
petitively, and that often works to make one of them retreat without
incurring the damage of a more powerful thrust from a hind leg. A
human example would be an agreement to use only conventional
weapons in fighting a battle, restricting the possibilities of damage
and injury to limited war.

Compromising and not insisting on full achievement of group or individual goals can often maintain a social web over time while avoiding destruction. Mathematical "hawk-dove" games simulate real life
interactions that result in costs and benefits for actors. They repre-

sent competition for a valued resource by fighting for it (hawks) or taking what's left (doves). Modeled over time, payoffs for each depend on the frequency of each in a population. If hawks take over completely (unlimited war), they and the doves become losers. By restricting complete takeovers, equilibrium emerges; both types win, but no one wins totally.[72]

Like the hawk-dove game, the prisoners' dilemma game helped investigators understand how cooperation may have evolved and how violent conflict was avoided through prehistory and history. Numerous game trials using different strategies have shown some strategies to be more successful than others over many repetitions projected through time. These trials offer clues to how cooperation evolves over many generations. Martin A. Nowak has been a central researcher in this area (outlined in Chapter 4).[73]

These games can involve direct reciprocity between two individuals who interact regularly; this is common in other animals and in humans. But more complex indirect reciprocity is particularly important to *Homo sapiens*. This involves repeated encounters among individuals through time, in which Person A's strategy with Person B depends not only on how B has treated A, but how B has treated others in the population. Reputation over time matters in human interactions because we have the memory and language to enable it. In the long run, helpful people have bigger payoffs, and the generous receive more. Of course, reality is much messier.

The strategy called *tit-for-tat with forgiveness* is persistent over many generations of games. But it eventually results in so many cooperators that a lone freeloader can readily take advantage, which spurs more freeloaders, hence producing a change in strategy. Another strategy that is successful in persisting over many encounters is *win-stay, lose-shift*. Here a player repeats the strategy if it works, but shifts to the opposite if it fails. Nowak points out that other possibilities for strategies may still be discovered.

As applied to war and peace, these mathematical models produce cyclical patterns in the long run, as noted by Ian Morris and other historians and archeologists who study the rise and fall of civilizations. We see it in biological evolution in the rise and fall of species. This notion differs from the idea of continual and gradual progress.

An additional means of pursuing peace is reconciliation, which refers to re-establishing cooperation after conflict. This has been observed in people and in other animals, frequently in our bonobo cousins but occasionally even in our more aggressive common chimpanzee cousins.

Christopher Boehm, whose hunter-gatherer sample enabled inferences about the frequency of intergroup violence, recently analyzed reconciliation behaviors in this sample. Those cultures featuring violent encounters regularly employed peacemaking strategies, noting that they were more successful when applied to conflicts within groups than to conflicts between groups.[74]

We can add specific peacemaking efforts to storytelling, gossip, humor, and song as means of social control among hunter-gatherers. Melvin Konner's and Sarah B. Hrdy's descriptions of gentle, firm guidance of children among hunter-gatherers, in contrast to harsher patterns seen more often in inegalitarian societies, may also have made relations easier in the former. With the birth of food production and the changes that followed, a new kind of hierarchy and dominance based on cultural inequality rendered these earlier informal modes of social control less effective.[75]

Intergroup alliances of larger kinds have been formed for the sole purpose of establishing or re-establishing peace in cultures around the world. There is evidence for some success with this strategy. Members of the European community came together peaceably by yielding sovereignty in limited areas, although this plan took a number of years to become a reality. The Thirteen Colonies of the early United States used the same strategy.

The Iroquois federation is one of the best-known examples of this strategy used in kin-based societies[76] In resource-rich eastern North America, after documented wars between chiefs, Deganawidah, a remarkable leader according to oral history, advocated reason and diplomacy to combine societies into a larger unit in approximately 1600 A.D. Five societies united to become the Iroquois Confederation, and a century later (documented in 1722) a sixth society was added. Deliberate, planned development of common rituals, trading of unlike goods, intermarriage among tribes, and a council that met annually to solve common problems, effectively substituted these institutions for former military organizations that had opposed each other.

Although these peaceful interactions applied only to societies within the confederation and not to those outside it, it extended the circle of peace. It was such a successful union that the Anglo founders of the original thirteen American colonies consulted Iroquois leaders about forming their own union.

Douglas P. Fry presents examples of similar coalitions on other continents. Coalitions among several upper Xingu River tribes in South America were created through peaceful means but only after vicious wars. The important fact is that people were able to organize them, and the coalitions promoted greater harmony and security for a while. More recently, formerly war-torn Rwanda demonstrated some success at active community building through a similar effort.[77]

The general strategy that defines our humanity and makes these specific strategies possible in the first place is *adaptability*. Its opposite is adaptive specialization. Human adaptability is reflected in the plasticity of human behavior and thinking. It has become clear from recent animal research that some nonhuman animals have far greater ability to behave flexibly in response to particular conditions than was previously realized. Robert Sapolsky, summarizing his two-phase, long-term study of behavioral changes within a particular troop of Hamadryas baboons, sees this precedent as significant for understanding ourselves.[78] Human adaptability, developed way beyond that of baboons, has a correspondingly larger untapped potential for developing creative alternatives to reducing war and achieving peace.

Anthropologist and primatologist Augustin Fuentes writes of the growing recognition of the role of flexibility in *niche construction*; this refers to ongoing interactions among natural, social, and biological actors that constitute a web within a larger environment. He identifies four dimensions important during human evolution: genetic, epigenetic, behavioral, and symbolic. Research is demonstrating that these together influence the details of individual development, population genetics, and cultural transmission, resulting in an updated picture of how we become who we are.

Because of our high degree of plasticity, Fuentes recommends caution in inferring too freely from the behavioral models of other primates to describe human trends. Either war or peace can emerge from the diversity and complexity of human behavior. He reminds us that "frequent coordinated intergroup violence" is recent compared to the totality of human evolution, and also when compared to evolution during the shorter tenure (approximately 200,000 years) of *Homo sapiens*. Evidence for human cooperation appeared much earlier in prehistory than evidence for organized war. Waging war uses this cooperative ability but the existence of war does not explain how cooperation originated. He concludes: "War and peace emerge from the interactions of patterns of cooperation, shared and disputed ecologies, social, economic, and symbolic histories, and the perceptions of human polities."[79]

So, our species, with its culture-language complex and the behavioral flexibility that it provides, has considerable potential for pursuing alternative paths toward intergroup peace. More than other animals, we can envision and reason about possible ways to increase tolerance and appreciation of others.

Looking at the entire landscape provides a reminder that during most social interactions and disagreements, we humans do not use physical violence and we do not start wars. Peace and negotiations are more commonplace than war, and most of us tolerate different opinions and problem-solve every day by using language. With a cultural emphasis on military preparation, conflicts, and war, it is easy to forget that in everyday life other options for resolving conflicts are used most of the time in most human exchanges. Peace is more normal than war, and people everywhere tolerate each other's differences. But this is rarely considered newsworthy.

Summary and Conclusions

Tribalism and war are intimate companions, and tribalism is alive and well today. It has not disappeared as we have become more enlightened, although it has decreased in some forms and in some pockets of the world. It is responsive to how people organize themselves and to how they acquire and share basic resources. As the world becomes more interconnected, some forms of tribalism become less important and others emerge. We look at some of these transformations in the next chapter.

War is an end-point, tribalism carried to its extreme. Incentives for violent intergroup conflict and the organization necessary for carrying it out on a large scale came largely after the beginning of food production, settled villages, and changing notions of property. These conditions eventually led to surpluses that enabled still more resources to be used for war. Increased differences in property and power eventually enlarged the scale and destruction of war, and encouraged sentiments toward supporting it. This happened through enculturating children and developing an ethos to support war; part of this was encouraging males to be tough and aggressive. The birth of civilization, like the birth of ingroup morality, had a dark side that we must recognize if we are to move forward, beyond tribalism.

What makes some societies more violent than others? Emphasis on violence and war varies from one kin-based society to another in relation to environmental and sociocultural institutions. The same connection holds for state-based societies.

Many researchers have noted an inverse association between the degree of violence and women's empowerment, participation and status in both kinship-based and state-based societies. These associations are not overwhelming in strength but are promising for thinking about ways to promote peace. The forms that social, economic, and governing institutions take can nudge societies toward more peaceable or less peaceable relationships between groups and toward lesser and greater degrees of tribalistic attitudes.

Lawrence H. Keeley proposed that another influence on a society's emphasis on war is its "neighborhood."[80] We see this today in areas of the world that are beset by intergroup violence, for example, in the Middle East and on the African continent where outside nations superimposed new political entities without regard for traditional boundaries. And we see the neighborhood influence in some areas of the United States where individuals come to feel that increasing weaponry will increase security because there are so many well-armed neighbors. Societies or communities surrounded by violent neighbors tend to increase their own violent responses. In this sense, tribalism begets tribalism.

The willingness to think highly of our own ideas—the certainty that we are right—seems to be an important factor in the likelihood of using violent solutions to solve problems. Euro-Americans need to take special caution in this regard since persons from this tradition have in recent centuries benefited from a tribalistic attitude toward people from other traditions. E.O. Wilson reminds us that modern states not only celebrate war but have supported totalitarian and terrorist regimes elsewhere.[81]

As people from other traditions become dominant world players, and as they frame and spread their world views, it remains to be seen whether other forms of tribalism come to the fore or whether the changing world becomes less tribalistic. Oppression of minority groups happens around the world, and all members of *Homo sapiens* need constant reminders of how our brains can deceive us and how to recognize and override our biases if we are to continue to survive and thrive as a species.

We must remember, too, that the lines separating terrorism, freedom-fighting, and counter-terrorism are thin indeed. And support of terrorism can be indirect. Exporting weapons, military planes, and other equipment to be used in war is an extremely profitable business in the short term. The phrase *collateral damage*, used sometimes to refer to unintended deaths by violence, has implications as repugnant as *ethnic cleansing*.

Any time tribalism restricts opportunities to pursue health and well-being to particular groups, certain people, or some countries, it becomes a major obstacle to meeting common human goals. Almost everyone has the capacity for generosity, open and flexible thinking, and extending empathy outward. Its strength varies with individuals and with circumstances and cultures. How we define and frame our notions of people from groups other than our own influences what we can accomplish and how well we can collaborate. How we organize resources, everyday work, and political decision-making influences our ability to reach common goals.

We can speak with more certainty about the consequences than the causes of war. Whatever else it may or may not accomplish, war has two invariable consequences: First, it destroys other living, breathing, feeling, and thinking human beings and often the homes and infrastructures that enable them to survive, work, raise families, and enjoy life. Second, it increases the rate of use and destruction of our earth's resources that are finite yet essential for all living creatures. So, in a real sense, war represents the ultimate "anti-life" proposition and activity. And modern war produces many times more environmental destruction than earlier wars did.

Tribalism is toxic to our own and many other species in today's world, and it breeds war. It is not group differences themselves that create war. It is tribalistic attitudes toward those differences: the certainty that our tribe is on the *right* side. With this attitude, group members overestimate the virtues of their own group and underestimate any possibility of wisdom in alternate ways of living or thinking about the world. In Carl Sagan's words:

> Whenever our ethnic or national prejudices are aroused, in times of scarcity, during challenges to national self-esteem or nerve, when we agonize about our diminished cosmic place and purpose, or when fanaticism is bubbling up around us— then, habits of thought familiar from ages past reach for the controls. The candle flame gutters. Its little pool of light trembles. Darkness gathers. The demons begin to stir.[82]

Recognizing the tendency toward tribalistic attitudes may help us to respect and listen to different points of view. Since we are all wrong much of the time, we might be able at least to agree not to harm others, and in that sense remove tribalism's fangs and become more likely to reach common ground. We have seen that all animals, including the human animal, have evolved or invented ways to limit expressions of physical aggression and to foster peace.

Although war is tied to tribalism, it is often not tied to real differences. A pointed example of the role of tribalism in many conflicts around the world comes from the Israeli-Palestinian conflict. Izzeldin Abuelaish made this very important point in his book, *I Shall Not Hate*, describing Israelis and Palestinians as poignantly similar in family and cultural values and patterns of self-expression, yet able to be drawn into perceiving only difference and enemy status in the "other" tribe. Abuelaish acquired his deep understanding and compassion from his childhood experience living in a Palestinian refugee camp, from later practicing as a physician to both Israelis and Palestinians, and from the awful air raid that killed three of his daughters and a niece, and destroyed his family home.

Following this tragic event, Abuelaish became an ambassador for listening, for tolerance of others' ideas, for forgiveness, and for healing. He came to advocate recognition of the valuable role for women as peacemakers.[83] And he came to understand how easily a very few individuals can shape the opinions of citizens and international perceptions about groups other than their own.

I have attempted to show in this chapter that tribal emotions and attitudes and our capacity for violence are only one piece of our biological heritage. These impulses evolved in our ancestors who lived in scattered, small groups for mutual safety in a dangerous open environment. This required group living and cooperation. The capacity for cooperation, for reasoning with each other, and for widening our circles of caring and cooperation enabled our ancestors to become modern *Homo sapiens*. The emotions and attitudes that move us to care for others and treat each other as we would want to be treated define our humanity, even as they coexist with our more destructive tribalistic emotions.

Was tribalism perhaps less important among some early, nomadic, egalitarian hunter-gatherers living under conditions of low population density? With the egalitarian and sharing ethos, and observed gentleness with children, freedom to move easily, and openness to spontaneity of expression in similar contemporary groups, human creativity perhaps had freer rein than it did after the Neolithic Revolution, just as open conversation and the absence of powerful leaders may have enabled a kind of informal democracy to be practiced.

Informal, leaderless decision-making by consensus observed by ethnographers as lengthy discussions by men and women in several of these societies suggest that informal democracy existed prior to state-based societies.[84] It may have taken literacy and the printing press to disseminate democratic notions widely, but the germs of freedom of thought and creativity are as old as *Homo sapiens* and part of our biological legacy.

We might wonder whether conditions of high population density and increased competition for resources can coexist with an atmosphere of peace, harmony, and creativity. There are many unanswered questions regarding war and peace.

Even today, determining the frequency of violent deaths and deaths in war is an ongoing challenge, with differences in opinions about the accuracy of different databases as well as how they are analyzed. Certainly the discussion will continue. What will matter is whether we use our considerable capacity to reason, move forward, work with each other, and agree not to do deliberate harm, even when we do not share the same viewpoints.

In the next chapter, I suggest that the hope for the future of our species depends on our moving beyond tribalism toward a clearer understanding of our strengths and weaknesses. We can use our evolutionary gifts to modify social institutions, habits of thought, and values to reflect and to emphasize our common strengths rather than exaggerating differences between groups. It is human diversity that gives *Homo sapiens* its flexibility as a species and the potential to overcome the difficulties we face on a shared planet.

PART IV

HUMAN PROSPECTS

One blue sky above us, one ocean lapping all our shore
One earth so green and round, who could ask for more?
And because I love you I'll give it one more try
To show my rainbow race, it's too soon to die.

Go tell, go tell all the little children
Tell all the mothers and fathers too
Now's our last chance to learn to share
What's been given to me and you

 —Pete Seeger[1]

We stand now where two roads diverge. But unlike the roads in Robert Frost's familiar poem, they are not equally fair. The road we have long been traveling is deceptively easy, a smooth superhighway on which we progress with great speed, but at its end lies disaster. The other fork of the road—the road "less traveled by"—offers our last, our only chance to reach a destination that assures the preservation of our earth.

 —Rachel Carson, 1962[2]

In Chapter 9, I propose that our future as a species depends on overcoming the ancient tribalistic perceptions and emotions that divide us. Evolution endowed us with the capacity to extend social sentiments to all people and beyond, using our double evolutionary legacy of intelligence and empathy. Language-based culture gives our species its greatest strength—adaptability—which enables us to move *beyond tribalism.* We have the means to overcome our status as a belea-guered species.

How can we do this? First, we must become aware of our own biases. All of us have them, and many are hidden even to ourselves. Second, we must come to understand and accept that diverse ways of thinking and behaving are our strength as a species.

In this chapter, I suggest a range of specific "prescriptions" for modifying how we think about and organize institutions. We need to work toward reducing extreme economic and political disparities that further the divisions among us and pursue a common goal of pre-serving the resources on which we all depend. We must train our-selves to perceive human variety as the source of this capacity to con-struct solutions to the complex challenges that we face.

Chapter 10 looks at consciousness and the notion of free will in the context of evolution. Its second part looks at complexity, pro-gress, and the human trajectory. Finally, I explore the question of meaning, a topic of interest to philosophers and others who attempt to make sense of our place in the natural world. Over the years, there have been many ways that individuals have viewed the question of meaning. The search itself is one path toward meaning: Asking ques-tions, searching for answers, and celebrating that there will always be more to explore.

9

Beyond Tribalism:
Bringing People Together Again

Some would say that it is too idealistic to believe in a society based on tolerance and the sanctity of human life, where borders, nationalities and ideologies are of marginal importance. To those I say, this is not idealism, but rather realism, because history has taught us that war rarely resolves our differences. Force does not heal old wounds; it opens new ones. . . .

Imagine the legacy we could leave to our children. Imagine that such a world is within our grasp.

—Mohamed ElBaradei, 2005[1]

We are, in the end, stewards of the future at a time when our shared future is imperiled by economic divisions, shortsightedness, and a growing ecological crisis. We have great tasks ahead. . . We have a high responsibility to our children and other generations that will come. Let us begin anew.

—Jeffrey Sachs, 2011[2]

Thinking about Tribalism and the Future

Will there be a future for our species? The following facts about our species provide a starting point for seeking an answer:

- We are animals with intact animal drives, emotions, and ancient neurochemistry.

- We are social animals and products of multilevel selection.

- We care for others and we value fair play. Although we favor members of our own "tribes," we are able to extend these social sentiments outward under many circumstances.

- We are thinkers with an incredible ability to learn and to create. Through culture, we adapt to and modify our material and social environments.

- For the past 10,000 years, our species has multiplied many times in population and has accelerated extraction of energy from the earth, diverting it largely to our benefit.

- The earth and its resources are finite, and all living things are interconnected as part of the natural world.

We *Homo sapiens* are social animals extraordinaire, and like the eusocial insects, we have complex societies. Unlike them, we are torn between our desire to pursue individual interests and the desire to cooperate with and act generously toward others. These conflicting human attributes place us in a dilemma that few, if any, other animals face. I call us a "beleaguered species" because of this. I use this label also because we are approaching a point of no return according to scientists from diverse disciplines. We must live with our opposing impulses and emotions. Yet we have the capacity to reason and enough scientific knowledge about our world to act for the benefit our entire species, for humanity as a whole. On the other hand, we also have the ability to rationalize behaviors that are self-serving or based on specific group interests, even if they reduce the long-term chances for our species to survive and thrive.

The features that enabled us to dominate the earth produced our current dilemma. The disconnect between our human trajectory and that of the rest of nature is related to the speed of cultural evolution, which far outstrips the rate of change in the rest of nature. Our defining features—a large, complex brain, bipedalism, and multipurpose hands and fingers—enabled elaborate culture-building, efficient resource extraction, and accelerating depletion of sources of energy within the earth.[3]

Why is this important? From the largest perspective, the universe's point of view (if it could have one), the end of us *Homo sapiens* would only be the beginning of a new stage in the evolution (or devolution) of life on earth, or a new stage in the history of everything. Our universe, and even our planet Earth, will continue long after we are gone. Species come and go. The average mammalian species survives for three to four million years.[4] And the one-million to two-million year tenure of early members of genus *Homo* was far longer than the tenure of *Homo sapiens* thus far, approximately 200,000 years. Other species have survived much longer.

Some have suggested that our species could survive as a much tinier population, even following mass starvation or a human-produced holocaust. Yet if the human population became too small, there might not be the critical mass needed to generate invention and the spread of new adaptations. The hypothesized earlier human population bottlenecks were associated with (1) the bipedalism-childbirth-childcare adaptations faced by our early *Homo* ancestors; (2) the early phases of behavioral modernity (*Homo sapiens*) around 100,000 to 70,000 years ago in southern Africa; and (3) the transition to plant and animal domestication that defines the Neolithic. If another should occur, few of us would be here to see the result.

A different outcome for current trends set in place by our species might be an evolutionary transition into a different kind of human. We could become an intelligent animal who is less adapted to face-to-face relationships and social sentiments based on empathy, but more dependent on relationships mediated through technology, such as hybrids that combine organic and robotic parts. These new humans may or may not use our long-acquired social sentiments and the neurochemicals that drive them. Writers have produced a plethora of other possible outcomes.[5]

Although the universe as a whole is indifferent to human survival, most of us members of the species do care, at least for present and foreseeable generations. What will our fate be if we fail to take action, if we fail to manage our more destructive tendencies and our increased extraction of resources? Most scientists agree that we are in a tough spot right now, perhaps on the brink of disaster. Many are warning us, but too few with resources and political clout are listening. This may be how our species will self-destruct; we may not be smart enough, or wise enough, to figure out how to cooperate, move forward, and prevent this outcome for our beleaguered species.

In this chapter I propose that we have the capacity to use the same tool that has brought us to the brink—our culture-language complex—to construct mechanisms that can reduce the chances of our self-destruction. Emotions, those movers of all creatures, have two faces in that they can be expressed destructively or constructively. We are, after all, flexible animals, capable of changing behaviors through learning. Will we use this capacity for thinking and scientific understanding to modify our actions for a better chance at a positive outcome?

Tribalism and Arrogance

Tribalism, described in Chapter 8 as a product of our biological and sociocultural evolution, is a significant obstacle in our path toward a viable future. The following points summarize its roots.

- It evolved as a product of our being small, helpless, relatively weak primates who needed strong group ties and protection to survive.

- It utilizes the ancient mammalian emotions of bonding, trust, and their opposites, separation and fear of separation.

- It employs social emotions and the human capacity for sympathy and empathy that encourage identification with a group.

- These emotions of togetherness move us toward tribalistic thinking, while reducing our cognitive resistance to it.

- Our brain-based capacity for keeping track around 150 individuals limits the size of our closest face-to-face groups.

Our tendency toward tribalism, this legacy from our ancestors, works against our ability to survive as a species today because it emphasizes group differences. Claims about the superiority of one group in comparison to others breeds conflict that easily becomes violent when another group claims the same superiority. War frequently erupts, itself greatly increasing the rate at which we utilize and destroy the earth's limited resources, remarkable human inventions and constructions, and the lives of fellow human beings. I hope to have conveyed by this point the thesis of this book: Tribalism must be overcome, or at least its results controlled, for our species and others to continue surviving and thriving on our shared planet.

In Chapter 8, I described war as the ultimate expression of tribalism. War decreases the hard-won biological and cultural diversity that enables our adaptability, our evolutionary potential, and our strength as a species. Think of the lives, the cultural treasures, the languages, and the bodies of knowledge that have been lost already. Today's scientists, for example, are struggling to retrieve and re-create knowledge of rain forest medicine before it is completely lost. If we see our species as valuable, if we see human life as valuable, we must join others to move beyond tribalism and reach out to all peoples to solve our common problems.

Conflict is inevitable and even desirable in a species whose members can disagree, listen to each other, and think. But violent solutions are based on primitive and emotional responses that are connected to an underlying toxic sense of superiority. This attitude feeds tribalism, even though differences among us provide our strength as a species.

Tribalism is related to our peculiar evolutionary history. We humans evolved the ability to view ourselves as a unique species, as members of a unique sociocultural group, and as unique individuals. At each of these three levels, we perceive ourselves as special.

- Species level: We favor *Homo sapiens* over other animals. Another term for this is *anthropocentrism*.

- Sociocultural level: We favor our own group over other human groups. This is *tribalism*. American exceptionalism exemplifies this category.

- Individual level: We tend to see our personal accomplishments as due to effort, talent, and skill, while often attributing failures to outside factors. We often take the opposite position when thinking of successes and failures of others. This is called *egocentrism*, or narcissism, and has been amply supported by many studies.

I suggest that each of these perceptions of our uniqueness might be understood as forms of *arrogance*. Tribalism, or group arrogance, is abetted by arrogance at the other two levels.

Our tendency toward individual arrogance was covered in Chapter 2, in discussing the need to foster its opposite in doing science, i.e., scientific skepticism laced with humility toward one's own ideas. This arrogance lurks in the background; we readily rationalize and justify our own perceptions and thinking. Human concern with reputation and status works in this direction also.

Adam Smith two centuries ago spoke of this when he stated: "The over-weening conceit which the greater part of men have of their own abilities, is an ancient evil remarked by the philosophers and moralists of all ages."[6] The ancient notion of the tragic flaw of a hero, the biblical notion of pride coming before a fall, and the naming of pride as one of the deadly sins were early acknowledgements of this common human trait.

Robert Wright in *The Moral Animal* argues that honest, clearheaded self-evaluation is beyond the abilities of most of us, observing that we detect and remember others' flaws and debts to us more easily than we remember our own.[7] Similarly, in conflicts, including divorce and war, both sides feel aggrieved and believe in the other side's guilt, often demonizing the enemy. Such biases are mostly unconscious.

Species arrogance might be defined as the idea that we humans have the right to control the rest of nature. The Neolithic-born ideology of mankind's acquiring "dominion over the earth" did help us do just that, and it may also have aided bias toward thinking that we can ignore damage to the rest of nature as our environment changes. In this way, we move closer to a short-sighted "tragedy of the commons" that biologists and historians have long recognized in other endeavors.

In his day, Charles Darwin commented that artificial selection, which he practiced himself, might be a bit presumptuous, that it might not result in products as reliable as those produced through much longer periods of natural selection.[8] Perhaps we moderns should heed his wisdom regarding human limitations: Should we act more cautiously in utilizing technologies that seem promising without carefully investigating possibilities for long-term consequences? A bias toward short-term profitability often gets in the way of reasoned approaches to choices regarding technologies.

Could the idea of inevitable human progress represent another form of species arrogance, an opiate of sorts for our situation? Stephen Pinker demonstrated that in some ways we have made progress in reducing violence, while recognizing that such a trend is fragile and dependent on how we *Homo sapiens* continue to act. While hoping that the reduction of violence is an ongoing trend, I remain skeptical about our ability to put together the ideas and policies that will prevent us from destroying either ourselves or the environment that enables our survival. I fear that some of the emphasis on how we are improving may represent wishful thinking. As a species, we seem to have a brain bias that favors optimism.[9]

Views that attribute world progress to our Western Euro-American culture may represent a form of tribalism not unlike that of earlier Western explorers, anthropologists, missionaries, and others who viewed their own tradition as the pinnacle of achievement and possessed a cultural blindness to its drawbacks. Even careful thinkers and scholars are products of bias and often fail to give serious attention to alternative perspectives.

Over time, human actions around the world perpetrated by powerful, large-scale states in different prehistoric and historic periods had widespread adverse consequences. European colonial empires, for example, resulted in destroying cultures, partly through deliberate re-enculturation of surviving children and partly as unintended consequences of pursuing other goals. Resources were extracted in large quantities. Conquered people lost not only their cultural and family ties, but also the resources that could assist them in building something new. The consequences of these actions are still being felt today by millions of individuals. Many current "small wars" represent long-term effects of imposing new, highly stratified Leviathans on top of small-scale societies without respect to original boundaries.[10]

In this book I have used tribalism to refer to valuing the interests of one's own group and devaluing those of other people. Tribalistic cultures take as given that their society's interests are primary and take precedence over those of other groups. When tribalism is combined with disproportionate resources and power, as measured by ownership of land, media, corporations, and military technology, then those groups have influence far greater than that of groups without this coupling. They can publicize and disseminate their views, and can confuse or mislead the public, as Adam Smith warned long ago.

Our specific human evolutionary heritage enabled us to extend group membership more widely than that of other animals. While fear and distrust of outsiders is part of this heritage, it does not describe the whole story. Our evolution resulted in our capacity for caring, empathy, altruism, and the ability to reason and make decisions about how to manage our impulses and emotions. Human language is part of this legacy. It has been used to exaggerate differences between groups, to promote fear, and even to manufacture differences and fear where none existed before. But language can also be used to communicate and celebrate our common humanity. We can speak, write, and use language as a tool for formulating plans for working together to solve problems that affect all of us.

In the next sections, I attempt to apply this tool to current realities by outlining some strategies that could help our species think about and work together to negotiate a future for ourselves and our fellow co-habitants of planet Earth.

How We Can Move Beyond Tribalism

There are ways to employ human behavioral flexibility to modify our behaviors and increase the probability of a viable future for ourselves and other creatures. To accomplish this, we must orient ourselves to a rapidly changing environmental, technological, and social reality. This requires managing human conflicts in the face of our biological imperatives and current conditions, including a world population of over 7 billion, adverse effects on the ecosystem, expanding urbanization, and a decreasing sense of community.

None of us knows what the future will bring. Yet we have options that have the potential to influence the outcome. We can tweak or modify certain styles of thinking and responses to situations that provoke ancient fears and attitudes. We can apply our strengths, our capacity for empathy and reasoning, toward searching for ways to listen to each other across boundaries that divide us and cooperate to find solutions to shared problems. Using these tools, we have a chance at fulfilling the old dream of beating swords into plowshares, at least some of the time.

This is possible because we are cultural as well as biological animals. Cultural changes can happen and be transmitted more quickly and widely, and to many more people, than genetic changes can. We can enhance understanding of ourselves by studying, reading, and doing science. With effort, we can modify the neural circuitry of our brains. How we behave and who we are arise from and influence brain activity. In this way, everything we do makes a difference: music-making, reading philosophy, doing science, or providing food for others. The ability to modify our behaviors, thinking styles, brains, institutions, and technologies provides hope for our species and our planet.

Given this capacity to change, I present some practical prescriptions that may help us to move beyond tribalism. I group these roughly into three general, overlapping categories that include mental, institutional, and general society-wide or global strategies. Most are not new ideas; I have used a variety of resources while adding interpretations of my own.

Mental Prescriptions: Training Our Brains

These tweaks have the goal of understanding our primitive, irrational, excessively competitive tribal impulses to gain control over them, and to utilize our equally human cooperative impulses. Human nature is a composite of what our brains do; our behavioral plasticity enabled us to become the adaptable creatures that we are.

1. Understand the role of evolution.

This is important in shaping our perceptions, automatic and ancient impulses, thinking styles and biases, and even how we interpret these responses. All of us share the capacity for tribalistic feelings and thinking and the tendency to rationalize thoughts and feelings. Knowing how this tendency originated can encourage us to resist such impulses. We need to rely on evidence-based statements and learn to differentiate these from appeals to our emotions that are contrary to empirically-based knowledge.

2. Change responses.

This is done through practicing deliberate substitution of slower, reflective thinking (brain system 2) for immediate, reflexive responses (brain system 1). We can change even long-standing habits with hard work. Neuroscientists continue to demonstrate brain plasticity; brain chemistry and circuitry can be modified through deliberate changes in behaviors.[11]

3. Maintain skepticism.

We do this by considering our motives and responses. We tend to attribute good motives to ourselves and project the "demon" outward, and skepticism about our own emotion-driven motives can help counteract this tendency. As a species, we are often oversensitive to environmental cues. Like fear, this was an important tool for survival of a helpless ape in the face of danger, but also like fear, hypersensitivity can escalate responses to stimuli that in reality do not call for such a response.

To practice skepticism toward our impulses, Robert Wright suggests that we realize and admit how easily we deceive ourselves and others. He specifies guidelines for becoming alert to tribalistic biases: (1) discount moral indignation by 50 percent; (2) suspect any indifference to suffering; (3) be especially careful to suspect any negative feelings about members of outgroups; and (4) be wary of the tendency to behave less considerately to low-status people while being more tolerant of foibles of high-status people. Wright understands how difficult this is, concluding: "We are potentially moral animals—which is more than any other animal can say—but we aren't naturally moral animals. To be moral animals, we must realize how thoroughly we are not."[12]

4. Modify how we frame our responses to negative events.

We can do this by employing values that include humanity as a whole rather than a specific tribe or category. This enlarged perspective provides a frame more conducive to harmony and peace. For an example, consider the attacks in the United States on September 11, 2001, and their consequences. The George W. Bush administration reacted by declaring that four countries made up an "axis of evil," and then attacking two countries. He thereby missed an opportunity, during which the United States had the sympathy of many peoples around the world, to approach these events in a more productive way.

Philosopher Simon Critchley remarked, "When we act out of revenge, revenge is what we will receive in return. The wheel of violence and counterviolence spins without end and leads inevitably to destruction."[13] Since these events, American debt soared, additional lives were lost or altered, and more of our planet's resources were squandered for no benefit to anyone. This violent reaction can be contrasted with the 2011 Norwegian response to a tragedy that was smaller in scale but similar in that innocent civilians were killed in an act of terrorism.[14] These events had important differences, but we might learn something from the contrast in responses.

5. Act more like bonobos, less like chimpanzees.

What ancient or modern world religion actually preaches killing each other? Any species that does this would of course not survive. Exhibiting fangs and claws is not conducive to survival on the lifeboat earth that we inhabit. Neither are swords, guns, bombs, or military drones. Neither is the constant bickering of a species that models itself after chimpanzees. Let us be more bonobo-like. After all, these two closest relatives of ours offer two different models of our common ancestor, and the jury is still out on which we most closely resemble (see comparison, Chapter 5). We may never know with certainty. Given this, we may as well choose a model that resembles where we need to go as a species.

6. Learn from our mistakes.

Are we willing to admit that we have made mistakes, and that we keep making the same ones despite evidence that our choices have not worked? We must remind ourselves that mistakes can help us move forward. They can then be reframed as positive life events because we can learn from them. Given the human concern for maintaining a good reputation, perhaps we need also to devise more effective ways to save face, and to allow others to save face, while acknowledging mistakes.

7. Widen time and space perspectives.

Darwin, many years ago, envisioned an expanding of our "moral sentiments" outward to encompass an ever larger group:

> As man advances in civilization, and small tribes are united into larger communities, the simplest reason would tell each individual that he ought to extend his social instincts and sympathies to all the members of the same nation, though personally unknown to him. This point being once reached, there is only an artificial barrier to prevent his sympathies extending to the men of all nations and races.[15]

He recognized the difficulties in attempting this in his time, but he also recognized that once our sympathies become "more tender and widely diffused" they could become part of ordinary life. He may have expected this to come about as a natural consequence of human development. And it *has* happened to an extent. We regularly meet and greet individuals from diverse backgrounds as we conduct international business, travel in planes, and encounter strangers daily on the streets of cosmopolitan cities. We can share Darwin's vision, while recognizing that his optimistic prediction has not yet been realized.

Philosopher Peter Singer follows Darwin in advocating extending the circle of caring to other living creatures. Some have suggested that we humans cannot do this because we are bound with greater emotion to our kin and close associates (the 150 that we recognize personally) than to strangers.[16] Yet we are flexible animals, and we are able to make decisions and develop institutions that can nudge individuals toward a wider outlook, more respect, and more positive behaviors toward others.

8. Practice evolutionary ethics.

Evolutionary ethics is based on the idea that moral behavior evolved through natural selection and that prescriptive ethics, or how people ought to act, need to be based on what is universal to the human condition. This ethical stance would be based on the biologically-based moral sense that all of us share, despite differences between specific cultural norms for appropriate behavior. Philosopher Sam Harris's ethical goal of enhancing the well-being of self-conscious creatures reflects this application to all of humanity. It draws from our built-in human ability to cooperate, to share, to treat others justly, to mind read, and to feel empathy for others. Befriending others is as much a part of our biological heritage as is the capacity for violence.

Michael Shermer prefers the phrase "provisional ethics" because it expresses the idea that, as we gain knowledge, the specifics of ethical guidelines can change in line with empirical reality. He recognizes that systems of ethics are necessarily imperfect: We are, in his view, a bonobo-chimpanzee behavioral hybrid of sorts, acting more like bonobos within our own groups, but often resembling common chimpanzees in our behaviors toward outgroups.[17]

This description of evolutionary ethics does not assume that whatever traits are natural to us are morally good. We can use reason and scientific knowledge about our biology and our behavior to determine which guidelines for living increase well-being for ourselves and others in the long run. We take pleasure in nurturing and teaching young children, who have an extraordinary ability to learn from observing our behaviors, associations, and words.

9. Encourage creativity.

Anthropologists Timothy Ingold and Elizabeth Hallam envision every human behavior as a creative act; they see the living of a life itself as improvisation.[18] Rather than viewing creativity as an end point, as something extraordinary and unusual, these authors view it as an ongoing process. Life is about movement, about development, about *becoming* in the context of changing conditions. Human culture is all about responding in innovative ways and creating solutions to problems. Ingold suggests that every time we practice something learned, we infuse it with our own creativity and make it different from what came before. Modifying a story or adding nuances to a performance is a kind of improvisation or creative unfolding of something new, responsive to its particular context.[19] As a cello player, he describes music as a current that the player rides; the musician participates in the flow that *is* the music.

Creativity may be grounded in our propensity to play and in the relaxation of normal restraints that it allows (described in Chapters 4 and 7). Such conditions may enable "aha" moments, daydreaming, and thinking "outside the box." Neuroscientist Jonah Lehrer presents a similar idea in *Imagine*, proposing that persistent concentration and focus with interludes of freedom from mental constraint (e.g., physical activity) can be precursors of creative ideas.[20] This appreciation of creative, diverse, and changeable human stories might then promote religious and ethnic tolerance.

10. Use music and other arts to unify groups.

In Chapter 7, I described the ability of music and other arts to move people. Some music has specific religious themes, but music also celebrates or commemorates natural phenomena and historical events. And sacred music often tells a story that is applicable to humanity as a whole, not just to those who possess a particular belief system. The sentiments it inspires are often universal rather than sectarian: sadness, joy, yearning, pathos, frantic activity, rest, and harmony or peace. Just as celebrating with and engaging in music and dance helps to unify and activate smaller groups, perhaps with ever more rapid communication it can unite all of us.

Because music's capacity to inspire is not dependent on a particular tribal orientation, it is a particularly good candidate for unifying people from diverse backgrounds. Atheists, agnostics, and believers from diverse traditions can feel awe, glory, and "hallelujah" impulses that may be associated with the gods, animal spirits, the beauty or elegance of nature, the cosmos itself, or simply with the joy and wonder of being alive. Of course, music also has been used to motivate people to fight and kill; it can be used for positive or for negative purposes.

Music can inspire us to be more universal in our aspirations, hopes, and dreams for the world that we live in. It can encourage us to expand our circles of caring. Expanding our musical tastes and integrating different musical traditions can nudge us toward feeling like one huge tribe, the human tribe. These traditions are increasingly spreading around the world and even merging. Collaboration among musicians, visual artists, and poets of various traditions and genres, from Inuit to Australian to African to Asian to European is an exciting and hopeful development.

In this regard, I am fond of the phrase *music of the spheres* even though the phrase itself stemmed from an inaccurate cosmology. It evokes in me a sense of harmony (a musical word) and peace. There is room to glean what truths and what beauty we can from traditional music, artwork, and narratives. Appreciating the unifying, evolutionary narrative of how we became human can work with traditional and collaborative art to encourage valuing our differences. Harmony is achieved through weaving diverse strands of melody into a whole. Perhaps if we can see the beauty of each melodic strand, we can learn to develop a global appreciation for the resulting harmony.

Institutional Prescriptions: Modifying Group Practices

There are limits to using thinking and emotion in isolation as tools for extending human caring outward. Sociocultural institutions can foster either expansion or contraction of a framework for our thoughts and feelings about others.

Since most of my anthropological study focused on traditional, small-scale cultures, I do not pretend to be an expert on the institutions that dominate today's world. My interest in where we are going

as a species, however, has introduced me to the writings of economists, political scientists, historians, and others who *do* focus on these
institutions. The prescriptions I offer are based on this work of others, placed in an anthropological, biocultural frame. Many fields of
study are converging in a kind of consilience (E.O. Wilson's word)
that includes the biological and social sciences, philosophy, the arts,
and even mathematics, attesting to the power of an evolutionary, holistic approach to understanding the present as well as the past.

1. Modify Traditional Institutions To Extend Personal Ties.

Kinship, marriage, and friendship can extend ties to a multicultural and international community as diverse groups communicate,
meet, and sometimes mate and marry. Prehistorically and historically,
kinship has worked in this way. Today's rapid communication and
travel enable and ease this crossing of multiple boundaries among
groups of all kinds. Individuals come together not only through marriage and family, but through a variety of pairings and friendships
across traditional barriers.

Improvements in technology, enabling rapid international
communication, extends one's possibilities for connecting with others without regard for physical location. Expansion of communication began among humans through spoken language, drumming,
writing, the printing press, typewriters, and on to diverse ways enabled through the Internet. This is growing apace around the world as
devices proliferate in areas previously not interconnected. Rapid development in this area has already introduced unexpected changes to
economic and political institutions and ideologies.

2. Modify Economic Institutions and Ideology.

The idea behind modifying economic institutions is that they influence how well people can manage their lives. Anthropologists traditionally defined economics broadly, to include all means by which
members of a society are provisioned with goods, that is, how people
gather or produce what they need and how it is distributed. Used in

this sense, it does not refer to a particular philosophy or ideological economic position. Also, anthropology's holistic perspective views political and economic organization as connected, not as separate institutions. All people need food and other goods. Control of goods and control over people go together.

Increasing international trade

This had its beginnings in reciprocal exchange between small groups. Evidence for prehistoric trade comes from discovery of artifacts and natural materials in areas where they did not originate. The earliest members of *Homo sapiens* had trade networks. Later, the wheel, the chariot, boats, and efficient energy extraction led eventually to the transportation and communication systems of today's international economy. Lawrence H. Keeley showed that, in the past, trading unlike items was more effective than trading similar items toward fostering peace among trading groups.[21]

In a vastly interconnected world such as ours, economic interdependence and acceptance of international guidelines for trade could decrease violent suppression of people and even war. This would fit with Emile Durkheim's notion of interdependence as *organic solidarity* based on comparison with a biological organism. Today, however, countries are economically interdependent, yet violence and war persist and weapons of war are increasingly dangerous. Using trade rather than war to compete was touched on in the previous chapter, and I will return to it later in this chapter. Perhaps trade needs to benefit all parties enough to motivate each to put efforts into avoiding conflict.

Increasing economic opportunities for women

Wherever implemented, this has resulted in profound changes, including a decrease in birth rates, an increase in women's ability to provide for their children, and an increase in their status and authority in the family and in society as a whole. Widening the reach of this change holds promise for the future, and perhaps for prospects toward a more peaceful world.

Institutional nudging toward wise economic choices

Institutions can be structured to nudge individuals toward making healthful and future oriented choices (see Richard H. Thaler and Cass R. Sunstein's book *Nudge*).[22] These authors suggest, for example, that new employees be given the opportunity to opt out rather than needing to opt in to retirement savings plans. This results in a larger proportion of employees having savings, benefiting them in the long run. Much deliberate nudging takes the form of advertising, demonstrating that this tool can be used to further well-being, or for other purposes entirely.

Tweaking the business model

Businesses can be brought more into alignment with human biology and psychology. Harvard Law Professor Yochai Benkler in *The Penguin and the Leviathan*,[23] borrowing from evolutionary biology and neuroscience, argues that the notion of economic gain as the sole motivator of human behavior is a leap of faith based on accepting Hobbesian philosophy combined with a narrow interpretation of Adam Smith's work. Benkler sees material gain (often referred to as "the bottom line") as only one of the several motivations that drive us. A second motivation is empathy combined with caring for others, and a third is concern with fairness. Economist Elinor Ostrom's research in this area demonstrates that using money incentives alone "crowds out" other motives that contribute to getting jobs done collaboratively and efficiently. For some tasks, she argues, trust makes more of a difference than costly incentives, penalties, and subsidies.[24]

The basic idea is that the business model of the past few decades is inconsistent with what we know about human biology and psychology. This is connected to reciprocity (see Chapter 5). In their interdisciplinary work utilizing field and laboratory research from biology, anthropology, sociology, economics, and social psychology,

Herbert Gintis and colleagues review the results of extensive research, concluding that neither biology nor culture alone could have
yielded the complicated mix of human motives and means that define
us.[25] And this outcome would not have resulted from selfish, "*Homo
economicus*" motives alone.

Like Benkler and others, they demonstrate the importance of
multiple motivations and apply this to today's world of business and
leadership. Along the same line, Alan Fiske describes and classifies
human exchanges, illustrating the complexity of economic relationships and their roots in several motives.[26] This current understanding,
I think, emphasizes the value of the broad understanding that economic relationships are embedded in social relationships, as described by anthropologist Marshall Sahlins decades ago.

Benkler's research analyzes Internet use and reciprocity exhibited
on free public sites. Site participation is based on interest, desire to
demonstrate knowledge or competence, and pleasure in interacting
with others who share similar passions. Given recent disputes regarding freedom and restrictions on publications, this could change, but
at the moment, networking is a powerful tool for collaboration, and
Benkler's research continues.[27]

He concludes that corporations that have succeeded over the
long term recognize and incorporate motives other than the bottom
line into their way of doing business. Unwillingness to recognize anything but material motivation, he suggests, not only encouraged
CEOs in recent decades to emphasize short-term gain for their companies but also resulted in a form of self-selection. With this, individuals drawn to become CEOs in that business environment were often those who are driven by personal gain alone. This may have contributed to financial meltdowns.

In contrast, he cites Toyota's bottom-up (as opposed to top-
down) management style as part of its success and viability through
several economic downturns. This organizational model included union workers on problem-solving teams and encouraged innovation

during lunchtime brainstorming meetings. The company used similar teamwork ideas with suppliers. Treatment of employees and partners as human beings with diverse motives and talents resulted in more productive employees, improved products, positive relationships with suppliers, and greater business longevity.[28]

Viewing economic gain as the only goal of business, then, is short-sighted. Increasingly economists, philosophers, and others are becoming open to other ways of thinking about reciprocal human exchanges. Evolutionary sciences and information sharing through the Internet are helping to reframe incentives for collaboration. In the real world, contributing to a project gives people satisfaction and a sense of having accomplished something worthwhile. And it boosts trust and a contributor's reputation, important to all humans. Cooperation and social living require trust among group members; this is critical to self-esteem and to economic productivity.

3.   Reframe Political Institutions and Ideology.

We regularly fail to use evolution's gift of empathy in international relations. Instead, nation-states, like individuals and smaller groups, often emphasize historical conflicts and resentments rather than seeking common ground on which to build a workable future. This tribalistic thinking reduces the chances (and those of coming generations) of having a future at all. Recall that the institution of war— tribalism writ large—was enabled by the rebirth and spread of hierarchy (inequality). If we want to survive as a species, we need to get beyond our past histories.

Substituting win-win for win-lose political strategies

Robert Wright and numerous others have described *nonzero sum* or *win-win* solutions to problems.[29] *Zero-sum* or *win-lose* strategies are interactions or competitions in which one party wins and the other loses. Win-win strategies, in contrast, result in both parties receiving benefits.

Experimental work and development of interactive computer programs that simulate natural selection demonstrate that win-win strategies work better in the long run than win-lose strategies. The research of Martin A. Nowak and other mathematicians has demonstrated the survival value of altruism, as expressed in generosity and cooperativeness, and reciprocity related to a basic sense of fairness.[30] *Financial Times* foreign affairs columnist Gideon Rachman outlines a number of current global problems that would be solvable with non-zero-sum, win-win strategies. These outcomes would benefit all major powers and our species as a whole.[31] Such a strategy offers great promise for moving beyond tribalism.

One example of consequences of a win-lose strategy is the United States acting as global police. In a 2011 *New York Times* blog, Robert Wright suggests that security strategies emphasizing this stance while not engaging serious international collaboration resulted in a growing worldwide reputation of the United States as "global bully." It seems to have increased terrorist responses in a self-perpetuating vicious circle, a kind of inter-tribal revenge. This expression of tribalism blinds policy-makers and citizens to how the rest of the world sees this country, contributing to further destructiveness. Instead of promoting economic and political cooperation, we often get stuck in a win-lose, or perhaps more accurately, a lose-lose game. Many are horrified by events around the world, but few have a clear vision or strategy of what might be done.

Moving toward global governance

Wright and others who are looking for solutions to common problems are recognizing that only if we view various security threats as part of a worldwide issue requiring collective action can we design strategies that could begin to break the cycle of hatred and revenge. He states, "Once everybody is in the same boat, either they learn how to get along or very bad things happen. ... [Without this], there is a chance of chaos on an unprecedented scale."[32] A 2014 report from the World Economic Forum makes the same point, warning of the increasing probability for major disaster unless global solutions can be applied.[33] So it seems clear that we humans need a new framework for thinking about our collective future. And it seems that win-win strategies will be critical to its effectiveness.

These are not new ideas; global governance was the basis for organizations such as the World Federalist Movement, which emerged between 1937 and 1947 in Europe as local groups advocating increased world unity formed and merged. At first it advocated Euro-American-based governance. Its supporters now advocate the establishment of a global federalist system. The League of Nations and the United Nations were also organized with global peacemaking in mind.

Recognizing that the world is changing dramatically and that domination by the United States is temporary is essential for building a viable future. The recent trend of legislators to second-guess voters and laws and to obstruct rather that govern has paralyzed the ability to solve public problems. I sometimes wonder if jealousies and hatreds expressed readily are a last gasp, a final protest against loss of dominance in the world.

Existing but limited environmental, trade, and weapon agreements are places to start. Collaborating in these areas would also enable sharing the cost of international policing or security. The European Union (EU) is another start, imperfect of course, but nations within it are not fighting each other.

In the section on tribalism and war in the last chapter, I described historian Ian Morris's hope that competition through war could be replaced by economic competition. But he also acknowledges that conflicts could as easily "flip into counterproductive war on a scale to dwarf anything the world has seen before. Either way, the next fifty years will be the most important in human history."[34] I am as uncertain as Morris of the future. The better angels have not yet won the battle for human hearts and minds. I only hope that the notion that we are progressing toward peace will not indicate to anyone that we can be complacent about our future.

Constructing, executing, and enforcing laws that support justice

This is critical for government that aims and claims to be by the people and for the people. Fairness in formulating and applying legal guidelines for behavior, combined with training in administration of policies, can make a large difference to real-world violence.

Archeologist Lawrence H. Keeley described a kind of natural experiment that illustrates this point, contrasting settlement of the Canadian and the American West.[35] In Canada, well-trained Mounties administered justice even-handedly, treating infractions by indigenous populations and European immigrants the same, while settlement of the American West was haphazard and uneven. Indigenous societies were similar, the immigrant European-American people were similar, but the consequences of westward expansion were quite different. Perhaps other differences were at work also, but the contrast is clear: Canadian settlement happened relatively peacefully, while settlement of United States territory was often violent.

We see similar problems today with administration of justice across different populations within our society. As I was completing final revisions to this chapter, a tragedy was unfolding in Ferguson, Missouri, part of the St. Louis metropolitan community. The combination of events beginning with the August 9, 2014, confrontation between the police and Michael Brown, the still-controversial specifics of the interactions and witness stories, the killing itself with six shots, leaving the young man's body exposed on the ground for several hours, and the subsequent military presence would not have happened in a middle-class white community. And this incident was only one of similar events elsewhere in the U.S. in recent years.

These events in Ferguson illustrate and reinforce points made by legal scholar Michele Anderson, author of *The New Jim Crow*. She documents and describes how men of color are targeted by law enforcement for small drug crimes, which occur with the same frequen-

cy among middle class white men but have markedly different consequences, often no consequences at all from the legal system for the
latter category. Yet many young African-American men become part
of the huge prison population, thereafter facing restrictions on their
ability to support themselves or their families, obtain food, housing,
or employment; in addition, voting and other forms of participation
in the community are curtailed. In this situation, there are no options
available; there is often no way out if there has been an accusation
and arrest, even when the arrest has been shown to have no foundation.[36]

Anthropologist Alice Goffman describes the plight of a particular
cohort of African-American men in *On the Run*, (in press), reaching
similar conclusions from her years of participant observation; her
book was reviewed and is just being published.[37]

Current American society suffers under the significant influence
and power of well-funded individuals and lobbyists in the workings
of its government, whether in financing political campaigns or own-
ing and influencing media. The Citizens United court decision to
treat corporations as persons and money as speech in financing political campaigns[38] was another step toward disabling its functioning as
a democratic republic. For win-win outcomes in global or national
governance to be realized, they must be coupled with justice that is
administered evenhandedly. Anything less is a recipe for disaster over
the long haul.

Roy A. Rappaport's view of religious ritual as a tool for self-
regulation and self-organization is relevant here. Speaking of today's
world, he argues that all human regulatory hierarchies (including central governments) depend on individuals' perceptions that they are
working fairly well as defined by social norms. If institutions operate
badly and this becomes apparent to members of society, authority
will erode. He writes: "if authorities wish to maintain their sanctity,
which is to say their legitimacy, ... they must be sure that those regu-

latory structures remain in reasonable working order and are reasonably responsive to those subject to them."

Continuing, he argues that authority based on a "monetary epis-
temology" (profit is everything) is not viable in the long run.[39] Frans
de Waal makes a similar point, observing that fairness and justice are
essential if we want to live in a reasonably harmonious society. This
requires a certain level of trust among people belonging to it. In his
view, "one can't expect high levels of trust in a society with huge income disparities, huge insecurities, and a disenfranchised underclass."
Level of trust in a society also correlates with happiness; to support
this, de Waal cites experiments by Paul Zak and others.[40] This brings
us to the final category of strategies.

Reducing Extreme Inequality (Hierarchy)

Extreme differences in economic and political clout violate people's
sense of fairness and disrupt the balance that social living requires.
Because of rapid communication, people around the globe are aware
of this violation; the imbalance is no longer easily hidden. Increasing
the standard of living for those living in poverty may be critical for
moving forward in the United States and in the world as a whole.
Philosopher Benoît Dubreuil points out that people expect and tolerate a degree of income inequality and even are prepared for some un-
fair treatment, but acceptance of extreme differences has its limits.[41]
Without a sense of empowerment and the ability to work toward a
better life, individuals feel (and are) helpless, and this adversely affects their physical and mental health, family life, productivity of
work, confidence, and just about all else that makes us human.

Biologist and naturalist Geerat Vermeij offers this bit of biological realism for the theme of this section: "We are, and presumably
will remain, made of organic matter, and we live because we metabo-
lize; and all of this depends on the ready availability of life's essen-

tials. To deny this, it seems to me, is to engage in economic alche-my."[42]

These are not new ideas. Adam Smith recognized that good wag-es for laborers encourage hard work, decent health, cheerfulness, and diligence; his conclusions came from comparing prevailing wages and worker sentiment in England with those in Scotland during his life-time. He noted also that when profits are put back into industry, workers are encouraged, while the use of profits for personal luxuries and opulent dwellings has the opposite effect on workers, who are sensitive to issues of justice (fair play) by an employer. He warned the public to be wary of any proposal for change arising from the class of the very wealthy because that group's interests are biased by their so-cial position. He noted that profits were "highest in the countries ... going fastest to ruin."[43]

Repeatedly, he made this point in *The Wealth of Nations*, writing of the caution with which policy makers need to view this group of people. Economist Paul Krugman makes a similar point in a 2012 article regarding proposals to balance the U.S. budget.[44] Jeffrey Sachs, whose views are discussed in the next section, also recognizes these often-neglected contributions of Adam Smith.

I next note parallels between the United States today and Great Britain during the period of mercantilism which Adam Smith ana-lysed. Then, I review social mobility in today's United States, noting what it might take to improve chances for individuals and families to move forward, pursue education, contribute to society, and thereby increase health and well-being.

Past Mercantilism and Present Corporatocracy

These two institutions must have been cut from the same cloth. The Oxford dictionaries define historical mercantilism as "the economic theory that trade generates wealth and is stimulated by the accumula-tion of profitable balances, which a government should encourage by means of protectionism."[45] Jeffrey Sachs describes a twenty-first-century version of this in which a small, wealthy economic elite influences not only a single country but also governments and media around the world in what he calls a world *corporatocracy*.[46] In this current version that Adam Smith would hardly recognize as capitalism, influence is concentrated in the hands of a few, as it was during his years of writing about mercantilism.

Adam Smith's amazing scholarship extended to a lengthy discussion of England's empire building. He explained how the English government borrowed from rich merchants (further enriching that class), who subsequently squandered their wealth on luxuries and pageantry rather than putting it into production and jobs. The government became overconfident in the wealthy merchants, who themselves were overconfident about governmental support of their ventures. This reduced the merchants' motivation to save and invest, thereby increasing government debt. During wars to expand the empire, more resources were squandered, and on it went until England was forced to borrow from other nations.[47] I expect that executives of government-subsidized corporations and institutions in the United States and elsewhere might cringe to hear that this analysis came from the same person who spoke of the market's invisible hand.

And here we are today, with surcharges often added to bills for basic services so that customers further subsidize companies that keep their disproportionately high profits. Individual taxpayers rather than entrepreneurs take the risk when large, highly profitable corporations use tax-increment financing instead of investing their own profits back into production, as recommended by Smith. Often enough, tax-financed projects are not completed, and individual taxpayers (real persons) who supported them receive no benefit from their investment. In numerous other ways in the United States today, political and economic decisions are resulting in redistribution of income from poorer to wealthier citizens. Yet we know that people react negatively to perceived unfairness. As psychiatrist Leon McGahee points out, "when income inequality becomes endemic in a society, its members become unhappy and distrustful of each other," and this affects how society functions as a whole.[48]

The current American corporate system, then, receives considerable governmental support (entitlements) through bailouts and tax relief to an extent not seen since the gilded age, more than a century ago. It resembles the past British mercantilistic system described by Adam Smith far more than it resembles his proposal for a "free market" economy. In his time, state-supported merchants were attempting to decrease competition and raise funds for themselves, as are many corporacrats today.

Social Mobility

Evidence for growing rigidity of class differences in the United States comes from comparisons of past and present economic class mobility and educational opportunity and cost. Access to quality education is an important means of facilitating class mobility. In reality, there was more student aid, proportionately, in the 1940s and 1950s than there is for today's students. Current studies of math and reading scores show a stronger relationship between educational success and socioeconomic class than between education and race. Childhood poverty has a large impact on school success, regardless of ethnicity.

Another means of potentially tweaking social mobility to increase or decrease inequality is through changes in the tax structure and in other government-managed economic programs. In the United States today, the federal and some state legislatures are using every means available to directly or indirectly reduce the progressiveness of taxation, reduce the safety net for people in poverty, and keep the minimum wage at a level that does not allow families to afford a place to live. Examples of tax policies include reduced income tax rates for the wealthy, lower tax rates on investments than on wages, and increased sales taxes that result in a greater relative burden for all but the top earners.

These add insult to other attempts to reduce mobility such as passing laws that restrict access to voting, insisting on exclusively local funding for schools in poor communities, and reducing early childhood programs despite their proven success. All of these measures, however verbally justified, have the effect of increasing income inequality while decreasing opportunities for moving forward by even the most diligent individuals growing up in poverty.

Below is a list of documented areas in which inequality of opportunity creates obstacles to individuals and families attempting to rise above poverty or near-poverty in recent decades.

- Housing, food, energy
- Health and medical care
- Early childhood, elementary, and secondary education
- Income distribution
- Taxation
- Participation in decision-making
- Administration of justice, including policing, courts, sentencing

Scholars and leaders representing diverse areas recognize the risks in allowing these inequalities to persist and grow. Jeffrey Sachs, Senator Elizabeth Warren, Frans de Waal, Pope Francis, Paul Krugman, and others see extreme wealth and marked power asymmetries as contrary to the functioning of democratic and ethical institutions. Biologist E.O. Wilson notes the significance of growing inequality for our species as a whole. He too sees justice and fairness as critical to human well-being, while wondering whether the United States can manage such a transition, given the extent to which the problem has grown.

One could argue that equality of opportunity to pursue quality education, decent housing, and employment that provides a living wage, would also minimize the effects of tribalism on human lives. Strong support for public education, decent and affordable housing, a

clear separation of church and state, and access to other cultural institutions should minimize effects of group biases.

Privilege and Kinship

As described above, the United States today features the most extreme inequality of wealth and power among developed countries of
the world. Especially since the beginning of the Great Recession, in
2007, inequality has grown and social classes in the United States
have become increasingly rigid. I focus next on the role of education
in social mobility, and the attitudes and values associated with inequality.

One impetus for colonial settlement of the New World in the
seventeenth century was to break the ties of a kinship-based aristocracy. The emerging democratically organized republic emphasized the
ballot box (however flawed and noninclusive of women, slaves, and
indigenous people), and the idea that people would enjoy new opportunities without the entrenched hereditary aristocracies of the past.
Another aim of the founders of the United States was to ensure liberty, freedom from domination and exploitation by small groups of
powerful people supported by the close connection between governmental and religious authority.

This is why the framers of the Constitution and the Bill of Rights
included multiple safeguards to balance sources of authority—with
legislative, executive, and judiciary branches of government—and to
separate church and state. Public education was not mandated by the
Constitution, but state legislatures realized in early years that free
public education was an important means for enabling the democratic form of government to function effectively.

I find it ironic that the trend today away from public education
and toward greater economic disparity is fueling the growth of a new
hereditary aristocracy, with the same drawbacks that many colonists
fought against in the first place. Kinship, in the form of indirect nepotism, is regaining importance as an organizing principle, much like

the ancient civilizations following the birth of social inequality. The
increasing costs of opportunity and its relationship to education,
transportation, housing, and work supports entrenched hierarchy.
These important aspects of life are often tied to one's neighborhood
— and to whether one has a neighborhood at all. Their effects begin
at birth.

The Role of Education

Education was for many years an important means of social mobility
for Americans. Despite the often-stated view that any worthy student
who wants to can attend college, this has been eroded in recent years.
The tool of free, quality public education for all may be the most important feature of any society trying to function according to democratic principles. It is particularly critical today, in a world where scientific knowledge and literacy matter. Public education, however, has
been devalued and defunded in recent decades.

The wealthy often turn to private schools as public schools receive less support and as teachers have increasing paperwork loads,
fewer benefits, and less support and respect. Compounding these issues, access to safe and adequate homes, healthful food, and good
affordable health care is widely different in terms of socioeconomic
class.[49] These factors have demonstrable effects on a child's life, ability to learn, and opportunities.

Psychologists Stanley Greenspan and Stuart Shanker stress the
importance of meeting individual developmental needs and requirements for health and well-being, for enabling development of reflective and critical thinking in children. My personal experience working
with homeless children and others from impoverished families
opened my eyes to the enormity of the obstacles that hardship imposes on young children and their families. From a developmental
point of view, our future depends on how well and fairly we treat individuals, particularly children.[50] Economic opportunities also reduce

the likelihood of violent conflict and increase everyone's chances for a sustainable future.

The Attitude of Entitlement

From discourse and in the press, class membership seems often to be explained in terms of innate differences between people, as though it were natural for those with a large share of resources and power to be where they are, as though they arrived there only because of their superior behaviors or hard work. Meanwhile, those at the bottom may be accused of wanting lives based on government handouts, such as food stamps.

Government-based options for the wealthy include numerous tax shelters and loopholes, "corporate welfare" subsidies, reduced penalties for infractions of regulations that protect communities, and bankruptcy benefits and tax increment financing for wealthy corporations. Bankers and executives known to have promoted illegal practices receive bonuses and bailouts. Companies that fail to pay living wages get indirect governmental support when their employees qualify for low-income assistance *because* of their low wages.

These programs become subsidies for privileged individuals and corporations, allowing them to reap advantages from paying low wages. The consequences of policies that benefit the wealthiest among us have significant ill effects on the common good. And the wealthy beneficiaries of these practices do not receive the public ire that is heaped onto so-called "welfare cheats" and even union members attempting to maintain hard-earned salaries and benefits.

Additionally, the U.S. legal system offers advantage to lawbreakers who can afford to hire the most successful (and expensive) attorneys, and white-collar offenders receive the least onerous penalties even for crimes that cost their victims millions of dollars. Yet the poor, and especially nonwhite citizens, are too often arrested for little or no cause, or languish in prison for lesser crimes, as described by Michele Anderson and others and summarized above.

The "attitude of entitlement" often attributed to the poor, then, has in reality become endemic among some members of the wealthy class. To move forward, individual citizens and members of the press must recognize and publicize the negative effects of these practices and work toward more equitable and appropriate use of public resources.

Divide and Conquer

In Chapter 8, I suggested that *classism* can be considered a form of tribalism. We saw in Chapter 5 that class society originated following the development of food production, food storage, and accumulation of wealth. Human societies have struggled with it since that time.

The practices and attitudes described in the previous section support the notion of classism as a variety of tribalism. Other forms of modern tribalism that engage the emotions often mask the degree of class-based tribalism, whose basis is extreme economic and political inequality. Whether this masking is intentional or unintended, it functions as an effective divide-and-conquer strategy. This strategy is familiar to historians, who can vouch for its effectiveness in expanding empires while keeping small cultural groups opposing each other rather than joining together to work against an oppressive regime.

Extreme hierarchy abets tribalism along many fronts. With greater inequality of resources, top resource holders can wield the greatest power and influence on public policy. This can happen directly or indirectly. It can be seen when governments run and control business, as happens in totalitarian societies, and it can be seen in democratically organized societies when owners of great wealth have enough control of resources to disproportionately influence government and public opinion. In the latter, it can happen through funding of candidates for political positions, gerrymandering of voting districts, or ownership and control of media. This is increasingly the case in the United States in the early decades of the twenty-first century. The Supreme Court decision of 2010, Citizens United, gave a hefty boost to this influence, as described above.

In these ways, individuals and corporations can encourage tribalistic attitudes and manipulate related emotions to influence people. When this happens, democratic ideals may get lip service, but they are not realized in policy or practice. Former Secretary of Labor and current professor of public policy Robert Reich states this in a Huffington Post blog from January 19, 2014:[51]

> Unequal political power is the endgame of widening inequality—its most noxious and nefarious consequence, and the most fundamental threat to our democracy. Big money has now all but engulfed Washington and many state capitals—drowning out the voices of average Americans, filling the campaign chests of candidates who will do their bidding, financing attacks on organized labor, and bankrolling a vast empire of right-wing think-tanks and publicists that fill the airwaves with half-truths and distortions.

Moving beyond other forms of tribalism can become more difficult as societies develop extreme income inequality. Tribalistic attitudes held by ethnic or sectarian religious groups within a large, complex society are bound to be confounded when combined with overlapping socioeconomic classes: An individual's loyalty can be divided between class and ethnicity, and the effects can be powerful. Emphasizing divisions of race, religion, ethnicity, or even abortion rights, breeds fear around one or more of these issues. The fear easily distracts citizens from debating or protesting larger, far-reaching changes in policy or law. I sense that the encouragement of negative sentiment against immigrants may be an ongoing example of this tactic. Tribalistic fear of "others" can discourage individuals without power from joining those in similar situations to work toward common goals that could increase opportunities for all.

If Adam Smith were alive today, he would likely be appalled to see the extent to which his carefully reasoned thinking has been distorted and misused to manipulate public opinion and justify the huge economic and opportunity gaps between the rich and the poor in current American society. He argued specifically against such a gap in his time, and he decried the use of fear to manipulate public opinion (see Chapter 8).

Educated citizens are more likely to have the tools to recognize and not be unduly influenced by clever strategies and distortions such as those described here. But as public education gets less support, these tools are being eroded. Without truly democratic, adequately funded institutions that offer opportunities for all citizens, the playing field is not even, and the game is not fair. From extremes of unfairness, the seeds of tribalism grow.

We must also be aware of and work to avoid the dangers of a global economic elite, which, as outlined by business journalist Chrystia Freeland, shares with the U.S. elite a notion of entitlement and superiority.[52] Anthropologist Christopher Boehm points also to extreme wealth differences as a major driver of international conflict. In speaking of the free-rider (or freeloader) problem, he introduces the idea of "secondary free riders" who manage to get others to indirectly pay the cost of their free riding, so that they are not easily exposed or punished. Fitting examples would be those banking and financial industry executives who received large bonuses after they betrayed the public trust.

Since we were hunter-gatherers, people have been dealing with individual freeloaders. Might we call the current system one of *institutional freeloading*? There are measures that would discourage these inequalities and minimize the effects of economic and class tribalism and institutional freeloading. I next suggest that balance is as critical to achieving this. It is as important to the healthy functioning of societies as it is to living organisms.

Strategies for Restoring Balance

Restoring balance between the poles of competition and cooperation can further our chances of moving beyond tribalism. In almost every understanding of biological and social organisms, balance or homeostasis is important. Any interacting system can become imbalanced. The extremes of selfishness, altruism, competitiveness, adaptedness, and even adaptability can get an organism or an institution into trouble. Unfettered capitalism, unfettered communism, unfettered power, or unfettered religious sectarianism do not make for a viable society in the long run. Effective democratic institutions, with built-in restraints provided by regulation and balance of power, hold the best promise for improving human well-being.

We can compare this to the need for balance within an organism. This is achieved by mechanisms that regulate temperature, metabolic rate, concentration and proportion of electrolytes, growth and death of different cell types in the blood, bone marrow, and other organs. Similarly, the concentration and fluctuation of neurochemicals and hormones that respond to the organism's environment and influence its behaviors, in most cases achieving balance here. When imbalance occurs, when concentrations reach an abnormal or extreme level, a healthy organism responds by restoring balance. Disease or disorder results when self-regulating, homeostatic mechanisms fail.

Geerat Vermeij notes that natural selection has produced biological systems that work through central control, and others that use diffuse control. He compares centrally organized societies and economies to organisms with brains. Societies with economies organized by the kind of diffuse, "invisible hand" of the marketplace that Smith described with the assumption of fair competition and no preferential treatment for interest groups, are comparable to diffusely controlled organisms in the early phases of their evolution. In an open environment with plenty of resources, diffuse control can work.

But as we approach the limits of the earth's capacity, and as we reach a shift in capitalism to huge international corporations, a shift to central control may be necessary unless other means of curbing rigidity and promoting flexible solutions can be found. Vermeij summarizes it this way: "Natural selection is a process in which agencies of destruction and opportunity sort among alternatives according to how well those alternatives work ..."[53] This resembles Rappaport's notion of a dynamic homeostasis in the form of ritual with built-in mechanisms that respond to changing conditions.

Balance for us conflicted, bipolar apes encompasses personal, cognitive, emotional, economic, and political institutions. Perhaps to function well, human societies require enough competition to provide incentives for solving problems, balanced by enough generosity and cooperativeness of individuals to forego some individual desires for benefit to the community, the whole. This balance resembles Aristotle's notion of pursuing the *golden mean.*

International economist Jeffrey Sachs compares Aristotle to Buddha, his wise Asian counterpart, who also extolled a path that balances the extremes of individual and social needs, concerns for self and concerns for the whole, recognizing our dual tendencies and the need for compassion in human affairs.[54] We can recognize that balance is also connected to multilevel selection, by which individual selection proceeds through competition and kin or group selection proceeds by cooperation.

Finally, the need for balance can be seen in the contrasting human responses of impulsive or reflexive thinking and behavior (brain system 1) on the one hand, and reflective, thoughtful responses (brain system 2). Greene suggests a specific way these responses can be balanced. He advocates relying on our automatic setting (what feels right; individual conscience) when a dilemma involves one's personal interest as opposed to that of another person or group. When a dilemma is controversial, when groups have opposing stances on issues, one's conscience is unreliable and solutions require careful reflection about possible consequences. This reflection requires maintaining a healthy skepticism toward one's particular inclinations. This constitutes Greene's manual setting.[55]

Human evolution is an account of how we came to cooperate in new ways with the help of language-based culture, and capacities such as empathy and mind reading, while retaining a penchant for fairness that originated in mammalian morality. As we moved away from an egalitarian hunter-gatherer lifestyle to a more settled existence with larger populations and built-in inequalities, we retained a concern for fairness. The birth (and rebirth) of democratic ideas was an attempt to inject more fairness into state-based societies.

For democratic institutions to restore and maintain balance between the poles of competition and cooperation, they must be empowered to work democratically in real life, not just on paper. Complex societies, like complex biological organisms, need regulatory mechanisms to function in a balanced way. In our world today, this is sorely lacking.

Balance can happen when mixed human motivations are recognized and valued. Our behaviors, responses to challenges, transactions with others, and the incentives that move us are related to how our brains make sense of the world. This perspective is supported by converging research from the biological and social sciences (analyses summarized above), and insights from the humanities. The notion of different types of economic transactions fitting different kinds of relationships is in line also with Marshall Sahlins's original pairing of social distance with types of exchange (golden rule, silver rule, brass rule; see Chapter 7). These ideas about balance fit what we know of the complexities of human morality, today's political and economic forces, and our shared environment.

Totalitarianism (one might call it the opposite of balance) can emerge within any sociopolitical system that does not include limits to empowerment of particular groups. Such a group may be a social class, a specific political party, a branch of government, a corporation or collection of corporations, or any other group that gains control over material or personal resources that people need. Our human ability to deceive with words, and to be deceived by them, enables propaganda. With this, public opinion can, for a while, be manipulated to work against the public interest. Unless people are educated in critical thinking and in how to understand and evaluate evidence, the emergence of some form of totalitarian governance can easily become a reality.

In classical economic theory as outlined by Adam Smith, a market economy, with appropriate limitations, is designed to provide a win-win outcome over the long term. But in today's world, the largest and most profitable business transactions are not limited by the fairness ethic that he observed and advocated. As early as the mid-twentieth century, President Dwight D. Eisenhower recognized and named the vast military-industrial complex as an entity, warning Americans about the "potential for the rise of misplaced power" and the importance of "an alert and knowledgeable citizenry" to curb the ability of money to influence even research and scientific policy.[56]

His hopes for a peaceful, harmonious society for all citizens of the world were idealistic, but in stating this goal, he understood that we had a long way to go and that we were an imperfect society. In his farewell speech as president, he recommended that we look at our own institutions critically and be skeptical of our motives and the ease by which we can be diverted by the influences of powerful people and institutions. Sometimes we forget these warnings given by a president representing the Republican Party of his time.

In the twenty-first century, we have seen that a wealthier and smaller international elite influences governments and media of countries around the world; this elite forms the *corporatocracy* that Jeffrey Sachs[57] and Chrystia Freeland[58] describe from their different perspectives. In this completely revised version of capitalism, influence is concentrated rather than distributed into the small farms and businesses that Adam Smith would have recognized. Sachs describes the sequence of events that gave rise to this form of governance, which blurs the boundary between economic and political institutions.

Increasing inequality and greater social distance (decreasing balance) foster the hardening of social classes and decrease the health of democratic institutions. Tribalistic thinking is rigid thinking that relies on our human weaknesses, but often feels comfortable in times of uncertainty. But to be effective, democracy requires flexibility of thinking and openness to ideas from persons with different motivations, values, and points of view. A vibrant democracy has a heterogeneous population empowered by knowledge of how the world works, the science behind it, and where to turn to work out solutions to complex problems.

Frans de Waal calls his adopted country, the United States, a winner-take-all society whose differences in educational opportunities for rich and poor are especially striking to him, a native of the Netherlands, which emphasizes equality of opportunity. As a primatologist, he reminds us that other primates are sensitive to fairness and even to a "connection between effort and reward."[59] Mitigating extreme differences of wealth, power, and privilege can help to provide the balance we need. It is the degree of hierarchy—the extreme inequality—that provokes a strong sense of unfairness and is, therefore, a danger to a society.

The value of diverse talents and perspectives for dealing with a rapidly changing world can only be reaped when institutions are designed to enable individuals to make headway toward goals. Extreme differences in life chances adversely influence human health, well-being, level of trust, and violence. These influence one's ability to pursue those values specified in the preamble to the Declaration of Independence as "Life, Liberty, and the pursuit of Happiness." That such factors matter is evident in comparisons among nations and among individual states.

Human cooperativeness reflects our complex human motives, including our need to trust others. Our institutions work more effectively when they are based on the mixture of motivations that influence behaviors. Understanding the critical role of fairness and the negative impact of high income disparities on performance, health, and morale is important for achieving balance and preparing for a sustainable future.

Community participation is higher when income is more equally distributed. Policies to balance inequalities can help communities govern themselves by unleashing alternative human motives and enabling local problem solving, while preventing social breakdown. Balance is critical to preserving social order and harmony. The now-outdated assumption, institutionalized during the Ronald Reagan era, that we are driven by material self-interest alone, is simply not supported by evidence. Gintis and others predict that nations with extreme inequality will turn out not to be viable in the highly interdependent and global environment that is emerging.[60]

Communication is critical to cooperation. Language gave *Homo sapiens* a significant advantage over other animals. Edward Glaeser proposes that cities have become keys to our future as hubs of communication, economics, and population.[61] These hubs, in concentrating creative resources, can influence public health initiatives, generate innovative ideas, and organize planned growth that can enable a greener environment. He agrees with other experts that digital media can enhance our ability to collaborate on a large scale to solve problems if we choose to use them that way. On another hopeful note, women in the United States Senate are beginning to develop new strategies for communication and conciliation in their efforts to promote peace.[62]

How might we achieve greater balance so that we have a chance to succeed at moving beyond tribalism? Jeffrey Sachs offers a synthesis, showing how multiple human motivations can be tapped to make positive changes. In recognizing that our current problems are interconnected and worldwide in scope, he calls for a global approach to finding solutions, while offering particular suggestions for the United States, in which changes to education are critical.

He describes the historical transition "from decades of consensus and high achievement to an era of deep division and growing crisis."[63] Sachs understands our current ills to have economic, political, social, and psychological components, outlining each in *The Price of Civilization*. He identifies an economic triple bottom line in which efficiency, fairness, and sustainability are components. This requires governmental intervention at times of crisis to prevent disasters associated with the inevitable cyclical downturns, reinstating balance, and using scientific knowledge to construct plans for preventing and mitigating crises.

Sachs views the current divisiveness and unwillingness of factions to cooperate as major obstacles to achieving the needed balance, attributing this partly to the confusion of many Americans. Because decision making is driven by powerful corporate interests, particularly those representing energy and the media, news and even scientific knowledge become distorted, and average citizens do not hear or participate in meaningful deliberation. This situation results in people favoring and accepting policies that go against their best interests. Political spin has resulted in policies that benefit the wealthy, help the middle class barely if at all, and take from the poor what few resources they have. As most of us realize, the divisions are seriously interfering with both decision making and governing.[64]

Yet he also notes considerable consensus on core values, such as the need to take care of those unable to care for themselves and the right of individuals to be treated fairly in matters of law. But these core values are often hidden in masses of disinformation and emphases on irrelevant issues that are perpetuated by politicians and the media. Issues of trust and entitlement enter here also. The message often conveyed is that the poor could move out of poverty if only they wanted to and were willing to make the effort. In this view, people who are poor are undeserving, rather than deserving help.

Sachs describes seven "habits," or guidelines, for a government that would be based on the core values, those that we share.[65] All of these require long-term planning. And all have to do with achieving balance between cooperation and competition. He summarizes his point of view as follows:

> [The market ...] must be complemented with government institutions that accomplish three things: provide public goods such as infrastructure, scientific research, and market regulation; ensure the basic fairness of income distribution and long-term help for the poor to escape from poverty; and promote sustainability of the earth's fragile resources for the benefit of future generations.[66]

The overall thrust of his guidelines is to highlight public management as basic to the effective and efficient working of a complex society and to achieve a measure of balance that is now sorely lacking. A corporatocracy with different goals cannot achieve it. We have seen that a similar role for government was recognized by Adam Smith even in the eighteenth century.

Sachs suggests that a third political party might provide the best avenue for achieving these changes, which are about restoring competence and honesty to government, requiring combined economic and political reform. He places hope in the millennial generation, whose members he thinks understand, accept, and possess the diversity, the lack of vested interest, and the need to make major changes. They represent the future; they will be living in the world their elders have bequeathed them.

Steven Pinker makes a related point. He describes how governments set up to be democratic can fail and, as failed democracies, become autocracies. He uses the word *anocracy* to characterize inefficient and ineffective new states in the third world. Given this description, I wonder sometimes if our United States democracy is in danger of transforming itself into anocracy. Pinker suggests that future peace for our species must be based on three legs: democracy, openness to a global economy, and international organization that includes a key role for peacekeeping.[67]

Economist Jeremy Rifkin offers technological fixes for achieving balance that involve decentralization for greater efficiency in some areas. Simplified, his recommendations include (1) shifting to renewable energy, (2) modifying buildings to collect and transfer green power, (3) providing energy storage in existing local buildings and infrastructure, (4) developing continental interactive power grids and energy sharing to be modeled after the Internet, and (5) transitioning to electric plug-in and fuel cell vehicles using these grids. The "smart grid" is critical to this distributed economy in its capacity to coordinate various green energies. He compares it to nature and ties it to a network-based worldview, which encompasses a change in human priorities. This collaborative venture would depend on open communication and compatible educational and business values similar to those of Benkler and Sachs, which similarly emphasize our place in the biosphere.

Looking at insights and research conclusions from several disciplines, I see benefits from combining decentralization and centralization. Decentralization would emphasize use of local resources and green energy wherever possible. Centralization would emphasize collaboration and cooperation for effective and efficient global governance, water resources, prevention of illness, international guidelines for trade, pursuit of learning through education and research, and systems of justice.

Our highly social species dominates the earth through the capacities of our brains and our culture-language complex. This puts us in a unique position to use our biological legacy to engineer alternatives to violent conflict and prevent further devastation to the environment. As creatures of nature, we do not have unlimited reach into determining the future, but we do have a tremendous capacity to innovate, which brought us to our current situation.

Vermeij echoes the theme of balance in this statement: "If we could sever the link between prestige and material plenty, we humans could temper our collective use of resources without significantly compromising our standard of living."[68]

Finding Motivation to Apply Fixes

How can we possibly achieve these lofty goals and move beyond tribalism? Christopher Boehm offers several insights into uniting as a species.[69] He suggests that we merge the generosity and the refusal of individuals to be bullied (gleaned from our hunter-gatherer past) with effective global governance. To accomplish that, he thinks we may need to define a common enemy of some sort, while recognizing that it could take a major catastrophe to provide the degree of motivation needed to work toward a common goal. He offers several scenarios that might compel people to act.

Perhaps we could make that enemy a common, already existing threat that we face right now. Short of a catastrophic single disaster, might we redefine our enemy as worldwide environmental degradation? Could this be enough to push us to make plans, to stop bickering and destroying each other, and to work collectively?

The first step would have to be widespread acceptance that we have a real problem on our hands. The converging scientific consensus is that the human species has wrought huge changes to our atmosphere, oceans, and living organisms. In addition, these changes are not only progressing with time, but are interacting to increase the speed of the process. We are on the edge right now, pushing the limits of our sources of life, health, and well-being, with little wiggle room. For the interested reader, Jonathan Foley outlines specific environmental processes, each with a boundary or limit of safety.[70]

Analyzing ongoing changes helps scientists identify tipping points and clarify conditions through which human life and livelihood are irreparably threatened. These changes are easier to envision now than even a few years ago as the increasing frequency of extreme climatic events has made the likelihood of environmental change evident to more people. Denial has become more difficult. Our collective enemy is real and threatens destruction of the very resources that made possible our becoming human in the first place.

Atmospheric scientist Ken Caldeira's 2012 summary of climate change includes a graph depicting the projected direction of five variables. Of these, global temperature, atmospheric carbon dioxide, sea level, and total biomass on the earth, are increasing. But the fifth variable, biodiversity, is on the decrease. So far, he explains, we have seen only the early consequences of these trends, frequent, unusual storm patterns fueled by atmospheric warming over land and the melting of ice and snow at the poles.[71]

Many people do not recognize the significance of reduced biodiversity (the fifth variable noted by Caldeira) when thinking about our planet's future. Geerat Vermeij points out that, in developing large swaths of the biosphere into resources for *Homo sapiens*, we have created many isolated, island-type habitats whose species lack the diversity that provides raw material for further evolution. Whenever environmental stresses become severe, regions for sourcing new foods, medicines, and materials will have disappeared unless we focus efforts into reconstructing larger tracts of wilderness.[72]

In earlier chapters, we saw that most of the major events in human prehistory and history were instigated by major environmental events. In contrast to earlier crises, this time around, major and rapid climate change is happening to a vastly larger human population. Our atmosphere, oceans, fresh water, and soil are already compromised, and we lack new territory for occupation.

E.O. Wilson agrees, stating: "We are an evolutionary chimera, living on intelligence steered by the demands of animal instinct. This is the reason we are mindlessly dismantling the biosphere and, with it, our own prospects for permanent existence."[73] We almost did become extinct at several points along our evolutionary history, but managed to avoid it those times, partly through luck. Only time will tell how long we will manage to survive as a species.

Perhaps in those earlier times, it was only those human groups that could cooperate, think outside the box, and practice flexible resourcefulness that survived those crises. Or they might simply have been lucky. Today, we are modifying the earth that nurtures us in ways that we may not be wise enough or have time enough to appreciate.

Naturalists are reaching a consensus that earth is undergoing its sixth major extinction event. Some geologists have suggested changing the name *Holocene* (our current geological epoch) to *Anthropocene* because so many changes have been due in large part to human activity. Given the conditions, any massive natural or military disaster would further press the limits and loosen our hold on planet Earth. We might well commit *anthropocide* (my word).

There can be danger in too much pessimism. When we lose hope for the future, we can lose motivation to work for change because it seems hopeless. Perhaps here, too, we need to strike a balance. Aristotle's golden mean makes sense in seeking a balanced attitude that can help us see a path forward while guiding us through our present struggles. Tiny steps by many persons can make a difference.

Another bright side is that today we possess scientific knowledge and powerful technological tools that give us a *chance* to turn things around, or to plan how to adjust to changes as they occur. Such a plan requires some sacrifices, difficult choice for people whose lives are not immediately on the line. Changing course will require motivation, will, self-control, willingness to accept unpleasant truths, changes in lifestyle, and putting aside our biases. Yet only we have the capacity to make such changes. Can we do it? A better question: Will we do it?

Since 2012, many other scientists, science writers, and, recently, business leaders have brought the environmental crisis into public focus, providing not only clear evidence for its significance today and for the future, but offering concrete steps to delay if not reverse some of the damage that we have done. One renowned scientist and business leader, Amory B. Lovins, writes of the forces, including media, that spread inaccurate and unsupported messages to the public that minimize climate change, while other countries advance forward to develop clean, innovative solutions that are already making a difference in those countries. In addition to improving climate they are improving their chance to be part of a healthful international community.[74]

Without institutions to support and motivation to embrace worldwide cooperation, we must face the probability of our own demise. We each must give up the notion that only our own culture, religion, economic system, world view, and technology is the right one. And this brings us back to the scourge of war, so often the outcome of rampant tribalism. War is relevant to any discussion of the future.

Whenever we use human skills and talents to destroy the natural resources that we depend on, we only hasten the end of our tenure on earth. We destroy natural selection's gift to our species, the gift of diversity, and we destroy lives of fellow humans. Since we are ephemeral creatures, here for such a miniscule portion of time, why work so hard to speed up our demise? Can armed conflict make sense when it begets more war and increases environmental devastation?

Melvin Konner reviews cross-cultural studies showing that scarcity and fear of scarcity continue to be good predictors of war, as first proposed by Thomas Malthus. Konner argues that the currently popular anti-Malthusian stance ignores the repeated prehistoric and historic changes in available resources, overpopulation, and associated human suffering and loss of hope. Even with the current slowing of population growth, as human material expectations increase around the world, ecological imbalances that are conducive to war will continue. Unless we change these conditions, war and suffering will continue, as the many "small wars" since World War II demonstrate.

Konner offers some hope, too, suggesting that, although war and violence may be part of who we are, they can be tackled using a strategy similar to that developed for combating major diseases, comparable threats to life.[75] Rather than giving up on conquering disease, we instead utilize as many preventive and treatment tools as we can muster. Konner advocates formation of a Center for Conflict Control analogous to the Centers for Disease Control and Prevention. This organization could monitor and deal with conflicts while they are still small, before they have metastasized (my phrase). Such an approach requires recognizing that conflict is endemic, while understanding that political barriers are crossed regularly when investigating and treating human disease.

The paradox is that we are creatures who top all others in our capacity for behavioral flexibility. Violence and war are part of our evolutionary legacy, but they are only one part of it, and they will not save our species. Thinking back on the overall dynamic between specialization and adaptiveness as evolutionary strategies, I wonder if our current world-dominating complex culture represents a kind of specialized adaptation. Combining advanced technology and communication with an ideology that equates bigger with stronger may be a human version of the male peacock's tail. Like that glorious but cumbersome tail, our cultural extravagance has reached a point of threatening survival. Vermeij wisely reminds us: "Power is not permanent; it flits notoriously from place to place, from one party to another."[76]

On the hopeful side, organization into large, complex units does provide a means to pursue large, complex plans to act globally. Human pressure on the limits of our environment through sheer numbers, lifestyles, and degree of inequality of access to resources is a daunting problem. But the failure of human will may be the biggest problem of all for our beleaguered species. Excessively optimistic predictions such as salvation through development of "machine morality"[77] or colonizing other planets can woo us into avoiding the urgent situation facing our species right now.

Summary and Conclusions:
Beyond Tribalism and into the Future?

Thinkers in many disciplines have long attempted to define what makes us human and determine how it happened. We evolved the capacity to cooperate on a new level during several million years of the evolutionary maze stretching from our earliest ape ancestors to our becoming a single species, *Homo sapiens*. We differ from other apes in our usually civil behavior to strangers and in our ability to extend trust beyond our kin and beyond our homelands.

This happens regularly as we do business and visit on the streets of villages, towns, and cities around the world; as strangers pass and greet each other without rancor; in flight as passengers strike up conversations; and as part of international collaborations in science, medicine, the arts, work, and other projects. And it happens when people from different traditions meet, fall in love, marry, and have children. Even in war-torn areas, life goes on and most people continue to eat, love, have sex, marry, give birth, and care for families as well as they can. In most societies there is more peace than war going on—we have increased our numbers by surviving and reproducing.[78]

The ability to conceive of the future is also highly developed in *Homo sapiens* and is physiologically enabled by the cerebral cortex and particularly the prefrontal cortices of our brains. We can understand that we live on a planet with other people who have dreams like our own, and that we share it with other organisms. That our bodies contain more bacterial cells than total human cells exemplifies our biological interdependence with other species.

We live today in a world that is vastly different from that of our ancestors, and we need to be creative in adapting to it. Global interdependence is here to stay whether we like it or not. Our strength lies in human adaptability enabled by reflective brains and cultural variability. Darwin's statement about extending bonding outward is more critical now than ever before. Our survival depends on cooperating as one species and working against parochial tendencies and impulses that divide us and can destroy us.

Making ethical decisions cannot be easy. Life is complicated, and intertwining and contradictory conditions make it difficult to find a path forward. There are no perfect solutions for our imperfect species. We can only hope to keep our options open, to consider long-term consequences for each plan, and to identify and understand our own biases.

We have the capacity to move beyond tribalism and create a future for ourselves. We only need to make choices, one at a time, that move us in this direction. Will we make such choices? No one can answer that. But we can be alert to our built-in human weaknesses and attempt to utilize our strengths, remembering the following:

- Effective democracy depends on a healthy and well-educated populace. It thrives on dissent.

- The method of science, its attitude of questioning, and its basis in reasoning and empirical observation provides the most reliable path to knowledge that can lead to effective solutions to large problems. Skepticism laced with humility is critical, while intrusion of untestable ideologies into education cannot improve our quest.

- Great discrepancies in access to resources and opportunities breed discontent and extremism and activate impulsive responses. This is a recipe for tribalism and violence.

- A sense of fairness is biological. We, like other mammals, strive to be treated fairly. Societies and institutions that fail to meet this need cannot endure.

- We are dependent on our planet remaining compatible with life in its many forms. All of nature is interconnected and the loss of a small or large component, however insignificant it appears, has repercussions for other life forms. All of it is our environment.

Small-scale hunter-gatherer societies of our past were not utopian, as Henry Thoreau depicted, and it was probably a stretch to call that adaptation the "original affluent society." Hunter-gatherers were no more angels than we are, but their cultures do offer lessons that we might well heed as we face our present dilemmas. Perhaps their institutions and ideologies nudged them in a more generous direction than ours do. Their closeness to nature and to each other nurtured them, perhaps calmed them, and reminded them constantly of their own place in the larger world.

To accomplish a task as large as moving beyond tribalism, we must tinker with the basic emotions and impulses expressed in earlier centuries by tribalistic behavior. Through framing those impulses differently, we may be able to use ancient small-group emotions to move us to large-scale collaborative action against a more abstract threat to humanity. This type of tinkering is perhaps comparable to the epigenetic tinkering that modifies how genes are expressed in organisms.

Similarly, an emotion that moves us toward tribalism (a meme) does not inevitably lead us there or to violent intergroup conflict. Human culture might instead redirect its expression, working as a kind of *epimimetic* influence, a new way of using an old cultural theme. Timothy Ingold's notion (described in Chapter 7) of performance as a creative unfolding that uses existing material is a good example of epimimetic modification. Epimimetic tinkering with cultures may open pathways leading beyond tribalism and toward viewing and using diversity as a tool for change.

Only through accepting that we face major problems as a species can we hope to engender the degree of motivation required to make the difficult changes to our lifestyles that can warrant realistic optimism. Because no easy solutions exist, we must be flexible to suggestions that may not please us at first glance. We may need to search through the multitude of past and present human cultures for hints at navigating various obstacles on the path toward harmony in diversity. If we fail to find or invent such a pathway, tribalism may overcome us all.

Surely we are in for more surprises. Perhaps we humans will in our bumbling ways be reminded that there is *no* perfect society, *no* answer for living that will take us through everything that we will face as individuals, as communities, as countries, or even as a species. In a dynamic universe, with a dynamic but imperfect human understanding of life and how it works, we can only predict that nothing about life will stay the same. In one sense, we must live the questions, experience the obstacles and the dangers, and solve them one by one.

Perhaps we can then avoid Ian Morris's "Nightfall" (a word he borrowed from science fiction writer Isaac Asimov). If we are to have a future at all, we must acknowledge that changes are happening quickly, that the future is hard to predict, that further change is inevitable, and that denial will only put us deeper into the hole that we have dug (if you're in a hole, stop digging). We have carried our burden of ancient tribalistic tendencies for too long. To move beyond tribalism into a viable future, we need a novel approach.

10

Our Place in Nature: Where Is the Meaning?

Our deeds determine us, as much as we determine our deeds.
 —George Eliot, 1893[1]

The stakes in the broader adoption of an evolutionary perspective are more than philosophical. Understanding the history of our planet, both recently and in the deep past, is key to its intelligent stewardship, and to its preservation for human societies.
 —Sean B. Carroll, 2005[2]

What is our place in nature? We are creatures of nature, products of evolution like all other life on our planet. In a larger perspective, we are a tiny part of the cosmos. We are unique among Earth's creatures for possessing language and complex culture, through which we can try to understand and preserve the earth's bountiful resources *or* wreak havoc on them. We are capable of understanding that our fate as a species is tied to that of other living things and to the state of our planet.

We are able to ponder the very slim probability that our species, *Homo sapiens*, with its particular brain, came into existence at all and the even slimmer probability that any individual came to be.

This chapter is about defining our humanity in the context of nature. We look at self-consciousness, choice, and responsibility; then at our human trajectory and the notion of progress. Finally, I present my personal perspective on constructing meaning. This is simply a description of one way of thinking about meaning.

Self-Consciousness, Choice, and Responsibility

To understand human consciousness, we must return to our evolutionary roots, even to the emergence of life. Given the vague boundary between life and non-life, we might say simply that living things develop, grow, reproduce, and respond to their environments. In addition, species change over generations in response to their environments; they adapt and evolve.[3] The observable differences in organisms and their responses provide a means for us to speculate about the evolution of consciousness.

Organisms without brains possess mechanisms that respond to environmental changes. Responses are the first sign of rudimentary awareness, or proto-awareness, in living things. The earliest responses may have been movement in relation to a single condition such as temperature.

Sensing pain or pleasure may be a second level of awareness but this requires inference from behavior and an organism's chemistry. Pain and pleasure responses are identified mainly by observing movement or behavior; signals of pain appear easy to interpret in many other animals, but we can only infer pain in other organisms based on our own responses. Neurochemicals related to pain and pleasure are ancient, and all vertebrates have similar pain receptors, chemical transmitters, and brain areas that mediate what we call pain. Research is ongoing in this important area. Consciousness appears to be a continuum; there are not clear lines between degrees of consciousness, and there is not a consensus on its definition.

Another level of awareness is noticing one's responses to stimuli, which some connect to having a rudimentary sense of self. Judging from responses of different animals to mirrors, including elephants, great apes, dolphins, and some birds, this capacity to recognize one's self may indicate a degree of self-consciousness. This ability is less common in animals, an additional step from simple consciousness. We humans can report and reflect on our awareness, providing another pathway to understanding it.

In *Homo sapiens*, our brains not only enable each of us to experience one's self as an entity with emotions, ideas, purposes, and hopes, but they impel us to create self-narratives that are connected to an autobiographical memory. One commonly accepted narrative is that each one of us has the ability to act freely. We often refer to our bodies as if we are somehow different and separate from them, as in the statement, "My body is letting me down this week." This is part of the common idea of a dual self with both mind and body.

Moreover, we make choices that influence future events. Does this mean that we choose freely, that we have "free will"? This old question is not only of concern to philosophers; almost everyone has an opinion about free will. Scientists have joined philosophers in deciphering the sense of choosing freely that we experience in everyday life.

Without life, without a thinking brain, there is no self and no consciousness. The closest most of us come to imagining *unconsciousness* is by thinking of dreamless sleep and its contrast to wakefulness, but both are products of a living and working brain.

V. S. Ramachandran argues throughout *The Tell-Tale Brain* that although we are apes, we are more than "mere" apes, and that *self-consciousness* is basic to humanity.[4] Mirror neurons, in his view, are a key to this human development, although these neurons are found in many species with longer prehistories than our own. He argues that our uniqueness resides in how we *use* these neurons to empathize with others and to reflect on ourselves; this makes us self-conscious. He describes seven specific human *intuitions* that contribute to this sense of self: (1) unity; (2) continuity through time; (3) embodiment; (4) privacy of self; (5) social embedding (emotional links with others); (6) free will; and (7) self-awareness.

Philosopher Daniel Dennett defines a human self as the "center of narrative gravity" analogous to a physical center of gravity, an abstract point at which several variables converge.[5] This description of self emphasizes a bundle of things and activities interacting with each other simultaneously. From these multiple activities, each of us spins a mind or a self. Although one's consciousness feels continuous, in reality it has gaps, and so does a "self." As we think back on our lives, there are notable gaps in our memories; we remember (or misre-member) events, and later we remember our memories of those events. This accounts for differences among individuals who have experienced the same events in each other's company. Reconstruct-ing past events resembles how our brains take bits and pieces of visu-al information to form the integrated picture that we are conscious of seeing.

Along a similar line, neuroscientist Michael Gazzaniga[6] describes how, in an event we call *choosing*, muscle action happens first, and on-ly afterward do we conjure up a reason for the choice or action. This sequence has been confirmed repeatedly in experimental studies of brain activity. He attributes one's sense of having chosen freely to be the work of an *interpreter module* in the left hemisphere of most brains. Gazzaniga understands this abstract module as an emergent and complex whole, something with new properties not directly predicta-ble from its components alone. Local neural networks are spread throughout the brain. They economize on space by connecting with other networks rather than with individual neurons, forming hierar-chies of connection. These many interconnected networks work as a kind of coalition that gives each person a sense of self as an entity. While an actual unitary self seems to be an illusion, the *sense* of self is the basis for the widespread concept of a *soul*.

Neuroscientist Antonio Damasio views consciousness as an evolved process of our brains based on social emotions and self-regulation that use ancient pain-pleasure responses and neurochemi-cals (see Chapter 5 on the evolution of morality). Sensory input trav-els to the brain and produces emotions regarding the state of one's self. This brain activity produces a kind of map or pattern of this bodily state, with emotions as signals. In *Self Comes to Mind*, Damasio elaborates on his theme of emotions evolving as tools for regulating life, initially by sensing the environment and moving in response to stimuli. From this simple beginning in organisms without brains, there emerges a protoself with primordial or "body" feelings (his first stage of self-development). A second stage is a "core self" resulting from two-way interactions between organism and environment, each modifying the other. A third stage is the autobiographical self that characterizes human brains.[7]

My understanding is that this third evolutionary stage involves a kind of pattern of images (Damasio's map) that emerges and becomes (or produces) consciousness. In contrast, the earlier core self has only "flickers" of images, or pulses of consciousness, without pattern. He explains that parts of the brain stem, thalamus, and cortex interact to produce the "triad of wakefulness, mind, and self" that constitutes human consciousness. In this, the thalamus is a kind of broker between the cortex and the brain stem; another key player is the anterior cingulate cortex (ACC) that lies within the outer cortex. This ACC surrounds and is part of the limbic system whose components encircle the brain stem.

Physical and mental states are different faces of the same thing. Damasio follows Sigmund Freud in seeing the mind as a largely unconscious product of evolution that we know only partly through our "narrow window of consciousness" which, while limited, does help our brains to organize experiences. A conscious mind emerges from this mapping project, but what becomes conscious is only a fraction of what is going on in our brain.

Neurophilosopher Patricia S. Churchland also writes about the importance of brain activities that happen below the level of consciousness. One is the mimicry of expressions and postures of persons we are with. Another is the unconscious use of signals and verbal expressions even when one presents a prepared speech. She suggests that language and speech stem from consciousness, rather than consciousness from language, a view she attributes to Dennett. Churchland notes that consciousness is widely distributed throughout the brain, and she emphasizes the importance of "rich club" neurons, which share many connections among them. When activated together, they result in conscious experience.[8]

Arguments about free will, then, are about self and consciousness. Most of us experience a *sense* of free will: That is, we feel as if we make choices freely, that we do indeed make decisions. Is this an illusion?

Baruch Spinoza was ahead of his times, several hundred years ago, when he proposed that everything in the universe is connected through multiple cause-and-effect relationships and that we live in a deterministic world.[9] In this conception, our actions and thoughts are part of a network. Given the current understanding of human choice resulting from prior bodily conditions and the unconscious sorting of impulses, memories, and emotions, our choices are not free. But they do have consequences that matter; they influence subsequent events. This is so because they are part of a complex network of causation; it is not evidence that we choose freely.

Knowing how this works and realizing its complexity, Churchland considers free will to be a moot concept. She notes that this scientific understanding is quite different from the everyday notion of free will that refers to behaviors that one has thought about and planned without obvious coercion.[10] E.O. Wilson places this issue in the evolutionary context of our having acquired our very humanity through the contradictory and simultaneous working of individual and group selection.[11] Ramachandran sums up the human predicament by noting that although science tells us differently, "we feel like angels trapped inside the bodies of beasts, forever craving transcendence."[12]

Gazzaniga offers another twist in untangling free will and human responsibility, which people often interpret as incompatible. Without free will, they say, we cannot be held responsible for our actions. He sees the notion of free will as a helpful illusion in relation to responsibility. We need to be held responsible for our choices even though they ultimately result from our particular histories and biological makeups. Individuals need protection from dangerous people, regardless of the reasons for their dangerousness. We must be considered responsible for our behavior because we live in societies with other people. The presumption of responsibility, like morality itself, depends on the fact of social living and is a matter of an unwritten (and sometimes written) social contract that we have with other members of society. It is not about assigning blame; it is about living in society. Solitary animals need neither morality nor responsibility to others, but social animals do.[13]

Journalist Robert Wright in *The Moral Animal* pointed to this paradoxical issue with his apt phrase contrasting "the intellectual groundlessness of blame, and the practical need for it."[14] As grounds for social policy, he suggests that determinism lends urgency to eliminating social conditions that lead to antisocial behaviors. Social life would be impossible if freeloaders were not somehow constrained. In this light, he, like Gazzaniga, sees responsibility as a contract between people rather than as a feature of our brains, and he sees the philosophical-scientific issue of determinism as irrelevant to this social contract.

Philosopher Sam Harris in *The Moral Landscape* adds to the discussion of decision making, consciousness, free will, and responsibility by noting that individual actions, perceived to be chosen or not, have consequences for one's biological functioning. For example, exercising willpower or developing goals interacts dynamically with and modifies brain circuits. Yet he too reminds us that in one sense "you are no more responsible for the next thing you think (and therefore *do*) than you are for the fact that you were born into this world." The fact that our sense of free will is illusory, he too suggests, ought to influence how we design systems of justice.[15] Albert Einstein expressed a similar point of view in 1932 as part of his Credo (see the final section of this chapter).

However we understand human choice, most of us would agree that we make choices that make a difference regardless of their cause. We have seen that particular environments can nudge us in directions that are more or less life-affirming, cooperative, and caring. Our environment includes the books we read, the activities we undertake, and the people with whom we associate. We have the capacity to make reasoned choices based on environmental factors such as these, even if we do not recognize all the factors that, together, cause a particular "choice," such as being drawn to a particular book.

Our awareness of unconscious and conscious brain activities can move us toward fostering positive ties with others, including other forms of life that share the planet and enable us to thrive. Even if we live in a universe governed by determinism and chance, our *sense* of free will and our ability to reason (and thereby understand and override our biases) can influence our future and that of others. All behaviors are responsive to social context, and the details of each brain's functioning are unique.

The Human Trajectory: Glory or Tragedy

From the point of view of the universe(s) or our solar system, each one of us *Homo sapiens* is only an infinitesimal speck in a flurry of activity. The life cycle of the speck has no meaning in the totality; or maybe it does in a statistical sense, in the same way that a butterfly flapping its wings may initiate a series of larger events. But generally, the idea of human progress in this very large context is not significant.

This context introduces another set of ideas important to understanding our place in nature: the fundamental thermodynamic laws of physics. The second law is relevant here: As the energy generated at the beginning of the universe is used in its ongoing evolution, less energy becomes available for use later.[16] Entropy is occurring constantly in our universe. This law came to be understood in the early years of industrialization in Europe, when it became clear that a perpetual motion machine could not be built. The loss of usable energy means the loss of organization in the natural world and in the universe as a whole.

What does this have to do with the human trajectory, and how does it relate to the ever increasing complexity of life, society, and culture? Through evolution of the universe and evolution of life, increasing organization has occurred. Disorganized energy has organized itself into atoms, elements, molecules, stars, planets, galaxies, and so on. Life, from small beginnings, increased, diversified, and came together in myriad joinings and splittings to result in all the organisms on earth today.

We *Homo sapiens* are just one among many of these organisms, but we have developed additional, cultural ways of utilizing energy. Our evolution into large-brained creatures involved capturing increasing amounts of energy; an early step was harnessing fire for cooking and warmth. Cultural evolution, like biological evolution, might be described, in part, by ever more efficient means of harnessing energy from earth's resources, and ultimately from its sun. Anthropologist Leslie A. White noted the importance of harnessing energy in his description of cultural evolution in *The Science of Culture* (1949) and subsequent publications.

With recent developments, researchers and writers from several fields are revisiting this understanding, and *complexity science* has emerged. This new field of study, still being defined, recognizes that complex entities occur often in the natural world. They evolve, and these varied, complex entities work in similar ways wherever they are found. A complex system is composed of smaller parts that interact to create a whole that behaves differently from any of its separate pieces. Such entities occur in the physical world (galaxies), in the biological world (multicellular organisms), and in groups of organisms (ant colonies and human societies). We looked at models of human reciprocity earlier. This was one example of how complexity science frames and analyzes systems mathematically or statistically.

The concept of complexity leads back to the relationship between progress and energy. Progress is sometimes defined by increasing complexity. Although cultural evolution may appear to be inevitably moving toward greater organization and progress, this is a local and a temporary phenomenon. Smaller and simpler forms of life, such as viruses and single-celled bacteria, continue to adapt and evolve while remaining single cells, and, based on their proliferation and influence in the natural world, we may question the everyday notion that equates evolutionary success with size and complexity. Only time will tell whether increasing cultural complexity is a long-term trend or is simply where we sit now in a much larger series of events. C. Leon McGahee writes: "As environments, niches, and competitors change, then so will natural selection of various adaptations change. In a dark world, creatures dispense with eyes or other visual detectors."[17] In this example, evolution has reduced complexity.

We humans may be stuck with complexity to an extent. Large organisms and large societies require increased organization and more roles to achieve the organization. For example, consider the human brain with its neurons organized into nested interconnected clusters (Chapter 3). Sociocultural complexity similarly requires multiple roles. Yet the *extreme* differences in human political and economic resources that is present today may not be viable in the long run. In a sociocultural system whose components are living people with biological, psychological, and social needs, it is the degree of difference in life chances that violates the need for balance.

Some scientists and science writers express more confidence than others in our human future, perhaps representing a kind of cosmic optimism. Robert Wright, in his book *The Evolution of God*, speaks of evolving toward something, perhaps larger cooperative groups with a kind of "mind" and a "non-zero-sum" trajectory.[18] Quantum physicist David Deutsch proposes in *The Beginning of Infinity* that we *Homo sapiens* may be ushering in a new phase of development characterized by the evolution of ideas (i.e., begetting ideas) in dynamic and open societies, creating new knowledge. He stresses the centrality of disagreement for stimulating thinking and the importance of tolerating and learning from contrasting views. Like Stephen Pinker, Deutsch credits the European Enlightenment with introducing the idea of human progress.[19] Both scientists, however, warn of ongoing threats to these hopeful trajectories.

The notion that our species will be able to bypass its problems by moving elsewhere in the universe or by evolving a consciousness beyond our biological selves could endanger our chance for survival in the long run if it causes us to be complacent about current conditions. We are, after all, biological creatures, products of organic evolution and subject to conditions that have grown and nourished us here on Planet Earth. We are firmly ensconced in it, not set apart or above it as we might wish to be. We will, of course, inevitably become extinct; but why make it come sooner than it needs to?

On the issue of human progress, Ian Morris explains that exploding globalization, rocketing changes in technology, and shifts in the balance of power that marked the 1990s, gave rise to the uncertainty that plagues us today. As the American economy stumbles and as China's economy strides forward, we may be moving back to a more familiar multipolar world. He notes the "alarming" similarities of today's world (with *Pax Americana* dominating but being challenged) to the situation of *Pax Britannica* a century ago, which required only one person with a pistol to ignite a world war. He concludes by expressing uncertainty about our human trajectory.[20] It could end in tragedy or glory.

From a different angle, primatologist Frans de Waal cautions us Westerners about giving ourselves too much credit for progress toward a better world, pointing out that:

> The antiquity of fairness is under-appreciated by those who regard it as a noble principle of recent origin, formulated by

wise men during the French Enlightenment. I seriously doubt that we will ever appreciate the human condition by looking back a couple of centuries rather than millions of years.[21]

So, it is wise to question our progress. Change is inevitable, and it is both challenging and threatening. Change of some sort is our only hope as life conditions on earth approach a tipping point. Suggested prescriptions for how to change have upsides and downsides. This is why balance and flexibility are critical. The full consequences of change can never be known in advance; another reason for celebrating variety is that it fosters adaptability. When one proposed solution does not work, a very different one can be considered and may work better. But the possibility of "nightfall" and the certainty of inevitable worldwide changes can hardly be denied.

The human trajectory has created a paradox. Our generalized primate features gave rise eventually to a large, convoluted, multilayered and interconnected brain, a biological device enabling greater adaptability through language and culture. Yet this same capacity enabled arrogance about our place in nature. In blinding us to appreciating the complexity of the world that we live in and depend on, it is bound to have unexpected consequences. "American exceptionalism" exemplifies this prideful attitude, particularly when it is belied by less than stellar achievements in medicine, education, and the well-being of its people.

Looking back, we can see that arrogance has been at the root of many failures in historical societies; failures of nations, policies, institutions, and leaders of institutions and corporations. It can be an enemy of justice and progress in science. Our very humanity, our language with its arbitrary symbols and ability to speak of things and ideas that are not present, allows us to be the most deceitful animal, and we easily deceive ourselves as well as others.

This history highlights the importance of maintaining an attitude of skepticism and humility toward our own ideas and pronouncements. We must remember that we are bipolar (de Waal) or Janus-faced apes (Barash and de Waal), saints and sinners (E.O. Wilson), or angels and demons (Pinker). As an evolved tool enabling human adaptability, our large, reorganized brains gave humanity this double whammy of an evolutionary legacy, known also as the human condition.

We might reflect on Darwin's wisdom; he retained his basic skepticism, applying it generously to his own ideas and carefully crafted conclusions. His sense of humility in relation to the natural world remained strong despite his membership in a leisured class and his brilliance as a biologist. The continuing value of his analysis and theory in the light of advances in evolutionary biology since his time is a product of this self-directed skepticism. We must follow his example and remind ourselves that explaining past events (*postdicting*) is often in error, and predicting itself is a monumental challenge, given our built-in biases.

While attempting to hang on to a bit of hope, I am skeptical that we are on a path toward inclusive humanism because tribalism remains strong and appears in some ways to be gaining force. Expecting a more peaceful world to emerge as a matter of course is dangerous and perhaps a fantasy. We have the capacity to build such a world, but it will not happen without hard work, listening to others, worldwide planning, and collaboration.

Furthering cooperation and reducing violent conflict are critical for any such hope to be realized. Reducing violence and war would give humankind and other living things a chance to delay our demise, certainly a good outcome for all creatures on earth. I do not see this as a way to overcome the basic law of entropy or to make our species immortal. On this, I appreciate, once more, Melvin Konner's reminder that "disorder continually licks at the edges of orderly organic systems."[22] This disorder (or randomness) has provided the raw material for natural selection, and in that sense it has allowed the local growth of complexity.

Too much certainty about the "truth" of Western-biased views of humanity and its assumed mandate to lead the world toward continual human progress poses dangers for us all. We are a young species, and we have developed innumerable ways to be deceitful, to oppress, to kill, and to do these things impersonally and from a distance. Even if the proportions of deaths through violence and war have been reduced through time, the sheer numbers of deaths by violence have been appallingly large in recent centuries.

Moreover, we still possess the technological knowledge to destroy everyone on the planet, and we continue to build our destructive arsenal. It makes no sense to congratulate ourselves when we do not yet know whether any measured reduction in the rate of violence is a temporary glitch, a trend, or a portion of a longer cycle. We can instead apply our empathy and our technological achievements to building a more ethical, humanitarian, and life-preserving culture, as a number of persons, organizations, and a few countries have begun to do even in the face of formidable odds.

Biological and cultural evolution are opportunistic processes. Some creatures adapt by reducing complexity, others by increasing it, and still others by staying stable in their specialized environments. In human evolution, environmental changes played a large role in driving key transitions. To predict that complexity or universal self-consciousness might be an end-point of our evolution, however comforting it might be on the surface, simply does not make sense to me in light of how the evolutionary process works.

A related paradox is this: The many organisms on our planet, all evolved through natural selection, have taken different paths. Some evolutionary lines moved toward specialization of features with tight fits to particular ecological niches. If such a niche disappears, so does that well-adapted species if it can't evolve quickly enough. Other evolutionary branches underwent changes that were not so niche-based, such as more efficient means for moving around, harnessing energy, and organizing behavior (central nervous system). The generalized features of our early primate ancestors put early hominins on a path that resulted in a degree of adaptability that enabled them (us) to populate and dominate planet Earth, at least for a while.

But our brains and our related culture-language complex vastly accelerated the rate of change in the environment. The capacity to live anywhere and to alter our surroundings so completely led to a high degree of species-arrogance. I wonder if our high-energy adaptation itself might represent a bizarre form of species-specialization—a narrowing of our niche—that will inevitably make us *less* adaptable to a changing world. In this regard, Geerat Vermeij reminds us that the earth's top consumers (like dinosaurs) have been the most prone to disappearance during each mass extinction.[23]

I return to several contrasts. In open societies (in contrast to closed ones), listening to diverse points of view is critical. This is related to adaptability (in contrast to adaptive specialization). Cooperation requires willingness to open our minds to competing ideas, which translates into human behavioral flexibility. In this book, I have outlined how cooperation and flexibility evolved, and how they are critical for success in our highly interconnected world. The trend of increased economic inequality and increased numbers of lethally armed camps can hardly help our species survive and prosper in the long run. Whenever human skills and resources are used for the destruction of resources that sustain us, we hasten the end of our tenure on earth.

We do not yet know whether the evolution of our large brains and culture-language complex will end in glory or tragedy for us. It enabled us to populate all corners of the earth and decipher many of its secrets. At the same time, it enabled us to "build castles in the air" *and* to live in those castles in contradiction to what the environment can support. Now we are beginning to pay the very high rent.[24] No one knows whether we can handle it.

I give Carl Sagan the last cautionary words on this topic of human progress; his thoughts from 1996 are still relevant in 2015:

We've arranged a global civilization in which most crucial el-ements—transportation, communications, and all other indus-tries; agriculture, medicine, education, entertainment, protect-ing the environment; and even the key democratic institution of voting—profoundly depend on science and technology. We have also arranged things so that almost no one understands science and technology. This is a prescription for disaster. We might get away with it for a while, but sooner or later this combustible mixture of ignorance and power is going to blow up in our faces.[25]

Making Meaning:

The Human Condition, Mystery and Awe

Home is always home for someone; but there is no Absolute Home in general.

    —Herbert Fingarette[26]

Everything about the human condition is rooted in biology: all insti-tutions, behaviors, and ideas. Evolution has made biology compre-hensible, and there is beauty in this understanding, and in the narra-tive that describes it. Our humanity results from a very long and complex multilevel evolutionary process.

A *sense* of meaning, like the *sense* of free will, is a product of our brains. Within our common humanity, each of us has been shaped by the entire heritage of life on our planet, a unique interacting set of genetic, epigenetic, microbial, prenatal and childhood environments, as well as all that surrounds us as adults. Yet we share common, spe-cies-wide, empathy-based connections to others and the potential to extend this connection outward.

Knowing this can help us modify our institutions in a way that encourages and helps to spread conditions that foster harmony over conflict, win-win over win-lose solutions, and preservation of our earth's resources. Although an individual human life may be ultimately meaningless in the vastness of the universe, we can each work to-ward and achieve goals. All animals behave in goal-directed ways, but only we humans can formulate and record these goals in a self-conscious way. Can we make more of a difference to the universe than a butterfly can by beating its wings in a particular place and time? Perhaps not.

There are no answers; there are only questions. This is an agnostic point of view in regard to knowledge. Thomas Huxley coined the word *agnostic* in an essay he penned in 1889.[27] In it, he argued in favor of accepting uncertainty unless a phenomenon can be backed up by clear evidence. Science is about assessing evidence and drawing conclusions while remaining skeptical and open to new observations and ideas. Geerat Vermeij reminds us that "the values and purposes we rightly cherish are no less wondrous and essential when they emerge from natural evolutionary processes ..."[28]

What we *Homo sapiens* can do is rejoice in the wonder of the natural world and the universe. We can rejoice also in the curiosity that impels us to try to understand how it all happened, and we can share this excitement with others. We can rejoice in our discovery of ways to penetrate the mysteries by using an ever-changing, human-produced scientific narrative that advances knowledge. Finally, each of us can rejoice in the planet that will continue to nurture us if we in turn nurture it.

Evidence for the importance of the natural world to human happiness and to a sense of peace has been accumulating in recent years. Nature does appear to nurture us emotionally. Anthropologist Spencer Wells describes his response to time spent with Julius, a Western-educated Hadzabe man (a speaker of the ancient "click" language) who today has chosen to maintain his ancestral way of life during a portion of each year.[29] While traveling with Julius and his local hunter-gatherer band, Wells reports experiencing a refreshing sense of release from the tensions built into his usual lifestyle.

This prompts the question of whether civilization has made us more or less *civilized*. Writer Pico Iyer in a piece aptly entitled "The Joy of Quiet" describes how some well-heeled people are choosing to spend time in expensive resorts in natural settings, which advertise their lack of television and Internet access.[30] Douglas Rushkoff, in *Present Shock*, makes a similar point, suggesting that the constant onslaught of stimuli prevents many of us from considering the flow from past into the future. This sense of "distracted present," of being pulled and constantly derailed from ongoing tasks,[31] is very different from the sentiment described by Wells as release from present worries.

Rushkoff shows how our surroundings, including the many machines through which we negotiate the world, often nudge us toward impulsive rather than carefully considered choices and responses. Economic and political campaigns of various kinds aim to influence our behavior rather than stimulate our reasoning about complex issues. This orientation affects almost everything — how we view life, how we make economic decisions, and how we do science. In some, present shock engenders a longing for closure of some kind. This echoes anthropologist T. M. Luhrmann's understanding of the attraction of evangelical movements in today's accelerated world (described in Chapter 7).

For me, quest into mystery, quest for meaning, living the questions and searching for answers, itself makes meaning. I like to think that I am in good company. Albert Einstein perceived beauty in mystery itself, as expressed in his Credo of 1932:

> The most beautiful and deepest experience a man can have is the sense of the mysterious. It is the underlying principle of religion as well as all serious endeavor in art and science ... To sense that behind anything that can be experienced there is a something that our minds cannot grasp, whose beauty and sublimity reaches us only indirectly: this is religiousness. In this sense I am religious. To me it suffices to wonder at these

secrets and to attempt humbly to grasp with my mind a mere image of the lofty structure of all there is.[32]

In his own way, my technologically savvy grandson echoed the spirit of this idea when he was quite young. Upon seeing the majestic Pacific Ocean for the first time, he exclaimed: "Nature is even more awesome than technology!"

I propose that we can find meaning in the questions and in the challenges that we face. Part of our evolutionary legacy is the range and flexibility of our behavior and thought, related to our culture-language complex, and further back to our heritage of becoming bipedal, terrestrial tool-makers and users. This heritage gave us the capacity to ask questions and explore the mysteries of the universe(s). We have constructed numerous and variable cultures that meet human needs in different ways. Just as genetic variety provides the raw material for biological evolution, cultural and behavioral variety provides the raw material for innovating, for creating prosocial and humanitarian institutions, and for using our twin gifts of reasoning and empathy.

David Barash, in viewing our human behavioral repertoire, comments: "The good news is that every human being—as a result of being human—is capable of overcoming the tyranny of the natural. 'We Shall Overcome,' indeed! In fact, the capability of overcoming may be a reasonable definition of what it means to be human."[33]

On this note, I present four general conclusions:

- All life is rare and precious, and it is interconnected in ways that we do not yet fully understand and appreciate.

- Each of us is exquisitely self-conscious, improbable, and, like all other organisms, unique.

- *Homo sapiens* is one small part of an interdependent, complex, and changing natural world on a small planet.

- We must think globally, not tribally, because tribalism can be fatal.

In the long run, our species will benefit from diversity; we will move into the future only if we develop ways to live in harmony with each other and find beauty in our many traditions. This diverse cultural heritage gives us the means to think outside the box of constraints that bind each of us to a particular thought tradition. Our differences combined with our capacity to communicate easily and quickly across cultures is an *asset,* a powerful tool for creating a peaceful world. Perhaps we are witnessing the beginnings of this in the efforts of young people of many traditions to reach out to others around the world with ideas, with helping hands, and through telling stories and making music and art together.

On an individual level, there are numerous ways that each of us can construct meaning and achieve a sense of inner peace. This is a personal enterprise; there is no one-size-fits-all solution. We vary in our inclinations, our personalities, and the biological, social, cultural, and individual forces that have shaped us, including the internal processes of each of our complex, intertwined neural networks. Fortunately, there are different ways of looking at the world and our place in it; there are many ways of being human.[34] Because of this, it behooves us to foster openness and tolerance toward others. Encouraging variable ideas can promote our adaptability as a species. Too much certainty about the mysteries of life can be dangerous because we are likely to be wrong.

Because we are products of it, we are all beholden to nature. In their stories and myths, hunting and gathering peoples often express gratitude to the animals and plants and to the sun, rain, and earth that nurture them. We need to cultivate a similar attitude that will encourage us to preserve and care for our planet. A shift in attitude does not require that we attribute intention to the world for giving us life; it requires only that we acknowledge that we originated in nature and are part of its large web of interdependence. To survive and thrive, we must think globally and live with gratitude, respect, and humility toward the natural world.

For me, the hope of life resides in its renewal or resurrection each spring, and in each new species that evolves on our earth. Life continues in different forms. We individuals live within our children's and friends' lives, within the lives of others that we have touched, and within the lives of the creatures that our molecules help to form after we die. In this way, we all become recycled parts of the earth.

The scientific story of evolution and the many life forms resulting from it—the evolutionary narrative—to me is more beautiful than any myth that our human imaginations have dreamed up. The natural phenomena of our universe, the beauty in nature, and its sounds—"the music of the spheres"—provide a constant source of wonder, mystery, and questions to ask and to live. I feel fortunate to experience this; such emotions, after all, motivate and move us, make us feel alive, and nudge us to seek solutions for our beleaguered species and for our earth.

Scientists and naturalists from around the world have expressed similar responses to this understanding. Vermeij brings it together when he states: "Each of us has but one life to live on one habitable planet. It is both a privilege and a responsibility to celebrate, understand, and protect this world."[35] Edward O. Wilson expresses a similar sentiment by wanting to substitute this evidence-based, scientific origin story of the earth and its inhabitants for the origin myths of particular religions that are by definition tribalistic. In his view, these traditions invariably separate their followers from humanity as a whole by placing moral value on particular groups and leaders who promote particular agendas.[36] In other words, they lend themselves to tribalism.

Understanding who we are reminds us of the importance of compassion: We rarely consider how fortunate we are to have made it to this present moment, to be regularly reading books, taking care of ourselves and others, working, playing, and loving. We readily give ourselves credit for our successes, but we often blame outside circumstances for our failures. We easily forget that chance circumstances have much to do with our successes *and* our failures. We can never truly understand where another human being has been, what that person's life feels like, or how difficult it may have been. For this reason too, we must work hard to accept those with different values and different priorities.

Where do human judgments of others come from? They are products of individual psychological development and values, of particular group norms that each of us acquires in childhood, of occupying a particular place and time in history, and of our entire heritage as small groups of weak mammals during the Pliocene and Pleistocene environments. Hence, the need for compassion.

In this second decade of the twenty-first century, we are at an exciting and important turning point for understanding what it means to be human and discovering what our future might bring. Rapid advances in the science of human behavior and the ability to analyze data from ancient biological and cultural remains have brought us to this point.

We *Homo sapiens* are capable of moving forward in our behavior and thinking by understanding (1) our human assets and vulnerabilities, (2) our dependence on the planet that nurtures us, and (3) the need to build a long-term future. We can influence the workings of our own brains by how we act and even how we talk to ourselves. We can build institutions that foster cooperation. We can practice opposing or at least overriding our tribal tendencies. We can move beyond tribalism and toward a sustainable globalism. The question becomes: *Will* we muster the strength to do so?

I close with Charles Darwin's own concluding words from *On the Origin of Species*:

> It is interesting to contemplate an entangled bank, clothed with many plants of many kinds, with birds singing on the bushes, with various insects flitting about, and with worms crawling through the damp earth, and to reflect that these elaborately constructed forms, so different from each other,

and dependent on each other in so complex a manner, have all been produced by laws acting around us ... There is grandeur in this view of life, with its several powers, having been originally breathed into a few forms or into one; and that, whilst this planet has gone cycling on according to the fixed law of gravity, from so simple a beginning endless forms most beautiful and most wonderful have been, and are being, evolved.[37]

A Final Note

We have explored how our species evolved as part of the natural world, how we lived for the first several million years of our tenure on earth, and what kind of animal we are today. The emergence of a large brain-culture-language complex changed the human animal around 200,000 years ago following the early phases of hominin evolution. Then came a second revolutionary cultural development: the birth of food production beginning about 11,000 years ago. The beginning of industrialization only 350 years ago was followed by the energy and information revolution within the past half-century.

Each event accelerated the rate of change, increasing the disconnect between generations and creating a degree of future shock and even present shock for individuals.

Part of our evolutionary legacy is a dual aspect of our being human—living with the contradictory threads running through the evolution of all life on earth and through our specific heritage as individualistic members of our symbolic, social, interdependent species. This differs from the old philosophical dualism of separate body and mind, since each person is an interconnected bodily whole. Understanding the conflicting threads within us and how they came about can suggest ways to move beyond tribalism.

Human institutions universally include kinship, religion or ideology, and political and economic activities related to a range of cultural values from fierce egalitarianism to norms of inequality. These nudge us toward viewing the world in particular ways that often blind us to seeing a larger, more comprehensive view of ourselves.

No one knows whether the outcome will be tragedy or sustainable continuation of our species into the future. But it will depend in large part on our collective actions, how we manage our tribalistic impulses, and whether we muster the courage and determination to recognize our common humanity and our common fate on the planet we share.

Annotated Bibliography

Alexander, Michelle, *The New Jim Crow: Mass Incarceration in the Age of Colorblindness*. New York: The New Press, 2011 (first edition, 2010).
   A legal scholar describes the emergence of a new form of systematic discrimination, in which African American males at each stage of the legal process are targeted and denied rights compared to their white peers.

Barash, David P., *Natural Selections: Selfish Altruists, Honest Liars, and Other Realities of Evolution*. New York: Bellevue Literary Press, 2008.
   A light-hearted look at Janus-faced humanity, offering hope based on our human strengths.

Benkler, Yochai, *The Penguin and the Leviathan: How Cooperation Triumphs over Self-Interest*. New York: Crown Business Publishing Group (Random House), 2011.
   Human motivations are varied; and looking at economic decisions as based on "the bottom line" alone is short-sighted.

Carroll, Sean B., *Endless Forms Most Beautiful: The New Science of Evo Devo*. New York: W. W. Norton, 2005.
   A geneticist outlines evolutionary developmental biology as a key to understanding how small genetic changes can make large differences in organisms.

Churchland, Patricia, *Touching a Nerve: The Self as Brain*. New York, W. W. Norton and Company, 2013.
   A neurophilosopher outlines human brain evolution and the roots of morality, combining insights from philosophy and neuroscience.

Dunbar, Robin, *Grooming, Gossip, and the Evolution of Language*, Cambridge, Massachusetts: Harvard University Press, 1996.
   This anthropologist proposes that human language replaced grooming as a form of bonding among early humans.

Elliot, Lise, *Pink Brain, Blue Brain: How Small Differences Can Grow into Troublesome Gaps—and What We Can Do about It*. New York, Houghton, Mifflin, Harcourt 2009.

How female and male brains and behaviors develop through interactions of genetic and chemical factors within specific cultural contexts.

Greene, Joshua, *Moral Tribes: Emotion, Reason, and the Gap between Us and Them*. New York: The Penguin Press, 2013.
A lucid explanation of interactions of emotions and thinking in human affairs, and the roles that individual and group identities and interests play in the whole, from a modernized utilitarian point of view.

Hrdy, Sarah Blaffer, *Mothers and Others: The Evolutionary Origins of Mutual Understanding*. Cambridge, Massachusetts: The Belknap Press, 2009.
An account of how we became human through "caring and sharing," extending care of children by mothers to include other nurturing caregivers., thereby making empathy a defining human trait.

Hosseini, Khaled, *A Thousand Splendid Suns*, New York: Riverhead Books (Penguin), 2007.
This compelling novel follows a young girl valiantly facing tribalistic attitudes and behaviors that take the forms of sexism and extreme religious sectarianism combined, in a country torn by both.

Judson, Olivia, *Dr. Tatiana's Sex Advice to All Creation*. New York: Henry Holt and Company, 2002.
Biologist Judson becomes an advice columnist for a wide variety of creatures, with entertaining insights into human evolution, behavior, and society.

Sachs, Jeffrey D., *The Price of Civilization: Reawakening American Virtue and Prosperity*. New York: Random House, 2011.
The current world situation in environmental, historical and economic context, with practical steps toward increasing the effectiveness of governance, economic sustainability, and justice.

Stringer, Chris, *Lone Survivor: How We Came to Be the Only Human on Earth*. New York, Henry Holt and Company, Times Books, 2012.
A British paleoanthropologist overviews human evolution, with emphasis on genus *Homo*, migrations and mixtures of populations.

Tattersall, Ian, *Masters of the Planet: The Search for Our Human Origins*. New York: Palgrave Macmillan, 2012.
An excellent overview of human evolution from our ancient ape ancestors to *Homo sapiens* by paleoanthropologist and curator emeritus at the American Museum of Natural History.

Vedantam, Shankar, *The Hidden Brain: How Our Unconscious Minds Elect Presidents, Control Markets, Wage Wars, and Save Our Lives*. New York: Spiegel and Grau (Random House), 2010.
   An exploration of the role of bias in the conduct of everyday life; directly relevant to tribalism.

Vermeij, Geerat J., *The Evolutionary World: How Adaptation Explains Everything from Seashells to Civilization*. New York: St. Martin's Press, 2010.
   A naturalist-biologist eloquently describes the natural world and natural selection, and how we humans are embedded in nature.

de Waal, Frans, *The Age of Empathy: Nature's Lessons for a Kinder Society*. New York: Harmony Books, 2009.
   A primatologist's perspective on human cooperation and altruism, competition and conflict, in comparison to behavior in other social primates.

Wilson, Edward O., *The Social Conquest of Earth*. New York: Liveright Publishing Corporation, 2012.
   A renowned biologist compares the evolution of human societies to that of ant colonies, reintroducing Darwin's group selection as an important way to understand both.

Notes

Preface

1. Wilson 2012:13.
2. Taylor 2010. Anthropologist author of book entitled *The Artificial Ape*.
3. Dennett 1995:346.

PART I: INTRODUCTION: LIVING THE QUESTIONS

1. Darwin 2006 [1859]:759.

Chapter 1 Science, Evolution, Biology and Culture

1. Wilson 2012:295.
2. Craig 2005:49–67; Solomon and Higgins 1996:56–68.
3. Al-Khalili 2011. Ibn al-Haytham (Alhazen) is author of the highly acclaimed, ancient and groundbreaking text, *Book of Optics*, cited in Al-Khalili. Ibn al-Haytham also clarified the scientific endeavor in terms of method and the attitude toward data and ideas; see Al-Khalili 2011:152–171.
4. I borrow this use of "involution" from Geertz 1963.
5. This happened during the opening of the third meeting of The British Association for the Advancement of Science. See Snyder 2011:2–3.
6. *Merriam-Webster's Collegiate Encyclopedia* 2000:1151.
7. See physicist David Deutsch 2011:111–113.
8. Sabra 2003.
9. Darwin 1794, 1796.
10. Researchers Peter and Rosemary Grant, chronicled in Weiner 1994.
11. Darwin 2006 [1859]:441–760.
12. Darwin 2006 [1859]:489; Darwin's theory is almost identical to a proposal Alfred Wallace made at the same time.
13. Malthus 1993 [1798].
14. Eldredge 2005:43, 46–47, 85–88.
15. For one of many summaries of this, see Wilson 2012:198.
16. This is associated with biologists Julian Huxley, Ernst Mayr, Theodosius Dobzhansky, George Gaylord Simpson, and others. See Campbell 1996; Carroll 2009:277–278.
17. Carroll 2005. I assume full responsibility for errors in this summary. Throughout this book, I utilize Carroll's spelling of Evo Devo. Carroll also has provided

a brief and clear description of DNA and proteins, and DNA sequencing and analysis for the non-scientist in Carroll 2009, especially boxed material on 252, 254, 256.

18. Stringer 2012; for summary of dating and imaging techniques and findings, see 36–80.
19. Konner 2010:749.
20. Churchland 2013:137.
21. Ridley 1993:1, 17–19.
22. Zimmer 2008.
23. Smith 2009 [1790]:13–21; quotation:13–14.
24. Darwin 2006 [1871]:798–806, 818–838.
25. Smith, 1937 [1776].
26. Smith 2009 [1790]:31.
27. de Waal 2009:233, Note 45.
28. The old term preadaptation was Darwin's and the newer one exaptation was coined by Stephen Jay Gould and Elisabeth S. Vrba to clarify confusion associated with the original term. See Gould and Vrba 1982:4–15.
29. Tattersall 2012:210. His partial quotation: "all genetic innovations … must arise initially not as adaptations to a particular lifestyle, but as exaptations; features that must necessarily be co-opted post hoc into a new use."
30. Ridley 1993:17–19; quotation:17.
31. Sahlins and Service 1960:93–122.
32. Sahlins and Service 1960:99–100.
33. Morris 2010, especially 12–13, 24–36, 32–3, 46–7, 82–3, 160–161, Ch. 12, and Appendix. See further discussion in Chapter 10 of this book.
34. Vermeij 2010:203–205, 207, 218–224.
35. Lloyd 2009.
36. Dobzhansky 1973:125–129.
37. Richerson and Boyd 2005:237 (chapter title).

PART II: THE HUMAN ANIMAL EVOLVING

1. Lorenz 2002 [1963]:222.

Chapter 2 The Bipedal Ape

1. Vermeij, Geerat. 2010:262
2. For a clear description of classification of life forms and fossil forms in particular, see Tattersall 2008:27–35.
3. Tattersall 2012; Stringer 2012.
4. A summary of reproduction can be found in Ridley 1993:16–17, 23–51.
5. Shubin 2009:160–164.
6. The cladistic scheme groups the lemurs and lorises into the Strepsirhini (literally, wet-nosed) suborder and places tarsiers with monkeys and apes in the Haplorhini suborder. See Jurmain et al. 2000:118–119.

7. None of these apes, in contrast to monkeys, possess tails. Dental patterns of New World monkeys include three premolars; many of them also possess prehensile tails. Old World monkeys and apes, in contrast, have only two premolar teeth on each side and have downward pointing nostrils.

8. For more information on commonalities of all animals, see Shubin 2009 and Carroll 2005.

9. Radford 2011.

10. Wood and Guth 2008.

11. Wilson 2012. His list of preadaptations include (1) dwelling on land, (2) large body size, (3) origin of grasping hands and fingers that could manipulate, (4) upright posture, (5) shift to a meaty diet and advantage placed on cooperation, (6) controlled use of fire, (7) cooking, (8) campsites and nest guarding as precursor to eusociality, and (9) division of labor facilitated by existing dominance factors (e.g., male/female, age, "personality"). Note that this conception is similar to that presented here and in the next chapter.

12. Tattersall 2008:11–12, 23–28, 6–69.

13. Stringer and Andrews 2005: Timeline, 12–13; Geological Timescales, 27–29; Dating the Past, 131. These charts and tables coordinate geological events with human prehistory events.

14. Stringer 2012; and Tattersall 2012.

15. Sahelanthropus tchadensis, Orrorin tugenensis, and Ardipithecus ramidus are full designations; see Tattersall 2012:6–14. The importance of these fossils is not set in stone. Some paleoanthropologists dispute the sweeping claims for incomplete and shattered fossils, and this applies to others assigned to the hominin branch. See Wood and Harrison 2011.

16. Jha 2011.

17. Larsen 2003:1903–1904; Lee 2005:219–232.

18. Berger et al. 2010.

19. Sometimes called "Paranthropus" as a group.

20. Tattersall 2012:72–73.

21. Harmon 2013:42–49.

22. Gibbons 2012b:538–539.

23. Hypothesis that our common ancestor with all great apes was important in evolution of bipedalism, as evidenced by modern arboreal orangutan's semi-upright navigation: Thorpe, Holder, and Cropton 2007:1328–1331.

24. Ian Tattersall 2012:14–19.

25. Hopkin 2004:415–418.

26. Wrangham 2009, see especially 37–194.

27. Bramble and Lieberman 2004:345–352.

28. Watson 2012.

29. We sometimes harbor a third species, the body louse (Pediculus humanus corporis), which clings to clothing rather than hair. It is closely related to the head louse (Pediculus humanus capitis) and less close to the pubic louse (Phthririus pubis).

30. Stringer 2012:202–204. The DNA of human pubic lice is closely related to gorilla lice, while our human head lice resemble chimpanzee lice (and those that infested our more recent common ancestor).

31. Jablonski 2012, see especially 9–63; Jablonski and Chaplin 2000:57–106; Jablonski 2012:24–46.

32. Tattersall 2012:119–124.

33. Wilford 2013.

34. Falk 2011. Falk describes the *Homo floresiensis* ("Hobbit") controversy and research. These early people survived until 18,000 years ago and perhaps much later, at least according to persistent descriptions of tiny people in the historical past. Also see Stringer 2012:82–85.
35. Oakley 1972.
36. Napier 1956:902–913.
37. Young 2003:165–174.
38. Kivell et al. 2011:1411–1417.
39. Dart 1949:1–16.
40. Adovasio et al. 2007:57–58, 76–78, 85–88.
41. A fossil originally discovered in 2008 by Lee Berger. (His young son Matthew uncovered the first bone and wisely alerted his father.) Recent summary by science writer Wong 2012:30–39.
42. Rosenberg and Trevathan 2002:1199–1206. Also see Adovasio et al., 2007:62–71.
43. DeSilva 2011:1022–1027; Lewton 2012:198.

Chapter 3 The Brainy Ape

1. Pugh, George E. 1977: 54 (Attributed to author's father, Emerson M. Pugh).
2. Watson 1992: iii (Foreword).
3. Robson 2011:40–45.
4. Taylor 2010:13–32, 72–73.
5. Seung 2012:33, 110–115, 179–184.
6. Roth and Dicke 2005:250–257.
7. Wilson 2012:24, 32, 46, and throughout book.
8. Tattersall 2012. See figures on pages 5 and 129–134. This source provides a coherent overview and discussion of ongoing controversies, updated to early 2012.
9. Summarized in Dunbar 1996. Also see Stringer 2012:113–117.
10. Dunbar and Shultz 2007:649–658.
11. For examples, see Gazzaniga 2011:150.
12. Sol and Price, 2008:170–177.
13. Tattersall 2012:186.
14. Linden 2007.
15. Seung 2010:3–34.
16. Seung 2010:33–5, 104–110, 124–131.
17. Falk, 1992:6–8.
18. Gazzaniga 2011:32–44, 60–70.
19. Gibbons 2012c.
20. Zimmer 2011. Here he cites research by Carl Wray on glucose transport genes.
21. Churchland 2013:87.
22. Pollard 2009:44–49.
23. Montagu 1955:13–27.
24. Ramachandran 2011:37–38.
25. Konner 2010:58–61, 125, 130–136, 138, 140–143.
26. Hawkes et al. 2000:2–22.
27. Konner 2010:108–112,128–133, 400.
28. Stringer 2012:59–70.

29. This symposium resulted in a book of the same name that became a classic in anthropology (Lee and DeVore 1968).
30. Oakley 1972.
31. Dahlberg 1981.
32. Hart and Sussman 2005.
33. Adovasio 2007:177–183.
34. Hrdy 2009:38–63. She uses remainder of book to provide a wealth of evidence for her hypothesis.
35. Konner 2010:142–144, 241–259.
36. Dissanayake 2000; Falk 2009.
37. Hrdy 2009:120–124.
38. Hawkes 2003:380–400. And see subsequent report of mathematical modeling and computer simulation of this hypothesis. Using chimpanzee data and adding some grandparent care over time seem to support this hypothesis, since it did increase lifespans over 60 generations, even ignoring the pair bonding and increases in brain size that also occurred in the human branch.
39. Gazzaniga 2011. See Chapters 1, 2, and final chapter.
40. Stringer 2012:49–54, 230, 251–252.
41. Stringer 2012:49–54, 105–107, 126–141, 147–160.
42. Tattersall 2012:160–184; Pennisi 2013:799.
43. Also see online results from *National Geographic*, The Genographic Project. https://genographic.nationalgeographic.com/denisovan. Accessed 12/7/14; regularly updated.
44. Hammer 2013:66–71.
45. Stringer 2012:262–278; quotation:267.
46. Morris 2010:63–64.
47. Marean 2010:55–61.
48. Wilford 2012b.
49. Balter 2011a.
50. Lombard and Haidle 2012:232–264.
51. Stringer 2012:67–70; 86–107,127–141, 211–234; Tattersall 2012:185–204.
52. For example, Nubian look-alike ancient tools (Sudan) in Oman dated to around 100,000 years ago, reported by Underwood 2011.
53. Balter 2011b.
54. Wilford 2011:26–27, 43–55.
55. Tattersall 2012:146–158; Stringer 2012:246–247, 267–278.

Chapter 4 The Moral Mammal

1. Churchland 2011:190.
2. Twain 1897:654.
3. Shapiro 2007; and see Ricardo and Szostak 2009:54–61.
4. Cox and Bonner 2001:448–449.
5. Wilson 2012:242–252.
6. Hrdy 2009: 1–4; 1–30; quotation:1.
7. Damasio 2003: 170–174; quotation:156.
8. Damasio 2010.
9. Churchland 2011:8–81, 119–126, 145–151.
10. Vedantam 2010.

11. de Waal 2005. Heading of his Chapter 6:215.
12. Barash 2013:25–37.
13. Bekoff 2001:81–90; Bekoff and Pierce 2010:16–17.
14. Olson and Spelke 2008:222–231.
15. Greenspan and Shanker 2004:212–223.
16. Bellah 2011:74–91.
17. The Christmas Miracle 2008.
18. Origin not quite clear; often reported to be proverb from Igbo and Yoruba people of Nigeria, but also found in other communities.
19. Dunbar 1996.
20. Tomasello et al. 2009.
21. Angier 2011.
22. Nowak with Roger Highfield 2011. For the general reader, I recommend especially the Preface and Chapters 1, 2, 3, 4, followed by Chapters 10, 11, and 14.
23. Nowak 2011:269, 282–284; quotation: 282.
24. Gintis, Bowles, Boyd, and Fehr. 2005:3-39. See Reference section for other contributors to these ideas in this volume.
25. Gintis et al. 2005:3–39, quotation.30.
26. Fiske 1992:689–723.

PART III: PEOPLE IN GROUPS

1. Tattersall, Ian. 2012:229.

Chapter 5 From Foraging Bands to the Digital Age

1. Smith, Adam. 1937 [1776]:674.
2. Gintis et al. 2005: 277. From thirteenth century Edda.
3. White 1949; White 1959.
4. On current attempts to make sense of classification and understanding cultural evolution, see Mesoudi et al. 2006:329–347; discussion 347–383.
5. Service 1962.
6. Childe 1951 [1936].
7. Hey 2010:921–933.
8. Johnson 2012. Also see Gibbons 2012a.
9. Hrdy 2009:172.
10. For comparing bonobos and chimpanzees, in addition to above sources in notes 5 and 6, also see de Waal 2009:24, 91, 203; de Waal 2005; Raffaele 2010:129–181, 136–138, 153–161; and Konner 2010:100–107, 430–434, 453–462.
11. Johnson 2012. Quotation from final paragraph of piece.
12. Pinker 2011:39–40.
13. Kelly 2007.
14. See discussion in Keeley 1996:170–171.
15. Besides those cited, see Boehm 2012; Hrdy 2009; Konner 2010.
16. Dubreuil 2010:88–9; 228–229.

17. Lee and Daly 2004:1–22.
18. Hrdy 2009; Konner 2010; See Footnote 26.
19. Boehm 2012:78–82.
20. Sahlins 1972:1–39.
21. Boehm 2012:24–35, 95–100, 115–128.
22. Boehm 136–147, 178, 198, 200–209, 321–322.
23. See Konner 2010:42–44, for summary of evolutionary "compromises" in competition, cooperation, reciprocal altruism and delayed reciprocity, cheating and its detection, the role of reputation and balancing these factors in early human societies.
24. Lee and Daly 2004:5, 14–16; quotation:5. They cite Tim Ingold for discussion in a later chapter within the volume.
25. Gintis et al. 2005:26.
26. Endicott 2004:411–418. For latter point, see pp. 416–417.
27. See Kelly 2007:297–302.
28. Hrdy 2009:126–441, 100–101; Konner 2010:381–398, 435–439, 578, 470 (Table 17.3).
29. Gurven 2006:158–192; Kaplan and Gurven 2005:75–113.
30. See in particular Adovasio 2007:78–88, 148–192, 243–279.
31. Morris 2010:85–97.
32. Rosen and Rivera-Collazo 2012. Their hypothesis, Theory of Adaptive Change (TAC) or Resilience Theory, contrasts with an earlier proposition of economic vulnerability and collapse of forager economies in the context of food production.
33. Tattersall 2008:122–124.
34. Pinker 2011:475.
35. For example, see Snodgrass 2011. Also see from same series Lieberman 2011.
36. Wells 2010.
37. Sahlins 1972:35–37.
38. Childe 1951 [1936].
39. Smith 1937 [1776]:47–49, 669–681; quotation:49.
40. Rudmin 1996:115–153; see 148–149 particularly.
41. Rudmin 2006.
42. See Kelly 2007:293–331.
43. Keeley 1996:170–180.
44. Kelly 2007.
45. Diamond 1999:405–410; and Sachs 2011.
46. Morris 2010:50, 142–157, 225: quotation:27. Also see discussion of energy capture beginning on p. 626 of his Appendix.
47. Piketty 2014. Also see review by Krugman 2014.

Chapter 6 Holding People Together: Kinship

1. Zihlman, Adrienne L. 1981:97.
2. Lodge, David. 1989 [1965]:57.
3. See Judson 2002, 153–165.
4. Ridley 1993:19.
5. For a clear discussion, see Zimmer 2008.
6. Phillips 2012.

Notes

7. Reported in Greenspan and Shanker 2004:154–55.
8. Gavrilets 2012:9923–9928.
9. Summarized by Edgar 2014:63–67.
10. Dunbar 1996:92–95.
11. Konner 2010:260–328, 335–345. See 264–276 for detailed evidence.; Hrdy 2009:199–203.
12. Konner 2010:270–274.
13. Konner 2010:262, 315–318.
14. Eliot 2009:2–3 and continuing theme through book.
15. Pinker and Spelke 2005.
16. Eliot 2009:7.
17. Balter 2013b.
18. Churchland 2011:8–81, 119–126, 145–151.
19. Konner 2010:749.
20. Chapais 2008:135–166; quotation:151.
21. Silk 2012.
22. Chapais 2008. See description of each, pp. 127–129:(1) Multimale-multifemale group composition, (2) Kin-group outbreeding, (3) Uterine kinship, (4) Incest avoidance, (5) Stable breeding bonds, (6) Agnatic kinship, (7) Bilateral affinity, (8) The tribe, (9) Postmarital residence patterns, (10) The brother-sister kinship complex, (11) Descent, (12) Matrimonial exchange.
23. And see Walker et al. 2011.
24. Balter 2013a.
25. Tomasello et al. 2009; quotation:53 (Joan Silk response).
26. Greenspan and Shanker 2004:155, regarding Tai Forest chimpanzee studies. Also see Tomasello et al. 2009:60–62, 80–82.
27. Silk 2012; Silk 2005.
28. Sahlins 2011:2–19.
29. Sahlins 1972:82, 92–99,191–205.
30. Mauss 1954:3, 18, 66.
31. Mauss 1954:30.
32. Kelly, Robert 2007:181.
33. Carsten 2004; Carsten 2000:1–20. She credits anthropologist David Schneider with first noting this change in discussing effects of colonialism and the industrial age.
34. Gat 2006:5–10.
35. Gat 2006:663–673.
36. Keeley 1996:50–51, 121–126, 150–157.
37. Kelly 2000. See especially 44–65 and 122–127.
38. *Science Encyclopedia* n.d.; Collier 2003:377–379. Accounts of more recent informants, however, are most likely biased by conditions in their times. Certainly, these earlier anthropologists, notably E. E. Evans-Pritchard and Meyer Fortes, produced very detailed and nuanced descriptions and analyses of the people among whom they lived in the early to middle nineteenth century.
39. Sahlins 1972:168–172, 181–183, 221–128.
40. Sahlins 1968:203–120.
41. Gat 2006, 17–25.
42. Gelfand et al. 2011:1100–1104.
43. Konner 2010:460–475.
44. Hrdy 2009:134–174, 233–272; Konner 2010:441–451, 540–544, on cooperative parenting, stress, and resilience within families.

45. Konner 2010:468.
46. Konner 2010:468–474; quotation:473.
47. This happens with avunculocal residence, in which a couple resides with the husband's mother's brother's family; here a strong sister-brother relationship centers on groups of males related through a line of women.
48. Zelman 1977:714–733.
49. Kelly 2007:165.
50. Chapais 2008:217–228.
51. Pinker 2011:684–689; quotation:583.
52. Abuelaish 2010.

Chapter 7 Holding People Together: Religion

1. Shermer, Michael. 2011:5.
2. Nietzsche, Friedrich. 1998 [1889]:58.
3. Geertz 1972:167–178.
4. See Chapter 3 of this book, and for new technologies for analysis, see Stringer 2012:220.
5. Robin Dunbar makes this point also; see Dunbar 1996:103–104. Also see Tattersall 2011. Tattersall (2011) speaks of the role of mystery as impetus to science and religion and of the importance of individual differences in this. Even in this sentiment, we individual *Homo sapiens* are variable.
6. Durkheim 1961 [1912].
7. For a summary, see Lessa and Vogt 1958, Section 10: "Dynamics in Religion" (multiple authors) 496–543.
8. On the role of evolutionary biology, see Wilson 2002:5–46.
9. Luhrmann 2012:300–312; quotation:312.
10. Luhrmann 2012:202–213; quotation:311.
11. Luhrmann et al. 2010:66–78; Luhrmann, et al. 2013:161-162, 171-174.
12. Sacks 2012.
13. Many anthropological sources from Durkheim 1961 [1912], to Radin 1937, to Douglas and Lewis 1970 support this view. Also see other work cited here.
14. Luhrmann 2012:301–302; and see 300–315, Appendix.
15. Boyer 2001:191–192, 240, 253.
16. Rappaport 1968. Similar ritual "dance" in other animals also conveys a message of fitness.
17. This is expressed in the unattributed quotation that Leslie A. White uses to begin his essay on the symbol (1949:22) "In the Word was the Beginning ... the beginning of Man and of Culture." Tattersall uses part of the same quotation as a chapter title (2012:14).
18. Rappaport 2000:280–287, 303–326, 378–461.
19. Wilford 2012a.
20. Levitin 2006:1–12.
21. Patel 2010, Ch. 3.
22. Levitin 2006:248–267.
23. Also see summary of work by archeologist and evolutionary anthropologist Steven Mithen in Schrock 2009:32–37.
24. Schrock 2009 summarizes Mithen's work:32–37.
25. Darwin 2006 [1871]:1207–1209, 808–812.

26. de Waal 2009:64–65; quotation:65.
27. Miller 2000:3–15, 258–283.
28. Dunbar 1996; see especially 139–151.
29. Sacks 2007:214–223, 233–258,335–352.
30. Durkheim 1961 [1912].
31. Also mentioned in Falk 2009 and Hrdy 2009.
32. Hrdy 2009:121.
33. Falk 2009 and Hrdy 2009; Dissanayake 2000 and 2008:169–195.
34. Angier 2012.
35. Brown and Parsons 2008:78–83.
36. From McGowan 2012:16–22.
37. Ramachandran 2011:234–244.
38. Dissanayake 2008b:241–263.
39. Boyer 2001:246–248.
40. Boyer 2001:51–91, 137–167. He emphasizes cognitive processes that lead to religious concepts throughout his book.
41. Boyer 2001:329–330.
42. Vedantam 2010:25–26.
43. Norenzayan and Shariff 2008:58–62; Norenzayan 2013.
44. Boehm 2012:202–204.
45. Smith 1937 [1776]:722, 726–727, 750–766.
46. Sapolsky 2006:161–170. This essay originally appeared in Discovery magazine 2005; text may have been slightly revised for this collection.
47. Wright 2009.
48. de Waal 2009:206.
49. Lovelady:2012.
50. See Haidt 2012:11–13, 123–127, 146–153.
51. Bellah 2011:96, 111.
52. Greenspan and Shanker 2004:182–84, 212–23.
53. Tomasello et al. 2009:3–100; see also S. Spelke, forum participant in same volume: 149–172.
54. Shakespeare n.d. (1998):32.
55. Wilson 2012:10.
56. Goodenough 1998:xv–xvii, 167–174.
57. Bellah 2011: Especially see Chapters 6–9.

Chapter 8 Pulling People Apart: Tribalism

1. Gaiman, 2011:207.
2. Neill 2009:22–23.
3. Allport 1954.
4. Hewstone 2003.
5. Vedantam 2010. See pp. 188–229, on the Obama election.
6. Self-testing of bias in several areas is available through the "Implicit Association Test" at the website of *Project Implicit*: http://projectimplicit.net/about. php. Also see Jablonski 2012:100.
7. Nesdale 1999.
8. See McKown and Weinstein 2013:498–515.
9. Yong 2013:76–80; Yong cites articles that provide additional detail.

10. Vedantam 2010.
11. Winkler 2009. Also see Nesdale et al. 2005:652–663; Vedantam 2010:60–81.
12. Kahneman 2011.
13. Eagleman 2011:12–19, 101–144.
14. Greene 2013:15, 194–199; quotation:26.
15. Shermer 2011:259–279. On these pages he names and briefly summarizes 12 major biases, concluding the chapter with a list of additional ones.
16. Gazzaniga 2011:202–212.
17. Shermer 2011:87.
18. Bloom 2010:8–18; quotation:12.
19. Konner 2006:1–30. See especially 17–22.
20. Orwell, George 1949 (1950, 1977); used on multiple pages.
21. Douglas 1966.
22. See Haidt 2006:233–243.
23. For example, Townsend 2011. This column in the St. Louis Post-Dispatch concerns a meeting scheduled by the St. Louis Chapter of ACT for hearing a recorded lecture on the Fort Hood Massacre perpetrated by Nidal Hasan. The short piece used the kind of dehumanizing language discussed in this chapter. In contrast, there were no such meetings regarding other massacres, for example, in Newtown, Connecticut.
24. Pinker 2011:320–343.
25. Harris 2010:32–33.
26. Patzia. Xenophanes (c. 570—c. 478 BCE). Internet Encyclopedia of Philosophy.
27. Harris 1968:41–42; quotation:41.
28. Jablonski 2012:106–108.
29. Darwin 2006 [1859]:917.
30. Tattersall and DeSalle 2011.
31. Livingstone 1962:279–281.
32. Connor 2010, interview of Spencer Wells. Also see Stringer 2012:44–48.
33. Jorde and Wooding 2004:s28–s33.
34. Brahic 2014:10–11. Also see Pickrell et al. 2014.
35. Stringer 2012:234–239.
36. Darwin 2006 [1871]:905, 907–911, 913–918, 1231–1235.
37. Jablonski 2012:27–33.
38. Jablonski and Chaplin 2000:57–106; Jablonski 2012:23–46; 93–102.
39. Jablonski 2012:46.
40. Montagu 1942.
41. Jablonski 2012:74–79.
42. Smith, 1937 [1776]:13–16; quotation:15.
43. Pinker 2011:40–58, 31–36.
44. Jablonski 2012:129–130. Her Chapter 9, 117–133, is entitled: "Skin Color in the Age of Exploration."
45. Smith 2013.
46. Experiments with groups of five-year-old children that assign them randomly to two groups wearing different colored shirts demonstrate that even such artificial, "minimal group affiliations" can engender group-based favoritism; children valued and shared more readily with those in their own group than with children in the other group. See Dunham and Baron 2011:793–811.
47. Jorde and Wooding 2004:s28–s33. For a lay-friendly discussion of this issue, see Tattersall and DeSalle 2011:160–184.

48. Yong 2013:76–80.
49. Cochran and Harpending 2009; see especially 14 ff, 179–186, 201–224, 225 ff.
50. I also question the conclusion that U.S. students, for example, are two standard deviations smarter than their grandparents' generation. Children today have considerably different experiences from those two generations older; they have more experience with figures and shapes found on tests and on digital media, and less experience with problems faced by their elders. This is known as the Flynn effect.
51. Konner 2010:200–201.
52. de Waal 2009:22.
53. Smith 1937 [1776]:750.
54. Konner 2010:708–712; Konner 2006.
55. Konner 2006:1–39. See especially 22–25, 26–30.
56. Williams 2013.
57. Pinker 2011:36. Throughout his book, Pinker classifies all societies as anarchies or states. Dual classifications can be helpful, but I prefer the terms kinship-based and state-based to denote this dichotomy between societies because these reflect the reality of organization and diversity within the former. (See my Chapter 7 for my discussion of the role of kinship as a basis for organization). Kinship is an organizer of small-scale societies, and it is a key to understanding transitions from egalitarian to hierarchal societies, as well as the intermediate transitions between bands, tribes, chiefdoms, and states, as described in my Chapter 6.
58. Sussman 2013:97–111; quotation:97.
59. Bowles 2009:1293–1298.
60. Chagnon 2009. But note: Anthropologist Jonathan Hill (personal communication, 2012), another Amazonian ethnographer, describes the Yanomamo as "remnants" of long-term Western expansion and encroachment on the complex Amazonian ecosystem rather than as a pristine pre-Western society. He sees their famous "fierceness" partially a result of their having been pushed, through colonial domination, into an increasingly smaller territory.
61. Fry 2012.
62. Ferguson 2013:112–141.
63. Boehm 2012:78–83, 108–109, 134–140, and throughout remainder of book.
64. Turchin 2010:1–37; Boyd, Gintis, Bowles, and Richerson 2005: 215–227.
65. Morris 2012:9–37. Morris pursues this general argument to the end of this article, pp. 11–33, 23–26 regarding cycles of wars. Compares threats to Pax Americana paralleling earlier threats and breakup of Pax Britannica, 32–33; quotation:28.
66. Morris 2012: ibid. He summarizes (14):"Anthropology and archaeology suggest that while some societies are less violent than others, every human group sometimes resorts to violence to settle its disputes … However, the shift toward bigger, safer, richer societies began in a very specific part of the planet, between roughly 20° and 35° North in the Old World and 15° South and 20° North in the New … I like to call this zone the lucky latitudes."
67. Morris 2012: quotation:30–31.
68. Prado 2014.
69. Sheridan 2013.
70. Pinker 2011:296–297.
71. Verbeek 2013:54–77, especially 58–59.
72. Hannah Kokko 2013:38–53. And Fry and Szala 2013:451–470.

73. Nowak 2011.
74. These most recent conclusions reported in Boehm 2013:315–340.
75. Boehm 2012:78–83, 108–109, 134–140, and throughout remainder of book.
76. Editors of *Encyclopedia Britannica* 2013. And see Fry 2013:543–558.
77. Wolfenden 2011:1–2. And see Doughty 2014:780–794.
78. Sapolsky 2013:421–438.
79. Fuentes 2013:78–94; quotations:91, 92.
80. Keeley 1996.
81. Wilson 2012:62–76. See his Chapter 8, entitled "War as Humanity's Hereditary Curse," especially 62–66.
82. Sagan 1996:26–27.
83. Abuelaish 2010:7, 35–70, 101, 134–137, 196–203.
84. de Waal 2009:185.

PART IV: HUMAN PROSPECTS

1. Seeger n.d.
2. Carson 2002:277.

Chapter 9 Beyond Tribalism

1. ElBaradei 2005.
2. Sachs. 2011:263.
3. See Wilson 2012:14–16.
4. Tattersall 2014:56.
5. See Hrdy 2009:293–294.
6. Smith 1937 [1776]:107.
7. Wright 1994:267–269, and the entirety of his Chapter 13, "Deception and Self-Deception."
8. Darwin 2006 [1859]:503:"if feeble man can do much by his powers of artificial selection, I can see no limit to the amount of change, to the beauty and infinite complexity of the co-adaptations between all organic beings, one with another and with their physical conditions of life, which may be effected in the long course of time by nature's power of selection."
9. Sharot 2011.
10. Hill 2009:149–150, 156.
11. Linden 2011:3–20; 65–66.
12. Wright 1994:342–344; quotation:344.
13. Critchley 2011.
14. Hegarty 2013.
15. Darwin 2006 [1871]:384.
16. Asma 2013.
17. Shermer 2011:224–225.
18. Hallam and Ingold 2007:1–24.
19. Ingold 2011.
20. Lehrer 2012:86–93, 110–111.

21. Keeley 1996:157, 152–156.
22. Thaler and Sunstein 2008.
23. Benkler 2011a:5–21, 34–54, 162–168, 236–237. All chapters support main points.
24. Ostrom 2005:253–275.
25. Gintis et al. 2005.
26. Fiske 1992:689–723.
27. Benkler 2011b.
28. Benkler 2011a; see 202–212 for discussion of Toyota experience.
29. Wright 2001.
30. Nowak and Highfield 2011.
31. Rachman 2011.
32. See Wright 2001:209–239, 334 (tribalism and global governance) and footnote 26; and see Wright 2009:411–430; quotation:427.
33. Global Risks 2014.
34. Morris 2012:33.
35. Keeley 1996:152–156.
36. Alexander 2011. NPR Podcast, 2012. Book review by Schuessler 2012. Also see Jones 2013, Introduction and Epilogue, for overview of related research.
37. See Schuessler 2014.
38. Toobin 2014.
39. Rappaport 2000:429–446; quotation:430.
40. de Waal 2009:192.
41. Dubreuil 2010:23–24, 183–189.
42. Vermeij 2010:255.
43. Smith 1937 [1776]:79–86, 249–250, 388–389, 625–626, 862–79, 899–900. From p. 250 "The proposal of any new law or regulation of commerce which comes from this order, ought always to be listened to with great precaution, and ought never to be adopted till after having been long and carefully examined, not only with the most scrupulous, but with the most suspicious attention. It comes from an order of men, whose interest is never exactly the same with that of the public, who have generally an interest to deceive and even to oppress the public, and who accordingly have, upon many occasions, both deceived and oppressed it."
44. Krugman 2012.
45. *Oxford Dictionaries*.
46. Sachs 2011:105, 130–131.
47. Smith 1937 [1776]: especially 625, 862–879, 899–900.
48. Personal communication.
49. A wonderful source for clear information about all of these issues is Sachs 2011.
50. See Greenspan and Shanker 2004:425, 437–439, 455.
51. Reich 2014.
52. Freeland 2012.
53. Vermeij 2010. See especially 83–86, 98–105; quotation:105.
54. Sachs 2011:9–10, 162–163.
55. Greene 2013:211–225, 293–304.
56. Eisenhower 1961.
57. Sachs 2011:105, 130–131.
58. Freeland 2012.
59. de Waal 2009:188–200; quotation:97.

60. Gintis et al. 2005:270, 392, 395; Fong, Bowles, and Gintis 2005:277–302; Kahan 2005:339–378; Bowles and Gintis 2005: 379–398.
61. Glaeser 2011:50–55.
62. Summarized in Steinhauer 2013.
63. Sachs 2011:26.
64. Sachs 2011:49–131; quotation:82.
65. Sachs 2011: Chapter 12, 237–250. His seven habits for governance:(1) Set clear goals and benchmarks. (2) Mobilize expertise (use scientists' input on science-based issues), (3) Make multi-year plans, (4) Be mindful of the far future (generations beyond legislators), (5) End the corporatocracy (through changing rules for financing of campaigns and media time, and eliminating the revolving door between legislators and lobbyists, and associated economic perks); (6) Restore public management (in place of private contractors); (7) Decentralize (some specific policy decisions and administration).
66. Sachs 2011:46.
67. Pinker 2011:310–315.
68. Vermeij 2010:260–261.
69. Boehm 2012:343–360, 205 on "secondary free riders"
70. Foley 2010:54–57, and see 58–60, "Solutions to Environmental Threats," offering multi-author suggestions for solutions relating to each process identified by Foley, collected by Scientific American.
71. Caldeira 2012:78–83.
72. Vermeij 2010 : see especially 202–203.
73. Wilson 2012:13.
74. Lovins 2014. Also see Lovins 2011.
75. Konner 2006:1–39.
76. Vermeij 2010: especially 205–223; quotation:205.
77. Allen 2011.
78. Keeley 1996:178.

Chapter 10 Our Place in Nature

1. Eliot 1893:61.
2. Carroll 2005:301.
3. Campbell 1996:6.
4. Ramachandran 2011:117–135, 247–288; on aspects of self:250–253.
5. Dennett 1991:410, 418, 423.
6. Gazzaniga 2011:114, 127–142; 66–69.
7. Damasio 2010:71–72, 174–178 252–263, 296–317.
8. Churchland 2013:195–198, 233–36, 245–252. And see her Chapter 8.
9. Damasio 2003:172–175.
10. Churchland 2013:178–183.
11. Wilson 2012:288.
12. Ramachandran 2011:291.
13. Gazzaniga 2011:179–225.
14. Wright 1994:348–359; quotation:357.
15. Harris 2010:102–112; quotation:104.

16. C. P. Stone's humorous capsule summary of the first three laws is probably the most famous:#1 You cannot win. #2 You cannot break even. #3 You cannot get out of the game.
17. Personal communication. February 15, 2014.
18. Wright 2009; see especially 410–483. Also see Wright 2001.
19. Deutsch 2011; see 78–106, 125–147, 196–222, 369–417, 422–431, 440–442.
20. Morris 2012:9–37; see 32–33; quotation:33.
21. de Waal 2009:185. Also see Boehm 2012.
22. Konner 2010:13.
23. Vermeij 2010:247.
24. From an old joke (source unknown): Neurotics build castles in the air, psychotics live in them, and psychiatrists collect the rent.
25. Sagan 1996:26.
26. Bellah 2011:605; quoting Fingarette 1963.
27. Huxley 1889.
28. Vermeij 2010:109.
29. Wells 2010:184–203.
30. Iyer 2011.
31. Rushkoff 2013.
32. Einstein 1932.
33. Barash 2008:103.
34. When asked why he believed in God, prominent physician and author Jerome Groopman responded: "Why believe? I have no rational answer. The question seems to be in the domain of why do we love someone? You could reduce it to certain components, perhaps refer to neurotransmitters but somehow the answer seems to transcend the truly knowable. This is the cognitive dissonance that people like me live with, and with which we often struggle." (cited in Shermer 2011:185).
35. Vermeij 2010:263.
36. Wilson 2012:291–293; quotation:293.
37. Darwin 2006 [1859]:760.

References

Abuelaish, Izzeldin. 2010. I Shall Not Hate: A Gaza Doctor's Journey on the Road to Peace and Human Dignity. New York: Walker and Company.

Adovasio, J. M., Olga Soffer, and Jake Page. 2007. *The Invisible Sex: Uncovering the True Roles of Women in Prehistory*. Washington, DC: Smithsonian Books.

Al-Khalili, Jim. 2011. *The House of Wisdom: How Arabic Science Saved Ancient Knowledge and Gave Us the Renaissance*. New York: Penguin Press.

Allen, Colin. 2011. The Future of Moral Machines. *The New York Times* Opinionator, December 25, 2011.

Alexander, Michelle, *The New Jim Crow: Mass Incarceration in the Age of Colorblindness*. New York: The New Press, 2011 (first edition, 2010).

Allport, Gordon. 1954. *The Nature of Prejudice*. New York: Perseus Book Group.

Angier, Natalie. 2011. Thirst for Fairness May Have Helped Us Survive. *The New York Times*, July 5, 2011.

———. 2012. Insights from the Youngest Minds. Interview with Elizabeth S. Spelke. *The New York Times*, April 30, 2012.

Asma, Stephen T. 2013. The Myth of Universal Love. *The New York Times* Opinionator, January 5, 2013.

Balter, Michael. 2011a. Earliest Human Beds Found in South Africa. *ScienceNow*, December 8, 2011.

———. 2011b. When Humans First Plied the Deep Blue Sea. *ScienceNow*, November 24, 2011.

———. 2013a. Ancient Foragers and Farmers Hit It Off. *ScienceNow*, February 11, 2013.

———. 2013b. Monogamy May Have Evolved to Prevent Infanticide. *ScienceNow*, July 29, 2013.

Barash, David P. 2008. *Natural Selections: Selfish Altruists, Honest Liars, and Other Realities of Evolution*. New York: Bellevue Literary Press.

———. 2013. Evolution and Peace: A Janus Connection. In *War, Peace, and Human Nature: The Convergence of Evolutionary and Cultural Views*. Douglas P. Fry, Ed., 25–37. Oxford: Oxford University Press.

Bekoff, Marc. 2001. Social Play Behaviour: Cooperation, Fairness, Trust, and the Evolution of Morality. *Journal of Consciousness Studies* 8 (2): 81–90.

Bekoff, Marc, and Jessica Pierce. 2010. The Ethical Dog. *Scientific American Mind*, March/April: 16–17.

Bellah, Robert N. 2011. *Religion in Human Evolution: From the Paleolithic to the Axial Age*. Cambridge, MA: Belknap Press of Harvard University Press.

Benkler, Yochai. 2011a. *The Penguin and the Leviathan: The Triumph of Cooperation over Self-Interest*. New York: Crown Business (Random House).

———.2011b A Free Irresponsible Press: Wikileaks and the Battle over the Soul of the Networked Fourth Estate, 46 Harv. C.R.-C.L. L. Rev. 311 (2011). *Harvard Civil Rights-Civil Liberties LawReview*. 1/2514. http://harvardcrcl.org/wp-content/uploads/2009/06/Benkler.pdf Accessed 10/31/14.

Berger, Lee R., et al. 2010. *Australopithecus sediba*: A New Species of *Homo*-like Australopith from South Africa. *Science* 328(5975): 195–204.

Blake, Edgar 2014. Powers of Two, *Scientific American*, September 2014: 63-67.

Bloom, Paul. 2010. *How Pleasure Works: The New Science of Why We Like What We Like*. New York: W. W. Norton and Company.

Boehm, Christopher. 2012. *Moral Origins: The Evolution of Virtue, Altruism, and Shame*. Philadelphia: Basic Books.

———. 2013. The Biocultural Evolution of Conflict Resolution between Groups. In *War, Peace, and Human Nature: The Convergence of Evolutionary and Cultural Views*. Douglas P. Fry, Ed., 315–340. Oxford: Oxford University Press.

Bowles, Samuel. 2009. Did Warfare among Ancestral Hunter-Gatherers Affect the Evolution of Human Social Behaviors? *Science* 324(5932): 1293–1298.

Bowles, Samuel and Herbert Gintis. 2005. Social Capital, Moral Sentiments, and Community Governments. In *Moral Sentiments in Material Interests*. Gintis et al., Eds., 379–398. Cambridge, Massachusetts: The MIT Press.

Boyd, Robert, Herbert Gintis, Samuel Boyles, and Peter J. Richerson. 2005. The Evolution of Altruistic Punishment. In *Moral Sentiments in Material Interests*. Gintis et al., Eds., 215–227. Cambridge, Massachusetts: The MIT Press.

Boyer, Pascal. 2001. *Religion Explained: The Evolutionary Origins of Religious Thought*. New York: Basic Books: 191–2, 240, 253.

Brahic, Catherine. 2014. The Return to Africa that Time Forgot. *NewScientist*, February 8, 2014: 10–11.

Bramble, Dennis M., and Daniel E. Lieberman. 2004. Endurance Running and the Evolution of *Homo*. *Nature* 432: 345–352.

Brown, Steven, and Lawrence M. Parsons. 2008. The Neuroscience of Dance. *Scientific American* 299(1): 78–83.

Campbell, Neil A. 1996. *Biology*. 4th edition. Menlo Park, CA: Benjamin/Cummings.

Caldeira, Ken. 2012. The Great Climate Experiment. *Scientific American*, September 2012: 78–83.

Carroll, Sean B. 2005. *Endless Forms Most Beautiful: The New Science of Evo Devo and the Animal Kingdom*. New York: W. W. Norton.

———. 2009. *Remarkable Creatures: Epic Adventures in the Search for the Origins of Species*. Orlando, FL: Houghton Mifflin Harcourt.

Carson, Rachel. 2002 [1962] *Silent Spring*. Anniversary Edition; Linda Lear, Edward O. Wilson. Eds. New York: Houghton Mifflin.

Carsten, Janet, Ed. 2000. *Cultures of Relatedness: New Approaches to the Study of Kinship*. Cambridge, MA: Cambridge University Press.

———. 2004. *After Kinship*. New Departures in Anthropology. Cambridge: Cambridge University Press.

Chagnon, Napoleon. 2009. *Yanomamo: The Fierce People*. Case Studies in Anthropology. Belmont, CA: Wadsworth Cengage Learning.

Chapais, Bernard. 2008. *Primeval Kinship: How Pair-Bonding Gave Birth to Human Society*. Cambridge, MA: Harvard University Press.

Childe, V. Gordon. 1951[1936]. *Man Makes Himself*. New York: New American Library.

Christmas Miracle, The. 2008. *The Guardian*, November 9, 2008.

Churchland, Patricia S. 2011. *Braintrust: What Neuroscience Tells Us about Morality.* Princeton, NJ: Princeton University Press.

————. 2013. *Touching a Nerve: The Self as Brain.* New York: W.W. Norton and Company.

Cochran, Gregory, and Henry Harpending. 2009. *The 10,000 Year Explosion: How Civilization Accelerated Human Evolution.* New York: Basic Books.

Collier, Jane F. 2003. Review of *Dividends of Kinship: Meanings and Uses of Social Relatedness* and *New Directions in Anthropological Kinship. American Anthropologist* 105(2): 377–379.

Connor, Steve. 2010. At Root, We're Still Hunters. Interview of Spencer Wells. *The Independent,* June 7, 2010.

Corey, Paul. 2014. Steven Pinker and the Ambivalence of Modernity. *Anamnesis Journal.* http://anamnesisjournal.com/2014/01/steven-pinker-ambivalence-modernity-critique-better-angels-nature-violence-declined/. Accessed July 7, 2014.

Cox, Edward, and John Bonner. 2001. The Advantages of Togetherness. *Science* 292(5516): 448–449.

Craig, Edward, Ed. 2005. *The Shorter Routledge Encyclopedia of Philosophy.* London: Routledge.

Critchley, Simon. 2011. The Cycle of Revenge. *The New York Times* Opinionator, September 8, 2011.

Dahlberg, Frances, Ed. 1981. *Woman the Gatherer.* New Haven, CT: Yale University Press.

Damasio, Antonio. 2003. *Looking for Spinoza: Joy, Sorrow, and the Feeling Brain.* Orlando, FL: Houghton Mifflin Harcourt.

————. 2010. *Self Comes to Mind: Constructing the Conscious Brain.* New York: Pantheon Books.

Dart, R. A. 1949. The Predatory Implement Technique of the Australopithecines. *American Journal of Physical Anthropology* 7: 1–16.

Darwin, Charles. 2006 [1859]. *On the Origin of Species.* In *From So Simple a Beginning: The Four Great Books of Charles Darwin.* Edward O. Wilson, Ed., 435–760. New York: W. W. Norton.

————. 2006 [1871]. *The Descent of Man, and Selection in Relation to Sex.* In *From So Simple a Beginning: The Four Great Books of Charles Darwin.* Edward O. Wilson, 767–1248. New York: W. W. Norton.

Darwin, Erasmus. 1794, 1796. Vols. 1–3 of *Zoonomia or the Laws of Organic Life.* Teddington, UK. http://www.gutenberg.org/files/15707/15707-h/15707-h.htm.

Dennett, Daniel C. 1991. *Consciousness Explained.* Boston: Little, Brown, and Co.

————. 1995. *Darwin's Dangerous Idea: Evolution and the Meanings of Life.* New York: Touchstone.

DeSilva, Jeremy M. 2011. A Shift toward Birthing Relatively Large Infants Early in Human Evolution. Proc Natl Acad Sci USA 108(3):1022–1027.

Deutsch, David. 2011. *The Beginning of Infinity: Explanations That Transform the World.* New York: Penguin.

de Waal, Frans. 2005. *Our Inner Ape.* New York: Riverhead Books (Penguin).

————. 2009. *The Age of Empathy: Nature's Lessons for a Kinder Society.* New York: Harmony Books.

Diamond, Jared. 1999. *Guns, Germs, and Steel: The Fates of Human Societies.* New York:

W. W. Norton Company.

Dissanayake, Ellen. 2000. *Art and Intimacy: How the Arts Began.* Seattle: University of Washington Press.

———. 2008a. If Music Is the Food of Love, What about Survival and Reproductive Success? *Musicae Scientiae,* Special Issue: Narrative in Music and Interaction: 169–195.

———. 2008b. The Arts after Darwin: Does Art Have an Origin and Adaptive Function? In *World Art Studies: Exploring Concepts and Approaches.* K. Zijlmans and W. van Damm, Eds., 241–263. Amsterdam: Valiz.

Dobzhansky, Theodosius. 1973. Nothing about Biology Makes Sense Except in the Light of Evolution. *American Biology Teacher* 35(3): 125–129.

Doughty, Kristin C. 2014. "Our Goal Is Not to Punish, but to Reconcile": Mediation in Postgenocide Rwanda. *American Anthropologist* 116 (4): 780–794.

Douglas, Mary. 1966. *Purity and Danger: An Analysis of Concepts of Pollution and Taboo.* Baltimore: Penguin Books.

Dubreuil, Benoît. 2010. *Human Evolution and the Origins of Hierarchies.* New York: Cambridge University Press

Dunbar, Robin. 1996. *Grooming, Gossip, and the Evolution of Language.* Cambridge, MA: Harvard University Press.

Dunbar, R[obin]. I. M., and Susanne Shultz, 2007. Understanding Primate Brain Evolution. *Philosophical Transactions of the Royal Society of London: Biological Sciences,* 362(1480): 649–658.

Dunham, Yarrow, and Andrew Scott Baron. 2011. Consequences of "Minimal" Group Affiliations in Children. *Child Development* 82(3): 793–811.

Durkheim, Emile. 1961 [1912]. *The Elementary Forms of the Religious Life.* Joseph Ward Swain, Trans. New York: Collier Books.

Eagleman, David. 2011. *Incognito: The Secret Lives of the Brain.* New York: Pantheon Books.

Editors of Encyclopedia Britannica. 2013. Iroquois Confederacy. http://www.britannica.com/Checked/topic/294660/Iroquois-Confederacy. Accessed June 14, 2014.

Einstein, Albert. 1932. My Credo. From Albert Einstein Archives, Hebrew University of Jerusalem, Israel. http://www.einstein-website.de/z_biography/credo.html. Accessed March 13, 2013.

Eisenhower, Dwight D. 1961. Farewell Speech. PDF of his typescript. http://www.eisenhower.archives.gov/research/online_documents/farewell_address/Reading_Copy.pdf. Accessed June 4, 2014.

ElBaradei, Mohamed. 2005. Nobel Lecture, Oslo, December 10, 2005. http://www.nobelprize.org/nobel_prizes/peace/laureates/2005/elbaradei-lecture-en.html. Accessed 7/30/14.

Eldredge, Niles. 2005. *Darwin: Discovering the Tree of Life.* New York: W. W. Norton.

Eliot, George. 1893. *Adam Bede.* Volume 2. Boston: Estes and Lauriat.

Eliot, Lise. 2009. *Pink Brain, Blue Brain: How Small Differences Grow Into Troublesome Gaps—And What We Can Do About It.* New York: Houghton, Mifflin, Harcourt.

Endicott, Karen L. 2004. Gender Relations in Hunter-Gatherer Societies. In *The Cambridge Encyclopedia of Hunters and Gatherers.* Richard B. Lee and Richard Daly, Eds., 411–18. New York: Cambridge University Press.

Falk, Dean. 1992. *Braindance: New Discoveries about Human Origins and Brain Evolution.*

New York: Henry Holt & Company.

—————. 2009. *Finding our Tongues: Mothers, Infants and the Origins of Language.* New York: Basic Books.

—————. 2011. *The Fossil Chronicles: How Two Controversial Discoveries Changed Our View of Human Evolution.* Berkley: University of California Press.

Ferguson, R. Brian. 2013. Pinker's List: Exaggerating Prehistoric War Mortality. In *War, Peace, and Human Nature: The Convergence of Evolutionary and Cultural Views*, Douglas P. Fry, Ed., 112–141. Oxford: Oxford University Press.

Fingarette, Herbert. 1963. *The Self in Transformation: Psychoanalysis, Philosophy, and the Life of the Spirit.* New York: Basic Books.

Fiske, Alan Page. 1992. The Four Elementary Forms of Sociality: A Framework for a Unified Theory of Social Relations. *Psychological Review* 99(4): 689–723.

Foley, Jonathan. 2010. Boundaries for a Healthy Planet. *Scientific American*, April 2010: 54–57.

Fong, Christina M., Samuel Bowles, and Herbert Gintis. 2005. Reciprocity and the Welfare State. In *Moral Sentiments and Material Interests.* Gintis et al. Eds., 277–302. Cambridge, Massachusetts: The MIT Press.

Freeland, Chrystia. 2012. *Plutocrats: The Rise of the New Global Super-Rich and the Fall of Everyone Else.* New York: The Penguin Press.

Fry, Douglas P. 2012. Peace in Our Time. Review of Steven Pinker, *The Better Angels of Our Nature.* In *Book Forum*, December/January 2012. www.bookforum.com/inprint/018_04/8575. Accessed July 2014.

—————. 2013. Cooperation for Survival. In *War, Peace, and Human Nature: The Convergence of Evolutionary and Cultural Views..* Douglas P. Fry, Ed., 543–558. Oxford: Oxford University Press.

Fry, Douglas P., and Anna Szala. 2013. The Evolution of Agonism. In *War, Peace, and Human Nature: The Convergence of Evolutionary and Cultural Views.* Douglas P. Fry. Ed., 451–470. Oxford: Oxford University Press.

Fuentes, Augustín. 2013. Cooperation, Conflict, and Niche Construction in the Genus *Homo*. In *War, Peace, and Human Nature: The Convergence of Evolutionary and Cultural Views..* Douglas P. Fry, Ed., 78–94. Oxford: Oxford University Press.

Gaiman, Neil American Gods, Tenth Anniversary edition. 2011. New York: HarperCollins Publishers, Mass Market Paperback.

Gat, Azar. 2006. *War in Human Civilization.* Oxford: Oxford University Press.

Gavrilets, Sergey. 2012. Human Origins and the Transition from Promiscuity to Pair-Bonding. *Proc Natl Acad Sci* USA 109(25): 9923–9928.

Gazzaniga, Michael. 2011. *Who's in Charge? Free Will and the Science of the Brain.* New York: Henry Holt and Company.

Geertz, Clifford. 1963. *Agricultural Involution: The Processes of Ecological Change in Indonesia.* Berkeley: University of California Press.

—————. 1972. Religion as a Cultural System. In *Reader in Comparative Religion: An Anthropological Approach.* 3rd edition.. William A. Lessa and Evon Z. Vogt, Eds., 167–178. Upper Saddle River, NJ: Pearson.

Gelfand, Michele J., and 44 others. 2011. Differences between Tight and Loose Cultures: A 33-Nation Study. *Science* 332(6033): 1100–1104.

Gibbons, Ann. 2012a. Bonobos Join Chimps as Closest Human Relatives. *Science-Now*, June 13, 2012.

—————. 2012b. For Early Hominins in Africa, Many Ways to Take a Walk. *Science*

336(4): 538–539.

———. 2012c. Raw Food Not Enough to Feed Big Brains. *ScienceNow*, October 22, 2012.

Gintis, Herbert, Samuel Bowles, Robert Boyd, and Ernst Fehr, Eds. 2005. *Moral Sentiments and Material Interests: The Foundations of Cooperation in Economic Life.* Cambridge, MA: The MIT Press.

Glaeser, Edward. 2011. Cities: Engines of Innovation. *Scientific American*, September 2011: 50–55.

Global Risks 2014, 9th edition. World Economic Forum Insight Report. http://www3.weforum.org/docs/WEF_GlobalRisks_Report_2014.pdf. Accessed August 1, 2014.

Goodenough, Ursula. 1998. *The Sacred Depths of Nature.* New York: Oxford University Press.

Gould, Stephen Jay, and Elisabeth S. Vrba. 1982. Exaptation: A Missing Term in the Science of Form. *Paleobiology* 8(1): 4–15.

Greenspan, Stanley I., and Stuart G Shanker. 2004. *The First Idea: How Symbols, Language, and Intelligence Evolved from Our Primate Ancestors to Modern Humans.* Cambridge, MA: DaCapo Press of Perseus.

Gurven, Michael. 2006. The Evolution of Contingent Cooperation. *Current Anthropology* 47(1): 185–192.

Haidt, Jonathan. 2006. *The Happiness Hypothesis: Finding Modern Truth in Ancient Wisdom.* New York: Basic Books.

———. 2012. *The Righteous Mind: Why Good People Are Divided by Politics and Religion.* New York: Pantheon Books.

Hallam, Elizabeth, and Tim Ingold, Eds. 2007. Creativity and Cultural Improvisation: An Introduction. *Creativity and Cultural Improvisation.* ASA Monographs, 44. Berg, Oxford International Publishers Ltd.

Hammer, Michael F. 2013. Human Hybrids. *Scientific American* 308(5): 66–71.

Harmon, Katherine. 2013. Shattered Ancestry. *Scientific American* 308(2): 42–49.

Harris, Marvin. 1968. *The Rise of Anthropological Theory: A History of Theories of Culture* New York: Thomas Y. Crowell and Company.

Harris, Sam. 2010. *The Moral Landscape: How Science Can Determine Human Values.* New York: Free Press.

Hart, Donna, and Robert W. Sussman. 2005. *Man the Hunted: Primates, Predators, and Human Evolution.* Cambridge, MA: Westview Press (Perseus).

Hawkes, John, Keith Hunley, Sang-Hee Lee, and Milford Wolpoff. 2000. Population Bottlenecks and Pleistocene Human Evolution. *Molecular Biology and Evolution* 17(1): 2–22.

Hawkes, Kristen. 2003. Grandmothers and the Evolution of Human Longevity. *American Journal of Human Biology* 15(3): 380–400.

Hegarty, Stephanie. 2013. Utoeya: How does a country recover from mass murder? BBC News; Health. June 22, 2013. www.bbc.co.uk/news/health-22951220. Accessed July 11, 2013.

Hewstone, Miles. 2003. The Contact Hypothesis. Intergroup Contact: Panacea for Prejudice? *The Psychologist* 16(7): 352–355.

Hey, Jody. 2010. The Divergence of Chimpanzee Species and Subspecies as Revealed in Multipopulation Isolation-with-Migration Analyses. *Molecular Biology and Evolution* 27: 921–933.

Hill, Jonathan D. 2009. *Made-from-Bone: Trickster Myths, Music, and History from the Amazon*. Urbana: University of Illinois Press.

Hopkin, Michael. 2004. Jaw-Dropping Theory of Human Evolution: Did Mankind Trade Chewing Power for a Bigger Brain? *Nature* 428: 415–418.

Hrdy, Sarah B. 1999. *Mother Nature: Maternal Instincts and How They Shape the Human Species*. New York: Ballantine Publishing Group.

———. 2009. *Mothers and Others: The Evolutionary Origins of Mutual Understanding*. Cambridge, MA: Belknap Press of Harvard University Press.

Huxley, Thomas. 1889. Agnosticism and Christianity. *The Nineteenth Century* 25 (1889): 937-964; and *Essays on Some Controverted Questions; Collected Essays Volume* 5: 309-365.

Implicit Association Test. http://projectimplicit.net/about.php. Accessed September 28, 2011.

Ingold, Tim. June 20, 2011, Lecture 3, Creativity—Abduction or Improvisation? http://podcasts.ox.ac.uk/creativity-lecture-3-creativity-abduction-or-improvis action-video. Accessed December 10, 2012.

Iyer, Pico. 2011. The Joy of Quiet. *The New York Times*, December 29, 2011.

Jablonski, Nina G. 2012. *Living Color: The Biological and Social Meaning of Skin Color*. Berkley: University of California Press.

Jablonski, Nina G., and George Chaplin. 2000. The Evolution of Human Skin Coloration. *Journal of Human Evolution* 39(1): 57–106.

Jha, Alok. 2011. Fossil Foot Bone Shows Our Ancestor Had Two Feet Firmly on the Ground. *The Guardian*, February 10, 2011.

Johnson, Eric Michael. 2012. The Better Bonobos of Our Nature. *Scientific American* June19, 2012. http://blogs.scientificamerican.com/primate-diaries/2012/06/19 the-better-bonobos-of-our-nature/.

Jones, Jacqueline. 2013. *A Dreadful Deceit: The Myth of Race from the Colonial Era to Obama's America*. New York: Basic Books.

Jorde, Lynn B., and Stephen P. Wooding. 2004. Genetic Variation, Classification, and "Race." *Nature Genetics* 36(11): s28–s33.

Judson, Olivia. 2002. *Dr. Tatiana's Sex Advice to All Creation*. New York: Henry Holt and Company.

Jurmain, Robert, Lynn Kilgore, and Wenda Trevathan. 2000. *Introduction to Physical Anthropology*. 8th Edition. Belmont, California: Wadsworth Thompson Learning.

Kahan, Dan M. 2005. The Logic of Reciprocity: Trust, Collective Action, and Law. In *Moral Sentiments in Material Interests*. Gintis et al., Eds., 339–378. Cambridge, Massachusetts: The MIT Press.

Kahneman, Daniel. 2011. *Thinking, Fast and Slow*. New York: Farrar, Strauss, and Giroux.

Kaplan, Hillard, and Michael Gurven. 2005. The Natural History of Human Food Sharing and Cooperation: A Review and a New Multi-Individual Approach to the Negotiation of Norms. In *Moral Sentiments and Material Interests*. Gintis et al. Eds., 75–113. Cambridge, Massachusetts: The MIT Press.

Keeley, Lawrence H. 1996. *War Before Civilization: The Myth of the Peaceful Savage*. Oxford: Oxford University Press.

Kelly, Raymond C. 2000. *Warless Societies and the Origin of War*. Ann Arbor: University of Michigan Press.

Kelly, Robert L. 2007. *The Foraging Spectrum: Diversity in Hunter-Gatherer Lifeways*.

New York: Percheron Press.

Kivell, Tracy L., Job M. Kibii, Steven E. Churchill, Peter Schmid, and Lee R. Berger. 2011. *Australopithecus sediba* Hand Demonstrates Mosaic Evolution of Locomotor and Manipulative Abilities. *Science* 333(6048):1411–1417.

Kokko, Hannah. 2013. Conflict and Restraint in Animal Species: Implications for War and Peace. In *War, Peace, and Human Nature: The Convergence of Evolutionary and Cultural Views.*. Douglas P. Fry, Ed., 38–53. Oxford: Oxford University Press.

Konner, Melvin. 2006. Human Nature, Ethnic Violence, and War. In *The Psychology of Resolving Global Conflicts: From War to Peace. Nature vs. Nurture* (Volume 1). Mari Fitzduff and Chris E. Stout Eds., 1–30. Westport, CT: Praeger Security International.

———. 2010. *The Evolution of Childhood: Relationships, Emotion, Mind.* Cambridge, MA: Belknap Press of Harvard University Press.

Krugman, Paul. 2012. Class Wars of 2012. *The New York Times*, November 29, 2012.

———. 2014. The Piketty Panic. *The New York Times*, April 24, 2014.

Larsen, Clark Spencer. 2003. Equality for the Sexes in Human Evolution? Early Hominid Sexual Dimorphism and Implications for Mating Systems and Social Behavior. Proc Natl Acad Sci USA 100(16): 1903–1904.

Lee, Richard B., and Irven DeVore, Eds. 1968. *Man the Hunter: The First Intensive Survey of a Single, Crucial Stage of Human Development—Man's Once Universal Hunting Way of Life.* Piscataway, NJ: Aldine Publishing Company.

Lee, Richard B., and Richard Daly. 2004. Introduction: Foragers and Others. In *The Cambridge Encyclopedia of Hunters and Gatherers.* Richard B. Lee and Richard Daly, Eds., 1–22. New York: Cambridge University Press.

Lee, S. H. 2005. Patterns of Size Sexual Dimorphism in *Australopithecus afarensis:* Another Look. *Journal of Comparative Human Biology* 56: 219–232.

Lehrer, Jonah. 2012. *Imagine: How Creativity Works.* New York: Houghton Mifflin Harcourt.

Lessa, William A., and Evon Z. Vogt. 1958. *Reader in Comparative Religion: An Anthropological Approach.* New York: Harper and Row.

Lévi-Strauss, Claude. 1963 Structural Anthropology. Translated from the French by Claire Jacobson and Brooke Grundfest Schoepf. New York: Basic Books.

Levitin, Daniel J. 2006. *This is Your Brain on Music: The Science of a Human Obsession.* New York: Plume (Penguin Group, U.S.A.).

Lewis, I. M. 1971. *Ecstatic Religion: An Anthropological Study of Spirit Possession and Shamanism.* Baltimore: Penguin Books.

Lewton, Kristi L. 2012. Complexity in Biological Anthropology in 2011: Species, Reproduction, and Sociality. *American Anthropologist* 114(2): 198.

Lieberman, Daniel E. 2011. Our Hunter-Gatherer Bodies. *The New York Times*, May 16, 2011.

Linden, David. 2007. *The Accidental Mind: How Brain Evolution Has Given Us Love, Memory, Dreams, and God.* Cambridge, MA: Belknap Press.

———. 2011. *The Compass of Pleasure: How Our Brains Make Fatty Foods, Orgasm, Exercise, Marijuana, Generosity, Vodka, Learning, and Gambling Feel So Good.* New York: Viking Press.

Livingstone, Frank B. 1962. On the Non-Existence of Human Races. *Current An-*

thropology 3(3): 279–281.

Lloyd, Christopher. 2009. *What on Earth Evolved? 100 Species That Changed the World.* New York: Bloomsbury.

Lombard, Marlize, and Miriam Noël Haidle. 2012. Thinking a Bow-and-Arrow Set: Cognitive Implications for Middle Stone Age Bow and Stone-Tipped Arrow Technology. *Cambridge Archaeological Journal* 22(2):232–264.

Lorenz, Konrad. 2002 [1963]. *On Aggression.* Classics Series. New York: Psychology Press.

Lovelady, Kate. 2012. Informal talk Forum St Louis Ethical Society. January 22, 2012.

Lovins, Amory B., and the Rocky Mountain Institute. Lecture presented on September 16, 2014, at Danforth Plant Center's 2014 Seeds of Change Conference. Lecture title taken from Lovins' 2011 book: *Reinventing Fire: Bold Business Solutions for the New Energy Era.* White River Junction, Vermont: Chelsea Green Publishing, 2011.

Luhrmann, T. M. 2012. *When God Talks Back: Understanding the American Evangelical Relationship with God.* New York: Alfred A. Knopf.

Luhrmann, T. M., Howard Nusbaum, and Ronald Thisted. 2010. The Absorption Hypothesis: Learning to Hear God in Evangelical Christianity. *American Anthropologist* 112(1): 66–78.

Luhrmann, T. M., Howard Nusbaum, and Ronald Thisted. 2013. "Lord, Teach Us To Pray": Prayer, Practice, Affects, Cognitive Processing. *Journal of Cognition and Culture.* 13:159–177.

Malthus, Thomas. 1993 [1798]. *Essay on the Principle of Population.* Geoffrey Gilbert, Ed. Oxford: Oxford University Press.

Marean, Curtis W. 2010. When the Sea Saved Humanity. *Scientific American* 303(2): 55–61.

Mauss, Marcel. 1954. *The Gift: Forms and Functions of Exchange in Archaic Societies.* Ian Cunnison, trans. London: Cohen & West.

McGowan, Kat. 2013. "Brainsong": Interview of Rodolfo Llinás. In special issue of *Discover, The Mind,* Spring 2013: 16–22.

McKibben, Bill. 2010. Breaking the Growth Habit. *Scientific American,* April 2010: 61–65.

McKown, Clark, and Rhona S. Weinstein. 2003. The Development and Consequences of Stereotype Consciousness in Middle Childhood. *Child Development* 74(2):498–515.

Merriam-Webster's Collegiate Encyclopedia. 2000. Springfield, MA: Merriam-Webster, Inc.

Mesoudi, Alex, Andrew Whiten, and Kevin N. Laland. 2006. Towards a Unified Science of Cultural Evolution. *Behavioral and Brain Sciences* 29(4): 329–347; 347–383. PMID: 17094820; http://www.ncbi.nlm.nih.gov/pubmed/17094820.

Miller, Geoffrey. 2000. *The Mating Mind: How Sexual Choice Shaped the Evolution of Human Nature.* New York: Doubleday.

Montagu, Ashley. 1942. *Man's Most Dangerous Myth: The Fallacy of Race.* New York: Columbia University Press.

———. 1955. Time, Morphology, and Neoteny in the Evolution of Man. *American Anthropologist* 57: 13–27.

Morris, Ian. 2010. *Why the West Rules—For Now: The Patterns of History, and What They*

Reveal about the Future. New York: Farrar, Straus, and Giroux.

———. 2012. The Evolution of War. *Cliodynamics The Journal of Theoretical and Mathematical History*, 3(1): 9–37.

Napier, John Russell.1962 The Evolution of the Hand. *Scientific American*, December 1962, 56-62.

National Geographic, The Genographic Project, Why Am I Denisovan? https://genographic.nationalgeographic.com/denisovan/ Accessed 2/28/2014.

Neill, James. 2009. *The Origins and Role of Same-Sex Relations in Human Societies.* Jefferson, NC: McFarland and Company.

Nesdale, Drew. 1999. Social Identity and Ethnic Prejudice in Children. Paper presented at the Culture, Race, and Community: Making It Work in the New Millennium forum, Melbourne, August 18, 1999. Accessed 2011 at http://www.vtmh.org.au/docs/csc/drewnesdale.pdf.

Nesdale, Drew, Anne Maass, Kevin Durkin, and Judith Griffiths. 2005. Group Norms, Threat, and Children's Racial Prejudice. *Child Development* 76(3): 652–663.

Nietzsche, Friedrich. 1998 [1889]. *Twilight of the Idols.* Duncan Large, Ed. Oxford World's Classics. Oxford: Oxford University Press.

Norenzayan, Ara. 2013. *Big Gods: How Religion Transformed Cooperation and Conflict.* Princeton, NJ: Princeton University Press.

Norenzayan, Ara, and Azim Shariff. 2008. The Origin and Evolution of Religious Prosociality. *Science* 322(5898): 58–62.

Nowak, Martin A., with Roger Highfield. 2011. *SuperCooperators: Altruism, Evolution, and Why We Need Each Other to Succeed.* New York: Free Press.

NPR. 2012. NPR Books podcast-interview with Alexander, Fresh Air, January 16, 2012. "Legal Scholar: Jim Crow Still Exists In America." Accessed August 28, 2014, at http://www.npr.org/2012/01/16/145175694/legal-scholar-jim-crow-still-exists-in-america.

Oakley, Kenneth P. 1972. *Man the Tool-Maker.* 6th edition. New York: Natural History Museum Publications.

Olson, Kristina R., and Elizabeth S. Spelke. 2008. Foundations of Cooperation in Young Children. *Cognition* 108: 222–231. Accessed at www.sciencedirect.com.

Orwell, George. 1949 (original) (1950, copyright renewed 1970). *1984.* New York: Signet Classic (New American Library, Penguin).

Ostrom, Elinor. 2005. Policies That Crowd out Reciprocity and Collective Action. In *Moral Sentiments and Material Interests.* Herbert Gintis, Samuel Bowles, Robert Boyd, and Ernst Fehr, Eds., 253–275. Cambridge, Massachusetts: The MIT Press.

Oxford Dictionaries. Oxford University Press. http://www.oxforddictionaries.com/us/definition/english/mercantilism. Accessed November 24, 2012.

Patel, Aniruddh. 2010. Music, Biological Evolution, and the Brain. In *Emerging Disciplines.* Bailar M., Ed., 91–144. Houston: Rice University Press.

Patzia, Michael. Xenophanes (c. 570—c. 478 BCE). In *Internet Encyclopedia of Philosophy.* A Peer-Reviewed Academic Resource. Last revised February 21, 2014. Accessed March 20, 2014, at http://www.iep.utm.edu/xenoph/.

Paulson, Steve. 2010. *Atoms and Eden: Conversations on Religion and Science.* Oxford: Oxford University Press.

Pennisi, Elizabeth. 2013. More Genomes from Denisova Cave Show Mixing of

Early Human Groups. *Science* 340(6134): 799.

Phillips, Melissa Lee. 2012. Bearing Sons Can Alter Your Mind. *ScienceNow*, September 26, 2012.

Pickrell, Joseph K., et al. 2014. Ancient West Eurasian Ancestry in Southern and Eastern Africa. Proc Natl Acad Sci USA doi: 10>1073/pnas.1313787111.

Piketty, Thomas. 2014. *Capital in the Twenty-First Century*. Arthur Goldhammer, trans. Cambridge, MA: Belknap Press of Harvard University Press.

Pinker, Steven. 2011. *The Better Angels of Our Nature: Why Violence Has Declined*. New York: Penguin Group.

Pinker, Steven, Vs. Elizabeth S. Spelke. 2005. The Science of Gender and Science. A Debate (April 22, 2005). *The Edge*. http://edge.org/events/the-science-of-gender-and-sciencepinker-vs-spelkea-debate. Accessed September 15, 2012.

Pollard, Katherine S. 2009. What Makes Us Human? *Scientific American* (May 2009): 44–49.

Prado, Jose L. Gomez del. 2014. The Privatization of War: Mercenaries, Private Military and Security Companies (PMSC). *Global Research*, U.N. Working Group on Mercenaries and Global Research. http://www.globalresearch.ca/the-privatization-of-war-mercenaries-private-military-and-security-companies-pmsc/21826.Accessed August 19, 2014.

Pugh, George E. 1977. *The Biological Origin of Human Values*. New York: Basic Books.

Rachman, Gideon. 2011. *Zero-Sum Future: American Power in an Age of Anxiety*. New York: Simon & Schuster.

Radford, Tim. 2011. What Fossils Teach Us about Human Evolution. *The Guardian*, April 24, 2011.

Radin, Paul. 1937. *Primitive Religion*.

Raffaele, Paul. 2010. *Among the Great Apes: Adventures on the Trail of Our Closest Relatives*. New York: HarperCollins.

Ramachandran, V. S. 2011. *The Tell-Tale Brain: A Neuroscientist's Quest for What Makes Us Human*. New York: W. W. Norton & Company.

Rappaport, Roy A. 1968. *Pigs for the Ancestors: Ritual in the Ecology of a New Guinea People*. New Haven, Yale University Press.

———. 2000. *Ritual and Religion in the Making of Humanity*. Cambridge, UK: Cambridge University Press.

Reich, Robert. 2014. David Brooks' Utter Ignorance about Inequality. *Huffington Post: The Blog*. http://www.huffingtonpost.com/robert-reich/david-brooks-inequality_b_4626943.html. Accessed January 19, 2014.

Ricardo, Alonso, and Jack W. Szostak. 2009. The Origin of Life on Earth. *Scientific American*, September: 54–61.

Richerson, Peter J., and Robert Boyd. 2005. *Not by Genes Alone: How Culture Transformed Human Evolution*. Chicago: University of Chicago Press.

Ridley, Matt. 1993. *The Red Queen: Sex and the Evolution of Human Nature*. New York: Penguin Putnam.

Robson, David. 2011. A Brief History of the Brain. *New Scientist* 211(2831): 40–45.

———. 2014. Sharp Thinking: How Shaping Tools Built Our Brains. *NewScientist*, March 1, 2014: 34–39.

Rosen, Arlene M., and Isabel Rivera-Collazo. 2012. Climate Change, Adaptive Cycles, and the Persistence of Foraging Economies during the Late Pleistocene/Holocene Transition in the Levant. Proc Natl Acad Sci USA 109 (10):3640–3645.

Rosenberg, Karen, and Wenda Trevathan. 2002. Birth, Obstetrics and Human Evolution. *BJOG: An International Journal of Obstetrics & Gynaecology* 109(11): 1199–1206.

Roth, Gerhard, and Ursula Dicke. 2005. Evolution of the Brain and Intelligence. *Trends in Cognitive Sciences* 9(5): 250–257.

Rudmin, Floyd W. 1996. Cross-Cultural Correlates of the Ownership of Private Property: Zelman's Gender Data Revisited. *Cross-Cultural Research* 30(2): 115–53.

———. 2006. Cross-Cultural Correlates of the Ownership of Private Property: A Summary of Five Studies. *The AnthroGlobe Journal* (online only) ISSN: 1481-3440. Accessed 10/28/13.

Rushkoff, Douglas. 2013. *Present Shock: When Everything Happens Now.* New York: Penguin Group.

Sabra, Abdelhamid I. 2003. Ibn al-Haytham. *Harvard Magazine.* September-October 2003.

Sachs, Jeffrey. 2011. *The Price of Civilization: Reawakening American Virtue and Prosperity.* New York: Random House.

Sacks, Oliver. 2007. *Musicophilia: Tales of Music and the Brain.* New York: Vintage Books.

———. 2012. *Hallucinations.* New York: Alfred A. Knopf.

Sagan, Carl. 1996. *The Demon-Haunted World: Science as a Candle in the Dark.* New York: A Ballantine Book.

Sahlins, Marshall. 1968. The Segmentary Lineage: An Organization of Predatory Expansion. In *Man in Adaptation: The Cultural Present.* Yehudi A. Cohen, Ed., 203–220. Chicago: Aldine Publishing Company.

———. 1972. *Stone Age Economics.* Chicago: Aldine-Atherton.

———. 2011. What Kinship Is (Part II). *Journal of the Royal Anthropological Institute* 17(2): 227–242.

Sapolsky, Robert M. 2006. The Cultural Desert. In *Monkeyluv: And Other Essays on Our Lives As Animals,* Robert M. Sapolsky, 161–170. New York: Scribner.

———. 2013. Rousseau with a Tail. In *War, Peace, and Human Nature: The Convergence of Evolutionary and Cultural Views.* Douglas P. Fry, Ed., 421–438. Oxford: Oxford University Press.

Schrock, Karen. 2009. Why Music Moves Us. *Scientific American Mind,* July/August: 32–37.

Schuessler, Jennifer. 2012. Drug Policy as Race Policy: Best Seller Galvanizes the Debate. Review of *The New Jim Crow* by Michelle Alexander. In *The New York Times,* March 6, 2012.

Schuessler, Jennifer, 2014, Fieldwork of Total Immersion. Review of Alice Goffman, *On the Run,* in press. New York Times, April 29, 2014,

Science Encyclopedia, Modernist Anthropological Theory of Family. http://science .jrank.org/pages/9306/Modernist-Anthropological-Theory-Family-Modernist-Study-Kinship.html. Accessed May 9, 2013.

Seeger, Pete. n.d. My Rainbow Race Lyrics (Lyrics.net) Retrieved November 2, 2014, from http://www.lyrics.net/lyric/2432622.

Service, Elman R. 1960. The Law of Evolutionary Potential. In *Evolution and Culture.* Marshall D. Sahlins and Elman R. Service, Eds., 93–122. Ann Arbor: University of Michigan Press.

————. 1962. *Primitive Social Organization: An Evolutionary Perspective.* New York: Random House.

Seung, Sebastian. 2012. *Connectome: How the Brain's Wiring Makes Us Who We Are.* New York: Houghton Mifflin Harcourt.

Shapiro, Robert. 2007. A Simpler Origin for Life. *Scientific American,* February 12, 2007: 46–57.

Shakespeare, William. 1998 [n.d.]. *As You Like It.* General Editor, Paul Negri, Editor this Volume V, Susan L. Rattiner. Unabridged from *The Caxton Edition of the Complete William Shakespeare.* London: Dover Thrift Edition.

Sharot, Tali. 2011. The Optimism Bias. *Current Biology* 21(23): R941–R945; doi 10.1016/j.cub.2011.10.030.

Sheridan, Kerry. 2013. Iraq Death Toll Reaches 500,000 Since Start of U.S.-Led Invasion, New Study Says. *The World Post,* October 15, 2013, updated January 23, 14. Accessed at http://www.huffingtonpost.com/2013/10/15/iraq-death-toll_n_4102855.html.

Shermer, Michael. 2011. *The Believing Brain: From Ghosts and Gods to Politics and Conspiracies—How We Construct Beliefs and Reinforce Them as Truths.* New York: Times Books.

Shubin, Neil. 2009. *Your Inner Fish: A Journey into the 3.5-Billion-Year History of the Human Body.* New York: Vintage Books.

Silk, Joan B. 2012. Interview by Sandra Aamodt. An Interview with Joan Silk: Primates are Social: The Evolution of Friendship, Strangers, and Gossip. *Being Human,* October 11, 2012. Accessed at http://www.beinghuman.org/article/interview-joan-silk-primates-are-social.

————. 2005. The Evolution of Cooperation in Primate Groups. In Gintis et al., Eds., 43–73 Cambridge, Massachusetts: The MIT Press.

Smith, Adam. 1937 [1776]. *An Inquiry into the Nature and Causes of the Wealth of Nations.* New York: Modern Library Edition.

————. 2009 [1790]. *The Theory of Moral Sentiments.* 6th edition. New York: Penguin.

Smith, Justin E. H. 2013. The Enlightenment's "Race" Problem, and Ours. *The New York Times* Opinionator, February 10, 2013.

Snodgrass, Josh. 2011. More Calories and Allergies. *The New York Times,* May 12, 2011.

Snyder, Laura J. 2011. *The Philosophical Breakfast Club: Four Remarkable Friends Who Transformed Science and Changed the World.* New York: Crown Publishing Group.

Sol, Daniel, and Trevor Price. 2008. Brain Size and the Diversification of Body Size in Birds. *The American Naturalist* 172: 170–177.

Solomon, Robert C., and Kathleen M. Higgins. 1996. *A Short History of Philosophy.* Oxford: Oxford University Press.

Steinhauer, Jennifer. 2013. Once Few, Women Hold More Power in Senate. *The New York Times,* March 21, 2013.

Stringer, Chris. 2012. *Lone Survivors: How We Came to be the Only Humans on Earth.* New York: Henry Holt Times Books.

Stringer, Chris, and Peter Andrews. 2005. *The Complete World of Human Evolution.* New York: Thames and Hudson.

Sussman, Robert W. 2013. Why the Legend of the Killer Ape Never Dies: The Enduring Power of Cultural Beliefs to Distort Our View of Human Nature. In

War, Peace, and Human Nature: The Convergence of Evolutionary and Cultural Views, Douglas P. Fry, Ed., 97–111. Oxford: Oxford University Press.

Tattersall, Ian. 2008. *The World from Beginnings to 4000 BCE*. Oxford: Oxford University Press.

———. 2011. Cooperation, Altruism, and Human Evolution. In *Origins of Altruism and Cooperation*. Robert W. Sussman and C. Robert Cloninger, Eds., 11–18. New York: Springer.

———. 2012. *Masters of the Planet: The Search for Our Human Origins*. New York: Palgrave Macmillan.

———. 2014. If I Had a Hammer. *Scientific American*. September 2014: 55-59.

Tattersall, Ian, and Rob DeSalle. 2011. *Race?: Debunking a Scientific Myth*. Texas A & M University Anthropology Series. College Station: Texas A & M University Press.

Taylor, Timothy. 2010. *The Artificial Ape: How Technology Changed the Course of Human Evolution*. New York: Palgrave Macmillan.

Thaler, Richard H., and Cass R. Sunstein. 2008. *Nudge: Improving Decisions About Health, Wealth, and Happiness*. New Haven, CT: Yale University Press.

Thorpe, S. K. S., R. L. Holder, and R. H. Cropton. 2007. Origin of Human Bipedalism as an Adaptation for Locomotion on Flexible Branches. *Science* 361(5829): 1328–1331.

Tomasello, Michael, with Carol Dweck, Joan Silk, Brian Skyrms, and Elizabeth Spelke. 2009. *Why We Cooperate*. Cambridge, MA: A Boston Review Book, MIT Press.

Toobin, Jeffrey. 2012. Money Unlimited: How Chief Justice Roberts Orchestrated the Citizens United Decision. *The New Yorker*, Annals of Law, May 21, 2012.

Townsend, Tim. 2011. Dehumanization of a Religious Group. *St. Louis Post Dispatch*, December 3, 2011.

Turchin, Peter. 2010 Warfare and the Evolution of Social Complexity: A Multilevel-Selection Approach. *Structure and Dynamics: eJournal of Anthropological and Related Sciences* 2(3):1-37. https://escholarship.org/uc/item/7j11945r, Accessed March 12, 2014.

Twain, Mark. 1897. *Following the Equator: A Journey Around the World*. Hartford, CT: American Publishing Company.

Underwood, Emily. 2011. Ancient Tools Point to Early Human Migration into Arabia. *ScienceNow*, November 30, 2011.

U.S. National Library of Medicine. *Genetics Home Reference: Your Guide to Understanding Genetic Conditions*. Website updated automatically. http://ghr.nlm.nih.gov. Accessed July 22, 2014.

van Gennep, Arnold. 1960 [1908]. *Rites of Passage*. Translated from French by Monika B. Vizedom and Gabrielle L. Caffee. Chicago: The University of Chicago Press.

Verbeek, Peter. 2013. An Ethological Perspective on War and Peace. In *War, Peace, and Human Nature: The Convergence of Evolutionary and Cultural Views*. Douglas P. Fry, Ed., 54–77. Oxford: Oxford University Press.

Vermeij, Geerat. 2010. *The Evolutionary World: How Adaptation Explains Everything from Seashells to Civilization*. New York: St. Martin's Press.

Walker, Robert S., Kim R. Hill, Mark V. Flinn, and Ryan M. Ellsworth. 2011. Evolutionary History of Hunter-Gatherer Marriage Practices. *Public Library of Science*

One 6(4); doi:10.1371/journal.pone.0019066.

Watson, James. 1992. Foreword to *Discovering the Brain*. Sandra Ackerman, Ed. Washington, DC: The National Academies Press.

Watson, Tracy. 2012. *Science* Shot: Standing Tall to Beat the Heat? *ScienceNow*, December 12, 2012.

Weiner, Jonathan. 1994. *The Beak of the Finch: A Story of Evolution in Our Time*. New York: Alfred A. Knopf.

Wells, Spencer. 2010. *Pandora's Seed: The Unforeseen Cost of Civilization*. New York: Random House.

White, Leslie A. 1949. *The Science of Culture: A Study of Man and Civilization*. New York: Grove Press.

———. 1959. *The Evolution of Culture: The Development of Civilization to the Fall of Rome*. New York: McGraw-Hill.

Wilford, John Noble. 2011. Fossil Teeth Put Humans in Europe Earlier Than Thought. *The New York Times*, November 2, 2011.

———. 2012a. Flute's Revised Age Dates the Sound of Music Earlier. *The New York Times*, May 29, 2012.

———. 2012b. Stone Tools Point to Creative Work by Early Humans in Africa. *The New York Times*, November 12, 2012.

———. 2013. Skull Fossil Suggests Simpler Human Lineage. *The New York Times*, October 17, 2013.

Williams, Garrath. 2013 (Update). Thomas Hobbes: Moral and Political Philosophy. *Internet Encyclopedia of Philosophy: A Peer-Reviewed Academic Resource*. Updated 06/25/2013, doi 10.1093/OBO/9780195396577-0096.

Wilson, David S. 2002. *Darwin's Cathedral: Evolution, Religion, and the Nature of Society*. Chicago: The University of Chicago Press.

Wilson, Edward O. 2012. *The Social Conquest of Earth*. New York: Liveright Publishing Corporation.

Winkler, Erin N. 2009. Children Are Not Colorblind: How Young Children Learn Race.http://www4.uwm.edu/letsci/africology/faculty/upload/children_colorblind.pdf. Accessed February 11, 2012.

Wolfenden, Katherine J. 2011. Ending Ethnic Conflict and Creating Positive Peace in Rwanda and Sierra Leone. *Student Pulse* 3(1):1–2.

Wood, Bernard, and Terry Harrison, The evolutionary context of the first hominins, *Nature*, 470 (February 17, 2011):347-352.

Wood, James, and Alex Guth. 2008. East Africa's Great Rift Valley. *Geology.com*. at http://geology.com/articles/east-africa-rift.shtml. Accessed April 22, 2012.

Wrangham, Richard. 2009. *Catching Fire: How Cooking Made Us Human*. New York: Basic Books/Perseus.

Wright, Robert. 1994. *The Moral Animal: Why We Are the Way We Are: The New Science of Evolutionary Psychology*. New York: Vintage Books.

———. 2001. *Nonzero: The Logic of Human Destiny*. New York: Vintage Books.

———. 2009. *Evolution of God*. New York: Little, Brown, and Company.

Vedantam, Shankar. 2010. *The Hidden Brain: How Our Unconscious Minds Elect Presidents, Control Markets, Wage Wars, and Save Our Lives*. New York: Spiegel & Grau.

Yong, Ed. 2013. Armor against Prejudice. *Scientific American* 308(6):76–80.

Young, Richard W. 2003. Evolution of the Human Hand: The Role of Throwing and Clubbing. *Journal of Anatomy*, 202(1):165–174.

Zelman, Elizabeth Crouch. 1977. Reproduction, Ritual, and Power. *American Ethnologist* 4(4): 714–733.

Zihlman, Adrienne L. 1981. Women as Shapers of Human Adaptation. In *Woman the Gatherer*. Frances Dahlberg, Ed., 75-120. New Haven, Connecticut; Yale University Press.

Zimmer, Carl. 2008. Mom and Dad Are Fighting in Your Genes—and in Your Brain. *Discover Magazine*, November, 2008.

———. 2011. A Body Fit for a Freaky-Big Brain. *Discover Magazine*, July-August 2011.

Index